D1547751

Rabbinic Political Theory

Chicago Studies in the History of Judaism

EDITED BY

William Scott Green and Calvin Goldscheider

Rabbinic Political Theory

Religion and Politics in the Mishnah

Jacob Neusner

The University of Chicago Press

Chicago and London

The University of Chicago Press, Chicago 60637
The University of Chicago Press, Ltd., London

00 99 98 97 96 95 94 93 92 91   5 4 3 2 1

Library of Congress Cataloging-in-Publication Data

Neusner, Jacob, 1932–
    Rabbinic political theory : religion and politics in the Mishnah /
Jacob Neusner.
      p. cm. — (Chicago studies in the history of Judaism)
    Includes bibliographical references and index.
    ISBN 0-226-57650-7 (cloth). — ISBN 0-226-57651-5 (pbk.).
    1. Politics in rabbinical literature. 2. Mishnah—Criticism,
interpretation, etc. I. Title. II. Series.
BM496.9.P64N48   1991
296.3'877'09015—dc20   90-45030
                                        CIP

JACOB NEUSNER is Graduate Research Professor of Humanities and Religous Studies at the University of South Florida, Tampa. His most recent book from the University of Chicago Press is *The Economics of the Mishnah*.

Contents

Preface

A politics theorizes an ongoing exercise of power, of coercion that includes legitimized violence. Here I show that politics addresses a religious issue and—more to the point—makes a religious statement, as much as, not uncommonly, religions take up political ones and engage in political action. How so? People expect from religion not only private solace but also final solutions to shared problems; that means they anticipate from religion acts of power, not only affirmations of conscience. As for the particular theory of politics we consider, it sets forth the imaginary structure and fabricated system of a working government conceived by a particular Judaism.[1] This Judaism is the one that finds its initial statement in the Mishnah.[2] Indeed, the Mishnah's politics is important precisely because the Mishnah formed the foundation document of all the Judaisms paramount from its time, ca. A.D. 200, to ours.[3]

What makes the politics of the Judaism studied here interesting is the highly political structure that encompasses issues of secular and this-worldly social power within a nurturing other-worldly and supernatural religious system. This Judaism's account of the ethos, ethics, and ethnos, or worldview, way of life, and social entity, that comprise it appeals to this-worldly political institutions and their functioning as an integral part of the representation of the social order it proposes to bring into being. The introduction spells out the purpose of this book and its program.

This of course is not the first study of "Jewish political theory" or "the politics of Judaism." But it is the first to read only a single document, in its context, and to insist that the systemic structure of that document be invoked in the description, analysis, and interpretation of every component of the document, including its politics. It is only by seeing the politics of the system within its systemic framework, and by interpreting the system as a whole in its historical and social context, that, in my view, we can make sense of the details of the politics in their correct perspective: systemic and historical, always first synchronic, and only then diachronic.

The contrary approach treats all writings by all Jews everywhere and at any time as unitary and all contexts as irrelevant, thus purporting to present "Jewish political theory," beginning to end, without differentiation of time, place, circumstance. That reading of the data forms an artificial construct that stands out of all relationship with particular time, place, circumstance, even out of dialogue with the very document that sets forth those data. Though manifestly wrong for any purpose other than forming a merely paraphrastic anthology of this and that on a given topic, that approach has guided every prior study of this subject. Its most recent manifestation typifies the genre. In his *The Judaic State: A Study in Rabbinic Political Theory,* Martin Sicker addresses various themes; he collects pertinent sayings on those themes from a variety of sources distributed over a considerable span of time and weaves them together in a sustained paraphrase and episodic observation.[4] Sicker's themes comprise the nature of man, the origins of political society, the individual and the polity, political authority and obligation, the structure of the polity, the priesthood, prophetic institution, the national executive, the monarchy, the king and the law, the judiciary, the magistrates. In fact, Sicker's themes are merely topics, and their relevance to politics is not argued but presupposed.

Clearly, Sicker has in mind a set of political categories—that is implicit in his program. But what theory of politics animates his theory of category formation? From its earliest pages the book assumes that "we all know" what we mean by politics, and that therefore political categories or classifications of data require no definition. From this perspective, politics becomes a subject matter, not a problem, and the task of political study is to collect and organize pertinent sayings about a given subject. Presumably, on that basis, Sicker has collected and arranged his sayings in a competent manner. Certainly, his method makes any detailed critique of his results redundant. But his study suffers because he ignores the historical context and intellectual circumstances that underpin the sayings he collects. Thus a comparison between Sicker's book and the work in hand will reveal the methodological distinctions between previous approaches and mine. It will reveal the significance of my reframing the field and will concurrently clarify why I insist that my primary readership lies in the history of religion, the history of political theory, and comparative politics.

Let me conclude by saying that while I mean to address problems of political theory here, in describing, analyzing, and interpreting the politics of the Judaism of the Mishnah, I also necessarily address issues of fictive theory and of fantasy. How so? In general, like religion, a politics begins within an imagination. Only much later, and in ways no one anticipates, does a political perspective find itself endowed with practical power. And not all imagined systems gain such power. Lacking full documentation, we thus cannot be sure what legitimate power was vested in the Jews in Palestine—that is to say, in Israel, the holy people, in the Land of Israel, the holy land—in the second century A.D. Indeed, we cannot be sure that any power at all was vested in the Jews when the politics we shall examine was included in the religious system set forth in the Mishnah. Nor can we even say how much legitimate violence, such as a political structure and system represent, was vested in the hands of the sages who imagined the system.

But luckily, these matters have no bearing on the theory of politics before us. We have as fundamental and irreducible fact only the system sages thought up, and the writing in which they set forth that system, encompassing among its principal topics a politics.

Let me here place this book into its larger context in my oeuvre. First, I have written a complete analysis and commentary to the Mishnah and the Tosefta, its complementary document, and cite some of that work here. My presentation of the document derives from my now completed *History of the Mishnaic Law*, in forty-three volumes (Leiden: E. J. Brill, 1974–1982), and another half-dozen volumes by students of mine, cited where referred to.

Second, this book in particular finds its place as the second component of my trilogy on the Mishnah's religious theory of the social order: the philosophy, politics, and economics of the Judaic system set forth by the framers of the Mishnah. The other two volumes are *The Economics of the Mishnah* (Chicago: University of Chicago Press, 1990) and *Judaism as Philosophy: The Method and Message of the Mishnah* (Columbia: University of South Carolina Press, 1991).

Clearly, what comes to closure in this book and its two companions is the description of the Judaism that the Mishnah and closely allied documents defined. What is the next phase in this ongoing history of the formation of Judaism in the classical period, that single and sole topic to which I have devoted every day of my life for nearly forty years, from entering the Jewish Theological Seminary of America in 1954 to the present day? The analysis of the philosophical character of the Mishnah places into perspective what I believe to be the character of the first phase, and therefore points toward the development of the second and third phases, of the Judaism of the dual Torah. The entire characterization of the first phase of the Judaism of the dual Torah, that is, the system attested by the Mishnah in particular, rests upon the results of this book and its two companions, on economics and politics respectively.

The comparison of the initial system of Judaism, that is, the politics, philosophy, and economics of the Judaic system of the Mishnah, with the next sequential and connected Judaic system, the one attested by the Talmud of the Land of Israel, Genesis Rabbah, and Leviticus Rabbah, comes next. The description of the economics, politics, and philosophy of that system, and the comparison of both systems for the first time, is worked out in my *Transformation of Judaism: From Philosophy to Religion* (Champaign-Urbana: University of Illinois Press, 1991).

A brief account of the results of that work will underscore the importance of the basic thesis offered in this one. When in the second phase we ask the same questions, e.g., concerning economics, politics, and philosophy, we perceive a process of category formation or reformation that signifies a movement away from philosophy altogether, a movement in which the inherited structure is preserved in form but reshaped in all essential aspects. The politics will change altogether; the economics will persist; the entire philosophical character and program will fall away, except within the narrow limits of the exegesis of specific Mishnah passages, and be replaced with a theological program in a form found theologically appropriate, as the philosophical program of the Mishnah comes to us in that list-making form that was found philosophically appropriate.

The characterization of the third phase, the one represented by the Talmud of Babylonia and associated writings, I can now readily imagine. The analysis will involve the Talmud of Babylonia and its companion Midrash compilations, Lamentations Rabbah, Esther Rabbah I, Song of Songs Rabbah, and Ruth Rabbah. My preliminary theory is contained within the overall title I presently contemplate for a series of analyses that will take more than a decade: *The Transformation of Judaism: From Religion to Theology.* But in saying so, I have gotten far ahead of my story. Only now some of the necessary *Vorstudien* of literature and special problems upon which such a synthesis is to be built have begun. The description of the named Midrash compilations has been accomplished, and the sustained literary analysis of the traits of the Babylonian Talmud's tractates is under way. But the issues of category formation have yet to be sorted out.

It remains to refer to what is excluded from my scholarly portfolio. It is original work on the philosophical tradition to which I make reference here. While in the final part of the book I refer to Aristotle's politics, I make no contribution to Aristotelian studies, even to the study of Aristotle's influence in the second century, when the Mishnah came into being. Scholars of the history of Greco-Roman philosophy in the second and third centuries will learn nothing about their subject in the pages of this book. I hope only to provide a standard textbook account of such matters which will suffice for the kind of comparison I believe is required.

Professor Alan Zuckerman, Department of Political Science and Program in Judaic Studies, Brown University, generously read and annotated every page of this book in its fourth draft. I revised the book in accord with his comments and questions and express my thanks for his generous help. The importance I attach to addressing political scientists in their own terms, so far as my sources permit and I am able, may be gauged from the high value I place on his critical reading.

Writing on this subject and its companions has required me to work out a style for which, in the area in which I work, I could locate no models. I had a good bit of difficulty in defining an appropriate prose for the task. I am therefore especially thankful to Dr. Caroline McCracken-Flesher, who served as literary editor for this book; she subjected the fifth draft to a complete line-by-line editorial revision. If the book has been saved from oppressive repetitiousness and cruel infelicity, it is because of her unsparing eye; I express my thanks for this latest among many services of a highly professional order to writing of mine or edited by me.

I am happy to express thanks also to my former colleagues at Brown University in Judaic Studies: Professors Ernest S. Frerichs, Calvin Goldscheider, and Wendell S. Dietrich. Now that I have left Brown, I salute them with a fond farewell. Professor Martha Nussbaum, Philosophy and Classics, gave me good advice and also shared her own excellent scholarship with me.

To Professor William Scott Green, University of Rochester, are owed special thanks. His editorial judgment as well as his scholarly acumen provided a rich resource of counsel. Had he not chosen a scholarly career, he could have achieved eminence in publishing. With such good friends and co-workers as these, work is fun.

The editors of this series, Professors Goldscheider and Green, devoted much time and work to this book. Professor Goldscheider paid close attention to the correct use of Weber's "Politics as a Vocation," which served as the starting point of my work. What is striking in this book is that the results—my account of the politics of this Judaism as a politics of hierarchization—prove identical with those that emerged out of quite separate work on the philosophy of this same Judaism, spelled out in *Judaism as Philosophy: The Method and Message of the Mishnah*. There I am able to show that Aristotelian method yields a Middle or Neo-Platonic proposition on the hierarchical order and unity of all being. The equivalent results for economics are already in print in *The Economics of the Mishnah*. The upshot is that the Judaism under study presents a theory of the social order which states precisely the same proposition in its treatment of each of the principal components of that order, philosophy, politics, and economics. That seems to me a noteworthy result.

I wrote the seventh and eighth drafts of this book in 1989–1990, during which I held a research fellowship from the National Endowment for the Humanities (FA 28396-89), in residence as a Member of the Institute for Advanced Study, with generous salary supplement provided by Brown University.

I take much pride in offering to the National Endowment for the Humanities my very hearty thanks for the recognition and material support that the fellowship afforded to me. I found the Endowment, particularly the Division of Fellowships and Seminars, always helpful and courteous in dealing with my application and express my admiration and appreciation to that thoroughly professional staff of public servants.

Brown University complemented that fellowship with substantial funds to make it possible for me to spend the entire academic year 1989–1990 in full-time research. In my twenty-two years at Brown University, now concluded, I always enjoyed the university's generous support for every research initiative that I undertook; I never took for granted the commitment of the university's scarce resources to my work in particular and now express the thanks commensurate to it.

The Institute for Advanced Studies, where I wrote the last drafts, provided a happy office and a congenial and stimulating environment in which to do this work. My special thanks go to the Members for 1989–1990.

JACOB NEUSNER

Our twenty-sixth wedding anniversary, March 15, 1990

School of Historical Studies
The Institute for Advanced Study
Princeton, New Jersey

Introduction

The politics expressed through the Mishnah's Judaism speaks of a social entity treated as a political one as well, of "Israel" classified as a state.[1] The Judaism of the Mishnah, a philosophical system in the form of a law code that reached closure in ca. A.D. 200, set forth for its social entity (called, as the social entity of every Judaism is called, "Israel") not merely a mythic and theological picture but also a political structure. When people would speak of "a state of (being) Israel," therefore, they would also address "the State of Israel," the Jewish state, understanding that they spoke of a political entity like other such political entities. Therefore this Judaism became in mind and imagination a state not only of (autonomous) being but also of (shared and social) doing, not alone of ontology but of society. That is why this Judaism defines a locus for inquiry into more than theological science, into, especially, social science: economics, politics, and philosophy.

But political religions are not the only kind of religion, or even the most common kind. Take the case of Christianity. Even after Christianity rose to the status of licit and, later, state religion (from Constantine onward), some Christianities still refrained from addressing the conception of a Christian politics at all. Bearing this in mind, we should not take Judaism's translation into a political religion for granted, even in our own time, where there exists a Jewish state strongly identified with (a) religious Judaism. And indeed, in the past every Judaism did not make up a Jewish state and so have a politics, nor did every Judaism through time invoke political categories and conceptions in the making of its systemic statements. Rather, in antiquity and in modern times we can locate Judaisms that in no way understood their "Israel" to form a political entity, that, for instance, did not endow their "Israel" with agencies capable of exercising power in the concrete form of legitimate violence.

This Judaism—the Judaism of the Mishnah and all the systems that flowed from it—by contrast did manifest power politically. And for the history of Judaism, that has made all the difference. From the period of the Mishnah, from Judaism's formative age to the present, the Jewish religion has realized its political potential in Judaisms across successive ages. That is, for the minds, intellects, and imaginations of this Judaism's religious leaders, the media of power offered an enduring and desirable option.

In this book I set forth a political theory, the ultimate rationality of which far transcends the range of power and the (mere) legitimate resort to violence to secure conformity to the social order.[2] At every point in the political theory I shall describe, analyze, and, through comparison and contrast, interpret in these pages, political theory bears its rightful share of an encompassing systemic message. The theory of legitimate violence that, in general, we identify as political can be understood only in that larger context. Politics in this Judaism (and in all subsequent systems as well) forms a dependent variable, to be explained by appeal to the nourishing religious theory of the social order, the system and its myths, not an independent variable to account for important aspects of the social order by merely dismissing them.

What is at stake in this portrait of a politics quite different from the familiar one? In the West politics is generally defined as the theory of legitimate violence, encompassing the institutions and persons that properly exercise violence: who tells whom what to do, who (rightly) does what to whom. But that theory of politics treats power as disembedded from other critical components of the social order. With the separation of religion and politics, the proper exercise of force proves difficult to explain. In antiquity religion, encompassing philosophy, was embedded in politics, and politics in economics, so that a coherent theory explained in a single way the definitive components of the social order. Today we treat religion as private and personal, politics as social and collective. Perspective on the disembedded politics of the modern age is gained when we examine a politics that is fully integrated with philosophy or religion, a political theory, structure, and system. The Mishnah provides us with a fully articulated example of a systematically integrated politics, hence my subtitle, "religion and politics in the Mishnah."

The received tradition of political theory deems religion a rationalization of power and eliminates from the range of plausible explanations of matters important components of society. The Mishnah's political theory, by contrast, accomplishes more than the mere sorting out of the material relationships within the state. The key generative problematic of the Mishnah is the interplay of divine will and the human will, and the relationships that require political scrutiny are between God and Israel, not among citizens or between the state and its citizens. Religion and politics are integrated, and in the pages of this book I spell out a striking example of how that integration shapes the political dimension of the social order—encompassing, of course, legitimate violence and those who, on earth and in heaven, exercise it.

In these pages, therefore, I mean to provide a generally intelligible example of a religious politics and to direct it principally to three loosely related fields and two freestanding ones: the history and comparison of religion, the history of political theory, and comparative politics on the one hand, and ancient history and Judaic studies (the last and least important direction for these pages) on the other. For all five fields of learning I propose to answer a question—a question aiming at the comparative study of religion and politics: if a religion could invent a state, what sort of politics would that religion produce? That is, of what would that religion's public policy consist? How would public policy take shape? By what legitimately violent means would that policy be enforced?

Let me specify those whom I mean to address. For those concerned with the history and comparison of religion, I offer an example of how a religion utilizes a theory of politics in the composition of its system. For historians of political theory, I present a fully exposed political theory set into the context of its larger intellectual framework. For them, I mean to explain why politics becomes important in the social theory of a religion and how religion affects political theory. And for those interested in comparative politics, I compare and contrast two political theories, the Mishnah's and Aristotle's. Why Aristotle's in particular? As I explain at length later on, the basis for comparing those two politics is that they share a single economic theory but diverge in their fundamental conceptions of political structure and order. Hence, from their shared traits of economic theory we have grounds for comparison, and from their differences in political theory we have grounds for contrast. So these three principal fields of theoretical inquiry that define my primary focus of discourse are here offered an example worked out for purposes of comparative study across religion and politics.

As I mentioned, two other fields of learning may derive benefit from this case and from my analysis of it. These are ancient history, with its narrow synchronic focus, and the more diachronic field of Judaic studies. Those who study ancient history—especially those concerned with the outlying subgroups of the Roman Empire in the centuries between Augustus and Constantine—may find here a path into the political intellect of some of those enemies of the Roman order to whom Ramsay MacMullen has directed attention.

As for scholars concerned with the history of Judaisms, I offer them a close analysis of the politics of a single Judaism, a Judaism seen entirely on its own. Up to now work on Jews' politics and the politics of Judaism has treated as an undifferentiated continuum all Jews and all politics put forth within all Judaic religious systems. In these pages I treat only one politics, invented by one group of thinkers. This allows me to place that politics within the framework of the larger system worked out by single philosophy.[3] I am able to explain, therefore, why a given Judaism found it necessary to set forth its systemic message through the medium of political thought.

In order to address colleagues in politics, I derive part of my basic theory about the principles of category formation pertinent to the study of politics from Max Weber's "Politics as a Vocation."[4] I appeal to a theory of politics that describes in general terms but within a single framework diverse political structures and systems. I began with Weber in my inquiry into the political categories of the Mishnah's system. The data that I identified in turn permitted me to set forth what I believe is the political structure and system that the

Mishnah's Judaism imagined and therefore to account for the importance accorded to politics and its issues by the framers of the particular Judaism that began with the Mishnah. Weber helped me to identify pertinent data, but, as my description and analysis of the data proceeded, I found his categories somewhat too limited to serve throughout. Weber's categories are systemically disembedded. Consequently they impose distortions on the politics of a system that absorbs politics within a larger system and makes its statement as much through politics as through economics and through philosophy and science. That is why Weber serves in this book as a guideline, rather than as the principal theoretical framework for my description, analysis, and interpretation of the Mishnah's politics.

Why do I ask historians of religion and political theory to take account of the Judaism set forth in the Mishnah in particular? The Mishnah is important to the study of a religious politics and a political religion for two reasons, one having to do with religion, the other with politics.

The Mishnah offers the first formulation of a Judaism that became paramount and, for a long time, normative. Thus for the history of religion the Mishnah (as much as the Hebrew Scriptures or Old Testament) provides a case in which a single piece of writing served to impose continuity upon the long history of diverse, if interrelated, religious systems of a single family.

And the Mishnah proves important to the study of politics—in particular, to the politics of a religion—because the Judaism that took its start in the Mishnah and that runs through to the present day has set forth an utterly political religion. Further, if we consider the power of religion to define politics, whether in Islam or Christianity or Judaism, whether in ages past or in the twenty-first century, historians of political theory and scholars of comparative politics surely must value a case for which, in detail and *de novo,* we are able to show precisely where and how and above all why—for what systemic purpose—a religion defines a politics.

To this point, I have treated the issue of a religion's politics as though the political religion were everywhere conceded to be a routine phenomenon. But how can we speak of the politics of a religion at all? In answer to that question, we turn to the question of a religious politics. In some religious traditions today—Islam everywhere, Roman Catholic Christianity in parts of Latin America, Spain, and Portugal, Judaism in the state of Israel—the participants know that religions have politics. In other traditions—Roman Catholic, Orthodox, and Protestant Christianity in the West, Reform and Conservative Judaism in the United States—participants do not concede that religions legitimately have, or ought to have, a politics at all. So far as in these settings we speak of a religion's politics, we mean who gets to be bishop of this diocese, or to whom that synagogue pulpit is assigned. But in this book, what we consider the politics of a religion is the political system that a religion, if it could, would frame for a state—any state.

Still, religion in its inward and mystical modes commonly finds itself not saddled with but contrasted against politics. A mystical religion is supposed not to engage in political life at all. For instance, "Render unto Caesar . . . " is understood to define Christianity as distinct from politics. And indeed, for long centuries no Christianity was a political religion—which is to say, none delivered its systemic message through a sustained and systematic theory of a politics. Calling Christ "King" did not bear political implications about the legitimate use of coercion such as politics requires (and as even Christianity, in due course, exhibited).

Similarly, today we see that intellectuals responding to other-worldly concerns more often than not indeed appeal to the this-worldly power of violence and therefore frame (in theory at least, but often in practice as well) a concrete and this-worldly politics. One such politics derives from liberation theology, for example. Moreover, the religious system actually appears to define the independent variable which accounts for the structure and system of the politics it puts forth. My sustained argument, in part 3, that the politics of Judaism forms part of a larger systemic statement and can be understood only in terms of the ineluctable question and self-evidently valid answer that frame the systemic statement—and that are not of a political character at all!—aims at the same conclusion: that religion forms the independent variable in the systemic analysis of religious systems of the social order.

Religious intellectuals, however focused in mind and imagination upon heavenly considerations, engage with the public interest and undertake to construct a politics encompassing ongoing institutions to acquire and sustain worldly power. Even mystics in one religious world after another prove remarkably practical in their assessment of the media of power for realizing their vision. Their vision practically and concretely shapes public affairs of women and men doing things together. Indeed, that fact characterizes all kinds of religious intellectuals. The formation of a politics of a religion comes forth from mystics, such as Bernard of Clairvaux, from prophets, such as Muhammed, and, as we shall see, from philosophers, such as the author of the Mishnah.

But if some religions make up and even realize a politics, that does not tell us what makes the politics of a religion interesting. What do we learn in the analysis of the politics of a religion, and how high are the stakes in this study? If we want to know why politics set forth high stakes for the study of the politics of a Judaism, for example, I see two points of fundamental importance.

First comes the simple and practical fact that religious imaginations—whether primarily prophetic, mystical, or philosophical—have set forth political systems in structure that in the passage of time have often turned out to impart shape to the everyday realities of the social order. Today we know religions whose political structures and systems were made up long ago and wholly in intellect, and which yet actively intervene in the formation, or reformation, of nation-states. Clearly, what begins in theory, in theology and in religious intellect, can emerge in the concrete realm of politics and the social system.[5]

Consequently, a case study of the kind of politics religious intellectuals made up for themselves within their larger design for the social world they proposed to bring into being claims acutely contemporary interest. And, as I shall show in chapters 3 through 8, the Mishnah does set out a clear account of a political structure and system, answering fundamental questions of politics in a systematic and orderly way. It is the kind of writing that sages could have taken along to any distant, unsettled land for reference on how to build the holy society that they would have had in mind. So the politics of a religion attracts our interest simply because, in the world as we know it, religion forms a fundamental constituent of political reality.

But there is a second point of acute interest, one that raises the stakes still higher. If through studying the politics of religion we learn about politics, in that same inquiry we learn still more about religion. Indeed, I should claim that if we do not study the politics of a religion that falls into the classification of a political religion, we do not understand much about that religion, for when a religion sets forth a politics, the politics will form the focus of that religion's intellectual energies and in the practical life will furthermore attract considerable and sustained attention. Specifically, in a political religion such as Judaism, we see how religion enjoys and (in at least the instance at hand) exercises the power to speak not only through theology or myth but also through politics.[6]

Why then do I insist that *if* a religion has a politics, then that politics demands analysis as a principal heuristic exercise? The reason is that what characterizes a well-crafted systemic statement of the social order is that every detail makes the system's main point. A system finds cogency in addressing a self-evidently valid response to a single urgent question. It follows that the details will bear the burden of the whole. So through politics as much as through theology, what the system wishes to say overall, it also says in detail.

But why through politics in particular? Answers to these questions help us to grasp the character of religion in its diverse manifestations: why did this system (in our case, this Judaism) bother to make up a politics at all? What type of religion will speak also through politics and what type will not? And that fundamental question yields these principal parts: what statement, part of the larger theory of the social order and system, did the politics serve to make, and why was politics the uniquely appropriate medium to convey that message? These are the questions concerning the institutionalization and utilization of state power in the foundation document of Judaism that, in my view, draw our interest and make the inquiry important.

It follows that at stake is our understanding not only of politics in the religious setting, but of religion in its own right. In asking how religions would invent and have invented politics and political systems, states and governments, we frame a question that religions do answer in their own terms.[7] If I frame the question in a systemic way, wanting to know the place of politics within the social order planned by a religion, the message the political component of the system sets forth, and the reason that that message requires formulation in political terms, it is therefore is for a simple reason. That way of inquiry—seeing things whole, as a coherent system and account of the social order—entirely accords with the way in which religions answer the question of power.

Let us now turn to the plan of this book. In chapters 1 and 2 I lay out the definitions for a politics, the politics of a religion, required for the rest of the work.

Then at some length, in chapter 2, I introduce the source for the system of Judaism analyzed here, the Mishnah.[8] Next, I spell out the Mishnah's particular politics and describe how it worked. In chapters 3 through 8 I set forth what I conceive to be the politics of Judaism as the Mishnah defines that politics: in chapters 3, 4, and 5 I lay out what I understand as its stable and static structure (myth, institutions, staff), and in chapters 6, 7, and 8 I go on to consider the dynamic workings of the system (passion, responsibility, proportion).

If in part 1 I present the structure, and in part 2 the system of the politics of Judaism, in part 3 I proceed to interpret the structure and system in an appropriate context of comparison and contrast. In this, the analytical and interpretative section of the book, I first propose a theory of comparison (chapter 9) and from that theory validate my choice of Aristotle as the author with whom I compare (chapter 10). I then compare the politics of Judaism with Aristotle's politics (chapter 11) and go on to characterize in comparative and contrastive context the politics of Judaism (chapter 12).

Of course, I operate comparatively and contrastively because I bear in mind that "who knows only one thing knows nothing."[9] Still, I take more than usual risks in choosing Aristotle's *Politics* as my text for comparison, for I am not an expert on classical philosophy.[10] Indeed, for Aristotle's *Politics* I rely on standard textbook descriptions—with attention to some first-class monographs, to be sure. I do not pretend to know first hand what is in fact not my field of learning at all. But despite my acknowledged limitations, the *Politics* of Aristotle[11] allows us to discern through its contrast with the politics of Judaism the choices sages made, the indicative traits peculiar to the system before us.

But what we shall see in this comparison bears interest beyond the case at hand. For instance, Aristotle's politics and economics appeal to precisely the same social metaphor, appealing to a single building block (the household) for the explanation of both aspects of the social order. In that sense Aristotle embeds economics within political economy. By contrast, the Mishnah's Judaism works out politics and economics each within its own social framework. In this sense, then, Judaism in the system of the Mishnah presents us with the anomaly of an economics separated out from a politics. In due course I shall set forth why I think the systems differ and what I think accounts for the difference. But that matter, of more than local interest, will become clear only in the comparison of Aristotle's and Judaism's economics and their respective politics.

With regard to the Jewish materials for comparison, let me stress that here I cite only a sample.[12] Still, in these pages I do present a considerable volume of abstracts. Obviously, I could have made this book much shorter if I had merely referred the reader to the Mishnah passages that I discuss. But the Mishnah, though important in Judaism, is not widely known. And certainly, the rather diverse audience I seek to address includes a majority who, before opening this book, have never heard of it at all. For their sake I present fairly sizable abstracts from the document itself and explain them in somewhat greater detail than authors in other fields, such as classics and biblical studies, commonly find necessary.

At two important points in the unfolding argument, I draw upon results from my earlier studies. Chapter 2 rests on *Self-Fulfilling Prophecy: Exile and Redemption in the History of Judaism* (Boston: Beacon Press, 1986); chapters 9, 10, 11, and 12 draw upon *The Economics of the Mishnah* (Chicago: University of Chicago Press, 1990). Indeed, chapter 10 goes over a matter discussed at much greater length in *Economics*.[13]

1

Defining a Politics and
the Politics of a Religion

Religion comprises what people *do* together, not just what they believe in the privacy of their hearts. In other words, religion functions socially. And since it operates within society, religion may therefore function politically. Consider: when a social entity exercises violence that it regards as legitimate, it translates itself into a fully empowered political structure; in that religious (and secular) systems address issues of the social order, explaining and legitimating power, a religion may and commonly does encompass the use of violence in maintaining that order. That is, religion takes on the power of politics, narrowly defined as the theory of legitimate violence, indicating who gets to tell whom what to do and why, and therefore also who gets what.

This point proves critical to my comparative study of Aristotle's and the Mishnah's political systems. Since politics encompasses the (possible) distribution of scarce resources (the "who gets what" part of the definition), I compare two systems the economics of which coincide in detail and in premise. Alike in economics, the systems prove quite unlike in politics, and I explain why. But that very narrow definition of politics will soon prove inadequate to the task of fully describing, explaining, and evaluating the Mishnah's system. The philosophical issues of politics raised both by Greek and Mishnaic political thought ask systemic questions about the uses of power. Defining politics in terms of the use of violence to achieve one's will eliminates important aspects of legitimate violence within human society by treating power as an independent topic of political and philosophical inquiry. Analyzing the Mishnah's and Aristotle's politics requires us to drop the post-Hobbesian definition as inadequate, and I show in these pages that that definition is inadequate as an ultimate definition of politics and also is inadequate to the variety of human history and experience.

Of course, the kinds of power effected in politics and in religion generally are thought to differ from one another. Religion focuses on supernatural power; politics deals with government, the state, and authority in the natural world of the here and the now. As M. I. Finley says, "state power is unique, overriding all other 'powers' within the society by its acknowledged right to exercise force, even to kill, when its representatives deem such action to be necessary." [1] Accordingly, in theory, the power of which religion speaks and that of concern to politics scarcely intersect. But the theory of what may be contradicts the facts of what was, since, before the seventeenth century, politics addressed systemic purposes and was not disembedded from the encompassing theory of the social order put forth by religion. Religion integrated politics, economics, and philosophy, imparting its character and purpose to them all, expressing its statement of self-evident truth through them all.

Judaism falls into the classification of a political religion because its foundation document, the Mishnah, sets forth a view of power and of the disposition of power in society that is fundamentally political. What makes this view political is that the system treats violence as legitimate when exercised by proper authority. Indeed, it specifies who may impose his will through coercion. [2] That is, the initial system of Judaism defines within the framework of the faith a political structure and system that are integral to its religious plan for the social order. In the first systemic statement beyond Scripture itself, this Judaism secured for the institutions of the social order the power to exercise legitimate violence for the social entity. The institutions of this particular Judaism permanently ration and rationalize the uses of that power.

It is certainly not a typical situation. Consider: not all prior Judaisms appealed to political categories. [3] In fact, after the Pentateuch few of them even set forth a politics. Moreover, from the writing down of the highly political fantasies of the Pentateuchal compilers (ca. 450 B.C.) to the formation of the Judaism that began with the Mishnah (ca. A.D. 200), no Judaism in the Land of Israel systematically incorporated politics within its system or framed any part of its statement in political categories. But this one did. In consequence, we classify it as a political religion and undertake to study the genus, political religion, through the species of a particular and appropriate Judaism.

To the sages of Judaism represented by the Mishnah, the separation of power in the form of legitimate violence from power in other forms, supernatural ones, for instance, proves implausible. To them, as to the Greco-Roman philosophical tradition in political theory, politics forms a component of the social order. Power is not to be separated from other critical elements of that same order. Politics and power cannot be treated as an independent topic of inquiry; for in antiquity, what we say about politics forms a chapter in a larger statement within our theory of the social order. Politics then is subordinated, contingent, instrumental. Treating politics as limited to the use of violence to achieve one's will proves a distinctively modern reading of matters; politics disembedded from economics and philosophy formed a point of analysis only with Hobbes's *Leviathan,* and economics was disembedded from politics only a century later. [4]

But it is precisely because we cannot take for granted the severing of the relationship between religion and political power that the Judaism analyzed here provides us with such an interesting case. Here I set forth a politics that is thoroughly integrated into a larger systemic structure and that bears a principal part of the systemic message. Rabbinic political theory, beginning with the Mishnah, integrated politics with economics and philosophy and provided a first-rate example of a political religion and a religious politics—both, equally. Here, of course, we focus only on the description, analysis, and interpretation of a political religion. Others will want to consider the same writings that I treat here within the framework of the representation of a religious politics.

For many religions, political power has no relevance; by contrast, this Judaism set forth as part of a large philosophical structure and system a political religion—a religious and also, therefore, a theological politics. Indeed, the power posited by the Judaism of the dual Torah in its initial document, and, as a matter of fact, by all Judaisms deriving from this formulation, exactly matches that described by Finley.

The Judaism of the dual Torah came to literary expression in the Mishnah.[5] From this philosophy in the form of a law code (closed at ca. A.D. 200), all subsequent Judaic systems claimed their provenance.[6] So it is of considerable importance that the Mishnah's philosophers invoke the power of the state legitimately to commit acts of violence, that they allow their concept of the Jewish state, or of Israel as political entity, the right to seize property, to maim, banish, ostracize, and kill. Why is it so important? They effectively formulate Judaism in their time and in the times to follow as wholly and completely political in precisely the accepted sense. In other words, they make it clear that when a religion invents a politics, as did the Judaism of the dual Torah in its initial formulation in the Mishnah, we may reasonably investigate the politics of that religion.

Of course, all religions speak of power, and thus of legitimate violence. In their view, power is exercised by or in behalf of god and his divine agencies. But religions talk politics in another manner, too. A religion's intellectuals claim to explain the workings of power. That is, they try to explain why things are the way they are. And in accounting for why legitimate power works, why things are as they are, they commonly propound a causative theory of how things began. Further, the assertion of how things began serves as an apologia for the religion's legitimate violence, for when we say how things originated, we implicitly claim that that is how things were when they were right, and therefore how they should be even now. This combination of circumstances explains why in this book we address the politics of a religion, that is to say, we analyze a political religion. It further explains why we cannot limit our analysis to data that directly concern coercion and violence, legitimate or otherwise, but must extend our interest to the consideration of all aspects of the social order that the Mishnah means to describe. We cannot treat politics as disembedded from myth and philosophy and economics.

In fact, in imagination and intellect the system builders of the Judaism in the Mishnah invented a political theory to bear a principal part of their systemic statement. That theory precipitated a system comprising, in correct position, proportion, and composition, the components of the social order. Its Judaism therefore comprises an ethos (an account of a worldview, in secular terms, a philosophy), an ethics (a prescription of a corresponding way of life, in secular terms, an economics[7]), and an ethnos (a definition of the social entity that finds definition in the one and description in the other). These three components sustain one another in explaining the whole of this Judaism's social order, in constituting the theoretical account of its system. In Judaism's foundation document they combine to define in the context of a Judaism what is meant by "Israel."

Indeed, until the advent of the nation-state, in important ways political systems that claimed to carry forward the politics of the Mishnah's Judaism did govern. The fictive politics of post-Temple Judaism's initial statement constituted the reference point for subsequently sorting out issues of power. That is, for long years they continued to define legitimate violence for the Jewish people—insofar as the Jews had any power at their disposal. True, in practice this politics was never quite that planned by the initial statement, but then, politics rarely follows the path projected by the founders. Certainly, the generative principles of post-Temple Judaism's initial formulation endured. Thus the answers we find here to the following questions—"By what right does one party tell another party what to do?" and "With what justice does the commanding party legitimately impose sanctions, including violent ones, upon the party that does not conform?"—apply across time.

Clearly, the Judaism that commenced with the Mishnah and that continues to predominate even now is political.[8] And why does that Judaism have a politics? Because its initial system made and effected its statement within political, as well as economic and philosophical, categories (among other intellectual media of thought and expression). It therefore designed a society in all its important conceptual components. It included (1) economics: the disposition of scarce resources,[9] (2) politics: the utilization of legitimate violence, and justification by appeal to (3) philosophy: the generative natural and supernatural rules.[10] And in attending to all three together, to the categorical imperatives of economics (the means for everyday living), to politics (the realization in concrete policy and action of the theory of the social entity), and to philosophy (the well-composed account of the worldview that animates the whole), Judaism managed to form an account of a complete social order.

Further, that initial Judaism established the boundaries inside which all successive systems within that same unfolding Judaism situated themselves. To the present day, the social forms of Judaism take positions on economic, political, and philosophical questions. The matter of politics, of course, is most blatant. How so? In contemporary times, important continuators of the Judaism of the Mishnah and its successor writings and systems try to accomplish their religious goals by appealing to politics, to the legitimate use of coercion.

It is the fact, then, that the power of the Mishnah's framers' imagination guided them in producing a well-crafted and encompassing politics, a theory of political institutions with power to make and effect public policy that was integral to their systemic program. And that theory of politics did form the reference point for the legitimate exercise of coercion such as, through nearly two thousand years, Jews' public institutions and political community carried on.

The Mishnah, and thus its politics, emerged at a transitional moment in the social world of Jews in Palestine. They came simultaneously to expression in the brief moment between the end of the old order, in A.D. 70, and the beginning of the new, A.D. 135 (although not brought to closure in writing until ca. A.D. 200); the moment between a period of many centuries during which Israel, in its Land of Israel, had constituted a political entity, and the period during which the Jews in Palestine lost most of their political power in the aftermath of Bar Kokhba's rebellion. That is, the Mishnah emerged between the end of the politics of political autonomy (if not complete independence), such as Jews sustained before 70 as a self-governing entity within the Roman system, and the politics of subordination and severe restriction of the political power to coerce obedience in this world.[11]

Since the world persisted in denying Jews civil power until 1948, when Jews formed the nation-state, when we examine the Mishnah's picture of the Jewish state, its political structure and system, we consider a fabrication, something that never was and, so far, never has been. Claiming to present how things originally had been and should be again, this invented politics described a world that never was as a model for a world that has not come into being.

So why, in that moment of suspended political activity between A.D. 70 and A.D. 135, should a group of sages set forth a grand design for politics? They did so because their design formed part of a still larger imaginary conception of the integrated life of the entire nation that sorted out the rules for structure and order in every component of that life, whether economic, political, hierarchical, philosophical, or theological. All components of the system as a whole found an appropriate locus, each detail embedded in one encompassing framework of conviction and value, along with every other component. And through many things these system builders managed to say one thing; through politics, as through economics and philosophy, the nourishing system made its one statement.

Thus, in describing, analyzing, and interpreting the system builders' implicit politics, we examine in the material context established by that concrete setting that one thing that the system as a whole meant to say, its self-evident answer to the question its framers selected as urgent and ineluctable. And this is what makes our study interesting—to see how in the parts we are able to discern the character and composition of a whole. With that perception in mind we can make sense of the politics that this religion invented and frame a theory on the workings of religious politics and political religions.[12]

In brief, the framers of the Mishnah set forth a picture of a state and a society in relationship with other states and other societies and under the rule, so they held, of the one God who ruled all states. Further, conforming with the theory at hand, they tacitly rejected the world in favor of the life within. They set forth a powerful affirmation of the capacity of the private person to sort things out in the formations of intention, will, imagination, and intellect. And yet, as we shall see, at every point they appealed not to private vision but to public policy. That explains why a theory of politics proved necessary to their systemic composition, why their imagined scheme, constructed wholly in mind, formed a political religion and a religious politics.[13] And that accounts for my picture, in parts 1 and 2, of the politics of Judaism, for the categorical imperatives that guide me to the data within the Mishnah that I deem to form the politics of that particular religious system.

Since the Mishnah, unlike Plato's *Republic* or Aristotle's *Politics,* is not broadly received as a treatise on politics, it remains to explain precisely what kind of data I claim do provide information on the politics of Judaism.[14] My criteria for selecting the data I examine derive from the theory of politics just now adumbrated. So far as politics is the theory of the exercise of legitimate power, dictating who may do what to whom and upon which basis, sanctions embody politics—imposing sanctions marks an extreme exercise of that power that works best when left tacit and implicit. At each critical point in my description of the politics of Judaism, therefore, I return to the Mishnah's account of sanctions. I regard as a principal contribution of this book my identification of sanctions as the entry point for political study of Judaism. Everything else flows from that selection of what is pertinent among a variety of available data.

The politics of Judaism invokes in vast detail the naked exercise of legitimate coercion. Coercion takes the form of judicial acts of killing, judicial infliction of injury, confiscation of valued property and services, ostracism and exclusion.[15] These penalties are specific to particular actions. Over and over again, we shall find in the details of the system's picture of sanctions the facts we require for the composition of the theory of politics we seek. For instance, its myth accounts for what political institution imposes which sanction. Then again, if we ask about the passion and purpose of the system and propose to identify the validating responsibilities assumed by the system, we repeatedly inquire into the representation of power in its naked forms. That is why in parts 2 and 3 I repeatedly appeal to the data supplied by sanctions in my description of the system's six principal components. There I claim, in the form of brute force legitimately exercised, to find the politics of Judaism.

What kind of politics, exactly, do we now describe? It is not a practical politics, one that describes how things actually happened, but only a utopian politics, a structure and system of a fictive and a fabricated kind. It is an intellectual's conception of a politics. In making up a politics, religious intellectuals' pictures of how things are supposed to be appeal to archaic systems. Politics then emerges as invention by Heaven or in the model of Heaven, not as a secular revision and reform of an existing system. To see religion—exemplified here by a Judaism in particular—in this way is to take religion seriously as a way of realizing, in classic documents, a large conception of the world. That is why we appropriately turn to a Judaism as an example of a religion that composes for itself a cogent account of the social order.

But if all we analyze is a politics of utopia, a structure built nowhere in particular and a system never actually realized in social governance, then why bother? Surely reality presents sufficient cases for political inquiry? We need not be detained by someone's fantasies too. To understand what is at stake in the question taken up here, finding out in some detail just how the framers of the theory of a social system invent a politics, we must undertake an experiment in imagination. This will show what we learn in an account of an imaginary politics, why even today political thought appeals not only to the *is* but to the *what if*.

What if, preparing to make the voyage to Jupiter, where we intended to build a new heaven, we had to invent a politics for the new planet from the debris of a ruined Earth? Consider the challenge of constructing a new and valid politics using whatever we might wish from available institutions and conceptions, and inventing what we needed. What sort of politics should we invent for our brave new world? Clearly, the problem is to discover the categorical imperatives, the strategy as to policy, for the formation of a world made up *de novo*. What should we take with us out of the past? And how within the utopian imagination should we organize the political system to govern the nascent state? So our fabricated politics provides data about the possibilities of invention—and also about the consequences.

We can assume, for instance, that the potential society, like the dying one, will require the legitimate exercise of power, even of violence, to hold together and sustain itself over time. Some people must exercise authority and so tell others what to do, and they will need a theory or story of legitimation for that power, that is, they will appeal to a political myth. Further, since the right to exercise power will be vested in offices and institutions and will have to be transmitted to persons qualified to staff those agencies, they will need a theory of the structure of political institutions and an account of the way to qualify for the bureaucracy. Finally, the travelers into the unknown of social organization will also take with them a theoretical picture of how the politics will actually function. That is to say, they will map the sources of passion, the outer limits of the arena of public and political responsibility, and the workings of public policy in proportion and proper balance.[16] And all of this will govern the map that in intellect and sensibility will guide the travelers as they venture into the uncharted spaces to build a new society, a new politics.

Of course, our refugees from planet Earth will think about other political issues besides those that I will specify as fundamental for Judaism. Just so, the second-century philosophers could have defined their politics in other categories entirely. At this stage, then, let me specify systemic issues that theoretically bear upon any politics—that surely would bear upon the politics of our new earth to be built in a distant heaven—but that I choose to omit from my study of Judaism. But first let me explain why I do not address them. My answer will clarify the entire enterprise. The most important omitted topic is this: what exactly did the politics of Judaism conceive the Jews to be? Were they a nation, a state, a region, an ethnos in the Greco-Roman sense? What choices were before the theorists, and what selection did they make among them? Our space travelers would assuredly answer that question for their people, but here, for the Jews, we shall not. Why? Because, first, the question is dealt with systematically elsewhere, and, second, while political, it plays no important part in the exposition of the politics of the "Israel" invented by the philosophers of the Mishnah.[17]

But there are other political questions that do make a difference and that, although they would surely be dealt with by a theoretical politics for a new world, I omit. These cover the definition in abstract terms of the body politic and include the nature of sovereignty, how it is acquired, how it should be exercised, the characteristics of good and bad government, and, in general, the relations between the ruler and the ruled. Why do I exclude these questions? The Mishnah's philosophers think in concrete ways about abstract questions; the issues of the body politic concerning sovereignty prove only abstract (at least, for them). Consequently, I cannot identify the epiphenomena, in concrete facts, of the applied reason that lead us back to the theory of the matter.

There is still a third range of political questions not dealt with here. The reasons why I bypass these illuminate the character of the analysis I propose to undertake. To be specific, I do not treat the Judaic political culture (i.e., "good breeding, courtesy, and urbanity . . . civility, etiquette, and correct behavior in both social and political contexts").[18] I omit it not because the Mishnah neglects it. In fact, the Mishnah richly describes the traits of the political culture. For instance, it depicts extensively the sage's training—and the sage, as civil servant, is the political instrument of power. He tells people what to do and invokes sanctions upon those who fail to keep the law. I neglect these weighty matters of the politics not because they are neglected or even because they bear little consequence, for that is not so. Rather, I choose not to address them because they are systemically inert issues. They contain information; they do not define systemic structure and composition. They provide interesting instruction; they do not address the generative problematic, which is to say, the acute and urgent questions, and they do not contain elements of the self-evidently valid answers to those questions. Thus I exclude some categories of political issues not because the Mishnah fails to provide opinions on them, but because the Mishnah's opinions do not lead us into the dynamics of the politics under study or clarify the character of the system that speaks through this politics. The reason, of course, is that the system is prior, selecting first its problems, then the data that require exegesis in the solution of those problems.

Accordingly, an analysis of the politics of a religious system therefore yields insight not into politics, but into the nature of that religious system. It reveals how that system delivers its message through the topics it selects for detailed analysis, what its message is, and why it chooses (in this case) politics as the appropriate medium for stating its message. But political culture in the politics of Judaism, though prominent, is essentially peripheral to the systemic problematic. That is why, in this context, the questions at hand fall entirely outside the frame of reference of the politics we shall examine.[19] So much for the nature of our inquiry, our analysis of a theory about theoretical politics, our accounting for what "we" should and would do, if in terms of power we could do anything at all.

Why focus upon the politics of Judaism in particular? Judaism's politics proves peculiarly congruent with the requirements of our mental experiment, for this politics speaks of a structure that never was and of a system, moreover, that never came into being. In the Mishnah we deal with intellectuals through their pure thought; here we know only how people imagined that things should be. The whole political structure and system of Judaism, as portrayed in the Mishnah, was fabricated by the document's authorship. At the time the Mishnah's sages made up their laws, as I suggested in my introduction, the politics to which they appealed bore no correspondence whatsoever to the politics they knew in the concrete exercise of power. To quote, somewhat anachronistically, "Brick served them as stone, and mud served them as mortar" (Gen. 11:3); they had nothing better with which to work, no facts, no experience, no problems that fell within their power for solution and resolution.

The facts of history show us why we find a politics thus congruent with our experiment's requirements in the Judaism of the Mishnah, why we find there a made-up politics for a utopian society.[20] In the middle second century, Rome incorporated the Land of Israel, as Palestine, into its imperial system. Further, Rome denied Jews access to their capital, Jerusalem. That is, the Romans permanently closed the Jews' cult center, their Temple. Yet at the same time, the Mishnah's authorship, Judaism's religious intellectuals, its philosophers, made up a politics. Despite their circumstances, which undermined their entire pursuit, they described a government comprising a king, a high priest, and an administration fully empowered to carry out the law through legitimate violence. It follows that if we want to know what it is like to weave a politics out of the gossamer threads of hopeful fantasy, we can do no better than to turn for thread to the skein of the Mishnah's politics.

As I have indicated, that theoretical task of inventing a state, of defining the institutions that bear responsibility for the social entity, of detailing the institutional functions for telling people what to do, for enforcing policy through sanctions (the legitimate manifestation of violence), defines the agenda of any politics. But what, precisely, will any politics, any theory of the legitimation of violence and its uses, need to dictate for its structure and system? Every politics needs a list of questions that require attention, a program of thought that guides its constitution in a new setting.[21] The new politics would have to set forth how power in the new age would be distributed. Through a constitution and bylaws, a description of institutions and their jurisdiction, or a law code, it would need to detail political institutions and their power, political classes and their responsibility, and, not least, a political system and its myth.

Once we ask for the topics that politics must take up—and that is, politics any time and anywhere—we move from an experiment in imagination to the identification of a political theory that will guide us in our initial stages of identifying relevant facts in the Mishnah. I find helpful the political theory of Max Weber in his "Politics as a Vocation." I find, in particular, six descriptive categories for political analysis that serve here as a starting point. These categories are as follows: (1) myth; (2) institutions; (3) administration; (4) passion; (5) responsibility; (6) proportion. They seem to me on the surface to cover principal constituents of any political structure and system, because they tell me how to know what politics is and how it works. These categories require that we see how a system explains for the generative motivation and legitimation of its politics. They tell me that I have to know what ongoing institutions and administrative organs manipulate power. They require me to look for the definitions of a system's political goals, how the system defines its arena for concrete action, and where the system derives its sense of order and cogency that make the whole work. Weber's catalog of political structures provides correct starting points only. From them I turn to the Mishnah's statements on matters Weber tells me concern politics. But when I take up these statements, I find that the Mishnah's political structure and system is not wholly symmetrical with Weber's categories, requiring the inclusion within the realm of politics of data of a less than tangible character in describing quite worldly issues of power and administration.

Let me give a brief account of what I have found important in Weber's definition of politics. He considers that politics encompasses "any kind of independent leadership in action." By politics Weber understands "only the leadership, or the influencing of the leadership, of a political association, hence, today, of a state." And a state is defined as a political association with access to the use of physical force, "a human community that (successfully) claims the monopoly of the legitimate use of physical force within a given territory. . . . Hence 'politics' for us means striving to share power or striving to influence the distribution of power, either among states or among groups within a state" (PV 77, 78).[22] A problem qualifies as political when "interests in the distribution, maintenance, or transfer of power are decisive for answering the questions and determining the decision."

Further, Weber says, "He who is active in politics strives for power either as a means in serving other aims or as 'power for power's sake,' that is, in order to enjoy the prestige-feeling that power gives" (PV 78). That observation frames for us the initial issue of a politics, one that must be dealt with before a political structure can be set forth. Weber asks the question in this way: "If the state is to exist, the dominated must obey the authority claimed by the powers that be." He goes on to ask, "When and why do men obey? Upon what inner justifications and upon what external means does this domination rest?" (PV 77–78). Here is a point on which the Mishnaic testimony proves particularly fresh, since we see within a religious politics a highly differentiated answer: there are different authorities, some worldly, some not, and obedience to each is going to be explained within a theory encompassing the whole.

That is why a religion's politics proves so suggestive, for it offers a principal mode for the legitimation of domination. One way of course is through appeal to the charisma of the prophet or general. But that category, so familiar in Weber's corpus, does not serve with the Mishnah, which is—if anything— a profoundly anticharismatic document, and yet which also predicates its politics upon a response to religious attitude and conviction. One reason that Weber serves better at the beginning than at the end of the description of a religious politics is his richer appreciation for the charismatic than for the routine, his reluctance to accord to myth and even theology the capacity to secure obedience that faith in the holy man precipitates. But when Weber asks, further, who is to exercise domination, we find in the Mishnah a quite appropriate corpus of data, since a variety of persons and institutions, each in its own realm, can tell others what to do and impose sanctions if they do not obey. Weber states matters as follows:

> Organized domination, which calls for continuous administration, requires that human conduct be conditioned to obedience towards those masters who claim to be bearers of legitimate power. . . . By virtue of this obedience, organized domination requires the control of those material goods which . . . in a given case are necessary for the use of physical violence. Thus organized domination requires control of the personal executive staff and the material implements of administration. The administrative staff, which externally represents the organization of political domination, is, of course, like any other organization, bound by obedience to the power-holder (PV 80).

Here the pertinent question is, what program does the system follow in staffing its institutions? I shall explain the classes of persons recruited for the administration and spell out how they are selected and trained for the work and what sort of positions are envisioned for them. The question then is, who manages and maintains the institutions of politics and secures long-term and broad obedience to the political structure? In this connection Weber writes, "In all political associations which are somehow extensive, that is, associations going beyond the sphere and range of the tasks of small rural districts . . . political organization is necessarily managed by men interested in the management of politics." When we can outline the program for staffing the institutions, we find a clear account of the political structure, seen from within. We shall dig down to the deepest layers of the system's foundations. There we find both why and also how the political classes sustain themselves, make the living that is required to permit them to service the power that they seek.

An account of the structure of a politics in general will tell us the answers to these three questions: what are the components of power, encompassing the myth of legitimacy, to which all users of power to coerce appeal? How do the institutions of power, that is, the political structures, take shape? Who makes up the political classes, how are they supported, and by what means do persons gain entry into the political classes of administration and bureaucracy, of leadership and domination? The answers to these three questions seem to me to form the principal components of an account of a political structure. And, as we shall see, in its somewhat odd way, the Mishnah will tell us the forms of power that it recognizes, how these forms of power to coerce are realized, and who exercises the power of coercion—telling whom what to do and why. So much for defining what we mean by Judaism's political structure, which is treated in part 2.

Now, what of the political system of Judaism, to which part 3 is addressed? Weber classifies not only political institutions but also their dynamics. He explores how a structure works, detailing the components of a functioning system. The politician realizes the system, the system preserves the occasion for the politician to do his work. What then are the elements in Weber's classification that serve in this study?

Weber considers the politician's qualities to be passion, a feeling of responsibility, and a sense of proportion. For the purposes of a political reading of the Mishnah, I translated these into systemic categories as follows: passion stands for why the politics works; responsibility for what the politics accomplishes; proportion for how the politics is imagined to function. Weber defines the virtues of the politician in language that we may easily translate into the functions of a system and hence utilize in our account of the politics of the Mishnah. He speaks of

> passion . . . in the sense of matter-of-factness, of passionate devotion to a cause, to the god or demon who is its overlord. . . . The politician inwardly has to overcome a quite trivial and all-too-human enemy: a quite vulgar vanity, the deadly enemy of all matter-of-fact devotion to a cause, and of all distance, in this case, of distance towards oneself.
>
> [The politician] works with the striving for power as an unavoidable means. Therefore 'power instinct' belongs indeed to his normal qualities. The sin against the lofty spirit of his vocation . . . begins where this striving for power ceases to be objective and becomes purely personal self-intoxication, instead of exclusively entering the service of the cause. For ultimately there are only two kinds of deadly sins in the field of politics: lack of objectivity and irresponsibility. . . . Irresponsibility . . . suggests that he enjoys power merely for power's sake without a substantive purpose (PV 115–16).

The matter of proportion is left by Weber without clear exposition. In my opinion his observations on the ethics of politics do point toward a good definition: "The decisive means for politics is violence. . . . Whoever contracts with violent means for whatever ends—and every politican does—is exposed to its specific consequences" (PV 121–24). That is to say, the correct proportion in the political system will weigh against one another the costs and benefits of the exercise of power. It will assess the relative effectiveness of violence and persuasion, threat and promise.

Clearly then an account of how a political system is supposed to work will tell us how to hold the whole together. Our task is without the exercise of naked power to persuade people to do what we want. Weber's judgment guides my inquiry on these points: "Politics is a strong and slow boring of hard boards." That explains why I follow up three questions: passion, or why the politics works; responsibility, or what the political component of the Judaic system is supposed to accomplish; and proportion, how the politics functions to achieve its goals.

Out of Weber, then, I have drawn organizing categories. But I have not limited my repertoire of pertinent data to those facts that serve within Weber's framework. I have had to transcend his limits, because his appreciation for the political dimensions of religion, and the religious dimensions of politics, proves incongruous with the facts of the Mishnah. The Mishnah organizes its discourse and sets forth its own system of classifications. Even where Weber's classifications serve—and this book begins with the postulate that they do serve, if in a limited way—the Mishnah's mode of category formation time and again presents us with important data that require recasting Weber's categories. But Weber allows us to come to the Mishnah with categories that can be readily understood, so that comparative studies can get under way in which the Mishnah, too, provides its corpus of pertinent examples in the inquiry into issues of general interest and intelligibility. True, political theory has long since made its judgment of Weber. But anyone who wishes to deal with a very specific system in such a way as to address common concerns has to begin somewhere beyond the particular system under study, and I know of no better starting point than Weber.

I mean, moreover, to contribute to the discussion Weber inaugurated in his "Religious Rejections of the World and Their Directions," with special reference to the political sphere.[23] For Weber, we recall, thought to comment upon the history of Judaism and of the Jews, and in some of the most embarassing parts of his oeuvre, he laid down judgments that have to be addressed. Specifically, Weber finds tension between the brotherly ethic of salvation religions and the political orders of the world. This tension comes about by the rise of universalist religions, which posit God's ruling the whole world. Weber writes:

> The gods of locality, tribe and polity were only concerned with the interests of their respective associations. They had to fight other gods like themselves, just as their communities fought, and they had to prove their divine powers in this very struggle. The problem only arose when these barriers of locality, tribe, and polity were shattered by universalist religions. . . . The problem of tensions with the po-

litical order emerged for redemption religions out of the basic demand for brotherliness. And in politics, as in economics, the more rational the political order became, the sharper the problems of these tensions became. . . .

The state's absolute end is to safeguard or to change the external and internal distribution of power; ultimately this end must seem meaningless to any universalist religion of salvation. This fact has held . . . even more so for foreign policy. It is absolutely essential for every political association to appeal to the naked violence of coercive means in the face of outsiders as well as in the face of internal enemies. It is only this very appeal to violence that constitutes a political association in our terminology. The state is an association that claims the monopoly of the legitimate use of violence and cannot be defined in any other manner (PV 334).

Here we see one important point at which Weber's theoretical framework proves not entirely serviceable in the analysis of the Mishnah's politics; moreover, the Mishnah's politics defines a realm of political analysis that Weber cannot in theory address. His notion that the state is defined by its claim upon a monopoly of the legitimate use of violence proves too narrow for political structures that recognize beyond themselves others capable of legitimately exercising violence. The Mishnah describes three structures that legitimately exercise violence, and none claims a monopoly. This triangular political structure calls into question the notion that the state finds its definition in its incapacity to share power. But a vast variety and range of political entities not only accommodate themselves to competing political structures, they concede the legitimacy of the competition. The complexity of the range of legitimate violence is scarcely recognized in Weber's definition of matters, and the system before us shows how political entities share power—a lesson that, in the politics of our own time, proves remarkably relevant.

Not only so, but even in his picture of Judaism, Weber errs. By the second century, the Mishnah's system addressed the world at large and, along with all other Judaisms, assuredly proposed a universalist account of how one God ruled all humanity in justice and love. And yet this Judaism in no way could perceive tension between religion and the rationalities of politics and economics. The whole held together in a single cogent system.

Consider: the Mishnah's framers resorted to a deeply political reading of existence in order to convey their vision of Israel and of the world as they proposed to reconstruct them both. Consequently they set forth a politics that addressed issues quite different from those that, in Weber's view, define matters. They produced a realm within, and yet a vision of the world that encompasses, the active, the highly interventionist, utilization of power. They took for granted that, in theory at least, the state they described legitimately used violence. So the tension Weber discerns between state power and religious vision in no way characterizes the system at hand. While Weber has taught us how to begin our work, in the end, the Mishnah's Judaism also will suggest that some rewriting of Weber may be in order.

But what sort of data, within the Mishnah, contribute to the description of the politics of Judaism? To identify those data we begin with considerations of the disposition and rationalization of the uses of power—who can tell whom what to do and why. This question rapidly is redefined in terms of sanctions. For the system describes a variety of political institutions and persons, and what the system selects as its principal point of exegesis is the differentiation between and among those who legitimately impose sanctions. If the question, who does what to whom, finds its answer in the theory of differentiation among those who impose sanctions, that theory transcends questions of power and addresses, rather, theological issues of God's relationship to humanity. Once we ask about legitimate power, therefore, we move past a restricted definition of politics altogether and find our way toward the systemic center, which is not political in its basic classification at all, but theological. That explains why I view the rabbinic political theory of the Mishnah as an exercise in sorting out the relationships between politics and religion, with religion the independent variable, politics the instrumental and contingent one. Where the system differentiates, there is its focus, and, consequently, my account of the political theory of the Mishnah, its picture of the relationship of religion to the social order, will commence with that same point of differentiation: the theological anthropology of a system that begins with the divine metaphor for humanity—"in our image, after our likeness."

Still, identifying the correct data, even concerning sanctions, within the Mishnah proves difficult because the Mishnah speaks very concretely about details of cases, but rarely abstractly about principles. Take the matter of the political myth, for example. Because of the systemic document's philosophical and literary traits, we do not know what stories people told to persuade the subsequent generation to obey the authority claimed by the powers that be. But we do know a great deal concerning precisely the actualities of the power exercised by those authorities. We must therefore move in our analysis from the concrete expressions of the legitimate use of violence backward toward the identification of those permitted to utilize violence, thence to the (likely) explanation for the right of those who do so to coerce others. We must trace our path from sanctions, to institutions, to myth. That will not only define the main components of the mythic foundations of the politics Judaism, it will also identify the institutional elements, the structure of that same politics.[24]

And the case of finding myth within sanctions provides the rule. At each point, we seek in the Mishnah for evidences of the concrete working of power in particular cases. When we know how power is legitimately exercised, we may work our way back from cases involving sanctions, the naked edge of power, to the theoretical system that sorts out the issues of politics. What we do, therefore, in the case of myth is to seek guidance in the conception of how power works as we uncover the conception of what validates power's working as it does. That is to say, to identify relevant evidence of the working of a myth is to return to our simple definition of politics. When we have surveyed what a given type of authority may legitimately do to secure conformity to the system and its rules, we may ask why authority may act in such a way, why it may use physical force to enforce the law and sustain the system. From the end product, the sanctions that are legitimately invoked, we may describe the myth of the politics of Judaism. And that is the rule throughout: from power in the form of sanctions we may derive a description of the political structure and system that accounts for those sanctions and organizes power for the purposes of the social order.

But the study of politics also requires the comparison of one politics with some other—for if we know only one thing, as I have suggested, we understand nothing. So once we have identified the case for description, we face the task of defining the categorical basis for description, analysis, and interpretation. There can be no analysis without comparison and contrast, and no interpretation out of context. But with what politics shall I compare and contrast the politics of Judaism, and how shall I define the context for interpretation? We gain the perspective required for the analysis and interpretation of that same structure and system in the politics of Aristotle.[25] Our choice of Aristotle's politics is far from random; it is rather pointed and particular. Two reasons require it.

First of all, we choose Aristotle because for him, as for the philosophers of the Mishnah, politics formed a medium of choice for making an important part of a coherent systemic statement. Aristotle sees politics as a fundamental component of his system. He says: "political science . . . legislates as to what we are to do and what we are to abstain from." As to the institutionalization of power, I cannot imagine a more ample definition of politics than that.[26] And the Mishnah's sages stand well within the philosophical mode of political thought that begins with Aristotle. Furthermore, each politics—the Mishnah's and Aristotle's—originates in intellectuals' theoretical and imaginative life. And within that life, each forms an instance of the concrete realization of a larger theory of matters.[27] Not only so, but the Mishnah's worldview and way of life came to expression in a world in which, as I have shown in my *Economics of Judaism,* the ideas of Aristotle were conventional and expressed commonplace truths among intellectuals.

Further, when I seek appropriate systems for comparison and contrast, I turn in particular to the material relationships within society, because in these relationships power is realized in concrete ways; it ceases to be a hopeless abstraction and becomes a concrete case of someone's telling someone else what to do and why. In my judgment, when we ask about power, we deal with questions not merely of control of custom or conscience, but of command of the means of production. Therefore I find fundamental how the social order sorts out the position and authority of the one who commands the means of production, how control of the irreducible minima of the means of production defines the social order. This also explains why political analysis comes only after economic analysis, why it depends upon the results of that prior inquiry into a social system's disposition of scarce resources and into the theory by which it controls the means of production (to name two critical questions of the social analysis of a system's economics). Only when I know who commands the means of production can I inquire about who tells whom what to do and why, who legitimately coerces others even through violence. When we turn to Aristotle and the Mishnah's philosophers we discover that both give the same answer about what category of "person" forms the commanding presence in control of the means of production.[28] For Aristotle and for the Mishnah's sages, the fundamental unit of economic thought and the generative social metaphor was the householder.[29] So the givens of the thought-world of the Mishnah's framers' theory of economics, embedded in a larger systemic plan, correspond point by point with the economic program of Aristotle.[30] And because the two systems appeal to precisely the same social metaphor, that of the householder and his establishment, the fundamental unit of production, they seem to me to sustain comparison.

But the two systems' similar location of the householder within their economics invites us to explain the likenesses and differences we discover thereby. Further, the point of comparison also offers a point for contrast. While the economics of Aristotle and the economics of Judaism both build on the place and power of the person ("class," "caste," economic interest) in control of the means of production, the social metaphors that animate the politics of the two systems part company. Aristotle in his *Politics* consistently starts with that same person ("class") when he considers issues of power. But the Mishnah's philosophers construct their politics with an altogether different set of building blocks. The householder, fundamental to their economics, does not form a subject of political discourse at all and in no way constitutes a political class or caste. In this sense, the economics of the Mishnah is separated out from its politics, whereas the economics and politics of Aristotle's system are embedded within a larger and nurturing, cogent theory of political economy. That is to say, for Aristotle, both economics and politics originate in the agglomeration of households into villages and of villages into the city or *polis* (the social metaphor of his thought on political question). But as we shall see, the politics of the philosophers of the Mishnah does not follow suit.

2

Defining a Judaism and the Judaism of the Mishnah

A Judaism is a religious system that appeals for authority to the Hebrew Scriptures, or Old Testament, in setting forth a way of life and a worldview for the social entity "Israel." Here, however, by "Judaism" I refer to one among the many Judaic systems produced over time. This is the Judaic religious system that appealed to the myth of the Torah, or divine revelation, in two media, written and oral. It is called "the one whole Torah [that is, revelation by God] to Moses, our rabbi." Together, the written Torah—the Hebrew Scriptures—and the oral Torah—preserved in the medium of memory—form the foundation of the Judaism considered here. Hence this particular Judaism can be termed "the Judaism of the dual Torah." Within this Judaism's mythic account of the holy writings of the canon, the Mishnah is identified as the first piece of writing that transcribed the originally oral part of the Torah. Between the mosaic of writings compiled ca. 450 B.C. by Ezra and identified as the Pentateuch (with the remaining writings as well), and the Mishnah (ca. A.D. 200), this Judaism identified no writings that formed part of its Torah. But after the Mishnah, it accepted a great many writings as canonical, that is to say as part of the Torah revealed by God to our lord (rabbenu) Moses at Mount Sinai.[1] The Mishnah, then, is important because, with the Hebrew Scriptures, it formed the foundation of the Judaism paramount from that time to the present.

Up to now I have used as though they were commonplace certain formulations that are not necessarily accessible to readers. For instance, I have spoken of "*a* Judaism," not "Judaism," of "a religious *system,*" not "a religion." Why have I invented the conception of "a Judaism"? There has not been a single, unitary, internally harmonious Judaism from the beginning to the present. My conception permits identification of coherent data and makes it unnecessary to form theological judgments of authenticity or truth in addressing conflicting data from different Judaisms. The alternative is, for example, to try to harmonize the Judaism of the Dead Sea Scrolls with the Judaism of the Mishnah, although these scarcely intersect. As for my formulation "religious system," I employ it to distinguish between a religion, which covers many things, and the operations of religion within society. A religious sytem addresses only the identifiable traits of society and culture defined here. My shifts in terminology are intended to permit more precise and accurate identification of our subject and avoid needless errors in conception.

But let me expand on what I mean by *a* Judaism and a religious *system*. A religious system is an account of the shared life of a social entity, an account that appeals to supernatural origin or authority. The system comprises a way of life and a worldview, that is, it includes the (1) ethos and (2) ethics of (3) an ethnos studied, in the terms of social science, as the (1) philosophy, (2) economics, and (3) politics of a religion.[2] The social entity (which may also constitute a political entity; for example, a state with access to legitimate violence to secure its goals) may be made up of any number of persons, and it may last for any length of time, from an hour to an epoch.[3] The power of a religious system is to hold the social entity together, to hold the society the system addresses, the individuals who compose the society, and the ordinary lives they lead, in ascending order of consequence. That system then forms a whole and well-composed structure, for systems endure in that eternal present that they create.[4] Although they evoke precedent, they do not have a history. So a system relates to context, but it exists in an enduring moment.

If we use the same criteria to define a Judaism, they reveal that Judaism as a religious system comprising (1) a theory of the social entity, the "Israel," constituted by the group of Jews who sustain that Judaism;[5] (2) a way of life characteristic of, perhaps particular to, that group of Jews; (3) a worldview that accounts for the group's forming a distinctive social entity and explains those indicative traits that define the entity. Within this definition, I see the formation of the system of a Judaism in three aspects: [1] the context of the social entity or group that constituted the Judaism (corresponding to the ethnos), [2] the components of the canon of that group, that is, of the literary analysis of Judaism as displayed in its sacred writings—as they emerge at a particular time and place (corresponding to the ethos), and [3] the system of questions and answers that served that group of Jews in conducting its everyday affairs (corresponding to the ethics). That context finds definition in the encompassing society, by contrast to which the distinctive social entity sees itself as different.

The encompassing world constitutes the framework within which a given Judaism takes shape. I call it the ecology of a Judaism. The social entity in the case of a Judaism always appeals to "Israel" and calls itself an (or the only) "Israel." Within the framework of a program to describe the social foundations of a Judaism, the principal points of inquiry are readily defined. I see the politics as a concrete and material statement of the social entity of the system, the economics as the equally practical expression of its way of life, and the philosophy, of course, as the medium through which the prevailing worldview addresses concrete and urgent questions of mind.

Since I claim to know the difference between one Judaism and another, I have now to explain how we may tell Judaisms apart, for readers will certainly ask, are Judaisms not continuous with one another, forming a linear system through time as (at the very least) one begets the next? You may ask, even though they exhibit difference, do all Judaisms not in the end appeal to a single set of beliefs that make of the many things one thing? The answer to these questions, when formulated descriptively, not theologically, is negative. Theology assumes a single Judaism, attested by a single canon, but description finds in the concrete facts of history no justification for the classification of all data within a single harmonious and linear system. It sees no justification for Judaism, only for Judaisms. Indeed, evidence undermines more than the notion of a single Judaism running down through time. Even when we select synchronic evidence, that evidence does not admit the notion of a single Judaism universally acknowledged and practiced. There is not now, and never has been, a linear and incremental history of one continuous Judaism, beginning, middle, end, for there has never been Judaism, only Judaisms. Whether we take the measure diachronically or synchronically, we come up with no single Judaism, continuing on through time and absorbing within itself all manner of differences. We undertake a long and fruitless task if we try (on a descriptive, not on a theological, basis) to harmonize all matters of faith and religious practice regarded by Jews in all times and places as authoritative.

But what if we forego harmonization and instead claim to pick and choose authentic from inauthentic, or normative from aberrational, within Judaism? Then we abandon all claim to description. Instead we evaluate as to truth, which is to say, we make theological judgments. In so doing, we impose the judgment of what is merely one Judaism upon all Judaisms. Within the framework of description, analysis, and interpretation, such theological judgments find no place. Indeed they upset the composition and composure of academic inquiry of a descriptive and analytical character. Accordingly, vast differences characteristic of elements of a single genus of religions (for example of the genus Judaism, the species Judaisms) require not harmonization, let alone theological triage, but respectful attention. Each Judaism therefore is to be examined on its own, within the stages of its development as written sources attest to those stages. The natural history of Judaism(s) permits no other procedure than generalization out of speciation.

How to begin? When we identify Judaisms in one circumstance or period after another, we begin by trying to locate, in the larger group of Jews, those social entities that see themselves and are seen by others as distinct. The social entities of special interest are the ones that present to themselves in a form accessible to us (e.g., writing) a clear account of who they are in distinction from all other Jews, of what they do that is different from what all other (and unsuitable) Jews do, and of why they do what distinguishes them from gentiles as well as other Jews. These, the indicative rules and the characteristic modes of exegesis and explanation, all together define their own distinctive, even "unique," Judaism, just as the social entity commonly defines itself as the unique "Israel." For a Judaism addresses a social group, an Israel, with the claim that because that group constitutes not *an* Israel but (the only) Israel, people are to conduct themselves in one way, rather than in some other. It follows that a principal issue of the system will be a theory of power, of its institutionalization and utilization, that is to say, of its structure and its system. So a Judaism, or a Judaic system, constitutes a clear and precise account of the source and rationalization of power in and through the life of a social group, the way of life and worldview of a group of Jews, however defined.

This stress on the multiplicity of Judaisms precipitates an obvious question. If there are only many Judaisms, and has never been one Judaism, how can we speak of *Judaism* at all? Perhaps we deal with various species of the genus religion, but not with species of the genus Judaism?[6] As a matter of fact, all Judaisms from the formation of the Pentateuch (ca. 450 B.C.) onward have recapitulated a single paradigmatic and definitive human experience and reworked that experience in its own circumstance and context. That single paradigmatic experience to which all Judaisms refer, everywhere and under all conditions, is a political experience of exile and return, destruction and restoration of the state in the specified territory of that state.[7] So is formed the paradigm set forth by the Pentateuch in the myth of patriarchal Israel gaining the land not unconditionally but contingently. Politics is not a given but a gift.[8]

The reason for this uniform paradigm among otherwise diverse Judaisms is simple. From the formation of the Pentateuch by Ezra in the aftermath of the return to Zion in the fifth century B.C., all Judaisms have identified the Torah or the Five Books of Moses as the written statement of God's will for "Israel, the Jewish people." (As a matter of fact, every Judaism also identifies "Israel" as its own social group). Specifically, each Judaism in one way or another has sorted out whatever social experience its "Israel" proposed to explain by appeal to the tension of exile and the remission of return, and Judaisms in general appeal to the fixed paradigm of Israel's exile and return. That singular and indicative appeal has formed an ecological fact for all Judaisms, as much as the Jews' continuing minority status and utopian situation defined issues to be addressed by any Judaism. As a matter of fact that framing of events into the pattern of exile and return represents an act of powerful imagination and interpretation, for on one person or group both went into "exile" and also "returned home"; no Jews after 568 B.C. actually experienced what in the aggregate Scripture says happened; none both went into exile and then came back to Jerusalem. So, to begin with, Scripture does not record a particular person's experience. Indeed, taken together exile and return constitute an invented experience. To establish it, diverse experiences have been sorted out, various persons have been chosen, and the whole has been worked into a system by those who selected history out of happenings, and models out of masses of persons.

Let me emphasize the lesson people claimed to learn out of the events they had chosen for their history. It was this: *the life of the group is uncertain, subject to conditions and stipulations; nothing is set and given, all things—* land and life itself—are a gift and an act of grace, not coerced, not earned, but merely given freely. Yet the events of that uncertain world, the pattern of exile and restoration, marked the group as special, different, select. And once the Persians' viceroy, Ezra, promulgated the Torah of Moses (ca. 450 B.C.), all subsequent Israels could refer to that experience as it had been set down and preserved as their formative norm. They could perceive Israel in the mythic terms of that "original" Israel, the Israel not of Genesis and Sinai that ended at the moment of entry into the promised land, but the "Israel" of the families that recorded as the rule and the norm the story of both the exile and the return. In that minority genealogy, that story of exile and return, of alienation and remission, imposed on the received stories or preexilic Israel, adumbrated time and again in the Five Books of Moses and addressed by the framers of that document in their work overall, we find that paradigmatic statement in which every Judaism, from then to now, found the structure and deep syntax of its social existence, the grammar of its intelligible message.

I dwell on this matter because the myth of exile and return (resentment and remission) took a political form. That is, it spoke of violence, both legitimate and illegitimate. The illegitimate violence comprised the destruction of a Temple and of the state and government that that Temple had realized. The legitimate violence, of course, came with the restoration. At that time, Ezra (and therefore Moses) used legitimate coercion and violence. Whereas in theological terms exile and return rehearsed the conditional moral existence of sin and punishment, suffering and atonement and reconciliation, in social terms it manifested the political group's uncertain and always conditional national destiny, its disintegration and renewal as a society properly able to coerce conformity to its calling.

That political moment captured within the Five Books of Moses, that is to say, the judgment of the generation of the return to Zion about what it conceives to have been its extraordinary experience of exile and return, informed the attitude of all the Judaisms and all the Israels beyond. That is, all the Judaisms that appealed to Ezra's writing and paradigm constituted politics along the lines taken by the Judaism he detailed. Accordingly, we identify as a fact of the diachronic ecology of all Judaisms that generative and definitive moment. And in so doing, we do precisely as all Judaisms have done. We look into that same Scripture. All Judaisms identify the Torah or the Five Books of Moses as the written statement of God's will for Israel.

But why not appeal to Moses instead of to Ezra to explain the fact that Judaisms fall into the classification of political religions? Why not appeal to Abraham, for that matter? Superficially it might seem that we should specify the story of creation (down through Abraham and Isaac and Jacob) as the formative and definitive moment recapitulated by all Judaisms. Or it might seem that Sinai offers that original point of definition "descended from Heaven." But recapitulating the events of a religion does not help us to understand that religion. Interpreting the story's events, identifying the point of origin of the story and relating the story's contents to its context, does. For the story tells not what happened on the occasion to which the story refers (the creation of the world, for instance) but how, long afterward and for their own reasons, people want to portray themselves. The tale therefore recapitulates that resentment, that obsessive and troubling point of origin, that the tale-telling group wishes to explain, transcend, transform.

Every Judaism, each tale-telling group, took as its task the recapitulation of the "original Judaism", and each located "original Judaism" through exile and return. And to them, exile and return formed political categories. Exile meant exile from statehood (statehood marked by the person of the monarch); return signified return to the capital of the government as well as the cult— indeed, it meant return under overtly political auspices, with Iranian troops to carry out the commands of the Jewish satrap. And the psychological counterpart of the political taxon sustained the politics. It invoked resentment of circumstance and also reconciliation with the human condition of a given "Israel." That is to say, each Judaism made its own distinctive statement of the generative and critical resentment contained within that questioning of the given, that deep understanding of the uncertain character of the existence of the group in its normal location and under circumstances of permanence that characterized the life of every other group but Israel (so far as the Judaic group understood things). What for everyone else seemed a given, for Israel was a gift. What all the nations knew as how things *must* be, Israel understood as how things *might not be*. For Israel there was exile and loss, alienation and resentment but—instead of annihilation—renewal, restoration, reconciliation, and (in theological language) redemption. So that paradigmatic experience, the one beginning in 586 B.C. and ending ca. 450 B.C., written down in that Torah of Moses, made its mark.

That pattern of appeal to political means and of defining Israel as a political entity permanently inscribed in the Torah at Sinai would define for all Israels over all time that matter of resentment demanding recapitulation: leaving home, coming home. What one systemic trait marks all Judaisms and sets them apart from all other religious systems, viewed jointly and severally? The religious ecology of Judaisms is dictated by that perpetual asking of the question, "who are we?" That trait of self-consciousness, that incapacity to accept the group as a given and its data—way of life, worldview, constituting the world of an Israel, a Jewish people, in the here and now—is the one thing that draws together Judaisms from beginning to end. Jews' persistent passion for self-definition characterizes all of the Judaisms they have made for themselves. What others take as the given the Jews perceive as the received, the special, the extraordinary. And that perception of the remarkable character of what to other groups is the absolute datum of all being requires explanation.

As we have seen, the union of politics and psychology sustained the indicative character of the initial paradigm. Ever since the formative pattern imposed that perpetual, self-conscious uncertainty, treating the life of the group as conditional and discontinuous, Jews have asked themselves who they are

and invented Judaisms to answer that question. Accordingly, on account of the
definitive paradigm affecting their group life in various contexts—ecology in
an intellectual form—no circumstances have permitted Jews to take for
granted their existence as a group. Looking back on Scripture and its message, Jews have ordinarily treated as special, subject to conditions and therefore uncertain, what in their view other groups enjoyed as unconditional and
simply given. Why the paradigm renewed itself is clear: this particular view of
matters generated expectations that could not be met, hence created resentment—and then provided comfort and hope that made it possible to cope with
that resentment.

Specifically, each Judaism retells in its own way and with its distinctive em-
phases the tale of the Five Books of Moses, the story of a no-people that becomes a people, a people that has what it gets only on condition, and a social
entity that can lose it all by virtue of its own sin. That is a terrifying, unset-
tling story for a social group to tell of itself, because it imposes acute self-
consciousness, chronic insecurity, upon what should be the level plane and
firm foundation of society. That is to say, the collection of diverse materials
joined into a single tale on the occasion of the original exile and restoration
because of the repetition in age succeeding age also precipitates the recapitulation of the interior experience of exile and restoration—always because of
sin and atonement. To conclude this picture of the paradigm common to all
Judaisms at the point at which we began, let me account for the systemic
power that will undergird the politics of any Judaism.

The power of Judaism(s) to form an independent variable in the life of
Israel(s) throughout all time and so to impose its imprint upon the politics,
also, of all Judaisms that set forth a politics, flows from an ever-renewed
source, resentment and the resolution of resentment. For the power of Judaisms derives from their capacity to form and reform a permanent social paradigm and to perpetuate a single corresponding psychological attitude and
experience. And how was (and is) this done? Promising what could not be
delivered, then providing solace for the consequent disappointment, the pentateuchal system, to which all subsequent systems appealed, precipitated in
age succeeding age the very conditions necessary for its own replication. Precipitating resentment and then remitting the consequent anguish, Judaisms
renew themselves. In the context of Judaisms, religion itself forms a self-
perpetuating fact of the ecology of religion.

From Judaisms in general, we come to the Judaism of the Mishnah, that is
to say, to the Judaic religious system that is first set forth in the Mishnah. The
Mishnah reached closure ca. A.D. 200, but in its initial intellectual layers it
reaches back to before 70. The bulk of the document, however, depends upon
conceptions first attested among second-century authorities.[9] In the aftermath
of a half century of political disasters that stretched from before 70 to after
135 and that overturned structures and systems valid for centuries, a group of
intellectuals set forth a grand design for an imagined reconstruction (forming

what ultimately appeared another half century later in the Mishnah). Their design encompassed in a single theory of all things the correct conduct of the life of society within the dominion of God. In providing for institutions and organizations of an enduring society, not merely for the inner life of individuals and families, the design quite naturally encompassed politics. It was a politics represented as a (mere) recapitulation of how things had been, how things (as a matter of fact) really were. But in fact it was a politics imagined, not reconstructed. The political imagination extending to political structures and institutions, and also to political systems and activities, expressed an essentially theological vision. That is why I claim to provide an instance of how religion invents politics.

Political in its very basic design, speaking of a social entity and its power to exercise legitimate violence in governing its own affairs, in the form of a law code the Mishnah presents as its social vision what is in fact the design for a social system. That is why I ask the Mishnah to tell us the political structure and system that it sets forth for the society its authorship imagines; that is why I promise to explain why it said what it said and why it imagined what it made up. For the law code at hand is not an account of how things were, but of how, out of the sherds and remnants of an indeterminate past, its authorship proposed to reconstruct the world. The Mishnah therefore constitutes a profoundly utopian document, in the tradition of the political theory in the form of a fantasy, a kind of *Staatsroman* of ancient times, to be compared therefore to Plato's *Republic* and Aristotle's *Politics*.[10] The Mishnah provides a sustained example of thinking in a systematic and orderly way about political questions about which, in reality, its authorship could do absolutely nothing.

But why politics in particular, and not, for example, teleology in eschatological form? Why ignore theological issues about the nature of God and address social issues about the utilization of power? These are questions of systemic analysis that require us to ask, "Why this, not that; this topic, not that topic?" in the systemic statement. And to answer those questions, we need to find out both how people thought and also what they meant to convey in choosing the topics they treated and in thinking about them as they did.[11]

Conducting an analysis of the imagined politics of the document allows us entry into a mode of thought that is utterly unaffected by the variables of practical life and public policy applied to concrete problems. Here we have an ideal example of a political structure and system that flows wholly from an imagination—but an imagination shaped by problems set by concrete reality, on the one side, and rigorous, disciplined, rational, philosophical modes of thought, on the other. That is, we perceive political theory in its most elegant setting, the human mind, the engaged intellect. For the Mishnah, a deeply philosophical document, manages to say one thing about many things. The work therefore falls well within the framework of classification defined by the modes of philosophical thought of antiquity.[12]

The document presents its discourses as thematic expositions with beginnings, middles, and ends, with principles and secondary developments. Throughout the Mishnah the preferred mode of presentation is through themes, spelled out along the lines of the logic imbedded in those themes. The Mishnah is divided into six principal divisions, each expounding a single, immense topic. The tractates of each division take up subtopics of the principal theme. The chapters then unfold along the lines of the logic of the necessary dissection of the division (as that logic appears to the framers). Intermediate divisions of these principal divisions (we might call them chapters of tractates) are to be discerned on the basis of internal evidence, through the confluence of theme and form. That is to say, a given intermediate division (a "chapter" of a tractate) will be marked by a particular, recurrent formal pattern in accord with which sentences are constructed, and also by a particular and distinct theme to which these sentences are addressed. When a new theme commences, a fresh formal pattern will be used. Within the intermediate divisions, we are able to recognize the components, or smallest whole units of thought (hereinafter, cognitive units), because there will be a recurrent pattern of sentence structure repeated time and again within the unit and a shifting at the commencement of the next theme. Each point at which the recurrent pattern commences marks the beginning of a new cognitive unit.

The Mishnah's logic of cogent discourse establishes propositions that rest upon philosophical bases. It operated, for example, by proposing a thesis and composing a list of facts that, perhaps through shared traits of a taxonomic order, prove the thesis. The Mishnah presents rules and treats stories, inclusive of history, as incidental and of merely taxonomic interest. Its logic is propositional, and its intellect does its work through a vast labor of classification, comparison, and contrast that generates governing rules and generalizations. The Pentateuch, by contrast, appeals to a different logic of cogent discourse. It is the cogency imparted by teleology, that is, a logic that provides an account of how things were in order to explain how things are and to set forth how they should be. This teleology takes the tabernacle in the wilderness as the model for (and modeled after) the Temple in the Jerusalem abuilding. The Mishnah speaks in a continuing present tense, saying only how things are, indifferent to the *were* and the *will-be*. The Pentateuch focuses upon self-conscious "Israel," saying who they were and what they must become to overcome how they now are. The Mishnah understands by "Israel" as much the individual as the nation. It identifies as its principal actors, the heroes of its narrative, not the family become a nation, but the priest and the householder, the woman and the slave, the adult and the child. It focuses on many castes and categories of person within an inward-looking, established, fully landed community. Given the Mishnah's authorship's interest in classifications and categories, in systematic hierarchization of an orderly world, one can hardly find odd its (re)definition of the subject matter and problematic of the systemic social entity.

That purpose is accomplished, in particular, though list making, which places on display the data of the like and the unlike and implicitly conveys the rule. it is this resort to list making that accounts for the rhetorical stress on groups of examples of a common principle. Once a series of three or five is established, the authorship assumes, the governing rule will be perceived. That explains why, in exposing the interior logic of its authorship's intellect, the Mishnah had to be a book of lists, with the implicit order, the nomothetic traits of a monothetic order, dictating the ordinarily unstated general and encompassing rule. And why all this? In order to make a single statement, endless times over, and to repeat in a mass of tangled detail precisely the same fundamental judgment. The Mishnah in its way is as blatantly repetitious in its fundamental statement as is the Pentateuch. If I had to specify a single mode of thought that for the Mishnah's authorship establishes connections between one fact and another, it is the search for points in common and therefore also points of contrast. We seek connection between fact and fact, sentence and sentence, in the subtle and balanced rhetoric of the Mishnah by comparing and contrasting two things that are like and not alike.

At the logical level, too, the Mishnah falls into the category of familiar philosophical thought. Once we seek regularities, we propose rules. What is like another thing falls under its rule, and what is not like the other falls under the opposite rule. Accordingly, as to the species of the genus, so far as they are alike, they share the same rule. So far as they are not alike, each follows a rule contrary to that governing the other. So the work of analysis is what produces connection, and therefore the drawing of conclusions derives from comparison and contrast—the *and,* the *equal.* The proposition that forms the conclusion concerns the essential likeness of the two offices, except where they are different, but the subterranean premise is that we can explain both likeness and difference by appeal to a principle of fundamental order and unity. These exercises yield lists of things that are alike and follow a given rule, and, when we have sets of such lists, we place them into proper arrangement, proportion, order, which is to say, into their (natural) hierarchy. (This point proves important in chapter 12). For instance, the high priest and king fall into a single genus, but speciation, based on traits particular to the king, then distinguishes the one from the other. (See chapter 12.) All of this exercise is conducted essentially independently of Scripture; the classifications derive from the system, are viewed as autonomous constructs; traits of things define classifications and dictate what is like and what is unlike. That is how the Mishnah's authorship finds it possible to say the same thing about many things.

So the Mishnah, seen whole, turns out to repeat in many ways a single encompassing proposition. Once the question is defined, the exegetical process takes over, with its infinite capacity to make details repeat a basic premise or proposition. But the systemic statement as a whole takes as urgent and obsessively reviews a set of questions deemed ineluctable. And in one way or another, those questions receive answers that are deemed self-evident. Accordingly, the Mishnah's system forms a closed circle. And as a matter of fact, the boundaries of the circle are political, the issues so framed that politics constitutes the principal force in the shaping of society and imagination alike; politics profoundly affects the conditions of religious belief and behavior.

As noted earlier, in the period in which the Mishnah came to closure, two political events, very well documented in a variety of writings and also in archaeology, defined the circumstances in which all Jews lived and therefore in which all Judaisms took shape. A stunning shift in the political circumstance of the Jews in the Land of Israel (Palestine) therefore affected thought about perennial questions. The first shift was represented by the destruction of the second Temple in A.D. 70, the second by the complete defeat, three generations later, of Bar Kokhba in the war to reconstruct the Temple (A.D. 135). The one fact we know for certain is that the Mishnah's authorship did their work after Bar Kokhba's defeat. If we work our way back from the answers set forth in the Mishnah to the question addressed by these same answers and implicit within them, we confront an obsession with order. That fact suggests a concern with chaos, such as followed the political revolution brought about by the massive defeats suffered by the Jews in the Land of Israel over a half century. The Temple had formed the locus for social hierarchization and organization; it lay in ruins. The city, Jerusalem, had served as the center for the life of the Jews in the country; it was no longer accessible. These events formed the question to which the Mishnah's orderly system provided the answer. The system of the Mishnah delivers the message that through order—through the reordering of Israelite life—Israel attains that sanctification that inheres in its very being. That is, quite logically the sages who produced the Mishnah gave an elaborate series of answers to the question of the right ordering and classification of all things in the worlds of society, nature, and supernature. And, in the nature of things, the answers appealed to both sound philosophy and revealed theology.

The Mishnah is divided into six divisions, covering sixty-three tractates with 531 chapters, and encompasses six large topics. This brings us to a rapid survey of the several parts of the system, the six divisions and their sixty-two tractates (exluding tractate Avot). In this survey we see in concrete and specific ways precisely what it means to speak of the Judaism of the Mishnah as a political structure and system, for what the Mishnah takes up for its topical program is the concrete expression of the power to dictate the conduct of the social entity. It is the rationing and rationalization of power.

The Division of Agriculture treats two topics: producing crops in accord with the Scriptural rules on the subject, and paying the required offerings and tithes to the priests, Levites, and poor. The principal point of the division is that the land is holy because God has a claim on both it and what it produces. God's claim must be honored by setting aside a portion of the produce for those for whom God has designated it. God's ownership must be acknowledged by observing the rules God has laid down for use of the land. The division is divided into rules for producing crops in a state of holiness (tractates Kilayim, Shebiit, Orlah) and rules for disposing of crops in accord with the rules of holiness (tractates Peah, Demai, Terumot, Maaserot, Maaser Sheni, Hallah, Bikkurim, Berakhot).

The Division of Appointed Times forms a system in which the advent of a holy day, such as the Sabbath of creation, sanctifies the life of the Israelite village by imposing on the village rules on the model of those of the Temple. Clearly, the purpose of this system is to align the moment of sanctification for the village and the home with the moment of sanctification of the Temple. The underlying and generative theory of this system is that the village is the mirror image of the Temple. If things are done in one way in the Temple, they will be done in the opposite way in the village. But taken together on the holy day, the village and the Temple form a continuum, a completed creation awaiting sanctification.

This division treats two quite distinct sets of problems. First, it considers what one does in the sacred space of the Temple during sacred time, as distinct from what one does in that same sacred space on ordinary, undifferentiated days. (The latter is worked out in the Division of Holy Things.) Second, the Division defines how, for the occasion of the holy day, one creates a corresponding space in one's own circumstance, and what one does, within that space, during sacred time. The issue of the Temple and cult on the special occasion of festivals is treated in tractates Pesahim, Sheqalim, Yoma, Sukkah, and Hagigah. Three further tractates, Rosh Hashshanah, Taanit, and Megillah complete the discussion. Shabbat, Erubin, Besah, and Moed Qatan delineate sacred space in the village. They delineate the limits within which one may move on the Sabbath and festival and specify those things which one may not do within that space in sacred time. While the twelve tractates of this division appear to fall into two distinct groups, joined merely by a common theme, in fact they relate through a shared, generative metaphor. This is the comparison, in the context of sacred time, of the spatial life of the Temple to the spatial life of the village, with activities and restrictions to be specified for each. As I have suggested, then, the Mishnah's purpose is to correlate the sanctity of the Temple, as defined by the holy day, with the restrictions of space and of action which make the life of the village different and holy within the holy day.

The Division of Women defines women within the social economy of Israel's supernatural and natural reality. Most notably, women acquire definition wholly in relationship to men, for it is men who impart form to the Israelite social economy. Nonetheless, the status of women is effected through both supernatural and natural (this-worldly) action, for what man and woman do on earth provokes a response in heaven. Since earthly actions and heavenly responses correspond exactly, women are defined and secured through and relative to men both in heaven and here on earth. But consequently, when a woman becomes or ceases to be holy to a particular man, when she enters or leaves a marital union, the instability in the personal relationship may destabilize society as well. For this reason, the Mishnah focuses on these moments when the woman enters or leaves male-dominated categories.

The formation of the marriage comes under discussion in Qiddushin and Ketubot, as well as in Yebamot. The rules for the duration of the marriage are scattered throughout but derive especially from parts of Ketubot, Nedarim, and Nazir, on the one side, and the paramount unit of Sotah, on the other. The dissolution of the marriage is dealt with in Gittin, as well as in Yebamot. Important throughout are the transfer of property as it goes along with the transfer of women (covered in Ketubot and to some measure in Qiddushin) and the proper documentation of such transfers (treated in Ketubot and Gittin). These critical issues turn upon the exchange of legal documents—writs of divorce, for example—and legal recognition of changes in the ownership of property, e.g., through the collection of the settlement of a marriage contract by a widow, through the provision of a dowry, or through the disposition of the property of a woman during the period in which she is married. Within this orderly world of documentary and procedural concerns a place is made for the disorderly conception of the marriage not formed by human volition but decreed in heaven, that is, the levirate connection. Yebamot states that heaven sanctifies a woman to a man (under the conditions of the levirate connection). What it says by indirection is that man sanctifies too. Man, like God, can sanctify that relationship between a man and a woman and can also effect the cessation of the sanctity of that same relationship. Five of the seven tractates of the Division of Women are devoted to the formation and dissolution of the marital bond. Of them, three treat what is done by man here on earth, that is, the formation of a marital bond through betrothal and marriage contract, and dissolution through divorce and its consequences (Qiddushin, Ketubot, and Gittin). One, Sotah, devotes itself to what is done by woman here on earth. And Yebamot, greatest of the seven in size and in formal and substantive brilliance, deals with the corresponding heavenly intervention into the formation and end of a marriage. That is, it explores the power of death to form and dissolve the marital bond. The other two tractates, Nedarim and Nazir, draw into one the two realms of reality, heaven and earth, as they work out the effects of vows—perhaps because vows taken by women and subject to the confirmation or abrogation of the father or husband make a deep impact upon the marital life of the woman who has taken them.

The Division of Damages comprises two logically related subsystems. One part presents rules for the normal conduct of civil society. These rules cover commerce, trade, real estate, and other matters of everyday intercourse, as well as mishaps, such as damages by chattels and persons, fraud, overcharge, interest, and the like, in that same context of everyday social life. The other part describes the institutions governing the normal conduct of civil society, that is, the courts of administration, and it details the penalties at the disposal of the government for enforcing the law. These two subjects form a single tight and systematic dissertation on the nature of Israelite society, on its economic, social, and political relationships as the Mishnah envisages them.

The main point of the division's first part is expressed in the sustained unfolding of the three Babas, Baba Qamma, Baba Mesia, and Baba Batra. It is that society's task to maintain perfect stasis, to preserve the prevailing situation, and to secure the stability of all relationships. To this end, in the interchanges of buying and selling, giving and taking, borrowing and lending, it is important that there be an essential equality of interchange. No party in the end should have more than what he had at the outset, and none should be the victim of a sizable shift in fortune and circumstance. All parties' rights to and in this stable and unchanging economy of society are to be preserved. When these rights are violated, so far as possible the law will secure the restoration of the antecedent status.

An appropriate appendix to the Babas lies in Abodah Zarah, which deals with the orderly governance of transactions and relationships between Israelite society and the outside world. Abodah Zarah maps out relationships which are subject to certain special considerations. These special considerations are necessary because Israelites may not derive benefit—even through commercial transactions—from anything which has served in the worship of an idol. While they cover both special occasions (fairs and festivals of idolatry), and general matters (what Israelites may buy and sell), the primary examples pertain to wine. These manifest for us what is at stake. As regards wine, the Mishnah supposes that gentiles routinely offer a libation from any wine to which they have access. It therefore takes for granted not only that wine over which gentiles have had control is forbidden for Israelite use, but also that such wine is prohibited for Israelites to buy and sell. That is, commercial transactions suffer limitations on account of extrinsic considerations of cultic taboos. And these detailed rulings concerning wine conclude what the Mishnah has to say about all those matters of civil and criminal law which together define everyday relationships within the Israelite nation and between that nation and all others in the world among whom, in Palestine as abroad, they lived side by side.

The other part of the division describes the institutions of Israelite government and politics. First it details the institutions and their jurisdiction (notably conceiving courts as both judicial and administrative agencies). Second, it discusses criminal penalties extensively. These penalties, detailed in tractate Sanhedrin, are three: death, banishment, and flogging. But it also details four ways by which a person convicted of a capital crime may be put to death and, indeed, organizes a vast amount of information on what sorts of capital crimes are punishable by which of the four modes of execution. What is important here is that although the information is alleged to derive from Scripture, the facts are many and the relevant verses few. Consequently the interest lies in what the Mishnah contributes to the exercise, a first-rate piece of organization and elucidation of available facts. (Where the facts come from we do not know.) In addition to these major foci, Sanhedrin describes the way in which trials are conducted in both monetary and capital cases and pays attention to the possibilities of perjury. The matter of banishment brings the Mishnah to a rather routine restatement regarding flogging and application of that mode of punishment and conclude the discussion.

The character and interests of the Division of Damages present probative evidence of the Mishnah's philosophers' larger program. These philosophers intended to create nothing less than a full-scale Israelite government, subject to the administration of sages. Their government is fully supplied with a constitution and bylaws (Sanhedrin, Makkot); it makes provision for a court system and procedures (Shebuot, Sanhedrin, Makkot) and offers full sets of laws governing civil society (Baba Qamma, Baba Mesia, Baba Batra) and criminal justice (Sanhedrin, Makkot). Moreover, this government mediates between its own community and the outside ("pagan") world. Through its system of laws it expresses its judgment of other societies and at the same time defines, protects, and defends its own society and social frontiers (Abodah Zarah). It even makes provision for procedures of remission to expiate its own errors (Horayot). These parts of the Mishnah provide us with the bulk—but by no means the whole—of the data for study in parts 2 and 3 of this book.

The Division of Holy Things presents a system of sacrifice and sanctuary. It details matters concerning the praxis of the altar and maintenance of the sanctuary. The praxis of the altar includes modes of sacrifice and the things set aside for sacrifice and so deemed consecrated. This topic extends through the following among the eleven tractates of the division: Zebahim and part of Hullin, Menahot, Temurah, Keritot, part of Meilah, Tamid, Qinnim. The maintenance of the sanctuary (inclusive of the personnel) is dealt with in Bekhorot, Arakhin, part of Meilah, Middot, and part of Hullin. Viewed from a distance, then, the tractates of Holy Things divide themselves into the following groups (in parentheses are tractates containing only scattered relevant materials): rules for the altar and the praxis of the cult—Zebahim Menahot, Hullin, Keritot, Tamid, Qinnim (Bekhorot, Meilah); rules for the altar and the animals set aside for the cult—Arakhin, Temurah, Meilah (Bekhorot); and rules for the altar and support of the Temple staff and buildings—Bekhorot, Middot (Hullin, Arakhin, Meilah, Tamid). Clearly, this division speaks of the sacrificial cult and the sanctuary in which the cult is conducted. The law pays special attention to the status of property belonging to the altar and to the sanctuary, both property to be utilized in the actual sacrificial rites and property whose value supports the cult and sanctuary in general. Both are deemed to be sanctified, that is, holy things. So the Division of Holy Things centers upon rules always applicable to the cult.

The Division of Purities presents a very simple system comprising three principal parts: sources of uncleanness (tractates Ohalot, Negaim, Niddah, Makhshirin, Zabim, Tebul Yom), objects and substances susceptible to uncleanness (Kelim, Tohorot, Uqsin), and modes of purification from uncleanness (Parah, Miqvaot, Yadayim). So it tells the story of what makes a given sort of object unclean and what makes it clean.

Viewed as a whole, the Division of Purities treats the interplay of persons, food, and liquids. Dry inanimate objects or food are not susceptible to uncleanness. What is wet is susceptible. So liquids activate the system. But what is unclean can be cleansed through the operation of liquids, specifically through immersion in fit water of requisite volume and in natural condition. So liquids deactivate the system, too. In fact, water in its unnatural condition, that is, water deliberately affected by human agency, imparts susceptibility to uncleanness, whereas water in its natural condition concludes the process by removing uncleanness. Persons too fall subject to uncleanness through liquid, specifically through body liquids. Women become unclean by flux when menstruating (Niddah), and fluid emission from the genitals (*zab*) renders either sex unclean (Zabim). Not surprisingly, a corpse's uncleanness results from a kind of effluent, a viscous gas which is imagined to flow like liquid. Even utensils can become unclean when they are receptacles able to contain liquid.

In sum, in material terms, liquid affects food, drink, utensils, and man. It has consequences for who may eat and drink what food and liquid, and what food and drink may be consumed in which pots and pans. (These loci are specified by tractates on utensils [Kelim] and on food and drink [Tohorot and Uqsin].) Yet its operation transcends the material base, for it is conditioned upon highly abstract notions. The invisible flow of fluidlike substances or powers serves to put food, drink, and receptacles into the status of uncleanness and to remove those things from that status.

In reviewing this account of the program of the Judaism of the Mishnah, the reader must wonder, what of Scripture? If, as we realize, all Judaisms appeal to the Hebrew Scriptures (Old Testament, written Torah), then should not an account of the politics of Judaism begin in that same generative document? And how can we legitimately read the Mishnah as an autonomous statement, and not merely as a secondary expansion and revision of the generative statement that is contained, for politics, in Exodus, Leviticus, and Deuteronomy? To answer that question and to show the autonomy of the Judaism of the Mishnah requires a brief survey of the Mishnah's relationship to Scripture. From that basis, we shall see how the authorship of the Mishnah has picked and chosen, how they have taken from Scripture whatever suited their purposes and contributed to the formation of their system. Clearly, once we see that picking and choosing has gone on, then the criteria for sorting out what pertains and what does not turn out to derive from the system that guides the choices, not from that system among which choices are made.

On the surface, Scripture plays little role in the Mishnaic system. The Mishnah's authorship rarely cites a verse of Scripture, refers to Scripture as an entity, links its own ideas to those of Scripture, or lays claim to originate in what Scripture has said, even by indirect or remote allusion to a scriptural verse of teaching. So, superficially, the Mishnah seems totally indifferent to Scripture. And the Mishnah's linguistic traits reinforce that impression, for amazingly, the framers of Mishnaic discourse never attempt to imitate the language of Scripture, as do the framers of the Essene writings at Qumran. Indeed, except in a very few cases (Leviticus 16, Yoma; Exodus 12, Pesahim), the Mishnah's framers find of no use whatever the redactional structure of Scripture that served the writer of the Temple scroll so well.

So formally, redactionally, and linguistically the Mishnah stands in splendid isolation from Scripture. Indeed, it is isolated in its very isolation from Scripture. Before the Mishnah, we find few anonymous books, received as holy and providing a base for a Judaism, in which the forms and formulations (specific verses) of Scripture play so slight a role. People who wrote holy books commonly imitated the Scripture's language. They cited concrete verses, or they claimed, at the very least, that direct revelation had come to them. That is, as in the angelic discourses of IV Ezra and Baruch, they claimed that their words stood on an equal footing with Scripture. By contrast, as I have suggested, in the Mishnah's sixty-two usable tractates (excluding Abot) we find no one pretending to talk like Moses and write like Moses, no one claiming to cite and correctly interpret things that Moses said, and no one even alleging to have had a revelation like that of Moses and so to stand on the mountain with Moses. There is none of this. So the claim of scriptural authority for the Mishnah's doctrines and institutions is difficult to locate within the internal evidence of the Mishnah itself.

Consequently, we need to pursue the facts of the Mishnah's relationship to Scripture before we proceed. They are as follows. First, some Mishnah tractates simply repeat in their own words precisely what Scripture has to say. At best, these serve to amplify and complete the basic ideas of Scripture. This category includes, for example, all the cultic tractates of the second divison, Appointed Times (times that tell what one is supposed to do in the Temple on the various special days of the year), the bulk of the cultic tractates in the fifth division, Holy Things, and all those tractates in the sixth division, Purities, which specify sources of uncleanness. Consider the last case, the uncleanness specified in Purities. Elsewhere I have demonstrated that every important statement in Niddah on menstrual uncleanness, the most fundamental notions of Zabim on the uncleanness of the person with flux referred to in Leviticus 15, and every detail in Negaim on the uncleanness of the person or house suffering the uncleanness described at Leviticus 13 and 14 serve only to restate the basic facts of Scripture and to complement those facts with other important ones.

Second, some tractates adopt facts from Scripture, but work them out in a way we could not predict from the facts themselves. For example, Scripture takes for granted that the red cow will be burned in a state of uncleanness, because it is burned outside the camp (Temple). That is, the priestly writers could not imagine that a state of cultic cleanness was to be attained outside of the cult. By contrast, tractate Parah holds as its absolute datum that cultic cleanness can be attained outside the "tent of meeting" (Temple) and that a state of cleanness can be achieved for the red cow even exceeding that cultic cleanness required in the Temple.

Third, many tractates either take up problems in no way suggested by Scripture or begin from facts at best merely relevant to facts of Scripture. In the former category, pursuing problems absent for scripture, fall Tohorot, on the cleanness of foods, with its companion, Uqsin; Demai, on doubtfully tithed produce; Tamid, on the conduct of the daily whole-offering; Baba Batra, on rules of real estate transactions and certain other commercial and property relationships. In the latter category, based in facts relevant to but not included in Scripture, fall, for example, Ohalot, which spins out its strange problems within the theory that a tent and a utensil are to be compared to one another(!); Kelim, on the susceptibility to uncleanness of various sorts of utensils; Miqvaot, on the sorts of water which effect purification from uncleanness; Ketubot and Gittin, on the documents of marriage and divorce. While both categories of tractates draw on facts from Scripture, the problems they confront in no way respond to problems important to Scripture. Rather, these categories reveal in the Mishnah a prior program of inquiry. First comes the problem or topic, then—if possible—comes attention to Scripture. That is, while the Mishnah's authorship draws richly upon the heritage of Scripture, its political structure and system in no way prove symmetrical to those of Scripture.

So there we have it. Some tractates merely repeat what we find in Scripture, some are totally independent of Scripture, and some fall in between. Clearly, we are no closer to defining Scripture's relationship to the Mishnah than we were when we described the state of thought on the very same questions in the third and fourth centuries. We find everything and its opposite. But to offer a final answer to the question of Scripture-Mishnah relationships, we have to take that fact seriously. On the one hand, the Mishnah in no way is so remote from Scripture as its formal omission of citations of verses of Scripture suggests. On the other hand, it can in no way be described as contingent upon and secondary to Scripture, as many of its third-century apologists claimed. But the right answer is not that it is somewhere in between. Scripture confronts the framers of the Mishnah as revelation, not merely as a source of facts. But the framers of the Mishnah had their own world with which to deal. They made statements in the framework and fellowship of their own age and generation. They were bound, therefore, to come to Scripture with a set of questions generated other than in Scripture. They brought their own ideas about what was going to be important in Scripture. And that is what justifies our asking about their structure and their system, not only about how they have reshaped the politics of ancient Israel as portrayed in scriptural stories and rules.

The philosophers of the Mishnah conceded to Scripture the highest authority. At the same time what they chose to hear within the authoritative statements of Scripture in the end formed a statement on its own. Consider: all Scripture is authoritative, but only some Scripture is relevant. That means the framers and philosophers of the Mishnah came to Scripture only when they had reason to, and when they came, they brought to it a program of questions and inquiries framed essentially among themselves. They were highly selective. Consequently, their program constitutes a statement *upon* the meaning of Scripture, not of its meaning.[13]

It would carry us far afield if we traced the fate of the Mishnah's specific structure and system from 200 to the present. And it would also prove beside the point, since the continuators of the Mishnah considered it not as a system but as a composite of authoritative details alone. Through the literature of exegesis, in applying its law, in codifying and restating its principles, they shaped the Mishnah into structures and systems of their own choosing. In fact, the Mishnah stands as a systemic structure for only a brief moment. To successive crises, new systemic compositions would respond with (to the believers) self-evident answers. What the Mishnah's authorship contributed to the later politics of Judaism, then, was not a set of facts or even a specific system. Rather, they contributed the simple proposition that a Judaism would constitute, whatever else it would be, an essentially political religious system.

PART ONE
THE STRUCTURE

3

Politics within the Judaic Myth

The principal structural components of Judaism's politics are easily defined. Just as a systemic myth expresses the teleology of a worldview, telling people why things are the way they are, a political myth expresses that element of a social entity's worldview that instructs people why coercive power is legitimate in forcing people to do what they are supposed to do. It presents the narrative equivalent of legitimate violence, because it means through the force of its teleological apologia to coerce conformity with the social order and its norms. As we shall see, the political institutions envisaged by a politics convey details of the way of life of the same entity that, in theory at least, exercises the coercive power to secure compliance with the rules. Finally, the management of politics delineates, within the social entity's ongoing affairs, how the institutions secure suitable and capable staff to carry out their public tasks. Politics defines the concrete and material component of the conception of a social system, and the theory of politics, defining both how things should be and also how they should be done, forms the critical element in a religious system.

The task undertaken by the political myth of Judaism is not only to make power specific and particular to cases. It is especially a labor of differentiation of power, indicating what agency or person has the power to precipitate the working of politics as legitimate violence at all.[1] When, therefore, we understand the differentiating force of myth that imparts to politics its activity and dynamism, we shall grasp what everywhere animates the structures of the politics and propels the system. In the case of the politics of Judaism, we shall work our way downward, into the depths of the system, toward a myth of taxonomy of power. Appealing to a myth of taxonomy, the system accomplishes its tasks by explaining why this, not that, by telling as its foundation story a myth of classification for the application of legitimate violence. The myth appeals in the end to the critical bases for the taxonomy, among institutions, of a generalized power to coerce. Let me make these somewhat abstract remarks more concrete.

Specifically, we analyze the mythic foundations of sanctions. And when we move from sanctions to the myth expressed and implicit in the application and legitimation of those sanctions, we see a complex but cogent politics sustained by a simple myth. This somewhat protracted survey of sanctions and their implications had best commence with a clear statement of what we shall now uncover.

The encompassing framework of rules, institutions, and sanctions is explained and validated by appeal to the myth of God's shared rule. That dominion, exercised by God and his surrogates on earth, is focused partly in the royal palace, partly in the Temple, and partly in the court. For us, the issue here is the differentiation of power, which is to say, which part falls where and why? Helpfully, the political myth of Judaism explains who exercises legitimate violence and under what conditions, and furthermore specifies the source for differentiation. The myth consequently serves a particular purpose—which is to answer that particular question. Indeed, the Judaic political myth comes to expression in its details of differentiation, which permit us to identify, and of course to answer, the generative question of politics.

Moving from the application of power to the explanation thereof, we find that the system focuses upon finding answers to the question of who imposes which sanction, and why. And those answers contain the myth, nowhere expressed, everywhere in full operation. So we begin with cases and end with cases, only in the midstages of analysis uncovering the narrative premises for our diverse cases that, when seen together, form the myth of politics in the initial structure of post-Temple Judaism. Through the examination of sanctions, we identify the foci of power. At that point we ask how power is differentiated.

In spelling out what the reader may now find somewhat enigmatic, I have skipped many stages in the argument and the examination of the evidence. So let us begin from the very beginning. How, exactly, do I propose to identify the political myth of Judaism? And precisely what data are supposed to attest to that myth?

Institutions of political persuasion and coercion dominate not only through physical but also through mental force, through psychological coercion or appeal to goodwill. So my inquiry's premise is not far to seek. I take as a given that a political myth animates the structure of a politics. But the authorship of the Mishnah has chosen other media for thought and expression than narrative and teleological ones. It is a philosophical, not a historical (fictive), account; it is conveyed through masses of detailed rules about small things. While the Mishnah through its cases amply informs us on the institutions of politics, the mythic framework within which persuasion and inner compliance are supposed to bring about submission to legitimate power scarcely emerges, remaining only implicit throughout.[2] But it is readily discerned when we ask the right questions. If we were to bring to the authorship of the Mishnah such questions as "who tells whom what to do?" they would point to the politics' imaginary king and its equally fictive high priest, with associated authorities. Here, they would tell us, are the institutions of politics—represented in personal rather than abstract form, to be sure. But if we were to say to them, "and tell us the story (in our language: the myth) that explains on what basis you persuade people to conform," they would find considerable difficulty in bringing to the fore the explicit mythic statements made by their writing.

How then are we to identify, on the basis of what the Mishnah does tell us, the generative myths to which the system is supposed to appeal? The answer derives from the definition of politics that governs this entire study. A myth, we recall, explains the exercise of legitimate power. Now, we know power comes to brutal expression when the state kills or maims someone or deprives a person of property through the imposition of legal sanctions for crime or sin.[3] In the absence of a myth of power, we therefore begin with power itself.[4] We shall work our way back from the facts of power to the intimations, within the record of legitimately violent sanctions, of the intellectual and even mythic sources of legitimation for the exercise and use of that legitimate violence. For it is at the point of imposing sanctions, of killing, injuring, denying property, excluding from society, that power operates in its naked form. Then how these legitimate exercises of violence are validated will set before us such concrete evidence of the myth. And so far as there is such evidence, that will identify the political myth of Judaism.[5]

Since the analysis of sources will prove somewhat abstruse, let me signal in advance the main line of argument. Analyzing myth by explaining sanctions draws our attention to the modes of legitimate violence that the system identifies. There we find four types of sanctions, each deriving from a distinct institution of political power, each bearing its own mythic explanation. The first comprises what God and the heavenly court can do to people. The second comprises what the earthly court can do to people. That type of sanction embodies the legitimate application of the worldly and physical kinds of violence of which political theory ordinarily speaks. The third comprises what the cult can do to the people. The cult through its requirements can deprive people of their property as legitimately as can a court. The fourth comprises conformity with consensus—self-imposed sanctions. Here the issue is, whose consensus, and defined by whom? Across these four types of sanction, four types of coercion are in play. They depend on violence of various kinds—psychological and social as much as physical. Clearly, then, the sanctions that are exercised by other than judicial-political agencies prove violent and legitimately coercive, even though the violence and coercion are not the same as those carried out by courts.

On this basis we can differentiate among types of sanctions—and hence trace evidences of how the differentiation is explained. Since our data focus upon who does what to whom, the myth of politics must explain why various types of sanctions are put into effect by diverse political agencies or institutions. As we shall see, the exercise of power, invariably and undifferentiatedly in the name and by the authority of God in heaven to be sure, is kept distinct. And the distinctions in this case signal important differences which then require explanation. Concrete application of legitimate violence by (1) Heaven covers different matters from parts of the political and social world governed by the policy and coercion of (2) the this-worldly political classes. And both sorts of violence have to be kept distinct from the sanction effected by (3) the community through the weight of attitude and public opinion. Here again we find a distinct set of penalties applied to a particular range of actions. When we have seen the several separate kinds of sanction and where they apply, we shall have a full account of the workings of politics as the application of power, and from that concrete picture we may, I think, identify the range of power and the mythic framework that has to have accommodated and legitimated diverse kinds of power.

Our task therefore is to figure out on the basis of sanctions' distinct realms, Heaven, earth, and the mediating range of the Temple and sacrifice, which party imposes sanctions for (in modern parlance) what crimes or sins. Where Heaven intervenes, do other authorities participate, and if so, what tells me which party takes charge and imposes its sanction? Is the system differentiated so that where earth is in charge, there is no pretense of appeal to Heaven? Or do we find cooperation in coextensive jurisdiction, such that one party penalizes an act under one circumstance, the other the same act under a different circumstance? A survey of the sanctions enables us to differentiate the components of the power structure before us. So we wonder whether each of these three estates that enjoy power and inflict sanctions of one kind or another—Heaven, earth, Temple in between—governs its own affairs without the intervention of the others, or whether, working together, each takes charge in collaboration with the other, so that power is parcelled out and institutions simultaneously differentiate themselves from one another and also intersect. The survey of sanctions will allow us to answer these questions and so identify the myth of politics and the exercise of power that Judaism promulgated through the Mishnah.[6]

What has been said about the relationship of the Mishnah to Scripture—the system makes its own choices within the available revelation—imposes the first task. We must address this obvious question: can we not simply open the Hebrew Scriptures and choose therein the operative political myth? No, we cannot. Why? First, the system builders choose what they find useful and ignore what they do not. Second, Scripture presents for a political myth pretty much everything and its opposite; it allows for government by the prophet (Moses), the king (David), the priest (Ezra). So if we are to appeal to Scripture in our search for myth, we can do so only by showing that, in the very context of the concrete exercise of power, the framers of the Mishnah turn to Scripture. They then will tell us where to look and why. In fact, our authorship does represent the entire system as the realization of God's dominion over Israel.

And this representation is specific and detailed. It thus justifies an inquiry, once we have identified the questions the myth must answer, into how we find responses to just those questions in Scripture.

Here, then, is one instance of the way in which Scripture provides a detail of a myth accompanying a detail of legitimate coercion. The following lists the number of law violations that one commits by making a profit, which is to say, collecting interest:

> Those who participate in a loan on interest violate a negative commandment: these are the lender, borrower, guarantor, and witnesses.
> Sages say, "Also the scribe."
> They violate the negative commandment, *You will not give him your money upon usury* [Lev. 25:37]; *You will not take usury from him* [Lev. 25:36]; *You shall not be a creditor to him* [Ex. 22:25]; *Nor shall you lay upon him usury* [Ex. 22:25]; and they violate the negative command, *You shall not put a stumbling block before the blind, but you shall fear your God. I am the Lord* [Lev. 19:14].
> M. Baba Mesia 5:11

We appeal to the Torah to justify obedience to law and to impose sanction for disobedience. But where is the myth that sustains obedience? Let me explain this question, which is critical to all that follows. On the basis of the passage just cited, we do not know what actually happens to me if I do participate in a loan on interest and so violate various rules of the Torah. More to the point, we do not know who imposes that penalty or effects it. That is to say, the generalized appeal to the law of the Torah and the assumed premise that one should obey that law and not violate it hardly tell me the morphology of the political myth at hand. They assume a myth that is not set forth, and they conceal those details in which the myth gains its sustaining vitality and power.

Clearly, simply knowing that everything is in accord with the Torah and that God wants Israel to keep the laws of the Torah does not reveal the systemically active component of the political myth. On the one hand, the propositions are too general; on the other hand, they do not address the critical question. The sequence of self-evident premises that runs (1) God revealed the Torah, (2) the political institutions and rules carry out the Torah, and therefore (3) people should conform, hardly sustains a concrete theory of *just* where and how God's authority serves the systemic construction at hand. The appeal to Scripture, therefore, reveals no incisive information about the Mishnah's validating myth.

This conclusion is reinforced by the references we find here and there to "the kingdom of Heaven"[7] that appeal to God's rule in an everyday framework. These form a mere allegation that, in general, what the political authorities tell people to do is what God wants them to do, which illuminates not at all. For example, at M. Ber. 2:5, to Gamaliel is attributed the statement, "I cannot heed you to suspend from myself the kingdom of Heaven even for one hour." Now as a matter of fact that is not a political context[8]—there is no threat of legitimate violence, for instance—for the saying has to do with reciting the *shema*. No political conclusions are drawn from that allegation. Quite to the contrary, Gamaliel, head of the collegium of sages, is not thereby represented as relinquishing power to Heaven, only as expressing his obedience to divine rule even when he does not have to. Indeed, "the kingdom of Heaven" does not form a political category, even though, as we shall see, in the politics of Judaism, all power flows from God's will and law, expressed in the Torah. In this Judaism the manipulation and application of power, allowing the impositions of drastic sanctions in support of the law, for instance, invariably flow through institutions, on earth and in Heaven, of a quite concrete and material character. "The kingdom of Heaven" may be within, but violate the law deliberately and wantonly and God will kill you sooner than you should otherwise have had to die. And, as a matter of fact, the Mishnah's framers rarely appeal in the context of politics and the legitimate exercise of violence to "the kingdom of Heaven," which, in this setting, does not form a political institution at all.

Indeed, from the pentateuchal writings we can hardly construct the *particular* politics, including the mythic component thereof, that operates in the Mishnah's (or any other) Judaism. First of all, the Pentateuch does not prepare us to make sense of the institutions that the politics of Judaism for its part designs—government by king and high priest rather than, as in the Pentateuch, prophet. Second, and concomitantly, the pentateuchal myth that legitimates coercion—rule by God's prophet, governance through explicitly revealed laws that God has dictated—plays no active and systemic role whatsoever in the formulation and presentation of the Mishnah's politics of Judaism. Rather, of the types of political authority contained within the scriptural repertoire, the Mishnah's philosophers reject prophetic and charismatic authority and deem critical authority exercised by the sage's disciple who has been carefully nurtured in rules, not in gifts of the spirit. The authority of sages in the politics of Judaism does not derive from charisma (revelation by God to the sage who makes a ruling in a given case, or even from general access to God for the sage). The myth we shall presently explore in no way falls into the classification of charismatic myth of politics.

True, everybody knows and believes that God has dictated the Torah to Moses. But the Mishnah's framers do not then satisfy themselves with a paraphrase of what God has said to Moses in the Torah. How might they had done so? The answer to that question provides perspective on what our authorship has done. The following allows us to see how matters might have been phrased—but never were:

A. *Now it happened that when Moses held up his hand, Israel prevailed, and when he let his hand fall, Amalek prevailed* [Ex. 17:11].

B. Now do Moses's hands make war or stop it?

C. But the purpose is to say this to you:

D. So long as the Israelites would set their eyes upward and submit their hearts to their Father in Heaven, they would grow stronger. And if not, they fell.

E. In like wise, you may say the following:

F. *Make yourself a firey serpent and set it on a standard, and it shall come to pass that every one who is bitten, when he sees it, shall live* [Num. 21:8].

G. Now does that serpent [on the standard] kill or give life? [Obviously not.]

H. But: So long as the Israelites would set their eyes upward and submit to their Father in Heaven, they would be healed. And if not, they would pine away.

M.R.H.

The silence now becomes eloquent. We look in vain in the pages of our systemic writing for a *single* example in which authorities ask people to raise their eyes on high and so to obey what said authorities command. Such a political myth may, however, be implicit. But when made explicit and systemically active, not left in its inert condition, the myth we seek by definition precipitates not obedience in general, but rather concrete decision-making processes, to be sure inclusive of obedience to those decisions once made. And we shall know the reason why.

More to the point, is God's direct intervention (e.g., as portrayed in Scripture) represented as a preferred or even available sanction? Yes and no, but mostly no. For in our system what is important is that the myth of God's intervention on an ad hoc and episodic basis in the life of the community hardly serves to explain obedience to the law in the here and now. What sort of evidence would indicate that God intervenes in such wise as to explain obedience to the law on an everyday basis? Invoking God's immediate presence, a word said, a miracle performed, would suffice. But in the entirety of the more than five hundred chapters of the Mishnah, no one ever prays to have God supply a decision in a particular case.[9] More to the point, no judge appeals to God to put to death a convicted felon. If the judge wants the felon killed, he kills him. When God intervenes, it is in the jurisdiction assigned to God, not the court. And then the penalty is a different one from execution.

It follows that an undifferentiated myth explaining the working of undifferentiated power by appeal to God's will, while relevant, is not exact and does not explain this system in its rich detail. How the available mythic materials explain the principles of differentiation now requires attention. The explanation must be both general and specific. That is to say, while the court

orders and carries out the execution, the politics works in such a way that all
three political institutions, God, the court, and the Temple, the three agencies
with the power to bestow or take away life and property and to inflict physical
pain and suffering, work together in a single continuum and in important ways
cooperate to deal with the same crimes or sins. The data to which we now turn
will tell us who does what to whom and why, and, in the reason why, we shall
uncover the political myth we seek.

Predictably, when we work our way through sanctions to recover the mythic
premises thereof, we begin with God's place in the institutionalization and
execution of legitimate violence. Of course, the repertoire of sanctions does
encompass God's direct intervention, but that is hardly a preferred alternative
or a common one. Still, God does commonly intervene when oaths are violated, for oaths are held to involve God and the person who invokes God's
name. Further, whereas when faced with an insufficiency of valid evidence
under strict rules of testimony, the earthly court cannot penalize serious
crime, the Heavenly court can and does impose a penalty. Clearly, then, God
serves to justify the politics and account for its origin. Although God is never
asked to join in making specific decisions and effecting policy in the everyday
politics of the state, deliberate violation of certain rules provokes God's or the
Heavenly court's direct intervention. Thus obedience to the law clearly represents submission to God in Heaven. Further, forms of Heavenly coercion such
as we shall presently survey suggest a complex mythic situation with more
subtle nuance than the claim that, overall, God rules would indicate. A politics of rules and regulations cannot admit God's ad hoc participation, and this
system did not do so. God joined in the system in a regular and routine way,
and the rules took for granted God's part in the politics of Judaism.

Precisely how does the intervention of God into the system come to concrete expression? By appeal to the rules handed down at Sinai as an ultimate
reference in legal questions, for instance. This is the case in the story about
R. Simeon of Mispah, who sowed his field with two types of wheat. Simeon's
problem is that he may have violated the law against sowing mixed seeds in a
single patch. When the matter came before Rabban Gamaliel, the passage
states:

C. They went up to the Chamber of Hewn Stone and asked [about the
    law regarding sowing two types of wheat in one field].
D. Said Nahum the Scribe, "I have received [the following ruling] from
    R. Miasha, who received it from his father, *who received [it] from
    the pairs, who received [it] from the prophets, [who received] the
    law [given] to Moses on Sinai,* regarding one who sows his field with
    two types of wheat."

                                        M. Peah. 2:6 (my emphasis)

Here, the law's legitimacy clearly depends on its descent by tradition from Sinai. But that general principle of descent from Sinai was invoked only rarely.[10] Indeed, R. Simeon's case undermines the Mishnah's relation to God's intervention. R. Simeon's problem is minor. Nothing important requires so drastic a claim to be made explicit. That is to say, it is a mere commonplace that the system appeals to Sinai.

But this is not a politics of revelation, for a politics of revelation consistently and immediately appeals to the myth that God works in the here and now, all the time, in concrete cases. That appeal is not common in the Mishnah's statement of its system, and consequently that appeal to the myth of revelation does not bear important political tasks and is not implicit here. Indeed I do not think it was present at all, except where Scripture made it so (e.g., with the ordeal inflicted on the wife accused of adultery). Why the persistent interest in legitimation other than through the revelation of the Torah for the immediate case? The answer to that question draws upon the traits of philosophers, who are interested in the prevailing rule governing all cases and the explanation for the exceptions, rather than upon those of historian-prophets, who are engaged by the exceptional case which is then represented as paradigmatic.[11] Our philosophers appeal to a myth to explain what is routine and orderly, and what they wish to explain is what is ordinary and everyday: institutions and rules, not cases and ad hoc decisions yielding no rule at all.

The traits of the politics of Judaism then emerge in the silences as much as in the acts of speech, in the characteristics of the myth as much as in its contents. The politics of Judaism appeals not to a charismatic but to a routine myth, in which is explained the orderly life of institutions and an administration, and by which are validated the rules and the workings of a political structure and system. True, as I have repeatedly emphasized, all of them are deemed to have been founded on revelation. But what kind of revelation? The answer derives from the fact that none of the political institutions appeal in the here and the now to God's irregular ("miraculous") intervention. Treatment of the rebellious elder and the false prophet as we shall see tells us quite the opposite. The political institutions not only did not invoke miraculous intervention to account for the imposition of sanctions, they would not and did not tolerate the claim that such could take place.

It is the regularity and order of God's participation in the politics that the character of the myth of the politics of Judaism maintains we have to understand and account for. Mere allegations in general that the law originates with God's revelation to Moses at Sinai do not serve to identify that middle-range myth that accounts for the structure and the system. If God is not sitting at the shoulder of the judge and telling the judge what to do (as the writers of Exodus 21ff. seem to suppose), then what legitimacy attaches to the judge's decision to give Mr. Smith's field over, or back, to Mr. Jones? And why (within the imaginary state at hand) should people support, sustain, and submit to authority? Sages' abstract language contains no answers to these questions. And yet sages' system presupposes routine and everyday obedience to power, not merely the utilization of legitimate violence to secure conformity. That is partly because the systemic statement to begin with tells very few stories. Matters that the pentateuchal writers expressed through narrating a very specific story about how God said thus and so to Moses in this particular case, rewarding the ones who obeyed and punishing those who did not, in the Mishnah come to expression in language of an allusive and philosophical, generalizing character.

Here, too, we discern the character of the myth even before we determine its contents. While we scarcely expect that this sort of writing is apt to spell out a myth, even though a myth infuses the system, we certainly can identify the components of the philosophical and theological explanation of the state that have taken mythic form.

Even here, to be sure, the evidence proves sparse. First, of course, in the mythic structure comes God, who commands and creates, laying out what humanity is to do, exercising the power to form the social world in which humanity is to obey. God then takes care of God's[12] particular concerns, and these focus upon *deliberate* violation of God's wishes. If a sin or crime is inadvertent, the penalties are of one order, if deliberate, of a different order. The most serious infraction of the law of the Torah is identified not by what is done but by the attitude of the sinner or criminal.[13] If one has deliberately violated God's rule, then God intervenes. If the violation is inadvertent, then the Temple imposes the sanction. And the difference is considerable. In the former case, God through the Heavenly court ends the felon's or sinner's life. Then a person who defies the laws—as these concern one's sexual conduct, attitude toward God, relationships within the family—will be penalized either (if necessary) by God or (if possible) by the earthly court. This means that the earthly court exercises God's power, and the myth of the system as a whole, so far as the earthly court forms the principal institutional form of the system, emerges not merely in a generality but in all its specificity. These particular judges, here and now, stand for God and exercise the power of God. In the latter case, the Temple takes over jurisdiction; a particular offering is called for, as the book of Leviticus specifies. But there is no need for God or the earthly court in God's name to take a position.

Now come the data of real power, the sanctions. We may divide sanctions just as the authorship of the Mishnah did, by simply reviewing the range of penalties for law-infraction as they occur.[14] These penalties, as we mentioned above, fall into four classifications: what Heaven does, what political institutions do, what religious institutions do, and what is left to the coercion of public opinion, that is, consensus, with special attention to the definition of that "public" that has effective opinion to begin with. The final realm of power, conferring or withholding approval, proves constricted and, in this context, not very consequential.

Let us begin with the familiar, with sanctions exercised by the earthly court as they are fully described in Mishnah-tractates Sanhedrin and Makkot. We will review at length the imposition of sanctions as it is represented by the earthly court, the Temple, the Heavenly court, the sages. This review allows us to identify the actors in the system of politics—those with power to impose sanctions, and the sanctions they can inflict. Only from this perspective will the initial statement of Judaism, in its own odd idiom, be able to make its points in the way its authorship has chosen. When we take up the myth to which that statement implicitly appeals, we shall have a clear notion of the character of the evidence, in rich detail, on which our judgment of the mythic substrate of the system has been composed.[15]

The most impressive mode of legitimate violence is killing; it certainly focuses our attention. The earthly court may justly kill a sinner or felon. This death-dealing priority accorded to the earthly court derives from the character of the power entrusted to that court. The earthly court enjoys full power to dispose of the property and life of all subject to its authority—in the context imagined by Judaism, of all residing in territory that comes under the state's control.

Imposing the death penalty is described in the following way:

A. Four modes of execution were given over to the court [in order of severity]:
B. (1) stoning, (2) burning, (3) decapitation, and (4) strangulation.
C. R. Simeon says, "(2) Burning, (1) stoning, (4) strangulation, and (3) decapitation."

M. San. 7:1

The passage leaves no doubt that the court could put people to death. Only the severity of suffering imposed by each mode of execution is in question. Thus, Simeon's hierarchy of punishments (C) differs from that of B in the degradation and suffering inflicted on the felon, not in the end result. The passage details four modes of execution, that is, four forms of legitimate violence.[16] In the account, the following is of special interest. I have emphasized the key words.

A. The religious requirement of decapitation [is carried out as follows]:
B. They would cut off his head with a sword,
C. just as the government does.
D. *R. Judah says, "This is disgusting."*
E. "But they put the head on a block and chop it off with an ax."
F. *They said to him, "There is no form of death more disgusting than this one."*

G. The religious requirement of strangulation [is carried out as follows:]
H. They would bury him in manure up to his armpits, and put a towel of
    hard material inside one of soft material, and wrap it around his neck.
I. This [witness] pulls it to him from one side, and that witness pulls it
    to him at the other side, until he perishes.

M. San. 7:3

In among all the practical detail, Judah's intervention stands out. It leaves no
doubt that carrying out the law ("way of life") realizes a particular worldview. Specifically, his language implies that the felon remains a human being,
in God's image. Clearly, then, at stake in the theoretical discussions at hand is
how to execute someone in a manner appropriate to his or her standing after
the likeness of God. This problem obviously presupposes that in imposing the
penalty in the first place and in carrying it out, the court acts wholly in conformity with God's will. This being the case, a political myth of a dominion belonging to God and carrying out God's plan and program certainly stands
behind the materials at hand.

But that observation still leaves us struggling with a mere commonplace.
On the strength of our knowledge that God stands behind the politics and that
the consideration that human beings are in God's image and after God's likeness applies even in inflicting the death penalty, we still cannot identify the
diverse media by which power is carried out. More to the point, we can hardly
distinguish one medium of power from another, which we must do if we are to
gain access to the myth that sustains what we shall soon see is the fully differentiated political structure before us.[17] We do well at this turning point to remember the theoretical basis for this entire inquiry: a politics is a theory of the
ongoing exercise of the power of coercion, including legitimate violence.[18]
Sanctions form the naked exercise of raw power—hence will require the protection and disguise of a heavy cloak of myth.

How to proceed? By close attention to the facts of power and by sorting out
the implications of those facts. A protracted journey through details of the law
of sanctions leads us to classify the sanctions and the sins or crimes to which
they apply. Such a classification will permit us to see how in detail the foci of
power are supposed to intersect or to relate: autonomous powers, connected
and related ones, or utterly continuous ones, joining Heaven to earth, for instance, in the person of this institutional representative or that one. What we
shall see is a system that treats Heaven, earth, and the mediating institution,
the Temple, as interrelated, thus connected, but that insists in vast detail upon
the distinct responsibilities and jurisdiction accorded to each. Once we have
perceived that fundamental fact, we may compose for ourselves the myth, or
at least the point and propositions of the myth, that accounted for the political
structures of Judaism and persuaded people to obey or conform even when
there was no immediate threat of penalty.

A survey of (1) types of sanctions, (2) the classifications of crimes or sins to which they apply, and (3) who imposes them yields these results. First come the death penalty on earth and its counterpart, which is extirpation (death before one's allotted time) imposed by Heaven:

HEAVEN	EARTH	TEMPLE	COMMUNITY
Extirpation for Deliberate Actions	Death Penalty	Death Penalty	
Sexual Crimes	*Sexual Crimes*		
incest	improper relationships		
violating sex taboos (bestiality, homosexuality)	incest		
Religious Crimes against God	*Religious Crimes against God*		
blasphemy	blasphemy		
idolatry	idolatry		
magic	magic		
sorcery	sorcery		
profaning Sabbath	profaning Sabbath		
Religious Sins, Deliberately Committed, against God	*Religious Sins against Family*		
unclean person who ate a Holy Thing	cursing parents		
uncleanness in sanctuary	*Social Crimes*		
violating food taboos	murder		
making offering outside of Temple	communal apostasy		
violating taboos of holy seasons	kidnapping		
replicating Temple incense or oil outside	*Social Sins*		
	public defiance of the court		
	false prophecy		

Next we deal with court inflicted sanctions carried out against property or person (e.g., fines against property, flogging or other social or physical violence short of death for the felon or sinner):

HEAVEN	EARTH	TEMPLE	COMMUNITY
	Flogging Exile	Obligatory Offering and/or Flogging for Inadvertent Action	Shunning
	manslaughter incest violation of menstrual taboo marriage in violation of caste rules violating food taboos removing dam with offspring violating negative commandments	uncleanness eating Temple food in violation of the law replicating Temple oil or incense outside violating Temple food taboos violating taboos of holy days (Passover, atonement) uncleanness (*zab, mesora, etc.*) scx with bondwoman unclean Nazirite false oath of testimony false oath of deposit	failure to repay moral obligation (debt cancelled by Sabbatical year) stubbornly rejecting majority view opposing majority will opposing patriarch

The operative distinction between inflicting a flogging and requiring a sacrifice (Temple sanctions against person or property) and the sanction of extirpation (Heavenly death penalty) is made explicit as follows: For those [transgressions] are people liable, for deliberately doing them, to the punishment of extirpation, and for accidentally doing them, to the bringing of a sin-offering, and for not being certain of whether or not one has done them, to a suspensive guilt-offering." (That distinction is suspended in a few instances, as indicated at M. Ker. 2:1–2.)

This summary yields a simple and clear fact, and on the basis of that simple fact we may now reconstruct the entire political myth on which the politics of Judaism rested. Let me emphasize: *some of the same crime or sins for which the Heavenly court imposes the penalty of extirpation are those for which, under appropriate circumstances (e.g., sufficient evidence admissible in court) the earthly court imposes the death penalty.* That is, the Heavenly court and the earthly court impose precisely the same sanctions for the same crimes or sins. The earthly court therefore forms down here the exact replica and counterpart, within a single system of power, of the Heavenly court up there. This no longer looms as an empty generalization; it is a concrete and systemically active and indicative detail, and the system speaks through its details.

But this is not the entire story. There is a second fact, equally indicative for our recovery of the substrate of myth. We note that there are crimes for which the earthly court imposes penalties, but for which the Heavenly court does not, as well vice versa. The earthly and Heavenly courts share jurisdiction over sexual crimes and over what I classify as serious religious crimes against God. The Heavenly court penalizes with its form of the death penalty religious sins against God, instances in which a person deliberately violates the taboos of sanctification.

And that fact calls our attention to a third partner in the distribution and application of power, the Temple with its system of sanctions that cover precisely the same acts subject to the jurisdiction of the Heavenly and earthly courts. The counterpart on earth is now not the earthly court but the Temple. This is the institution that, in theory, automatically receives the appropriate offering from the person who inadvertently violates these same taboos of sanctification. But this is an odd choice for the Mishnah, since there is now no Temple on earth. The juxtaposition appears then to involve courts and Temple, and the upshot is that both are equally matters of theory. In the theory at hand, then, the earthly court penalizes social crimes against the community that the Heavenly court, on the one side, and the Temple rites, on the other, do not take into account at all. These are murder, apostasy, kidnapping, public defiance of the court, and false prophecy. The earthly court further imposes sanctions on matters of particular concern to the Heavenly court, with special reference to taboos of sanctification (e.g., negative commandments). These three institutions, therefore, exercise concrete and material power, utilizing legitimate violence to kill someone, exacting penalties against property, and inflicting pain. The sages' modes of power, by contrast, stand quite apart, apply mainly to their own circle, and work through the intangible though no less effective means of inflicting shame or paying honor.

The facts we have in hand draw us back to the analysis of our differentiation of applied and practical power. In the nature of the facts before us, that differentiation tells us precisely for what the systemic myth will have to give its account. Power flows through three distinct but intersecting dominions, each with its own concern, all sharing some interests in common. The Heavenly court attends to deliberate defiance of Heaven, the Temple to inadvertent defiance of Heaven. The earthly court attends to matters subject to its jurisdiction by reason of sufficient evidence, proper witnesses, and the like, and these same matters will come under Heavenly jurisdiction when the earthly court finds itself unable to act. Accordingly, we have a tripartite system of sanctions—Heaven cooperating with the Temple in some matters, with the court in others, each bearing its own distinct media of enforcing the law as well. What then can we say concerning the systemic myth of politics? The forms of power and the modes of mediating legitimate violence draw our attention to a single political myth, one that we first confronted, if merely as a generality and commonplace to be sure, at the very outset. The unity of that myth is underlined by the simple fact that the earthly court enters into the process right alongside the Heavenly court and the Temple; as to blasphemy, idolatry, and magic, its jurisdiction prevails. So, as I have stressed, a single myth must serve all three correlated institutions.

It is the myth of God's authority infusing the institutions of Heaven and earth alike, an authority diffused among three principal foci or circles of power, Heaven's court, the earthly court, and the Temple in between. Each focus of power has its own jurisdiction and responsibility, Heaven above, earth beneath, the Temple in the position of mediation—transmitting as it does from earth to Heaven the penalties handed over as required. And all media of power in the matter of sanctions intersect at some points as well: a tripartite politics, a single myth drawing each component into relationship with a single source and origin of power, God's law set forth in the Torah. But the myth has not performed its task until it answers not only the question of why, but also the question of how. Specifically, the details of myth must address questions of the details of power. Who then tells whom to do what? And how are the relationships of dominion and dominance to compliance and obedience made permanent through myth?

We did not require this sustained survey to ascertain that God through the Torah has set forth laws and concerns. That generality now may be made quite specific, for it is where power is differentiated and parceled out that we see the workings of the political myth. So we ask, how do we know who tells whom to do, or suffer, what sanction or penalty? It is the power of myth to differentiate that defines the generative question. The key lies in the criterion by which each mode of power, earthly, mediating, and heavenly, identifies the cases over which it exercises jurisdiction. That criterion is the attitude of the human being who has done what he or she should not: did he act deliberately or unintentionally?

I repeat this with heavy emphasis: *the point of differentiation within the political structures, supernatural and natural alike, lies in the attitude and intention of a human being.* A person who comes into conflict with the system, rejecting the authority claimed by the powers that be, does so deliberately or inadvertently. The myth accounts in the end for the following hierarchization of action and penalty, infraction and sanction: (1) If the deed is deliberate, then one set of institutions exercises jurisdiction and utilizes supernatural power. (2) If the deed is inadvertent, another institution exercises jurisdiction and utilizes the power made available by that same supernatural being.

A sinner or criminal who has deliberately violated the law has by his or her action challenged the politics of Judaism. Consequently, God or God's surrogate imposes sanctions—extirpation (by the court on high) or death or other appropriate penalty (by the court on earth). A sinner or criminal who has inadvertently violated the law is penalized by the imposition of Temple sanctions, losing valued goods. People obey because God wants them to and has told them what to do, and when they do not obey, a differentiated political structure appeals to that single hierarchizing myth. The components of the myth are two: first, God's will, expressed in the law of the Torah, second, the human being's will, carried out in obedience to the law of the Torah or in defiance of that law.

Have we come so far and not yet told the story that the myth contains? I have now to explain and spell out the story that conveys the myth of politics in Judaism. It is not in the Mishnah at all. Do I find the mythic foundation in Scripture, which accounts for the uses and differentiation of power that the Mishnah's system portrays? Indeed I do, for, as we realize, the political myth of Judaism has to explain the differentiation of sins or crimes, with their associated penalties or punishments, and so sanctions of power. And in Scripture there is a very precise answer to the question of how to differentiate among sins or crimes and why to do so. Given the position of the system of the Mishnah, the point of differentiation must rest with one's attitude or intentionality. And indeed, I do have two stories of how the power of God conflicts with the power of humanity in such wise as to invoke the penalties and sanctions in precisely the differentiated modes we have before us. Where do I find such stories of the conflict of wills, God's and humanity's?

The first such story of power differentiated by the will of the human being in communion or conflict with the word of the commanding God comes to us from the Garden of Eden.[19] We cannot too often reread the following astonishing words:

> The Lord God took the man and placed him in the garden of Eden . . . and the Lord God commanded the man, saying, "Of every tree of the garden you are free to eat; but as for the tree of knowledge of good and bad, you must not eat of it; for as soon as you eat of it, you shall die."
> . . . When the woman saw that the tree was good for eating and a delight to the eyes, and that the tree was desirable as a source of wisdom, she took of its fruit and ate; she also gave some to her husband, and he ate. . . .
> The Lord God called out to the man and said to him, "Where are you?"
> He replied, "I heard the sound of You in the garden, and I was afraid, because I was naked, so I hid."
> Then He asked, "Who told you that you were naked? Did you eat of the tree from which I had forbidden you to eat?"
> . . . And the Lord God said to the woman, "What is this you have done!"
> So the Lord God banished him from the garden of Eden.

Now a reprise of the exchange among God, Adam, and Eve tells us that at stake was responsibility: not who has violated the law, but who bears responsibility for deliberately violating the law:

> "The woman You put at my side—she gave me of the tree, and I ate."
> "The serpent duped me, and I ate."
> Then the Lord God said to the serpent, "Because you did this . . ."

The ultimate responsibility lies with the one who acted deliberately, not under constraint or on account of deception or misinformation, as did Adam and Eve. Then the sanction applies most severely to the one who by intention and an act of will has violated God's intention and will.

Adducing this story by itself poses several problems. First, the storyteller does not allege that Adam intended to violate the commandment; he followed his wife. Second, the penalty is not extirpation but banishment. That is why to establish what I conceive to be the generative myth I turn to a second story of disobedience and its consequences, the tale of Moses' hitting the rock:

> The community was without water, and they joined against Moses and Aaron. . . . Moses and Aaron came away from the congregation to the entrance of the Tent of Meeting and fell on their faces. The Presence of the Lord appeared to them, and the Lord spoke to Moses, saying, "You and your brother Aaron take the rod and assemble the community, and before their very eyes order the rock to yield its water. Thus you shall produce water for them from the rock and provide drink for the congregation and their beasts."
>
> Moses took the rod from before the Lord as he had commanded him. Moses and Aaron assembled the congregation in front of the rock; and he said to them, "Listen, you rebels, shall we get water for you out of this rock?" And Moses raised his hand and struck the rock twice with his rod. Out came copious water, and the community and their beasts drank.
>
> But the Lord said to Moses and Aaron, "Because you did not trust me enough to affirm My sanctity in the sight of the Israelite people, therefore you shall not lead this congregation into the land that I have given them."
>
> Those are the waters of Meribah, meaning that the Israelites quarrelled with the Lord—through which He affirmed His sanctity.
>
> Numbers 20:1–13

Here we have not only intentional disobedience, but also the penalty of extirpation. Both this myth and the myth of the fall make the same point. They direct attention to the generative conception that at stake in power is the will of God over against the will of the human being, in particular the Israelite human being.

The political myth of Judaism now emerges in the Mishnah in all of its tedious detail as a reprise—in now consequential and necessary, stunning detail—of the story of God's commandment, humanity's disobedience, God's sanction for the sin or crime, and humanity's atonement and reconciliation. The Mishnah omits all explicit reference to myths that explain power and sanctions, but it invokes in its rich corpus of details the absolute given of the story of the distinction between what is deliberate and what is mitigated by an attitude that is not culpable, a distinction set forth in the tragedy of Adam and Eve, in the failure of Moses and Aaron, and in countless other passages in the Pentateuch, Prophetic Books, and Writings. Then the Mishnah's is a politics of life after Eden and outside of Eden. The upshot of the matter is that the political myth of Judaism sets forth the constraints of freedom, the human will brought to full and unfettered expression, imposed by the constraints of revelation, God's will made known.

At stake is what Adam and Eve, Moses and Aaron, and numerous others intend, propose, plan, for that is the point at which the politics intervenes, making its points of differentiation between and among its sanctions and the authorities that impose those penalties. For that power to explain difference, which is to say, the capacity to represent and account for hierarchy, we are required, in my opinion, to turn to the story of the fall of Adam and Eve from Eden and to counterpart stories. The reason is that the political myth derives from that same myth of origins its points of differentiation and explains by reference to the principal components of that myth—God's and humanity's will and power—the dynamics of the political system at hand. God commands, but humanity does what it then chooses, and in the interplay of those two protean forces, each power in its own right, the sanctions and penalties of the system apply.

Power comes from two conflicting forces, the commanding will of God and the free will of the human being. Power expressed in immediate sanctions is also mediated through these same forces, Heaven above, human beings below, with the Temple mediating between the two. Power works in the interplay between what God has set forth in the law of the Torah and what human beings do, whether intentionally, whether inadvertently, whether obediently, whether defiantly. That is why the politics of Judaism is a politics of Eden. True, as we shall now see, we listen in vain in the creation myth of Genesis for echoes resounding in the shape of the institutions such as those the politics of Judaism actually invents. But the points of differentation of one political institution from another will serve constantly to remind us of what, in the end, serves to distinguish this from that, to set forth not a generalized claim that God rules through whoever is around with a sword (or the right, that is, Roman sponsorship).

The careful descriptions of, and distinctions among, institutions, through a vastly and richly nuanced account of concrete and enduring institutions, will once more emphasize the main point. It is through discovering how people know that power lies here, not there, is exercised by this bureau, not that, that we find our way back to the myth of differentiation and hierarchization. In what is to follow, we shall see how effectively the politics of Judaism distinguishes one institution from another, just as, in our survey of sanctions, we recognize the points of intersection and of separation. At every point we shall therefore be reminded of the most formidable source of power, short of God, of all. That always is the will of the human being. And he and she are never mentioned as paramount actors, even though in this politics humanity is what is at issue. Only at the end, in chapter 12, shall we fully grasp what is at stake.

4

The Divine Plan
of Perfect Hierarchy

Given that the political myth of Judaism, appealing to the theme captured in the stories of Eden and its parallels to account for the conflict between the power of the will of God and the strength of the will of humanity, explains why divine power is mediated through three institutional media of divine intervention, we can expect institutional arrangements to express and emphasize that same division of institutions. But when we turn to the question of how power is parcelled out, that is to say, among the Heavenly court above, earthly court below, and Temple altar in the middle, we find that the theoretical picture of political institutions is out of phase. The political myth has taken pains to explain institutional distinctions that make little practical difference. But that underlines once again the highly theoretical character of the politics. Concrete issues of jurisdiction bear slight consequence when what is at stake is solely a message that politics as a theoretical structure and system is meant to bear. That fact underlines the problematic of the politics of this Judaism: why a politics at all? But we shall find our answer only when the entire structure and system lie before us, fully exposed in the contrast to another politics altogether.

The Mishnah's politics presents a picture of forms with slight account of functions. The initial post-Temple statement of a politics of any Judaism sets forth institutional arrangements but scarcely alludes to the political dynamics of the structure that is described. Why the theory of politics comprises a description of inert institutions, not of the practice of politics or even the rules of administration, requires explanation.

Furthermore, while the myth details who penalizes whom for doing what and why, in the Mishnah's account of institutional arrangements jurisdictional questions generally are bypassed. Take for example the way in which power is jointly administered by Heaven, earthly court, and Temple. The tripartite pattern of sanctions, some imposed by Heaven, some by an earthly court, some by the Temple *ex opere operato*, suggests that institutional forms of power will produce a three-part structure as well. Not only so, but it seems that the shared responsibility for certain sins or crimes, punishable, depending upon the human attitude, by one or another of the three institutions that administer power, should yield a clear account of how, in the here and now, the institutions are formed and—more to the point—differentiated (for example, as to jurisdiction). Quite to the contrary, the differentiation is only on the surface, when it is even conceded.

The politics of institutions is curious in yet another aspect. No criterion tells us when an office is vacant or how power is transferred other than through the death of the officeholder. True, genealogy dictates what caste will hold the Temple's power, but it does not specify which member of that caste will exercise it. The accidents of politics are assumed to explain who becomes king. But the theory ignores such critical issues as how one gains entry into the court or prepares to carry out duties, or how the system provides support for its administrators and bureaucrats. Such practical considerations in the management of political institutions do not enter the account.

So although the myth explains arrangements among institutions, it neglects to define the differences among institutions, the respective importance of those institutions, and how each functions in relationship to the other. Whether this omission arises from the inexperience of the Mishnah's framers and their remote and tenuous connection with real power cannot be said for certain. Of course, more often than not, the fertile imagination makes up for fallow experience. But lack of direct knowledge and limitations of imagination form inert, not active, data in the framing of a system. For evidence we will have to turn to systemic dynamics, not the mere accidents of time and circumstance. Here we can proceed with some confidence, for system builders tell us what they want us to know—whatever the source of that information. In this context, deliberate neglect of or indifference to a question indeed offers us options for explanation.

And there is, as a matter of fact, such an explanation for the Mishnah's framers' failure to detail the relationships among the three institutional foci of power: to them, in their fundamental conception, institutional distinctions do not yield important practical differences. That is, the relationships among heaven, earth, and altar are systemically inconsequential and are consequently neglected in the Mishnah. All three institutions are joined under the hegemony of sages; sages run them equally.

Here, of course, it becomes of interest to us to detail why these relationships prove inconsequential. Let me explain. The politics so portrays matters that the earthly court falls wholly into the hands of sages, the Temple is run by priests only under sages' tutelage, and the king, who stands submissive to the sages, as is right and proper, governs "with the approval" of sages and stands constantly alert to cultivate their goodwill. The institutions then are three, but the institutional forms of power conceal the single mode by which the society through sages' government actually is ruled. The formal description of the media of domination then conceals, rather than exposes, the true disposition of power as the politics of this Judaism proposes to set things up. And that brings us to a major structural oddity: the institutional arrangements do not correpond with the facts of power as the structure and system define those facts. Then why make the distinctions at all? It is to deliver a message concerning not politics, to which such differences ought to matter, but ontology, the human condition. The message is framed in social, also therefore political, terms; however, it is not a social message in a this-worldly sense, but an ontological one in a metaphysical sense.[1]

When properly understood, in fact, the portrait of political institutions yields a result strikingly congruent with the mythic account of power. True, as I said, we should anticipate a sustained account of the political institutions of Heaven, earth, and Temple. But our systemic statement describes in requisite detail only one political institution, the *bet din,* which we conventionally translate as "court." The court is represented as the point at which administration and application of power are joined together. And, as I shall show, the usage of this term suggests that its true translation should be nothing less than "government." In fact, in the politics of this Judaism we have unicameral locus of power—whatever happens, happens within the court. True, there is a king. But the political system of Judaism pays scarcely any attention to the royal regime. And as to the Temple, although the Mishnah provides substantial information about the conduct of sacrifices and the maintenance of the staff and buildings,[2] it manifests little interest in the institutional forms of power within the Temple. Instead, it falls back on listing the names of administrative officials. But as for the court—the effective agency of government and administration, run by sages and wholly in conformity with their rules and policies—about that court-government we are informed in rich and loving detail. This court, which tries sinners and criminals, also administers the law and governs the systemic "Israel" and hence should be regarded as the government, pure and simple.

To gain perspective on the political institutions as Judaism initially described them, we have therefore to imagine a politics in which the Supreme Court judges also serve as the faculty of the national university and cover all subjects treated by that faculty. We have also to envisage those same judges, or those subject to their approbation, to be the United States Congress, the president, the heads of all federal agencies and departments, and on and on. The entire government of Israel, the Jewish people, is imagined in our document to consist of persons who, while holding various offices, uniformly conform to a single professional code, uniformly submit to the authority of essentially the same standard of conviction and everyday conduct, and who thus prove interchangeable. That accounts for the disjuncture between the political myth that underlies the politics, on the one side, and the political institutions that, in theory, realize the politics, on the other. Scholar-administrator-clerk-judge-priest-king all are one. What difference, then, will it make whether one is a priest who obeys the sage, a king who obeys the sage, or a judge who is a disciple of a sage or subservient to the sage? The myth differentiates what matters: the authority of a given institution in response to the attitude of the party subject to the system. The myth ignores institutional arrangements that, in any event, make distinctions of no material difference.

That fact reciprocally accounts for the failure of the theory of institutions to draw upon the logic of the myth to account for earthly representations of power. That is to say, if institutions were to express the concrete reality required by the myth, then we should discern correspondences between Heaven and earth, between King and king, or Heavenly court and earthly court, with the Temple and its priesthood represented as intervening and mediating bodies. But the king/queen does not stand as counterpart to the King/Queen in Heaven; the earthly judges do their task without being compared to angels; the Temple priesthood is not treated as more than mortal. Not one line suggests that the Temple on earth matches or corresponds to the Temple in Heaven. Clearly, the myth has prepared us for institutional arrangements that we do not, in fact, find in the theory of institutions. Why? First, the myth concerns itself with the power embodied by attitude and realized within the workings of intentionality. Second, the sage is the one who should exercise that power, on the one side, or who, on the other, should invoke sanctions on earth, in the Temple, or in Heaven when that power is misused. The system therefore conveys its message not only in the myth, but also in its curious mode of representing a tripartite institutional arrangement. What the theory of political institutions does not tell us testifies as persuasively as what it does convey concerning the systemic purpose and message.[3]

Let me give a concrete fact to prove that the myth stands disjoined from the institutions that are supposed to find their explanation and validation in it. As we have observed, the myth treats the important question of how Heaven's sanctions correspond with those on earth, drawing into a single system a variety of penalties, according to the case, in conformity with the attitude of the involved sinner or felon. Since sanctions draw Heaven into relationship with earth, so that the exercise of power down here corresponds with the exercise of power up there, with the mediating position of the Temple holding the two together, we have to ask where, here on earth, is the counterpart to God, called in the liturgy "King of the universe." Take the king as the leading candidate. Structurally at least, we should want to identify the king as the earthly counterpart to the rule of Heaven. That identification would then leave the earthly court as the administrative counterpart to the Heavenly court in the administration of sanctions, and of course the earthly Temple links the two. Our theory of correspondences, then, should give us king to King, court to Court, and Temple in between. And it is the fact that the sages then correspond down here to God's Heavenly staff. But there is no corresponding figure, that is, the king down here, to match the King/Queen up there. Not only so, but the picture of institutions does not encompass the sages' agency, except so far as sages are assumed to control the courts, the monarchy, and the Temple anyhow.

So there are two points of considerable puzzlement here: no sustained picture of the monarchy as an institution, no clear account of the sages' differentiated institution—even while there is supposed to be a match between down here and up there. And that fact requires us to reconsider the uses of the political myth. The myth, we remember, sets forth Heaven with an earthly counterpart and a cultic intermediary. The one focus of power neglected by the myth is the sage, who exercises scarcely any power (that is, the power of legitimate violence or coercion) within the system of sanctions that adumbrates the myth. And yet, as I have stressed, in the representation of the institutional formations of power, the sage predominates, even though he has no institution of his own. The absence from the institutions of the politics of this Judaism of the one agency for which we should expect an elaborated and differentiated account is striking indeed.[4] Even though the court is imagined to be wholly in the hands of, and run by, sages, the Mishnah does not present a sustained and detailed account of the political institution of sages or focus upon how it works. Indeed, sages are represented as the ordinary agents of decision making in all three institutions of state, and it is merely taken for granted that all members of the court, which serves as the executive and legislative as much as the judicial branch of government, happen to be sages. The myth in many ways therefore proves asymmetrical to the institutions.

The reason is simple. The institutional arrangements are so represented as to constitute mere formalities. And that representation eloquently makes a point of systemic urgency. It is that true power is not institutional but invisible and intangible. If power consists in the determination of jurisdiction (Heaven, Temple, earthly court, for instance), then that is the form of power which institutions will have to embody. But in the myth, that power is intangible because it is a matter of attitude, conviction, sentiment, emotion. If power is invisible, then what difference do institutions of a material order make anyhow?

When institutions are described, therefore, it will be in a formal way. When we reach the institutions at which power really is lodged, the systemic description will concentrate upon the correct formation of intellect, sentiment, attitude, and emotion. Thus with regard to the Temple's institutional arrangements and personnel, for example, we shall be told—as indeed we are—the titles of the officeholders in the Temple. When we come to the hierarchization of king and high priest, we shall find a powerful demonstration about the superiority of the formal power of the monarch. But when we hear about who really matters, it will be in terms not of titles or formalities, but of belief, conviction, correct intentionality. And then, of course, we shall have to confront the sage, who, as I said, either runs institutions (courts, administration) or tells those who do run them what they must do. In my view this explains why within the systemic description the system builders appropriately tell us what they do about each party: systemically inert facts (to use my distinction, not theirs) about the epiphenomena of the system, systemically lively facts about the systemically active, critical components.

In turn, this explains why sages are not assigned an institutional focus at all. Priest and king reign, but sages rule. And they rule not by their control of institutions, but by what we should have to call their moral authority.[5] The king obeys, the priest conforms, because that is how they should behave. Not a line of the Mishnah tells us what happens if the king does not obey or the priest does not conform (precipitating a constitutional crisis would suffice). The premise, of course, is that then the king and priest are not legitimate or have not done things rightly. But that premise—implicit illegitimation—hardly adumbrates an institutional arrangement capable of effecting sages' judgment concerning the illegitimacy of an officeholder or his action. Even in theory the anticipated structure of power hardly corresponds with the portrait of institutions totally under sages' control that the Mishnah offers as the politics of this Judaism.

Since, in the politics of this Judaism, power accrues where there is no institutional differentiation, the forms of power conceal, rather than reveal, the substance of effective authority. Time and again we observe that real power lies with those who prepare, educate, qualify, and empower sages, but of sages in institutional arrangements we hear nothing, just as the mythic substrate of the system scarcely has referred to sages' party and inner regime. The implicit power of sages over one another through the media of approbation or "excommunication," that is, ostracism or internal banishment, itself is not explained, and in any case no everyday consequence is imputed to that power. Nor are we told, for instance, how the (sages') bureaucracy is supported and does its work, how the (sages') administration is taught and learned, how the politics carries out its tasks on an everyday basis. Consequently, from one viewpoint we may judge the initial statement of the politics of this Judaism to take up a disingenuous position on its topic, the institutionalization and utilization of power. But from another perspective we must conclude that the initial statement conveys, in silence and in speech, precisely what the system builders want us to know: differentiation makes no difference, because what matters in politics is what counts everywhere else too, and that is ontological, not political, at its foundations.

Silence on all questions of administration that penetrate into the actual (imagined) working of things proves congruent to the historical circumstances in which the Mishnah's political system as a whole was made up. For were the systemic statement to represent effective power, as distinct from the trappings of power, our authorship would call attention to the realities of a world in movement and assuredly out of sages' control, a world in which conflict dominates and difference matters. But the politics of this Judaism wants to show the exact opposite. It proposes to portray a world at rest, in which consensus governs and right attitude, amenable to persuasion and argument, dictates the answers to important questions—a world in which no difference pertains at all. How to represent the realities of power in conflict, the negotiation and brokerage required for effective decision making? This is an important problem, for institutions that can accommodate and utilize conflict and work toward consensus, rather than assuming ubiquitous conformity, express an account of a world, including a political world, quite unwanted within the Judaic social system sages proposed to invent. That explains why, I think, the politics at hand describes a steady-state world in which law is realized by universal conformity. So law is described without sustained and detailed attention to the ways and means of applying or deriving it.

In this context we can explain why the account of institutions concerns only those people who exercise legitimate power within the systemic framework, that is, Jews who rule by appeal to the Torah and apply the law of the Torah, not Jews who do not or who appeal to alien (gentile, Roman) sources of power. The politics of Judaism is no way acknowledges that Israel's authorities rule by the grace of any agency but Heaven; there is no foreign policy,[6] let alone an agency for dealing with a colonial office.[7] Nor is there provision within the institutional fantasy before us for dealing with recalcitrant or recusant Jews. Given the interests of the myth, we grasp the systemic purpose in making up a politics, and that has no relationship whatsoever with a world in which Israel is scattered and weak, not in control of any sizable territories and not capable of sustaining an enlandised and locative politics at all. The reason is not merely that the Jews were a weak and defeated nation, not in possession of large tracts of land in which to build a state, not recognized by the imperial government as a self-governing entity of any size and substance. The reason is that the system addressed a different circumstance altogether, identifying as urgent a question of its own choice, responding with an answer of its own invention.

This is not to suggest that the system builders pretend no world exists beyond their own framework. Quite to the contrary, time and again the systemic statement of institutional arrangements contains the amazing acknowledgment that the politics set forth does not fully exhaust the ongoing administration of power within the world it contemplates. But that admission in no way contradicts the statement that the system builders choose to make; rather, in this context other loci for power constitute inert facts, givens of the everyday world that are acknowledged without being accorded any considerable consequence. Consider the roles played in the Mishnah by authorities within Jewry who are no sages, and gentiles.

As the following suggests, the system builders could account for and cope with power that thus lay beyond the limits of the politics they proposed to define:

A. R. Simeon b. Aqashya says, "As the elders of the *am ha'ares* grow old, their understanding is loosened from them, as it is said, *He removes the speech of the trusty and takes away the understanding of the elders* [Job 12:20]."

B. "But sages of Torah are not that way. But while they are growing old, their understanding is strengthened for them, as it is said, *With aged men is wisdom and in length of days understanding* [Job 12:12]."

M. Qinnim 3:6

A. If tax collectors entered a house, the house is unclean. If a gentile is with them, they are believed to state, "We did not enter," but they are not believed to state, "We entered but did not touch anything."

B. Thieves who entered the house—unclean is only the place trodden by the feet of thieves.

C. And what do they render unclean? Food, liquid, and open clay utensils. But couches and seats and clay utensils bearing a tight seal are clean.

D. If there is a gentile with them or a woman, everything is held to be unclean.

M. Toh. 7:6

These discrete statements acknowledge competing forces, people who are not sages but who exercise power. First come other Jews who serve as "elders," which is to say, authorities who decide questions in such a way that people may be coerced to accept their decisions. Second come "tax collectors," Jewish or gentile, who work for someone, we know not whom (but who we can assume to be Rome). These two disparate forces, the Israel beyond the politics contemplated by this Judaism, the Rome acknowledged but never admitted within the circle of the system, represent power beyond the disposition of the system builders and therefore not accounted for by them. But why should the system builders take account of what makes no difference to their system? Outside powers do not present to the system ineluctable and urgent questions and therefore do not require important responses. The politics of Judaism deals with its questions, not someone else's. And only when the question is asked will it get its answer. That fact explains why, from this politics, we simply cannot construct a government and describe how it works. We know only about those political institutions that the system wishes to describe, not about all the other institutions the presence of which the system builders were prepared to acknowledge, let alone those that for one reason or the other the system did not choose even to acknowledge.

Proof that everywhere in the politics of this Judaism larger systemic interests intervene emerges in yet another trait of the descriptions of institutions. We have no account of the politics of those institutions, no picture of how, in the interplay of pressure, jurisdiction, executive interest, career ambition and advancement, above all, intersecting forces in conflict on policy, yield decisions, actions, a long-term program.[8] Except where institutional intervention is called for by some special circumstance, an account of the actual process of making and carrying out decisions scarcely plays a role. For that process represents disruption and disorder, brokerage and negotiation among conflicting forces and competing interests—precisely what this politics will not recognize and does not choose to accommodate. This explains, also, why the task of the court is to apply those laws that do not work on their own. The politics makes little place in the routine and the everyday for its own institutions, for the theory of politics before us assumes that laws ordinarily do enjoy compliance and work more or less on their own. Decision-making processes of this politics pertain mostly to cases and produce ad hoc rulings on specific situations. On that basis we can at best merely infer how politics actually worked. We can barely detect even how the politics' framers imagined that politics worked.

Take for instance local government. If we want to know how in the villages people reached and carried out decisions, we shall be disappointed by the premise of the following:

> Townsfolk who sold a street of a town buy with its proceeds a synagogue. If they sold a synagogue, they buy an ark. If they sold an ark, they buy wrappings.
>
> M. Meg. 3:1

In the following case as well, we find no local authority, rather a "they" that is supposed to conduct public life in accord with acknowledged requirements.

> A. How was fasting carried out?
> B. They bring the ark into the street of the town and put wood ashes on the ark, the head of the patriarch, and the head of the court.
> C. And each person puts ashes on his head. The eldest among them makes a speech of admonition.
>
> M. Taanit 2:1

The premise is that people obey the rule at hand. But what happens if they fail to do so? And how do they reach their decisions and carry them out in conformity to law? The townsfolk have reached a consensus, but have they then effected the decision in conformity to law, and to whom are they answerable if not? The passage at hand invites a variety of inquiries, none of which finds suitable response in the document. Yet it is clearly a political case, for it is assumed that the townsfolk form a political entity and own public property and can dispose of it as they like, within the framework of rules set forth by sages for that purpose. On that basis we should anticipate the representation, in the political writing at hand, of the institutional forms of power as these are realized in the village. But there is no picture at all of other than an inchoate consensus which is, more or less, "identical with the law." [9]

Local government is, unsurprisingly, portrayed as the work of sages, who operate through the medium of ad hoc decrees [10] rather than through day-to-day administration, which is essentially beyond imagining. [11] The assumption then is that the decrees will be followed, rather than enforced, and that all parties will conform. We have no notion of how the system imagines those who do not concur can be coerced. In the following, by contrast, the source of the "decree" clearly is sages, and this tells us that on the local scene, sages were supposed to exercise authority:

A. They do not decree a fast for the community to take place on the new moon, Hanukkah, or Purim.

M. Ta. 2:10

D. They decreed a fast in Lud. It rained before noon.
E. R. Tarfon said to them, "Go, eat, and drink, and celebrate a festival day." So they went and ate and drank and celebrated a festival day. Then they assembled at twilight and proclaimed the Great Hallel.

M. Ta. 3:9

A. As to bakers:
B. Sages required them to separate from their produce only an amount sufficient for priestly ration taken for tithe and dough offering. Shopkeepers are not permitted to sell doubtfully tithed produce.

M. Dem. 2:4

These items leave no doubt that sages were represented as local authorities. But the Mishnah's items also suggest that the government of village affairs is not routinely part of sages' duties. Local government is, rather, an ongoing institution that is not described at all. And yet while those who determined to continue the fast can have done so privately, what about the bakers? To them sages' decree represented a cost, and, as we shall see in due course, when sages made rulings about the administration of prices, then someone lost, and it was invariably the merchant or capitalist. Such a person could not have given up profits willingly and voluntarily, and, since the consumer or purchaser surely would not have paid more than required, coercion in some form and by some medium would have found a prominent place in the system. But there is simply no hint as to how that coercion, even by means of public opinion, could have been brought to bear. So the everyday administration of law and local affairs (economic as much as judicial), attributed to sages as bureaucrats and representatives of a government that could make decisions, is scarcely explained, and no organized domination through continuous administration is represented. Here is a case in which power is assumed but not explained.

We turn now from our discussion of sages' power over village government to their ability to enforce decisions of their court. As a party made up of educated males sages rule.[12] And properly trained for their task, with the right attitudes, sages staff the earthly court and make the decisions of life and death, property and wealth that that court is imagined to make. To show that such a court forms the institutional centerpiece of the politics, we turn, as is our way, to the matter of sanctions (in the present instance, these involve not life and death but—as we already recognize—everyday matters of prices, personal status, and the disposition of property). Any picture of the earthly court, which is to say, of the exercise of power in the here and now, must commence with evidence that an administration plays a critical role within the system. Here are representative decisions, among a fair number covered by the Mishnah, supposedly made by a court or its agency, governing such concrete and therefore critical issues as prices and markets and personal status:

A. R. Tarfon gave instructions in Lud: "Fraud is an overcharge of eight
    pieces of silver to a sela, one third of the purchase price."
B. So the merchants of Lud rejoiced.
C. He said to them, "All day long it is permitted to retract."
D. They said to him, "Let R. Tarfon leave us where we were."
E. And they reverted to conduct themselves in accord with the ruling
    of sages.

M. B. M. 4:3

Power to control prices, by decree imputed to sages, derives from their standing as officers of the court, not from their personal charisma. This is not only explicit in the law, but also a reasonable supposition, since the power to deprive persons of their property, for example of their right to get as high a price as they can for their goods and services, cannot derive solely from broad-based voluntary compliance to the law.

The power to determine the still more critical matter of personal status, moreover, is explicitly assigned to the court, even though in parallel cases individual sages are represented as reaching such decisions:

A. If the court instructed a woman to remarry, then the marriage is deliberately carried out on her part and the remarriage is not an inadvertent transgression and null.

M. Yeb. 10:1

A. A certain man performed *halisah* [the rite of removing the shoe, Deut. 25:1ff.] with his deceased childless brother's widow when the couple were by themselves in prison, and when the case came before R. Aqiba, he validated the rite.

M. Yeb. 12:5

A. A certain man in Asya was let down by a rope into the sea and they drew back up only his leg.
B. Sages said, "If the recovered part included from the knee and above, his wife may remarry, and if only from the knee and below, she may not."

M. Yeb. 16:4

What is important in these three entries [13] is the parallelism of the decisions of the court, Aqiba, and "sages." That trait shows that the system treats as equivalent the rulings of a court in general, a named sage, and a collectivity of sages. It follows that the court system falls wholly within the framework of sages and their decisions. These sages are empowered by the Torah, we know, and in particular by their knowledge of the law of the Torah as it has come down to them from prior courts ("administrations"). So the institutional forms of power take shape wholly within the framework of sages, and, on an everyday basis, the administration of legitimate power is assumed to lie in their hands.

That prevailing assumption nonetheless competes with other equally well founded assumptions. The first is that other authorities, besides sages, applied the law and made decisions.[14] The document's framers include evidence that sages were not the only, or necessarily the main, agencies of the administration of the social entity. But when they concede the existence of competing agencies, they include evidence that sages formed opinions concerning the work and rulings of those agencies, and when the politics of this Judaism turns to the description of the institutions of power, agencies other than the approved ones never play a role. So the representation of competing authorities makes the paramount point that sages really disposed of what others proposed.

Let us take note of part of an account of how a competing administration is described:[15]

A. Two judges of civil law were in Jerusalem: Admon and Hanan b. Abishalom.
B. Hanan lays down two rulings.
C. Admon lays down seven.
D. He who went overseas, and his wife [left at home] claims maintenance—

E. Hanan says, "Let her take an oath at the end, but let her not take an oath at the outset [that is, she takes an oath when she claims her marriage contract after her husband's death, or after he returns, that she has not held back any property of her husband]."

F. Sons of high priests disputed with him and ruled, "Let her take an oath at the outset and at the end."

G. Ruled R. Dosa b. Harkinas in accord with their opinion.

H. Said R. Yohanan b. Zakkai, "Well did Hanan rule. She should take an oath only at the end."

M. Ket. 13:1

This account of the two civil law judges and their rulings treats the entire case as a matter of fact. Each case report introduces opinions concerning the civil law judges' rulings of "sons of high priests," Dosa b. Harkinas, and Yohanan b. Zakkai giving a judgment of the whole. And that, of course, is the institutional judgment: whatever other courts made decisions, sages had the power to approve or disapprove of what they did.

Accordingly, at least three institutions of administration operate: the civil law judges, "sons of high priests," and a sage (Dosa, and then Yohanan b. Zakkai). The sage settles matters, concurring with Hanan against sons of high priests. This somewhat complex jurisdiction, with three courts addressing the same issues, covers matters wholly in the charge of sages' courts, at least so far as sages in the Mishnah represent their own courts. The courts govern the disposition of the property of an absent husband, support for a wife in the case of an absent husband, dividing an estate, claims in cases of bailment, contract violations, real estate cases, and deeds, bonds, and other commercial paper. Not a single area of law over which jurisdiction was conceded to the judges in Jerusalem and, as a matter of implicit fact, to the "sons of high priests" (presumably some sort of Temple court), falls outside of the jurisdiction of "the court," which is to say, the sages' court system. Accordingly, we deal with an account of a politics in which power is shared among competing authorities or administrative bodies.

But even that picture of an administration of Israel's affairs, involving not only sages' courts but also civil priestly courts, vastly overstates how much the politics of this Judaism finds itself willing to concede to competing authorities and their institutions. As a matter of fact, when it comes to describing the institutional forms of power as distinct from conceding the adventitious facts of how power presently is shared, only a single institution of administration is fully and normatively set on display. That is, once more, "the court." [16] The court comprised sages and disciples, the more experienced of whom made the decisions.

Consider this fantastic account of the principal institution of decision making:

A. The sanhedrin was [arranged] in the shape of a half of a round thresh-
ing floor [that is, as an amphitheater],

B. so that [the judges] should see one another,

C. And two judges' clerks stand before them, one at the right and one at
the left.

D. and they write down the arguments of those who vote to acquit and of
those who vote to convict.

E. R. Judah says, "Three: one writes the opinion of those who vote to
acquit, one writes the opinion of those who vote to convict, and the
third writes the opinions both of those who vote to acquit and of
those who vote to convict."

M. San. 4:3

On the surface we deal with a court of judges. But when we review the things
this court did, we realize that that is not so. The "court" in fact is a theoretical
model for the institutions that actually govern. A given number of members of
the court is required for decisions of one kind (e.g., judicial ones); another
number is needed for decisions of a different kind (e.g., political and administrative ones).

The members and procedures prove interchangeable, hence we have a unicameral institution based on sages, many or few. But the distinctive tasks assigned to the court made up of one number of sages as against another has also
to be taken into account in our consideration of the institutionalization of
power. The interchangeability of sages in the several distinct political functions is clear in the following, which tells how men are qualified for political
tasks:

A. And three rows of disciples of sages sit before them.

B. Each and every one knows his place.

C. [If] they found need to ordain [a disciple to serve on the court],

D. they ordained one who was sitting in the first row.

E. [Then] one who was sitting in the second row joins the first row, and
one who was sitting in the third row moves up to the second row.

F. And they select for themselves someone else from the crowd and set
him in the third row.

G. [The new disciple] did not take a seat in the place of the first party
[who had now joined in the court] but in the place that was appropriate for him [at the end of the third row].

M. San. 4:4

One enters the administration through discipleship. Everyone who was qualified could serve in any of the several courts, each with its own task and role.

So the sages are undifferentiated, while the institutions, distinguished by the number of members required for each, were very carefully differentiated from one another. Each one in his place, the disciples work their way up to the status of serving on the court, and the court, we see, is a combination of legislature, judiciary, and executive.[17]

How about a legislature? I can identify no lawmaking agency. The nearest counterpart is the council of state or great sanhedrin, because to it are entrusted the decisions assigned to the legislative arm in governments familiar to us. But the system scarcely concedes that legislation *de novo* is plausible, since its fundamental insistence is that everything comes from Sinai, that is, from Heaven. Law is not made but discovered in the Torah. So while occasional concessions to pressing need encompass the changing of established custom, the general picture excludes substantial legislative activity.[18] The appeal to tradition—people do not know the answer to a question, so they go to Jerusalem and ask whether anybody has a tradition on the subject—forms the counterpart to that political agency. But there was a council of state, with its seventy-one members, the large ("great") sanhedrin. The political task of policy-making, social and political, at home and abroad, fell into the hands, of course, of sages. The difference between the council of state and the local court, then, was simply that the former required the larger number of sages, seventy-one in all.

Let us consider first of all how the court functions as administration and council of state. At stake here are, first, the maintenance of social order against sedition and revolution; second, the use of the army and other instrumentalities of state; third, the government of the capital; fourth, the relationships between the central government and the provinces or outlying constituencies of the state ("tribes"):

A. (1) They judge a tribe, a false prophet [Deut. 18:20], and a high priest, only on the instructions of a court of seventy-one members.

B. (2) They call [the army] to wage a war fought by choice only on the instructions of a court of seventy-one.

C. (3) They make additions to the city [of Jerusalem] and to the courtyards [of the Temple] only on the instructions of a court of seventy-one.

D. (4) They set up sanhedrins for the tribes only on the instructions of a court of seventy-one.

E. (5) They declare a city to be "an apostate city" [Deut. 13:12ff.] only on the instructions of a court of seventy-one.

F. And they do not declare a city to be "an apostate city" on the frontier,

G. [nor do they declare] three [in one locale] to be [apostate cities],

H. but they do so in the case of one or two.

M. San. 1:5

The executive—the court of seventy-one members—takes charge of the maintenance of civil order. It disposes of sedition ("apostate city"), decides the administration of important offices of state ("a high priest"), and reaches decisions concerning foreign policy ("They call the army to wage a war"). As supreme authority, it also calls to judgment the activities of entire administrative districts or units of state ("tribes").

Judicial functions, we realize, are carried out by the same personnel, that is to say, members of "the court," though the number of personnel required varies for the function. In general, when "the court" is portrayed as a judiciary, from three to twenty-three judges are involved—three for settling property cases, twenty-three for capital cases. Here is the account of "the court" now seen as judiciary:

A. (1) Property cases [are decided] by three [judges];

B. (2) those concerning theft and damages, before three;

C. (3) [cases involving] compensation for full-damages, half-damages [Ex. 21:35], twofold restitution [Ex. 22:3], fourfold and fivefold restitution [Ex. 21:37], by three;

D. (4) "cases involving him who rapes [Deut. 32:28–29], him who seduces [Ex. 22:15–16], and *him who brings forth an evil name* [Deut. 22:19], by three," the words of R. Meir.

E. And sages say, "He who brings forth an evil name is [tried] before twenty-three,

F. "for there may be a capital case."

M. San. 1:1

A. (5) [Cases involving the penalty of] flogging [Deut. 25:2–3] are before three.

B. In the name of R. Ishmael they said, "Before twenty-three."

M. San. 1:2

A. (1) Cases involving the death penalty are judged before twenty-three judges.

B. (2) The beast who commits or is subjected to an act of sexual relations with a human being is judged by twenty-three,

C. since it is said, *And you will kill the woman and the beast* [Lev. 20:16].

D. and it says, *And the beast you will slay* [Lev. 20:15].

E. (3) An ox which is to be stoned is judged by twenty-three,

F. since it is said, *And the ox will be stoned, and also its master will be put to death* [Ex. 21:29].

G. Just as [the case of the master], leading to the death penalty [is adjudged], so is the [case of] the ox, [leading to] the death penalty.

H. The wolf, lion, bear, panther, leopard, and snake—a capital case affecting them is judged by twenty-three.

I.   R. Eliezer says, "Whoever kills them first acquires merit."

J.   R. Aqiba says, "Their capital case is judged by twenty-three."

M. San. 1:4

Here we see how the court system as a judiciary is imagined to organize its jurisdiction.[19] The important part is what is left scarcely stated: all courts are made up of sages. So all of the variations and diverse modes of organization rest upon the fundamental uniformity of the system, which finds its coherence in the mode by which personnel are educated, qualified, and selected for service. The details are essentially beside the point. Courts of diverse sizes are impaneled to deal with various kinds of cases. M. San. 1:4H–J dispute whether E applies to all other beasts or only to the ox. That is why I am not inclined to see H–J as a fourth, independent item on the list. The main point then is at B–D, E–G, as is clearly expressed by G. The same "court" that administers criminal cases deals with issues of public policy that we should identify with an administration or executive. So the court works out the calendar, atones for civil crimes that cannot be imputed to any specific person, makes decisions on matters of personal status (such as we noted above), assesses the value of property donated to the Temple and in that way asserts its rights over Temple affairs, and in other ways carries out tasks not ordinarily assigned to the judiciary.[20]

The upshot is precisely what I signaled earlier. The institutional distinctions make no difference in the actual management or manipulation of power. The tripartite plan of institutions—court, Temple, monarchy—proves a mere formality. Whatever the organizational structure, the system appealed to a uniform mode of domination. Sages, bearers of legitimate power, required obedience by reason of their preparation and, in a broad and very specific sense, particular knowledge, rather than because of their institutional affiliation. Physical violence and moral authority joined together in the person of the sage.

Indeed, having come this far we must wonder what difference administrative arrangements among competing foci of power, Heavenly, earthly, and intermediary, can have made. For the simple fact is that the institutional forms of power draw upon a single type of person who is empowered to carry out diverse tasks. That is to say, whether large or small, whether administrative and executive, judicial, or legislative (in the making of law), the "court" was always one and the same, namely, a formation of sages.

In the following we find an identification of "member of the court" with "the congregation," which in the context of Scripture meant "any male Israelite." But the definition of "any Israelite" in this context can mean only "sage," that is to say, a disciple who works his way up the rows of the half-circle to the front rank:

A. The great sanhedrin was [made up] seventy-one members,

B. and the small one was twenty-three.

C. And how do we know that the great sanhedrin was to have seventy-one members?

D. Since it is said, *Gather to me seventy men of the elders of Israel* [Num. 11:16].

E. Since Moses was in addition to them, lo, there were seventy-one.

F. R. Judah says, "It is seventy."

G. And how do we know that a small one is twenty-three?

H. Since it is said, *The congregation shall judge,* and *The congregation shall deliver* [Num. 35:24, 25]—

I. one congregation judges, and one congregation saves—thus there are twenty.

J. And how do we know that a congregation is ten? Since it is said, *How long shall I bear with this evil congregation* [of the ten spies] [Num. 14:27]—excluding Joshua and Caleb.

K. And how do we know that we should add three more?

L. From the implication of that which is said, *You shall not follow after the many to do evil* [Ex. 23:20], I derive the inference that I should be with them to do good.

M. If so, why is it said, *After the many to do evil?*

N. Your verdict of acquittal is not equivalent to your verdict of guilt.

O. Your verdict of acquittal may be on the vote of a majority of one, but your vote for guilt must be by a majority of two.

P. Since there cannot be a court of an even number of members [twenty-two], they add yet another—thus twenty-three.

M. San. 1:6

Evidently, the unit behind the system of institutionalization of executive, legislative, and judicial power derives from the type of person who serves in all three units and the foundation for that person's qualifications: a male Israelite who has come up through the processes of discipleship to join in the government of the community.

Yet—to return to our initial observation—the system of sanctions reveals that beside the sages there existed a civil authority, an earthly court. The account of the institutions of power clearly envisions a king and a high priest. Not only so, but the Mishnah is explicit in comparing the king to the high priest and in setting forth the charismatic privileges and standing imputed to each. It effects its comparisons in wholly personal terms, as we should anticipate, abstract conceptions being inaccessible to the system builders, but nonetheless, king and priest clearly were deemed institutions of enormous consequence.[21]

The king and high priest are set forth in such a way that the rights and immunities of each are compared to those assigned to the other. By consequence, the high priest is shown to be a subordinate figure, the king an autocephalous authority. If we work through the comparison's terms, it introduces us to the power and authority of both the king and the high priest. So let us consider the entire passage here. The comparison runs as follows:

A. A high priest (1) judges, and [others] judge him;
B. (2) gives testimony, and [others] give testimony about him;
C. (3) performs the rite of removing the shoe with his wife.
D. (4) [Others] enter levirate marriage with his wife, but he does not enter into levirate marriage,
E. because he is prohibited to marry a widow.
F. (5) [If] he suffers a death [in his family], he does not follow the bier.
G. "But when [the bearers of the bier] are not visible, he is visible; when they are visible, he is not.
H. "And he goes with them to the city gate," the words of R. Meir.
I. R. Judah says, "He never leaves the sanctuary,
J. since it says, *Nor shall he go out of the sanctuary* [Lev. 21:12]."
K. and when he gives comfort to others,
L. the accepted practice is for all the people to pass on after another, and the appointed [prefect of the priests] stands between him and the people.
M. And when he receives consolation from others,
N. all the people say to him, "Let us be your atonement."
O. And he says to them, "May you be blessed by Heaven."
P. (6) and when they provide him with the funeral meal,
Q. all the people sit on the ground, while he sits on a stool.

                                                              M. San. 2:1

A. (1) The king does not judge, and [others] do not judge him;
B. (2) does not give testimony, and [others] do not give testimony about him;
C. (3) does not perform the rite of removing the shoe, and others do not perform the rite of removing the shoe with his wife;
D. (4) does not enter into levirate marriage, nor [do his brothers] enter levirate marriage with his wife.
E. R. Judah says, "If he wanted to perform the rite of removing the shoe or to enter into levirate marriage, his memory is a blessing."
F. They said to him, "They pay no attention to him [if he expressed the wish to do so]."
G. [Others] do not marry his widow.
H. R. Judah says, "A king may marry the widow of a king."

I.   "For so we find in the case of David, that he marries the widow of Saul.

J.   "For it is said, *And I gave you your master's house and your master's wives into your embrace* [2 Sam. 12:8]."

A.   (5) [If] he suffers death in his family, he does not leave the gate of his palace.

B.   R. Judah says, "If he wants to go out after the bier, he goes out,

C.   "For thus we find in the case of David, that he went out after the bier of Abner,

D.   "since it is said, *And King David followed the bier* [2 Sam. 3:31]."

E.   They said to him, "This action was only to appease the people."

F.   (6) And when they provide him with the funeral meal, all the people sit on the ground, while he sits on a couch.

M. M. San. 2:3

The passage's contrast stands clear:[22] by reason of his genealogy, the high priest enjoys certain immunities in his person; the king, who exercises power above the community, stands immune from all rules that apply to the community. The two heads of state therefore are alike, but different—and the king is the superior figure. The high priest and the king form a single genus but two distinct species, and the variations between the species form a single set of taxonomic indicators. The one is like the other in these ways, unlike the other in those ways. The comparison of the two yields, therefore, the amazing judgment that a figure who is scarcely acknowledged, to whom is assigned no substantial bureaucracy or administration as counterpart to the temple's and the courts', is deemed utterly autocephalous: the state, above the law. That assessment can scarcely be squared with the inconsequential role assigned to the monarchy, but it does accord with the representation of the king and queen as humbly seeking sages' approval (a picture Josephus draws for historic time as well). Within the larger politics, therefore, the king serves to deliver the systemic message: the state, embodied by the king, enjoys full sovereignty, and the sages run the state. Citing verses of Scripture and underlining that the king is superior to the high priest but inferior to the Torah, which he must obey, reveals this important fact even while it is not made articulate: the king obeys the sages, who are the masters of the Torah.

The key to the monarchy lies in the rule that "the king does not judge, and [others] do not judge him, does not give testimony, and [others] do not give testimony about him." What then does the king do?

A.   [The king] calls out [the army to wage] a war fought by choice on the instructions of a court of seventy-one.

B. He [may exercise the right to] open a road for himself, and [others] may not stop him.

C. The royal road has no required measure.

D. All the people plunder and lay before him [what they have grabbed], and he takes the first portion.

E. *He should not multiply wives to himself* [Deut. 17:17]—only eighteen.

F. R. Judah says, "He may have as many as he wants, so long as they do not entice him [to abandon the Lord (Deut. 7:4)]."

G. R. Simeon says, "Even if there is only one who entices him [to abandon the Lord]—lo, this one should not marry her."

H. If so, why is it said, *He should not multiply wives to himself?*

I. Even though they should be like Abigail (1 Sam. 25:3].

J. *He should not multiply horses to himself* [Deut. 17:16]—only enough for his chariot.

K. *Neither shall he greatly multiply to himself silver and gold* [Deut. 17:16]—only enough to pay his army.

L. *And he writes out a scroll of the Torah for himself* [Deut. 17:17]—

M. When he goes to war, he takes it out with him; when he comes back, he brings it back with him; when he is in session in court, it is with him; when he is reclining, it is before him,

N. as it is said, *And it shall be with him, and he shall read in it all the days of his life* [Deut. 17:19].

M. San. 2:4

A. [Others may] not (1) ride on his horse, (2) sit on his throne, (3) handle his sceptre.

B. And [others may] (4) not watch him while he is getting a haircut, or (5) while he is nude, or (6) in the bathhouse,

C. since it is said, *You shall surely set him as king over you* [Deut. 17:15]—that reverence for him will be upon you.

M. San. 2:5

The main point, once more, is that the king stands subject to the torah, and (systemically speaking) everybody knows who says what the Torah requires.[23] It follows that the king reigns but does not rule; the sages rule through him. When a war is obligatory (for example, for conquest of the Land), the sages' court makes the decision. When war is optional, the king calls out the army— again, on the initiative of the court of seventy-one! Policy-making then scarcely belongs within the royal domain. True, the king remains in charge of public works, takes priority in collecting the spoils of war, maintains the army—but that is that. So far as we can see, the monarchy then takes charge of the infrastructure of the state, and even with that, in anything of conse- quence, he acts upon the instructions of the sanhedrin run by the sages. How the king supports his army and administration we are not told, nor does the account tell us how legitimate violence belongs within the domain of the king acting on his own. All we hear is that in his person he is superior to the high priest—except as the high priest's genealogical and caste privileges intervene—and that both king and high priest obey sages.

Given that our evidence assumes the king governed at the instructions of sages, faithfully doing whatever they told him to do, it is not hard to understand why the system builders recognized scarcely any need to discuss the monarchy and its tasks, why they did not detail the monarchy's procedures, its modes of collecting and disposing of taxes, dealing with foreign powers (a consideration utterly beyond the systemic imagination), maintaining and using an army, maintaining the infrastructure of the state, the economy, and the institutions of culture and social order—all the things kings were supposed to do. Indeed, if we seek in the initial statement of Judaism an account of the monarchy and the rules governing it, beyond the instructions of the law of the Torah (Deut. 17:15ff.), we look in vain, as we shall see in a moment. Since, as we have seen, the (sages') court made decisions on war and peace, civil order and suppression of sedition and revolution, the everyday governance of communities, and the administration of law and justice, we must wonder why the system includes a king at all.

The one thing the Mishnah makes explicit is that the monarchy serves at the pleasure of the sages. This point appears indisputable in the following:

B. At the end of the first festival day of the Festival [of Sukkot],

C. on the eighth year, [that is] at the end of the seventh year,

D. they make him a platform of wood, set in the courtyard.

E. And he sits on it,

F. as it is said, *At the end of every seven years in the set time* [Deut. 31:10].

G. The minister of the assembly takes a scroll of the Torah and hands it to the head of the assembly, and the head of the assembly hands it to the prefect, and the prefect hands it to the high priest, and the high priest hands it to the king, and the king stands and receives it.

H. But he reads sitting down.

I. Agrippa the King stood up and received it and read it standing up, and sages praised him on that account.

J. And when he came to the verse, *You may not put a foreigner over you, who is not your brother* [Deut. 17:15], his tears ran down from his eye.

K. They said to him, "Do not be afraid, Agrippa, you are our brother, you are our brother, you are our brother!"

L. He reads from the beginning of *These are the words* [Deut. 1:1] to *Hear O Israel* [Deut. 6:4], *And it will come to pass, if you hearken* [Deut. 11:13], and *You shall surely tithe* [Deut. 14:22], and *When*

you have made an end of tithing [Deut. 26:12–15], and the pericope
of the king [Deut. 17:14–20], and the blessings and the curses
[Deut. 27:15–26], and he completes the whole pericope.

M. With the same blessings with which the high priest blesses them
[M. 7:7F], the king blesses them.

N. But he says the blessing for the festivals instead of the blessing for
the forgiveness of sin.

M. Sotah 7:8

A. Helene the Queen:

B. Her son went off to war and she said, "If my son comes home from
war whole and in one piece, I shall be a Nazir for seven years."

C. Indeed her son did come home from war, and she was a Nazir for
seven years.

D. Then at the end of the seven years, she went up to the Land. The
House of Hillel instructed her to be a Nazir for another seven years.

E. Then at the end of the seven years, she contracted uncleanness.

F. So she turned out to be a Nazir for twenty-one years.

M. Naz. 3:6

Both stories portray the monarchy as humbly obedient to sages' rule. The
symbolic transaction in the former passage, with the king receiving the Torah,
reading in it, and pledging his fealty to it—hence also to those who could tell
him what it meant—underlines the principal message. The story about the
queen is of the same sort. But the symbolic transaction of having the king read
in the Torah, which the sage mastered and the king did not (if he did, he would
be a sage), with the king humbly obeying the sages' instructions and gladly
accepting, even obsequiously seeking, their approval—that transaction contains the entire story of administration. In the particular case at hand, the
sages ("they") then complete their part of the transaction, setting aside the
rule of the Torah for the king, who is a foreigner but whose rule they approve.
Since sages are explicitly represented as placing their own politics above the
law of the Torah, the true picture, as sages portray matters, emerges.

The same point about sages' paramount status in the politics of state and
administration applies to the priesthood. It is expressed with surpassing sim-
plicity in the following:

A. All are suitable to examine plagues, but the actual declaration of
uncleanness and cleanness is in the hands of a priest.

B. They say to him, "Say, 'Unclean,'" and he says, "Unclean";

C. "Say, 'Clean,'" and he says, "Clean."

M. Neg. 3:1

A. They would render the priest who burns the cow unclean, because of the Sadducees, so that they should not say, "It is done by one on whom the sun has set."

B. They [sages] placed their hands on him and said to him, "My lord, High Priest, immerse now," and he descended, immersed, emerged, dried off [and proceeded with the rite of burning the red cow].

M. Par. 3:8

A. [Seven days before the Day of Atonement] they handed [the high priest] over to elders belonging to the court, and they read for him the prescribed rite of the Day of Atonement.

B. And they say to him, "My lord, high priest, you read it with your own lips, lest you have forgotten, or never even learned it to begin with."

M. Yoma 1:3

A. The elders of the court handed him over to the elders of the priesthood, who brought him up to the upper chamber of Abtinas.

B. And they imposed an oath on him and took their leave and went along.

C. This is what they said to him: "My lord, high priest, we are agents of the court, and you are our agent and agent of the court.

D. "We abjure you by Him who caused His name to rest upon this house that you will not vary in any way from all we have instructed you."

M. Yoma 1:5

I cannot imagine a clearer way of saying that the priests run the Temple, but the sages run the priests. The picture of the dumb priest waiting for the sage to tell him what to say (M. Neg.) and what to do on the holiest day of the year (M. Yoma) bears an element of contempt. This is reinforced by the account of how the unnamed "they" deliberately impart uncleanness to the high priest and have him immerse before carrying out the rite, because "they" maintain that the rite be carried out by a priest who is in the status of one who has immersed on that selfsame day and awaits sunset for the completion of the purification rite. Here again, control of the cult lies not only in pronouncing decisions but in the more critical matter of applying the uncleanness-taboos. The high priest in his own view will have carried out the rite in a condition of cultic uncleanness and so be worthy of the death penalty. But he submits—so the picture at hand wants us to believe. So too, I find the oath imposed upon the high priest not to disobey the Torah that the sages have taught him equally contemptuous. A politics of sages' domination over the Temple cannot have come to more stunning expression than in this brief account.

But the portrait of matters proves somewhat more complicated for, as before, the systemic account does consider the simple fact that priests do not conform to the law. This is implicit at M. Yoma 1:5, and it is made explicit in connection with the rejection by priests of sages' opinions on matters of marriage. Here, priests upset both the rules of genealogy and the system. But sages sidestep the problem. They concede that, for now, priests control whom they accept in marriage (deciding the law of genealogy and caste in a way that sages do not approve), but their concession means little, for they assert that in the end, God will intervene and straighten matters out. Where it counts, sages will win. That is, whereas the politics explicitly takes account of disobedience, by calling God in time to come to set matters right, by painting a picture of sages' dominance with Heaven's assistance, it both accounts for interim competition and dismisses that competition. This seems to me little more than the message already set forth.

A. Testified R. Joshua and R. Judah b. Beterah concerning a widow of an Israelite family suspected of contamination with unfit genealogical stock, that she is valid for marriage into the priesthood. For a woman deriving from an Israelite family suspect of contamination with unfit genealogical stock is herself valid for being declared unclean or clean, being put out or being brought near.

B. Said Rabban Gamaliel, "We should accept your testimony, but what shall we do? For Rabban Yohanan b. Zakkai decreed against calling courts into session for such a matter. For the priests pay attention to you when it comes to putting someone out but not when it comes to drawing someone near."

M. Ed. 8:3

A. Said R. Joshua, "I have a tradition from Rabban Yohanan b. Zakkai, who heard it from his master, and his master from his master, as a law revealed to Moses at Sinai,

B. "that Elijah is not going to come to declare unclean or to declare clean, to put out or to draw near, but only to put out those who have been brought near [to marriage into the priestly caste] by force and to draw near those who have been put out by force."

M. Ed. 8:7

Where the priesthood remains in full charge, therefore, it concerns only whom they will agree to take in marriage, which is to say, the priests govern the issues of genealogy on which their caste-status and power rest. But the concession by the sages is merely formal, concerning who ultimately dictates whom priests will marry; power here is negative, and the sanction involves what priests will refuse to do and may not (so the politics allows) be forced to do.

All that has been said bears the implication that the Temple is represented as an institution of power in a this-worldly political sense. But is that actually the case? The examples at hand suggest otherwise, for the Temple is never represented as a political institution, nor the priesthood as a political class. The priesthood is acknowledged, conceded its role and its rights (in a fantasy of the Temple to be sure), but not accorded that command of power that the political classes in fact enjoy. In other words, the sages do not concede much. In the Mishnah's picture of the politics of its Israel, the Temple does not conduct political trials or impose this-worldly sanctions.[24] These are not political actions and do not invoke any kind of coercion exercised outside the framework of the caste itself. For what narrowly political, administrative tasks are represented as assigned to the priesthood? I find none conceded by the systemic account. And that observation conforms to the distinction between the monarchy and the priesthood, the king and the high priest. The king is political, the high priest is not. Both, to be sure, serve as surrogates and representatives of the sages, who now are represented as forming the institutions of state and as exercising all the power that mattered. Can we explain the distinctions before us by appealing to the everyday facts of history? Hardly. There was no Temple in Jerusalem, no king ruling Israel, when sages made up their system. The distinction then is systemic, important because of the message that the system wished to convey through the picture of the political institutions. And that message comes through repeatedly, and loud and clear.

Enough has been said to raise the question, is there any identification of an ongoing and permanent administration, that is, an institution in which sages as such—not merely as controlling personnel—organize, make decisions, and effect power? The answer, as we should now predict, is negative. And it had to be, for sages' governance effected right attitude and right thought, and the triviality that sages differed from one another on this and that required no institutional formulation and expression. Right-thinking people may well disagree on details; they may even vote. But the system knows no institution in which the sages, formed into a party, for instance, work out their differences and come to a common position on public policy. If, as we have seen, the politics of this Judaism represent matters such that sages form the "party" that controls the state, where and how does that party come to institutional form and expression?[25] The systemic statement is remarkably silent on that matter, yielding only the following:

A. These are some of the laws which they stated in the upper room of Hananiah b. Hezekiah b. Gurion when they went up to visit him.
B. They took a vote and the House of Shammai outnumbered the House of Hillel. And eighteen rules did they decree on that very day.

M. Shab. 1:4

The party knows no substantial institutions. People are supposed to meet casually on informal occasions, make up their minds, and vote. Other portrayals of the sages' agency ("party" seems anachronistic) in the decision-making process offer details of how decisions are reached. These suggest a somewhat more regular procedure. In the following, part of a larger set of controversy materials, we have an example of debate and vote in practice, with the debate summarized as positions assigned to names.[26]

    A. On that day did they vote and decide concerning
    B. a footbath—
    C. which holds from two *logs* to nine *qabs* and which was cracked,
    D. that it is susceptible to uncleanness through *midras* uncleanness [as an object suitable for a chair or a couch, that is, for sitting or lying].
    E. For R. Aqiba says, "A footbath is according to its name."

M. Yad. 4:1

The continuation of the passage shows us what matters in how the system portrays the decision-making process: sages debate and vote. And on what basis do they make up their minds? In the debate the appeal is to verses of Scripture, which serve to settle questions as readily as tradition.

Are sages in their debates then engaged in running the government and dictating the policies of the agencies of administration? Yes and no. The program of issues portrayed in the systemic writings is limited to matters that we should regard as extrapolitical, such as the personal standing of an Ammonite proselyte, the rule as to tithing of outlying territories, a law of the Temple.[27] These are not decisions having to do with peace and war, economics and disposition of power. But they are the kinds of decisions that, in the imagination of the system builders, Israel's politics retained authority and power to settle. Thus, although none of this has any bearing upon the great institutions of state and government, monarchy, Temple, court, the theory of the management of political institutions nonetheless emerges with great force: the institutional structure and program make no place for sages, but in the politics of this Judaism as set forth by the Mishnah, sages run things.[28]

The upshot is that, except for the court, the institutions set forth by the politics of this Judaism, both in Heaven and on earth, really represent formalities, symbols of slight substance. The picture that we should have drawn from the mythic portrait of the whole is radically revised by the interposition of sages in all three institutional representations. The institutions make no place for sages, any more than the sanctions encompass actions effected by sages. But, we now realize, sages dominate all institutions of power, at least so their politics maintains. First of all, the king, never portrayed as the earthly counterpart to God, even though God is routinely called King, is represented as a mere puppet of sages. Second, the earthly court is represented as wholly staffed by sages and governed by the rules they have learned within their circles. And, third, the Temple priests are instructed by sages. So while the politics sets forth an institutional system in which Heaven and earth and Temple collaborate in the disposition of power, the system does not work in such a way at all. So why include the priesthood and monarchy? Because, after all, Scripture does; the Mishnah encompasses the governance of the Temple (which its authorship assumes will be rebuilt) and also the restoration of the monarchy (I assume, of the house of David). The utopian vision encompasses everything and then concedes nothing. Sages will govern while the king reigns, and the high priest rules only in his holy precinct. And both king and priest rule fully in accord with sages' instructions.

As we look backward, we realize that the systemic document is remarkably reticent in telling us about institutions at all. But we know why. Since sages form the true systemic manipulators of power, telling king and priest what to do and wholly controlling the court which served as executive, legislature, and judiciary, institutional differentiation would indicate precisely what our authorship wants to neglect. An analogy drawn from modern times may serve to place into perspective the somewhat odd institutional politics in hand. We distinguish between government and party, that is, the institutions of government—Heaven, earth, Temple—and the party of sages that runs all three institutions and administers them. Then we have a dual system of power, the government and the party, with the latter forming an inner and governing structure in control of the institutions of the former. To say that the politics of this Judaism portrays a party government probably presents an anachronism, but it seems also a valid metaphor for what we do see before us. This is not to suggest that the politics of a judicial government, a kind of court-administration by judicial fiat, exhausts the institutional arrangements contemplated by Judaism. It is to say that the only political institution that matters is that court, unicameral in the deepest sense: executive, legislature, judiciary all at once.

And the court administration is unitary in a second sense, since it is made up of sages who serve interchangeably in the three roles in which power attains institutionalization. So all things depend upon the personnel, and the institutional arrangements represent formalities. The political system focuses, therefore, upon the forming of qualified and correct personalities, persons trained for the work by reason of right formation of intellect and attitude. And that draws us onward to the administration of the politics.

5

Administering the Social Order

Attention to the management of politics, to issues of personnel and administration, requires an account of how the institutions that permanently exercise power maintain themselves, of how they find, educate, and support a competent and effective staff, of how they build the required bureaucracy for the everyday and not merely episodic or notional administration of public policy. The picture of monarchy, Temple, and courts suffices for a sketch of government, but for a prologue to a working political system, an authorship that proposes to describe a social world in vast detail, as does the Mishnah's, surely will want to say more than that. Specifically, that authorship will inform us about the bureaucracy that makes the institutions work. It will detail how the king is chosen and educated, what sorts of offices and tasks characterize the administration of the Temple, and, above all, how the courts find the staff sufficiently versatile to do their work. True, a politics need not provide a detailed account of the curriculum of schools that prepare managers, such as court officials, but it has to make some arrangement for the ongoing staffing of institutions, for the assignment of tasks to this institution and not to that, for the everyday management of politics. And that arrangement will draw us deep into the details of the political structure and system.

Given the Mishnah's capacity to deliver its message principally through details, moreover, we surely do not ask too much when we seek a picture of the nitty-gritty of working government. But because of its interest in the mediation of power between Heaven and earth, in the enduring arrangements of a settled political system, we should want to know how these arrangements are secured through provision of correctly trained personnel. For instance, we might ask what sort of classes of persons are recruited for the administration, and what kinds of positions are envisioned for them? How are persons trained for their work, and to what kind of careers may they look forward? These questions lead us to inquire into the professionalism of politics, the spirit of the administration, for these are what give life and vitality to an otherwise lifeless account of merely the formal and implausible pigeonholing of power.

However, more than mere curiosity animates our inquiry into the values of the administration and the goals it seeks to attain. We deal with a system, of which politics is a sizable component. The systemic message, I have noted, comes to expression in details, for the Mishnah's systematic account of the politics of this Judaism proposes in vast detail to say not merely how the social order is to be arranged, but why. Given that purpose, we should expect the Mishnah's social arrangements of a political character to convey not merely titles of offices but also the teleology of politics, proximate purposes realized even in the selection and training of political functionaries. And in a measure, our systemic statement does not entirely disappoint us. But in the aggregate, as before, it is through silence, as much as through speech, that our authorship says what it wants. The character of the details in context, not merely the contents, bears the message.

Three distinct corps of administrators are required for the three distinct institutions, Temple, court, monarchy. Relying upon the initial document of post-Temple Judaism, we may depict the modes of administration of the first institution and the professionalism of the second, but concerning the third we have only silence. Specifically, we can produce a rich picture of the administration of the Temple, its source of funds, how it disburses its funds, the offices of the bureaucracy, and what bureaucrats do—we even have names of officeholders. While not complete and certainly not nuanced, our account of the personnel and administration of the Temple provides a reasonable theory of the management of that component of the politics of this Judaism. Further, we can derive with some confidence the professional ideal of the members of the court, that is to say, the principal managers and administrators of the business of the state and society. But we have no information regarding the monarchy. I find not a line concerning its staff, how they are trained, or the tasks assigned to them.

In omitting all reference to the monarchy and its staff, the political structure of Judaism acknowledges, but does not then account for, the way the administration of its politics' (theoretically) central component proceeds. Given that the monarchy constitutes the political structure that even by the document's own word controls state policy toward other nations, and toward the constituents of state (not "states" or "provinces" but "tribes" to be sure), this is the more surprising. The politics' remarkable indifference to the monarchy, an institution acknowledged but left without differentiation as to staff and structure, personnel and administration, points not so much to the fragmentary character of the picture, which is far too detailed to be held a mere sherd of some larger political picture. It draws attention, rather, to the severe limits that constrain the imagination of the authorship at hand.

True, evidently lacking all direct encounter with a monarchy, that is, with the acknowledged head of an independent or essentially autonomous state, that authorship cannot have had experience on which to draw. But this explains little, for the same authorship quite nicely made up vast tracts of rules on the Temple, in ruins as they wrote. They detailed rules for cultic cleanness—a matter of most abstract theory—rules even for the conduct of the ordeal imposed upon the wife accused of infidelity—a topic that the document itself states lacks practical precedent for centuries (if ever). And they treated diverse other topics that lay far beyond the horizons of everyday reality. So the explanation for the large lacuna about the politics' single most formidable figure (in the personalized terms of discourse at hand), the king, must emerge from the characterization of the system itself, not appeal to the intellectual resources or experience in the framing of public policy typical of the system builders. That is to say, seeing the system's political structures all together, we shall seek an explanation for details characteristic of one or another of its components. We will ask, "Why this, not that; why information on one bureaucracy, silence on another?" Only holding what we are told together with what we do not know will we retrieve a clear account of the whole.

To describe the system, let us turn first to the rich characterizations provided for two of the three political corps, the courts and the Temple. Here we can examine the Mishnah's manner of describing a bureaucracy and administration. Specifically, we can perceive the administration of the politics and public policy so far as these lie in the hands of the priesthood and the Temple. We begin with the Temple offices, then proceed to the tasks attached to them, and on to how these are financed. The offices and the officeholders are depicted at some specific point in time, as these:

A. These are they who are appointed who were in the sanctuary [as its officers]:

(1) Yohanan b. Pinhas is in charge of the seals.

(2) Ahiah is in charge of the drink-offerings.

(3) Matthew b. Samuel is in charge of the lots.

(4) Petahiah is in charge of the bird offerings—(Petahiah is the same as Mordecai, and why is he called Petahiah? Because he is able to open questions and expound them and knows seventy languages.)

(5) Ben Ahiah is in charge of bowel-sickness.

(6) Nehuniah digs ditches [for water].

(7) Gebini is the herald.

(8) Ben Gerber is in charge of closing the gates.

(9) Ben Bebai is in charge of the knout.

(10) Ben Arzah is in charge of the cymbals.

(11) Hugras b. Levi is in charge of the singing.

(12) The house of Garmu is in charge of making the Show Bread.

(13) The house of Abtinas is in charge of preparing the incense.

(14) Eleazar is in charge of the hangings.

(15) Pinhas is in charge of the clothing.

M. Sheq. 5:1

A. They appoint no fewer than three revenuers and seven supervisors.

B. And they do not appoint less than two people to a public position of supervision in property matters,

C. except for Ben Ahiah who is in charge of the bowel-sickness [M. Sheq. 5:1A5],

D. and Eleazar who is in charge of hangings [M. Sheq. 5:1A14].

E. For them did the majority of the congregation accept.

M. Sheq. 5:2

The Temple administration involved a variety of tasks. Officers for "seals" and "drink-offerings" sold to worshippers the *materia sacra* required for the offerings. One would pay a sum of money for a chit that could be exchanged with the officiating priest for the wine that would accompany one's offering. The one in charge of the "lots" would divide up among the officiating priests the right to carry out given tasks in the cult (slaughtering the beast, placing the sacrificial parts on the altar, and the like). The same officer would help the priests divide up the priestly emoluments, such as shares in the carcass of a beast, shares in the Show Bread. So the administration before us took charge of the goods and services for the public and for the priesthood, collecting funds and providing what the public needed to do its task, then assigning the work of the day to individual priests and also providing the priesthood with its income from the altar.

The catalog before us proceeds to other matters, some of which are not self-evidently defined. The water supply had its bureau head (Nehuniah). What Ben Ahiah did I cannot say, but presumably he headed some sort of office of public health. The maintenance of order lay in the hands of Ben Gerber and Ben Bebai. The music—cymbals, singing—had its offices, and the preparation of the bread and incense had its offices too. The Temple decor lay in the bureau headed by Eleazar, and the priestly costume in that headed by Pinhas. M. Sheqalim 5:2 refers to a higher level of administration, to supervisors. That is clear from C, D, which allude to the figures of M. 5:1 and indicate that these heads of bureaus also served in supervisory capacities, with public consensus. So the Temple administration yields substantial and precise differentiation among fifteen offices at the very least. These are, moreover, set forth in systematic and orderly fashion, covering services to the public, the required services for health, security, the music, the ancillary offerings, the stage-setting, the costumes. The analogy to the institutional bureaucracy, of course, leads us in our own setting to not the federal bureaucracy but, in the Washington scene, to the Kennedy Center. To this point, we seem to deal with the administration of an arts agency.

But that analogy proves grossly misleading, for as we shall now see, the Temple authorities bore responsibility for administration of highly public tasks involving maintenance of public order. The Temple took responsibility for what in our own setting we would call the civil religion of the state, that is to say, public events of a sacred order, under public, political sponsorship, in which the *polis* as such undertook celebration, commemoration, shared cognition of community. So the political analogy, as we shall now observe, is to be drawn to the Department of the Interior, so far as it organizes and supervises public celebrations on the Mall in Washington, or to those offices and bureaus of administration that run the inauguration of the new president.

To begin with, the personnel of the Temple administered the cult, as we should expect. It is not surprising that the account of the Temple's administration places the priesthood in full command of its own rites, as in the following instaces:

> A. Nittai and Teqoan brought dough offering from Beitar to the Land of Israel to give it to a priest, and the priesthood would not accept it from him.
>
> B. People from Alexandria brought their dough offering from Alexandria, and the priesthood would not accept it from them.
>
> M. Hallah 4:10
>
> A. The son of Antines brought firstborn animals up from Babylonia to the land of Israel to give to a priest,
>
> B. and the priesthood would not accept them from him.
>
> M. Hal. 4:11

But these rules are commonplaces and give no indication of why the politics pays ample attention to the details of Temple personnel and administration, down to the collection and disposition of the last penny.

A clear account of the details, however, will in fact yield a compelling answer to the question that proves paramount in our description of the management of politics: why does the politics attend to some bureaucracies and ignore others? Beyond performing the daily sacrifices and those for holy occasions, the Temple in fact facilitated public access to its celebrations; it enabled what we call "pilgrimage." Indeed, the political administration of the Temple bore responsibility, beyond the Temple walls, for securing access to the Temple and its celebrations for all those who lived at a distance.

This fact stands revealed in the following passage. In it, we see how the Mishnah sets forth the workings of an administration. It is worth dwelling on the account and following a fair part of the whole, for critical to my analysis of the description of politics' administration is the claim that the *traits* in the descriptions of monarchy, Temple, and courts bear the systemic message. Since, as I hold, the Temple's staff and procedures are subjected to the most detailed account, we do well to consider one such picture through the factual repertoire. On that account, I provide a somewhat more substantial set of abstracts than is ordinarily the case. When we see what the Mishnah has done to set forth the workings of the Temple administration in the critical matter of collecting revenues and dispersing them in achieving the goals of the structure, we shall realize what was not said about the counterpart activities of the monarchy (and, as a matter of fact, of the courts).

A. On the first day of Adar they make public announcement concerning [payment] of *sheqel*-dues and concerning the sowing of mixed seeds [Lev. 19:19, Deut. 22:9].

B. On the fifteenth day of the month they read the *Megillah* [Scroll of Esther] in walled cities.

C. And they repair the paths, roads, and immersion-pools.

D. And they carry out all public needs.

E. And they mark off the graves [so that people will not inadvertently suffer corpse-contamination].

F. And they go forth [to inspect the fields] on account of mixed seeds.

M. Sheq. 1:1

A. Said R. Judah, "In olden times [the agents] would uproot them [mixed seeds] and throw them before the [owners].

B. "When transgressors became many, they would uproot them and throw them into the roads.

C. "They [finally] ordained that they should declare ownerless the entire field [in which mixed seeds had been planted]."

M. Sheq. 1:2

Let us first clarify the details at hand, then turn to the broader issue. The sheqel falls due on the first day of Nisan, so there is public notice of one month. Warning also is given about uprooting mixed seeds. From the first of Nisan offerings are purchased from the funds, which now fall due. The rest of the unit speaks of other events of the same season, five tasks to be done on (or after) the fifteenth of Adar, B−F. If, F, it turns out that a farmer has planted mixed seeds in his vineyard, the punishment is as specified by Judah. The calendar is a Temple calendar, since the sheqel-dues go for the purchase of the public offerings, representative of the entire community, that the Temple makes. That makes M. Sheqalim 1:1C exceedingly interesting, since the Temple bears authority for the roads. And that means, and can only mean, that the Temple administration must secure for the nation as a whole access to the rites. The concern for the taboos prohibiting mixed seeds (A, F) and prohibiting corpse-contamination (E) link to the pilgrimage two further and quite distinct considerations, one concerning agricultural, the other uncleanness, taboos.

The Temple calendar proceeds to account for the collection of public funds owed by all eligible Israelites that maintain the Temple and its cult. This involves paying the half-sheqel. To provide the correct coinage, the services of *cambios*, "money changers' tables," are needed. This petty banking was critical to securing for the Temple not only scarce resources, but scarce resources in a form that the Temple administration could use to best advantage, namely, *specie*. In an economy in which specie was scarce and credit unavailable to most persons, paying the Temple tax, while negligible in cost, did depend upon making available the necessary instruments of exchange; the money changers did not collect funds but made it possible for people to pay them in the appropriate way.

A.   On the fifteenth of that same month [Adar] they set up money changers' tables in the provinces.
B.   On the twenty-fifth [of Adar] they set them up in the Temple.
C.   Once they were set up in the Temple, they began to exact pledges [from those who had not paid the tax in specie].
D.   From whom do they exact a pledge?
E.   Levites, Israelites, proselytes, and freed slaves,
F.   but not from women, slaves, and minors.
G.   Any minor in whose behalf the father began to pay the sheqel does not again cease [to pay].
H.   And they do not exact a pledge from priests,
I.   for the sake of peace.

M. Sheq. 1:3

The money changers in the provinces provided the half-sheqel, which was then handed over by individuals to the Temple revenuers. The people who wished to bring the tax to the Temple would do so in the last days prior to the month of Nisan, in which Passover fell, and that, of course, was the start of the Temple's pilgrimage cycle.

Now we ask whether the priests bore responsibility for their share in the publicly financed offerings:

A.   Said R. Judah, "Testified Ben Bukhri in Yabneh: 'Any priest who pays the sheqel does not sin.'
B.   "Said to him Rabban Yohanan ben Zakkai, 'Not so. But any priest who does not pay the sheqel sins.
C.   "But the priests expound this scriptural verse for their own benefit: *And every meal offering of the priest shall be wholly burned, it shall not be eaten* [Lev. 6:23].
D.   "Since the omer, Two Loaves, and Show Bread are ours, how [if we contribute] are they to be eaten?' "

M. Sheq. 1:4

Now, the text returns to its discussion about collecting the sheqel-text for the Temple (A–C; expanded by D–I; M. 1:3H–I bear in their wake the appendix of M. 1:4.) Here, it appears that money changers serve to change various coins into the sheqel required for the Temple tax. In the Temple the money changers take a pledge from one who has not yet paid his tax and, in exchange, give the required half-sheqel. Clearly, money changers are essential for the collection of this tax, which serves through the coming year to provide the offerings in the name of the community. Further, these passages show that the priests maintain that, by analogy to their meal offering, any offering purchased in whole or in part by funds deriving from priests must be wholly consumed by fire. If priests give money for, for example, offerings which Scripture specifically requires to be eaten (M. 1:4D), then the commandment to eat the offerings (see D) is contravened by the priests' providing money to purchase these same offerings. It follows that priests cannot contribute to the sheqel-offering. M. 1:3E and H–I reflect this opinion. Ben Bukhri's view is that if the priest gives the sheqel, it constitutes a gift to the community and no longer is his. So Ben Bukhri's theory accords with that of priests. The exposition of the Temple tax of a half-sheqel proceeds to some secondary considerations, which are spelled out in the next passage:

A. And these are liable to the surcharge:
B. Levites, Israelites, proselytes, and freed slaves,
C. but not priests, women, slaves, or minors.
D. He who pays the sheqel in behalf of a priest, woman, slave, or minor, is exempt [from the surcharge].
E. And if he paid the sheqel for himself and for his fellow, he is liable for a single surcharge [for himself].
F. R. Meir says, "Two surcharges."
G. He who pays a sela and takes back a sheqel in change is liable to two surcharges.

M. Sheq. 1:6

A. He who pays a sheqel [as a gift] for a poor man, for his neighbor, or for a fellow townsman, is exempt.
B. But if he lent [the money to them], he is liable.
C. Brothers who are partners who are liable to the surcharge are exempt from tithe of cattle.
D. But when they are liable to tithe of cattle, they are exempt from the surcharge.
E. And how much is the surcharge?
F. "A silver *ma'ah* [= 1/24th of a sela]," the words of R. Meir.
G. And sages say, "A half [a silver *ma'ah*]."

M. Sheq. 1:7

The Temple is owed a half-sheqel. But there are costs of changing the money to be paid. If someone pays over a sela worth two sheqels and gets a sheqel and a half back, he loses in the transaction the fee paid to the money changer. It follows that there is a surcharge owing from those who are re-

quired by law to pay the half-sheqel, B. But it is not exacted from those who
to begin with are not required by law to pay the half-sheqel. This point—that
those not obligated by law to pay the half-sheqel, but who choose to pay it, do
not have to pay the surcharge—is expanded at D: if someone who is liable to
the surcharge pays the half-sheqel for someone who is not liable, the former
does not have to pay the surcharge. The same point is made at E. Here, if
someone pays in his own behalf and also in behalf of his friend, he pays the
surcharge only for himself. Why? Meir believes that the surcharge is required
of anyone who owes the half-sheqel. Since the friend is liable to the half-
sheqel, he also should pay the surcharge. Further, although in the present case
the man has paid a single coin for the two, sages nonetheless require that he
has to pay the fee for the money changer, for the money changer is needed to
break the coin into the two half-sheqels required. But sages concur (G) that if
one pays over a sela, which is four sheqels, and takes back a sheqel (E), he
has to pay the two surcharges. One is for the sela which he paid over to the
sanctuary, and one is for the sheqel which he took back in change.

M. 1:7A–B make a further point: if the half-sheqel is paid as a gift, there is
no surcharge, just as we noted at M. 1:6D, E, but if one lends the money,
then there is no gift, and of course a surcharge is involved. C–D make yet
another secondary point. Partners who paid the sheqel together—half for
each—are liable to the surcharge (M. 1:6E). Our case involves brothers who
have inherited the father's estate and divided it. They then enter partnership.
They are liable to the surcharge if they pay the sheqel together, like any other
partners. Cattle they divided up and then contributed to the partnership does
not have to be tithed by these partners. When the estate has not yet been divided, while the cattle remain subject to the tithe as a single herd belonging to
the father's estate, the brothers do not have to tithe the cattle. Since they now
are not (yet) partners, they are in the status of the sons of a father who pays in
behalf of his children. Consequently, if the estate pays the half-sheqel for
each, they do not have to add the surcharge. Lastly, in Meir's opinion the
amount of the surcharge is one twelfth of a sheqel, one twenty-fourth of a sela.
That is, Meir wants a person to pay a half-sheqel and a sixth more. Sages want
half this quantity, a half-sheqel and a twelfth more.[1]

Why all this? If we want to explain why our authorship has given us such a
rich and detailed picture of the administration and bureaucracy of the Temple,
we must turn back to the details of the account; we must consider how Temple
funds are collected and utilized, and how Temple accounts are administered.
Let us focus on the detail of the half-sheqel and on the services of money
changers in providing that particular medium of exchange for the entire population. Clearly, money changers served essentially to collect the tax. They
changed diverse coinage into the sheqel required for the Temple tax, taking a
coin from one who had not yet paid his tax and converting it into the required
half-sheqel. Why? Because that tax, paid by all eligible Israelites, serves
through the coming year to provide the public daily whole-offerings in the

name of the community. But the changing of money was required only of Israelite males. For other Israelites it was voluntary. Of course, some who did not have to pay the tax could do so (women, slaves, or minors), but importantly, others, such as gentiles or Samaritans, were not allowed to pay it. While they could contribute freewill offerings, they could not participate in supplying the Temple tax of a half-sheqel. What was at stake? If we can answer this question, we can define the importance of the money changers in the Temple. The authorship of the Tosefta, a third-century amplification of the Mishnah, help us in our quest. In the Tosefta we read:

A. *Once they were set up in the Temple, they began to exact pledges from those who had not yet paid* [M. Sheqalim 1:3C].
B. They exact pledges from Israelites for their sheqels, so that the public offerings might be made [paid for] by using their funds.
C. This is like a man who got a sore on his foot, and the doctor had to force it and cut off his flesh so as to heal him. Thus did the Holy One, blessed be He, exact a pledge from Israelites for the payment of their sheqels, so that the public offerings might be made out of their funds.
D. For public offerings appease and effect atonement between Israel and their Father in Heaven.
E. Likewise we find of the heave-offering of sheqels which the Israelites paid in the wilderness,
F. as it is said, "And you shall take the atonement money from the people of Israel and shall appoint it for the service of the tent of meeting, that it may bring the people of Israel to remembrance before the Lord, so as to make atonement for yourselves" [Ex. 30:16].

Tosefta Sheqalim 1:6

The proof-text at F, Ex. 30:16, explicitly links the sheqel-offering in the wilderness to the sheqel-tax or offering in the Temple. Both attain atonement for sin. The parable (C) makes the connection explicit: the doctor has to force the sore and cut it off to heal the patient; the Holy One has to exact the pledge of the half-sheqel so as to make all Israelites responsible for the daily whole-offerings, which atone for Israel's sin. (The explanation for the payment of the sheqel-tax forms a chapter in the larger conception of the daily whole-offerings, a chapter commenced by Ex. 30:16's explicit statement that the daily whole-offering atones for the sin of each Israelite and all Israel every day.) These daily whole-offerings, then, derive from communal funds provided by every Israelite equally, and they serve all Israelites, individually and collectively, as atonement for sin.

So the money changers serve a holy purpose for Israel. Let me explain: given that most Jews, in the land of Israel and in exile, assumed that the daily whole offerings expiated sin and so restored the relationship between God and

Israel that sin spoiled, the half-sheqel, by allowing all Israelites to participate in the provision of the daily whole-offering, served to accomplish atonement for sin in behalf of the holy people as a whole. (This explains why gentiles and Samaritans may not pay the sheqel, while women, slaves, or minor Israelites may [M. Sheqalim 1 : 5A – B]: gentiles and Samaritans do not form part of "Israel" and therefore are unaffected by the expiation accomplished by the daily whole-offering.) Money changers, then, form an integral part in mechanism allowing atonement and expiation for sin; they enable every Israelite to participate in the cult.

So the details are important. In telling us all this, the framers also tell us why this, not that. In the nitty-gritty of the story of collecting the sheqel-tax, of its mechanisms and the persons who apply them, the authorship has delivered its message about the way in which the holy nation rights its relationship with God.

Evidently, the account of the Temple bureaucracy bears a substantial burden of the systemic message concerning the character of the nation and, consequently, the construction of its politics, down to the holders of offices. The politics is a politics of mediation between Heaven and earth, just as the picture of the mythic foundations of politics suggested and just as the account of the political institutions showed us. So the matter of personnel and administration, in regard to the institution of the Temple, bears in its odd way the same burden: the personnel of the Temple mediate between earth and Heaven by disposing of those products of the land and resources of the community that Heaven wishes to have transmitted upward in the Temple smoke and fire. The system's message concerning the administration of the Temple is the same as what it has to say about the institution of the Temple, and giving the kinds of details we have reviewed allows that message to come to the fore.

This brings us back to our original question, the extensive and very particular differentiation in the activities of the employees of the Temple. Can we account for not only the contents, as with the story of the Temple budget, but also the type of information we have here? The question takes on meaning when we recall that, in connection with the court, the only point of differentiation was in the *size* of a body authorized to act in a particular type of activity, to judge a case of a certain character. All court bodies are composed of persons of precisely the same education and qualification. Here, by contrast, one administrator differs from another. That contrast delivers the systemic message when speaking of management of institutions, as much as in the description of the institutions themselves, the contrast between Temple and court bore the same message. Let us now dwell on that point in turning to the management of the courts.

Since the description of the administrative institution called "the court" differentiates one office and function from another only by the number of administrators required to carry out a given task (three for one thing, five for another, twenty-three, seventy-one), we can hardly expect a detailed account of diverse tasks. We cannot expect to find, for example, a court officer in charge of writing writs of divorce or investigating charges of murder, equivalent to the priest "in charge of bird offerings." Such specialization as appears implicit in designating specialists for particular tasks would contradict the claim that the court official ("sage" in the mythic language at hand, "philosopher" in other contexts) can serve anywhere and do anything. The undifferentiated bureaucracy before us is represented therefore by a statement of its professionalism, the ideal of the bureaucrat—whether sitting on a court and deciding a case of felony or a conflict over real estate, whether in session concerning the determination of the holy calendar, whether (in theory) dictating to the Temple priesthood how to make its rulings, whether (in theory) instructing the king on when to go to war. A single professional ideal covered all activities, and adherence to that norm qualified the bureaucrat in whatever he undertook to do. So while the politics represents the priesthood as specialized in the manner in which technicians are specialized, this one knowing this work but assumed to know no other,[2] that one able to carry on either a menial task or a task of a merely technical character, the bureaucracy of the courts—that is to say, the government set forth by the politics of this Judaism—remains undifferentiated.

The qualification contained within the professional ideal of the government bureaucracy is gained through discipleship with a sage—and the sage becomes a sage by first serving as a disciple, learning the arts of government and administration by imitating a sage who was qualified in that same manner. That conception of the profession of course accords with the basic plank of the political platform of Judaism, which is that, on earth, the court forms the counterpart to Heaven's administration of the world. It follows that the sage models himself down here on the ruler(s) up there. The nexus is explicitly *not* in the Temple but in the Torah, for the sages' handbook, attached to the Mishnah though not part of the systemic statement, makes that point clear. It does so in a chapter of a document closely associated with the Mishnah.

Within the sixty-two tractates of the Mishnah that follow a fixed formal and rhetorical pattern in setting forth a sequence of concrete cases to generate implicit rules governing like and unlike, we do not find a statement of the professional ideal of the scribe or court official or sage. No tractate among the sixty-two that bear the formal traits of the Mishnah's legal discussions presents rules or facts or catalogues concerning the courts such as we find in Mishnah-tractate Sheqalim for the Temple administration and personnel. But when the Mishnah's sixty-two legal tractates had taken shape and it became clear that the document lacked a clear picture of its sponsorship, origin, and, therefore, claim to authority, a sixty-third tractate, tractate Avot, the Fathers or Founders, was formulated. Closed about a generation beyond the formation of the Mishnah's sixty-two tractates, this tractate provided the answer to the question of authority and, along the way, set forth the professional ideal of the sage.

Avot's apologia concerning authority is implicit, its account of the correct training and conduct of the court bureaucracy or sage, explicit. It assembles sayings from those attributed to authorities from Sinai through to those credited to the generation after the formation of the Mishnah, and it places all those sayings in the chain of tradition beginning with God's giving of the Torah to Moses at Sinai. This forms the implicit claim to authority, that is, from God to Moses and by a process of (oral) tradition thereafter. Many of these sayings that are set into the chain of tradition convey the professional ideal of the authorities identified as the Mishnah's masters, and all of them presuppose that we deal with those masters of the Torah who are qualified to staff the courts. The contents of a sizable proportion of the sayings attend to attitudes or actions particular to court administrators, judges, and teachers of disciples for such positions. This is why we turn to Avot not only to uncover the rationale for the Mishnah's authority (which, on our own, we have already discerned), but also to discover the rationalization of the uses of power by the particular authorities to whom the Mishnah refers, which is to say, the bureaucrats or, again in the systemic language, the "sages."

Tractate Avot begins, predictably, with the message that the sages' discipleship connects them, in a line of receiving and handing on what we should call "tradition," to Sinai. The line traces not what is said but from whom the tradition is received and by whom it is handed on. That is to say, as we shall now see, no authority in the chain of "tradition" says what a prior authority has said, but all authorities stand in a chain of "tradition," receiving and handing on from Sinai. Accordingly, the qualification of the sage, through education attained in discipleship, invokes the political myth that accounts for the courts' exercise of power here on earth. Since the sage stands in a line of "tradition" from Sinai, his power is valid.

But this line of descent also accounts for the sage's administration, for what he does, how he does it, and why. All things refer back to the correspondence between Heaven and earth. But the nexus now is not the altar fires and the smoke going upward from here to there. It is rather that separate and parallel link formed of the persons of Moses and Joshua, the prophets and men of the great assembly, and traced onward and down to the earthly politicians named in the Mishnah itself.

And herein lies the component critical to the professional ideal of the bureaucracy administering the court-government, namely, the claim that the Mishnah's authorities, the bureaucrats, carry forward in the everyday life of the earthly government precisely what they have learned through this chain that runs not backward in time and space to the (merely) historical revelation at Sinai, but upward in direction to Heaven. The political myth encountered in Tractate Avot chapters 1 and 2, with its direction of Israel's eyes to Heaven and its invocation of God's authority, finds its counterpart in the professional ideal of the personnel and administration of government in the component of the politics of Judaism realized by the courts. First the chain of tradition, with its heavy emphasis upon the correct intentionality and attitude of judges and court administrators:

1:1. Moses received the Torah at Sinai and handed it on to Joshua, Joshua to elders, and elders to prophets. And prophets handed it on to the men of the great assembly. They said three things, "Be prudent in judgment. Raise up many disciples. Make a fence for the Torah."

1:2. Simeon the Righteous was one of the last survivors of the great assembly. He would say, "On three things does the world stand: On the Torah, and on the Temple service, and on deeds of loving kindness."

1:3. Antigonus of Sokho received [the Torah] from Simeon the Righteous. He would say, "Do not be like servants who serve the master on condition of receiving a reward, but [be] like servants who serve the master not on condition of receiving a reward. And let the fear of Heaven be upon you."

1:4. Yosé ben Yoezer of Zeredah and Yosé ben Yohanan of Jerusalem received [the Torah] from them. Yosé ben Yoezer says, "Let your house be a gathering place for sages. And wallow in the dust of their feet, and drink in their words with gusto."

1:5. A. Yosé ben Yohanan of Jerusalem says, "Let your house be open wide. And seat the poor at your table ["make the poor members of your household"]. And don't talk too much with women" (He referred to a man's wife, all the more so is the rule to be applied to the wife of one's fellow.)

1:5. B. In this regard did sages say, "So long as a man talks too much with a woman, he brings trouble on himself, wastes time better spent on studying the Torah, and ends up an heir of Gehenna."

1:6. Joshua ben Perahyah and Nittai the Arbelite received [the Torah] from them. Joshua ben Perahyah says, "Set up a master for yourself. And get yourself a companion-disciple. And give everybody the benefit of the doubt."

1:7. Nittai the Arbelite says, "Keep away from a bad neighbor. And don't get involved with a bad person. And don't give up hope of retribution."

1:8. A. Judah ben Tabbai and Simeon ben Shetah received [the Torah] from them.

1:8. B. Judah ben Tabbai says, "Don't make yourself like one of those who advocate before judges [while you yourself are judging a case]. And when the litigants stand before you, regard them as guilty. But when they leave you, regard them as acquitted (when they have accepted your judgment)."

1:9. Simeon ben Shetah says, "Examine the witnesses with great care.

And watch what you say, lest they learn from what you say how
to lie."

1 : 10. Shemaiah and Abtalyon received [the Torah] from them. Shemaiah
says, "Love work. Hate authority. Don't get friendly with the
government."

1 : 11. Abtalyon says, "Sages, watch what you say, lest you become liable
to the punishment of exile, and go into exile to a place of bad
water, and disciples who follow you drink bad water and die, and
the name of Heaven be thereby profaned."

1 : 12. Hillel and Shammai received [the Torah] from them. Hillel says,
"Be disciples of Aaron, loving peace and pursuing grace, loving
people and drawing them near to the Torah."

1 : 13. A. He would say [in Aramaic]: "A name made great is a name destroyed, and one who does not add, subtracts."

1 : 13. B. "And who does not learn is liable to death. And the one who
uses the crown, passes away."

1 : 14. He would say, "If I am not for myself, who is for me? And when I
am for myself, what am I? And if not now, when?"

1 : 15. Shammai says, "Make your learning of the Torah a fixed obligation. Say little and do much. Greet everybody cheerfully."

1 : 16. Rabban Gamaliel says, "Set up a master for yourself. Avoid doubt.
Don't tithe by too much guesswork."

1 : 17. Simeon his son says, "All my life I grew up among the sages, and I
found nothing better for a person [the body] than silence. And not
the learning is the thing, but the doing. And whoever talks too
much causes sin."

1 : 18. Rabban Simeon ben Gamaliel says, "On three things does the
world stand: on justice, on truth, and on peace. As it is said, *Execute the judgment of truth and peace in your gates* [Zach. 8 : 16]."

M. Avot 1

The claim that we deal with the ideal of the professional court-officer—bureaucrat, administrator, judge—is borne out by what is attributed to the figures in the chain that links back to Sinai (that is, to God's revelation to Moses
of the Torah, including the law) and forward through discipleship to the most
current sages, namely the principal authorities of the Mishnah, Hillel and
Shammai (and by implication their houses or adherents, major authorities in
the Mishnah's construction). The joining of judgment and disciples, the specification of what is at stake in discipleship, the specification of the links in the
chain of tradition, to the master, to the fellow disciple, and to one's own disciples—all these portray the bureaucracy that the politics proposes to put into
power. The context of the whole, namely the courts, cannot be missed, since
sayings such as these are explicit: "Don't make yourself like one of those who
advocate before judges [while you yourself are judging a case]. And when the

litigants stand before you, regard them as guilty. But when they leave you, regard them as acquitted (when they have accepted your judgment). . . . Examine the witnesses with great care. And watch what you say, lest they learn from what you say how to lie."

The substance of the professional ideal of the bureaucracy emerges in sayings that follow. In due course, to be sure, these sayings would be set forth as the ideal of personal conduct of all disciples of sages, and that would come to mean all Israelites (or more accurately, all Israelite males). But in the context of the Mishnah's politics, these sayings originally addressed those who would judge cases, who would adjudicate conflicting claims. They addressed those who would coerce or persuade the *polis* at large, the political community, Israel, to conform to the political program at hand, to the law of the Torah revealed by God to Moses at Sinai. The sizable excerpt from Avot that follows demands sustained attention not only because of its content, but also because it manifests the stunning contrast between the representation of the sages, the personnel and administration of the court-government, and of the priests and Temple officials, on the one side, and of the monarchy, on the other. The comparison of Mishnah-tractate Sheqalim with tractate Avot (chapters 2, 3, and 4) contains the entire message that, through its treatment of personnel and administration, the system wishes to present. And, of course, the silence concerning the monarchy and its bureaucracy becomes all the more noteworthy.[3] Here is chapter 2.

2:1. Rabbi says, "What is the straight path which a person should choose for himself? Whatever is an ornament to the one who follows it, and an ornament in the view of others. Be meticulous in a small religious duty as in a large one, for you do not know what sort of reward is coming for any of the various religious duties. And reckon with the loss [required] in carrying out a religious duty against the reward for doing it; and the reward for committing a transgression against the loss for doing it. And keep your eye on three things, so you will not come into the clutches of transgression. Know what is above you. An eye which sees, and an ear which hears, and all your actions are written down in a book."

2:2. Rabban Gamaliel, a son of Rabbi Judah the Patriarch, says, "Fitting is learning in the Torah along with a craft, for the labor put into the two of them makes one forget sin. And all learning of the Torah which is not joined with labor is destined to be null and causes sin. And all who work with the community—let them work with them [the community] for the sake of Heaven. For the merit of the fathers strengthens them, and the righteousness which they do stands forever. And, as for you, I credit you with a great reward, as if you had done [all the work required by the community]."

2:3. "Be wary of the government, for they get friendly with a person only for their own convenience. They look like friends when it is to their benefit, but they do not stand by a person when he is in need."

2:4. He would say, "Make His wishes into your own wishes, so that He will make your wishes into His wishes. Put aside your wishes on account of His wishes, so that He will put aside the wishes of other people in favor of your wishes." Hillel says, "Do not walk out on the community. And do not have confidence in yourself until the day you die. And do not judge your companion until you are in his place. And do not say anything which cannot be heard, for in the end it will be heard. And do not say, 'When I have time, I shall study,' for you may never have time."

2:5. He would say, "A coarse person will never fear sin, nor will an *am haares* [one who has not studied Torah as a disciple] ever be pious, nor will a shy person learn, nor will an ignorant person teach, nor will anyone too occupied in business get wise. In a place where there are no individuals, try to be an individual."

2:6. Also, he saw a skull floating on the water and said to it [in Aramaic], "Because you drowned others, they drowned you, and in the end those who drowned you will be drowned."

2:7. He would say, "Lots of meat, lots of worms; lots of property, lots of worries; lots of women, lots of witchcraft; lots of slave girls, lots of lust; lots of slave boys, lots of robbery. Lots of the Torah, lots of life; lots of discipleship, lots of wisdom; lots of counsel, lots of understanding; lots of righteousness, lots of peace. [If] one has gotten a good name, he has gotten it for himself. [If] he has gotten teachings of the Torah, he has gotten himself life eternal."

2:8. A. Rabban Yohanan ben Zakkai received [the Torah] from Hillel and Shammai. He would say, "If you have learned much Torah, do not puff yourself up on that account, for it was for that purpose that you were created." He had five disciples, and these are they: Rabbi Eliezer ben Hyrcanus, Rabbi Joshua ben Hananiah, Rabbi Yosé the Priest, Rabbi Simeon ben Nethanel, and Rabbi Eleazar ben Arakh.

2:8. B. He would list their good qualities: "Rabbi Eliezer ben Hyrcanus—a plastered well, which does not lose a drop of water. Rabbi Joshua—happy is the one who gave birth to him. Rabbi Yosé—a pious man. Rabbi Simeon ben Nethanel—a man who fears sin, and Rabbi Eleazar ben Arakh—a surging spring."

2:8. C. He would say, "If all the sages of Israel were on one side of the scale, and Rabbi Eliezer ben Hyrcanus were on the other, he would outweigh all of them."

2:8. D. Abba Saul says in his name, "If all of the sages of Israel were on one side of the scale, and Rabbi Eliezer ben Hyrcanus was also with them, and Rabbi Eleazar [ben Arakh] were on the other side, he would outweigh all of them."

2:9. A. He said to them: "Go and see what is the straight path to which someone should stick."

2:9. B. Rabbi Eliezer says, "A generous spirit."

2:9. C. Rabbi Joshua says, "A good friend."

2:9. D. Rabbi Yosé says, "A good neighbor."

2:9. E. Rabbi Simeon says, "Foresight." Rabbi Eleazar says, "Goodwill."

2:9. F. He said to them, "I prefer the opinion of Rabbi Eleazar ben Arakh, because in what he says is included everything you say."

2:9. G. He said to them, "Go out and see what is the bad road, which someone should avoid."

2:9. H. Rabbi Eliezer says, "Envy."

2:9. I. Rabbi Joshua says, "A bad friend."

2:9. J. Rabbi Yosé says, "A bad neighbor."

2:9. K. Rabbi Simeon says, "A loan. All the same is a loan owed to a human being and a loan owed to the Omnipresent, the blessed, as it is said, *The wicked borrows and does not pay back, but the righteous person deals graciously and hands over* [what is owed (Ps. 37:21)]."

2:9. L. Rabbi Eleazar says, "Ill will."

2:9. M. He said to them: "I prefer the opinion of Rabbi Eleazar ben Arakh, because in what he says is included everything you say."

2:10. A. They [each] said three things.

2:10. B. Rabbi Eliezer says, "Let the respect owing to your companion be as precious to you as the respect owing to yourself. And don't be easy to anger. And repent one day before you die. And warm yourself by the fire of the sages, but be careful of their coals, so you don't get burned—for their bite is the bite of a fox, and their sting is the sting of a scorpion, and their hiss is like the hiss of a snake, and every thing they say is like fiery coals."

2:11. Rabbi Joshua says, "Envy, desire of bad things, and hatred for people push a person out of the world."

2:12. Rabbi Yosé says, "Let your companion's money be as precious to you as your own. And get yourself ready to learn the Torah, for it does not come as an inheritance to you. And may everything you do be for the sake of Heaven."

2:13. Rabbi Simeon says, "Be meticulous about the recitation of the Shema and the Prayer. And when you pray, don't treat your praying as a matter of routine; but let it be a [plea for] mercy and supplication before the Omnipresent, the blessed, as it is said, *For He is gracious and full of compassion, slow to anger and full of mercy, and repents of the evil* [Joel 2:13]. And never be evil in your own eyes."

2:14. Rabbi Eleazar says, "Be constant in learning of the Torah; And

know what to reply to an Epicurean; and know before whom you
work, for your employer can be depended upon to pay your wages
for what you do."

2:15. Rabbi Tarfon says, "The day is short, the work formidable, the
workers lazy, the wages high, the employer impatient."

2:16. He would say, "It's not your job to finish the work, but you are not
free to walk away from it. If you have learned much Torah, they
will give you a good reward. And your employer can be depended
upon to pay your wages for what you do. And know what sort of
reward is going to be given to the righteous in the coming time."

"Rabbi" (Avot 2:1) is assumed to represent Judah the Patriarch, the
Roman-recognized ruler of the Jews in the Land of Israel, meaning the
Roman-appointed ethnarch of the Jewish component of the population of Palestine, a mixed community then as now. His son, Gamaliel (2:2), who presumably flourished after the closure of the Mishnah's sixty-two tractates or at
the time of the concluding work on them, addresses a consideration otherwise
ignored, which is how the bureaucracy is to be supported. His view is that the
administrators are not to be paid but are to support themselves. The priests,
we recall, are supported by the funds of the Temple and also take a share in
the sacrifices. The equivalent here would have the judges take a fee for judging cases or take a cut in settlements. But the system does not contemplate a
paid bureaucracy at all, nor does it account for how disciples are to be supported in their years of service as apprentices to the sages or masters of the
senior generation. The work for and with the community is to be "for the sake
of Heaven"—which makes good sense when we recall that, on earth, the bureaucracy does work that corresponds to the tasks assigned to their counter-
part(s) in Heaven. Consequently, the administrator-judge may not take a
salary: "He who takes payment for judging—his judgments are null. He who
takes payment for testifying—this testimony is null," (M. Bekh. 4:6). So the
picture is uniform and coherent.

How could people work all day and then undertake the administration of the
tasks of the bureaucracy and courts? Although the question is not our particular concern, the literature that continued the Mishnah dealt with the problem
in one of three ways that are of some interest. First, some authorities imagined
that the bureaucracy would be supported magically. That is to say, if people
"studied Torah," then *ex opere operato* their needs would "somehow" be
met. That view appears in the next passage, when R. Nehunia b. Haqqaneh
says, "From whoever accepts upon himself the yoke of the Torah do they remove the yoke of the state and the yoke of hard labor. And upon whoever
removes from himself the yoke of the Torah do they lay the yoke of the state
and the yoke of hard labor." Second, other authorities speculated that rich
people would provide the money in exchange for the merit they gained by
supporting the class of sages. And third, some authorities maintained that one

could, indeed, accept fees—not for one's services, but for the time lost by performing those services. Here, a neat fiction solved the problem. But in the context of the politics at hand, these three quite practical (if perhaps fanciful) solutions find no place. How so? When sages made the point that the earthly court was staffed by bureaucrats who formed the complement and counterpart to the administration of the Heavenly court, to them the problem of how the bureaucracy was to be paid seemed not only impertinent, but also systemically dissonant.

This Heaven-to-earth correspondence predominates, emerging time and again (e.g., 2:4). Or consider the way 2:8ff. draw our attention back to the chain of tradition of chapter 1. We recall that that chain ends with the patriarch, Gamaliel, and his son, Simeon, and these figures then form the continuation from Hillel and Shammai. But now Yohanan b. Zakkai takes over from Hillel and Shammai. The point, important in another context, is more to be noted in this one: the inner politics of the administration of the country, in the hands of the patriarch, through the bureaucracy represented by sages, forms no focus of sustained interest in the systemic document and hardly demands our attention. It was a matter of practical administration, not a major issue of public policy as the political theory represents matters. The interest in the character and quality of mind of disciples takes over, and that provides yet another notion of how the politics characterizes the training of the required personnel of the proposed system.

The sayings attributed to individual sages, as distinct from those assigned to such principals of the system as the patriarchs and the archetypal sage-and-disciple-circle (Yohanan b. Zakkai and his disciples), emphasize traits not of the practical profession but of those who staff the bureaucracy, that is to say, it emphasized the sage's mental and spiritual characteristics. These form political qualifications not only because the tasks to be performed involve the exercise of power, but also because of the mythic substrate that sustains the system as a whole. In terms of the political myth, one not only does as Heaven does, one also conforms to the pattern of Heaven in one's intellect, personality, heart, soul, and spirit. Accordingly, the professional ideal of the bureaucracy happens also to set forward the traits that every (male) Israelite should exhibit.[4] This is made explicit by Simeon b. Gamaliel when he says, "Under all circumstances should a man on his own act like a disciple of a sage" (M. Pes. 4:5).

The bulk of the sayings in tractate Avot chapter 2 represent commonplaces, in which time and again people in many different ways say essentially the same thing. But for our purposes, one thing of interest is repeated. This is the claim that Torah provides a living. That is to say, if people master their learning, somehow they will get what they need. Evidently, Torah bears an enchanted quality in this world. Moreover, the stakes in Torah study are very high, for God is present when Torah is exchanged. And, it goes without saying, much, though not all, of the work of Torah study leads to making decisions; despite the repeated warnings not to get involved in judging cases, in fact the bulk of the sayings address themselves to people who do just that. We have, then, a formidable account of the ideal of the professional politician, that is, the administrator, legislator, and judge of the Israel to whom the Mishnah speaks. There is not, of course, a remotely parallel statement for the king and his staff, the high priest and his caste.

This brings us back to the initial characterization of how the system represents the management of politics. When dealing with the priesthood, the portrait is differentiated, but the distinctions are trivial. When addressing the staff of the courts, the picture is general and noble in its ideal. Why? The Temple official is a technician, but the court bureaucrat is not merely a judge or scribe in charge of technicalities of legal documents (though he must be at least that). He is a philosopher, trained in the tradition that God has revealed, embodying in his person the ideals of that tradition—he is modeled in the image of the Heavenly likeness. He serves, indeed, as the model for the conduct and personality of every male Israelite. So obedience to the sage on earth, participation in the political system sustained by his rule and, above all, submission to his powers of persuasion and coercion form, in the terms of the bureaucracy and its personnel, restatements of the myth that sustains the politics as a whole. In light of the professional ideal before us, it ceases to be amazing that we know much more about sages' authority than we do about their ongoing institutions and how these are differentiated, the titles sages bear, the functions they perform.

The contrast between the representation of the Temple priesthood and its differentiated administration, and the sages' professional ideal, now has to explain not only what we are told, but also what we are not told: the priesthood is given tasks but no ideal because the priesthood does what sages teach them to do, and the system recognizes no encompassing administration other than that of the sages; the sages' ideal, instructing the sage how to behave under all circumstances, scarcely sustains differentiation as to context, task, or circumstance, for it governs behavior in all situations and for all purposes. That is, in each case we are told what the system wants us to know, because the politics bears the prevailing systemic message and in its terms and for its purposes makes a systemic statement in no way particular to politics at all.

Then why no bureaucracy for the monarchy? And where are the king's ministers, agencies, and administrators? The same theory of the structure of the politics of this Judaism that explains why we know what we are told must also tell us why we do not know what is passed over in silence.

The reason why the monarchy seems neglected is that it in fact bears no systemic position within the politics at hand. Details about the royal government and administration, having no systemic message, will not be supplied— if they bear no meaning, how can anyone make them up, and why bother? And to understand, we must recall how the institutional arrangements represented the monarchy to begin with.[5] The systemic consideration is that the monarchy corresponded, on earth, to the rule of God in Heaven. The king here appears structurally the counterpart of the King on high. And the administration and bureaucracy of the King on high (represented by the agents of Heaven who, for instance, imposed the sentence of extirpation), find their counterpart in the administration and bureaucracy of the courts on earth. The place of the monarchy, well-situated in the institutional arrangements of this politics, is therefore such as to exclude the possibility of providing to the monarchy an administration and personnel for the bureaucracy even in theory.

This observation moreover draws our attention back to the account of the political institutions. We recall that we know how the Temple administration was supposed to be supported, and we also have some idea of how people imagined sages would be paid for their political work. But the monarchy is assigned no income nor means of outside support. So we now observe three significant facts about the traits of the description of the institutions and management of politics: (1) payment for one bureaucracy, (2) support on some other basis for a second, and (3) silence as to the source of the budget of the third.

To conclude: a single picture of the politics allows us to explain these contradictory details. On the one side, there cannot have been a picture of a royal administration alongside a Temple administration and a court administration because there was no place for such a picture in the framework of the theory. The very reason that the king fits into the institutional setup at all accounts for the omission of the staff and services required by the royal institution in the picture surveyed here. What explains the absence of a royal bureaucracy (animated, as in the case of sages, perhaps, not by professional self-interest but by a high professional ideal) accounts also for the necessary inclusion, if in trivial and unimportant ways, of a picture of the Temple's bureaucracy. For there was not only ample place but real need for a picture of the administration of the offices that linked earth to Heaven. The tripartite myth, yielding a three-part structure of political institutions, requires pictures of only two administrations and their personnel. The one bureaucracy given shape and substance, the Temple's, is represented precisely as the system builders wished. The second, the court's, is portrayed in quite other terms, as an ideal in its professional standards to which all male Israelites must aspire. And the silence on the third also proves eloquent, indeed bearing with extraordinary power in its very silence the system's stunning political message.

PART TWO
THE SYSTEM

6

Passion

Sanctification

The politics of Judaism presents not merely a static theory of myth, institutional structures, and bureaucracies, but a dynamic account of the working of a political system. To gain access to the passion that animates the system, we seek entry at precisely the point at which we approached the institutional structure itself, namely, the account of sanctions. Why? As a matter of fact, the system not only offers that picture of sanctions that provides access to its political structures,[1] it also explains the purpose of the more important points at which legitimate violence, injury or death inflicted by the state for violation of the law, or retribution from Heaven in the same connection, pertains. The politics encompasses an explanation of what is at stake and how the system not only justifies itself but also motivates its agencies to action.[2] The representation of sanctions thus presents its passion.

So when we explore the passion that animates the system, we pursue it, too, through the politics' picture of punishment; we consider how and why sanctions work. Here we find the deepest concerns of the system expressed at the very moment at which legitimate violence is supposed to be inflicted. It is as if the authorship chose when describing how persons suffered a penalty for their crimes or sins, to explain what legitimates otherwise illegitimate violence. And, time and again, they refer to this single cause: the nature of the human being, the character of Israel. So the passion of the politics forms an account of the anthropology of the Judaism before us.[3]

One point must register at the very outset. We shall see that the positive force of passion competes with no negative power, that is, with no negative driving force of ambition or passion. Vanity plays no role for sages; envy animates no priests; jealousy drives no monarch. All are assumed to be devoted to the cause of Heaven.[4] At no point does the authorship imagine that ambition, envy, self-aggrandizing interest play any role. That is why no one in the systemic picture, for instance, aspires to office.

This phenomenon matches the system's disinterest in political change, in the beginnings and endings of terms of office, and in the transfer of power. As we recall, kings gain office by means never addressed. Priests are born into theirs. Every Israelite male is encouraged to aspire to take on the "name" or discipline of the disciple of a sage, and all are equally capable of doing so, but no one is represented as seeking after the political responsibilities of the courts, fully exercised by sages.[5]

Yet it also explains what motivates the system in the absence of individual ambition, envy, and self-aggrandizement. The system draws its momentum from a fundamental theory of humanity. Passion flows from the implicit theology that explains, on the one hand, how the human being is constituted in relationship to God, and on the other hand, how Israel is constituted as a political entity in relationship to Heaven.

Sanctions and penalties affirm this concept of passion. Their operations reveal that the human being is in God's image and after God's likeness and, when quite legitimately injured or killed by political power, remains in that image and after that likeness. (That is, the exercises of legitimate violence and coercion aim to secure the holy society not from disruption but from sin or crime.) As we shall see, when God enters the picture, God's point of passionate concern proves equally to express convictions of a theological-anthropological character. So what really makes the system work is a sustained, even obsessive concern with issues of life and individual, but also national, death in the context of man's relationship with God. The ultimate sanction, denial of life in the world to come, that is, life beyond death, forms the generative source of a fierce and passionate devotion to the politics of sanctification. Indeed, when the full story has emerged through evidence yet to be adduced, readers will realize that what has been said thus far concerning man's relation to God is a mere understatement.

Admittedly, identifying the theory behind the passion that makes the system work is a judgment call. Others may plausibly identify different sources for systemic dynamics. Yet my claim, that at every point the program of sanctions invokes a well-framed and articulated theory concerning relationships between God and Israel and between God and the individual, finds ample demonstration in the representation of sanctions. That in merely literary terms is precisely the point at which power takes on concrete form and reality: this one is put to death, that one is beaten, the third dies midway through life. In such passages in the Mishnah, and there alone, we find explicit appeal to God's image and likeness as the model for the human being. Accordingly, politics being an account of the disposition of power—who is allowed to do what to whom—sanctions form a set of indicative facts. The real and personal exercise of brute force, now deemed legitimate, and the equally brutal application of power, now held to be right and proper, surely mark the cutting edge of power.

On that basis I maintain that the passion of the politics flows from the definition of the human being, and of Israel, in God's image. People are to act as God wants them to because they are in the model and after the likeness of God. Israel's society is to order itself as a holy nation because Israel is meant to be a community of human beings who are like God. Consequently, power applies at those very points where the social order and the individual pattern of action conflict with the divine image, the Heavenly likeness, of the human being and of Israel the nation. And that is not a static but a dynamic likeness, because, as will become clear, the focus of the entire system does not come to rest on the here and now. Rather, the systemic portrait of humanity invokes this life and immortality, this world and the world to come. And each of the penalties that conveys the political anthropology, consequently the political passion, speaks of the moment but also of the indeterminate future.

Take, for instance, the pictures of punishment by judicial killing or by the infliction of personal injury through flogging. These accounts are so executed as to specify the operative consideration throughout. That is, we receive not the reason why, but the mode by which sanctions such as these are applied. That conveys what defines the primary concern. The implicit conviction, I think, maintains that how the state in the performance of its tasks kills or injures private persons defines the character and conscience of the state. And what defines that conscience? The political ambition of the politics of this Judaism is to form of Israel a holy community and to make of the Israelite what that person always is, which is the this-worldly representation of God's image and likeness. Political Israel, then, is to form on earth what the Heavenly court comprises in Heaven. The political system expresses the anthropology that sees the individual Israelite on earth in the context of the model of God in Heaven. The Israelite always stands for, calls to mind, God in Heaven. These twin principles come to expression even, or especially, when the political system finds itself required to inflict punishment on political entities within Israel, on the one side, and on individual Israelites, on the other. Now let us move from theory to evidence.[6]

The single most drastic exercise of power is judicial termination of a human life. Not surprisingly, therefore, it is in that very context that we find the first, and most important, point. It is simply that the convicted felon is in God's image and after God's likeness, as is the felon's victim in the case of murder. Consequently, the taking of life rights the balance. But, we immediately notice, precisely what is weighed against what introduces a complicating conception.

A. How do they admonish witnesses in capital cases?
B. They would bring them in and admonish them [as follows]: "Perhaps it is your intention to give testimony (1) on the basis of supposition, (2) hearsay, or (3) of what one witness has told another.
C. "[or you may be thinking], 'We heard it from a reliable person.'
D. "Or, you may not know that in the end we are going to interrogate you with appropriate interrogation and examination.
E. "You should know that the laws governing a trial for property cases are different from the laws governing a trial for capital cases.
F. "In the case of a trial for property cases, a person pays money and achieves atonement for himself. In capital cases [the accused's]

blood and the blood of all those who were destined to be born from him [who was wrongfully convicted] are held against him [who testifies falsely] to the end of time.

G.   "For so we find in the case of Cain who slew his brother, as it is said, *The bloods of your brother cry* [Gen. 4:10].

H.   "It does not say, 'The *blood* of your brother,' but 'The *bloods* of your brother'—his blood and the blood of all those who were destined to be born from him."

I.   Another matter: *The bloods of your brother*—for his blood was spattered on trees and stones.

J.   Therefore man was created alone, (1) to teach you that whoever destroys a single Israelite soul is deemed by Scripture as if he had destroyed a whole world.

K.   And whoever saves a single Israelite soul is deemed by Scripture as if he had saved a whole world.

L.   And (2) it was also for the sake of peace among people, so that someone should not say to his fellow, "My father is greater than your father."

M.   And (3) it was also on account of the *minim,* so that the *minim* should not say, "There are many domains in Heaven."

N.   And (4) to portray the grandeur of the Holy One, blessed be He. For a person mints many coins with a single seal, and they are all alike one another. But the King of kings of kings, the Holy One, blessed be He, minted all human beings with that seal of His with which He made the first person, yet not one of them is like anyone else. Therefore everyone is obligated to maintain, "On my account the world was created."

O.   Now perhaps you [witnesses] would like now to say, "What business have we got with this trouble?"

P.   But it already has been written, *He being a witness, whether he has seen or known, if he does not speak it, then he shall bear his iniquity* [Lev. 5:1].

Q.   And perhaps you might want to claim, "What business is it of ours to convict this man of a capital crime?"

R.   But has it not already been said, *When the wicked perish there is rejoicing* [Prov. 11:10].

M. San. 4:5

Why put the man to death? The balance that has been upset is in the future. The murdered person will have no heirs, so the murderer is to have no more heirs. The future stops now. "A whole world" has been destroyed; the correct penalty can only be the same. This is the first hint at what we shall discover to be the centerpiece and recurrent point of obsession, the determinate future which lies beyond the grave.

Clearly, in assessing issues of political passion, we move beyond the limits of a merely secular or this-worldly state with its king, Temple, and courts. The borders of politics encompass not only space but time. In truth, with its utopian rather than locative quality, here is a system with not much concern for space (other than Jerusalem, then everywhere else without differentiation or hierarchization), but with concern for time, for it covers a great span of time indeed, time hierarchized in fundamental dimension.[7]

The third, equally striking point, important in this same context, is that the fate of the felon after the execution forms the centerpiece of interest. The sanction, then, applies only in the here and now. But, as I said, again we see that the system finds its point of deepest concern with what is going to happen later on, a matter to which we shall return at the end. For, as we shall see presently, that passionate interest in what follows the execution, the condition of the felon after death in relationship to God, identifies for us the source of passion, which, as I said, concerns not what is but what will be. The politics of Judaism is a politics of the future, and teleology (but without articulation as eschatology![8]) informs its passion.

Just what future is at stake? It is other-worldly, for, as we have observed, and as the next passage suggests, the world to come constitutes a paramount consideration in the execution of a felon. And, as we shall see presently, the future that imparts to Judaism's politics a decidedly teleological character encompasses not a this-worldly, historical era but always and only an other-worldly one that happens after time has ended and death has taken up all things. A system that seeks stability and the right ordering of society bears within itself a profoundly disruptive apocalyptic teleology indeed. Here is a clear statement of the right ordering of the individual's life through his confession prior to execution and, in the same context, also of the fundamental principle that the felon is in God's image and is to be treated in that way. I give the context, defined by M. San. 6:1–2 and 4, and then the substance of the matter follows.

A. [When] the trial is over [and the felon is convicted], they take him out to stone him.

B. The place of stoning was well outside the court, as it is said, *Bring forth him who cursed to a place outside the camp [Lev. 24:14]*.

C. One person stands at the door of the courthouse, with flags in his hand, and a horseman is some distance from him, so that he is able to see him.

D. [If] one of the judges said, "I have something to say in favor of acquittal," the one at the door waves the flags, and the horseman races off and stops [the execution].

E. And even if [the convicted party] says, "I have something to say in favor of my own acquittal," they bring him back,

F. even four or five times,

G.   so long as there is substance in what he has to say.

H.   [If] they then found him innocent, they dismiss him.

I.   And if not, he goes out to be stoned.

J.   And a herald goes before him, crying out, "Mr. So-and-so, son of Mr. So-and-so, is going out to be stoned because he committed such-and-such a transgression, and Mr. So-and-so and Mr. So-and-so are the witnesses against him. Now anyone who knows grounds for acquittal—let him come and speak in his behalf!"

M. San. 6:1

A.   [When] he was ten cubits from the place of stoning, they say to him, "Confess," for it is usual for those about to be put to death to confess.

B.   For whoever confesses has a share in the world to come.

C.   For so we find concerning Achan, to whom Joshua said, *My son, I pray you, give glory to the Lord, the God Israel, and confess to him, [and tell me now what you have done; hide it not from me.] And Achan answered Joshua and said, Truly have I sinned against the Lord, the God Israel, and thus and thus I have done* [Josh. 7:19]. And how do we know that his confession achieved atonement for him? For it is said, *And Joshua said, Why have you troubled us? The Lord will trouble you this day* [Josh. 7:25]—*This day* the Lord will trouble you, but you will not be troubled in the world to come.

D.   And if he does not know how to confess, they say to him, "Say as follows: 'Let my death be atonement for all of my transgressions.'"

E.   R. Judah says, "If he knew that he had been subjected to perjury, he says, 'Let my death be atonement for all my sins, except for this particular sin [of which I have been convicted by false testimony]!'"

F.   They said to him, "If so, then everyone is going to say that, so as to clear themselves."

M. San. 6:2

A.   The place of stoning was twice the height of a man.

B.   One of the witnesses pushed him over from the hips, so [hard] that he turned upward [in his fall].

C.   He turns him over his hips again [to see whether he has died].

D.   [If] he had died thereby, that sufficed.

E.   If not, the second [witness] takes a stone and puts it on his heart.

F.   [If] he had died thereby, it sufficed.

G.   And if not, stoning him is [the duty] of all Israelites, as it is said, *The hand of the witnesses shall be first upon him to put him to death, and afterward the hand of all the people* [Deut. 17:7].

H.   "All those who are stoned are hanged on a tree [afterward]," the words of R. Eliezer.

I.   And sages say, "Only the blasphemer and the one who worships an idol are hanged."

J.   "As to man, they hang him facing the people, and as to a woman, her face is toward the tree," the words of R. Eliezer.

K.   And sages say, "The man is hanged, but the woman is not hanged."

L.   Said to them R. Eliezer, "And did not Simeon b. Shatah hang women in Ashkelon?"

M.   They said to him, "He hanged eighty women, and they do not judge even two on a single day!"

N.   How do they hang him?

O.   They drive a post into the ground, and a beam juts out from it, and they tie together his two hands, and thus do they hang him.

P.   R. Yosé says, "The post leans against a wall, and then one suspends him the way butchers do it."

Q.   And they untie him forthwith.

R.   And if he is left overnight, one transgresses a negative commandment on his account, as it is said, *His body shall not remain all night on the tree, but you will surely bury him on the same day, for he who is hanged is a curse against God* [Deut. 21:23].

S.   That is to say, on what account has this one been hanged?

T.   Because he cursed the Name, so the Name of Heaven turned out to be profaned.[9]

M. San. 6:4

At several points the convicted felon is asked to confess his sin. This will secure for him his place in the world to come. So the felon, a sinner in a system which knows no distinction between the holy and the merely civil, is expected to set matters right with Heaven. Heaven's interest is served also in the disposition of the felon's body, which must be treated with respect since it is like the body of God.

That point of correspondence is stressed in yet another way, since in what follows Meir explicitly maintains that God personally suffers when a felon is executed or when a human being's corpse is mistreated. Once more, I give not only the passage but the larger context, so that the relationship of theology to law can be immediately discerned. First comes the theology, then the concrete detail of everyday conduct, which is explained by the theology and which realizes that same theology.

A.   Said R. Meir, "When a person is distressed, what words does the Presence of God say? As it were: 'My head is in pain, my arm is in pain.'

B.   "If thus is the Omnipresent distressed on account of the blood of the wicked when it is shed, how much the more so on account of the blood of the righteous!"

C.   And not this only, but whoever allows his deceased to stay unburied overnight transgresses a negative commandment.

D. But [if] one kept [a corpse] overnight for its own honor, [e.g.,] to bring a bier for it and shrouds, he does not transgress on its account.

E. And they did not bury [the felon] in the burial grounds of his ancestors.

F. But there were two graveyards made ready for the use of the court, one for those who were beheaded or strangled, and one for those who were stoned or burned.

M. San. 6:5

A. When the flesh had rotted, they [then do] collect the bones and bury them in their appropriate place.

B. And the relatives [of the felon] come and inquire after the welfare of the judges and of the witnesses,

C. as if to say, "We have nothing against you, for you judged honestly."

D. And they did not go into mourning.

E. But they observe a private grief, for grief is only in the heart.

M. San. 6:6

God participates in the execution, supervising the use of legitimate power even unto death.

Since the systemic statement introduces into accounts of how capital sanctions are applied an explanation of the teleology of the sanction, we should anticipate the same when we consider how people are flogged. When inflicting that most commonplace penalty, the paramount consideration is to keep in mind that the sinner or felon is an Israelite, subejct to merit, the descendant of generations of Israelites and ancestor of many descendants. Why all this matters awaits explanation. As before, we address not only the teleological explanation for the sanction but also the context in which that explanation is represented, which is the description of the sanction itself. In this way we see the close relationship between the law of the sanction and its theology.

A. How do they flog him?

B. One ties his two hands on either side of a pillar,

C. and the minister of the community grabs his clothing—

D. if it is torn, it is torn, and if it is ripped to pieces, it is ripped to pieces—

E. until he bares his chest.

F. A stone is set down behind him, on which the minister of the community stands.

G. And a strap of calf hide is in his hand, doubled and redoubled, with two straps that rise and fall [fastened] to it.

M. Mak. 3:12

A. Its handle is a handbreadth long and a handbreadth wide,

B. and its end must reach to his belly button.

C. And he hits him with a third of the stripes in front and two thirds behind.

D. And he does not hit [the victim] while he is either standing or sitting, but bending low,

E. as it is said, *And the judge will cause him to lie down* [Deut. 25:2].

F. And he who hits him hits with one hand, with all his might.

M. Mak. 3:13

A. And a reader reads: *If you will not observe to do . . . the Lord will have your stripes pronounced, and the stripes of your seed* [Deut. 28:58ff.] (and he goes back to the beginning of the passage). *And you will observe the words of this covenant* [Deut. 29:9], and he finishes with, *But he is full of compassion and forgave their iniquity* [Ps. 78:38], and he goes back to the beginning of the passage.

B. And if the victim dies under the hand of the one who does the flogging, the latter is exempt from punishment.

C. [But if] he added even a single stripe and the victim died, lo, this one goes into exile on his account.

D. If the victim dirtied himself, whether with excrement or urine, he is exempt [from further blows].

E. R. Judah says, "In the case of a man, with excrement; and in the case of a woman, with urine."

M. Mak. 3:14

A. "All those who are liable to extirpation who have been flogged are exempt from their liability to extirpation,

B. "As it is said, *And your brother seem vile to you* [Deut. 25:3]—

C. "Once he has been flogged, lo, he is tantamount to your brother," the words of R. Hanania b. Gamaliel.

D. Said R. Hanania b. Gamaliel, "Now if one who does a single transgression—[Heaven] takes his soul on that account,

E. "he who performs a single religious duty—how much the more so that his soul will be saved for [handed over to] him on that account"

F. R. Simeon says, "From its own passage we may learn that,

G. "for it is written, *Even the souls that do them shall be cut off* [Lev. 18:29].

H. "And it is said, *Which if a man do he shall live by them* [Lev. 18:4].

I. "Lo, whoever sits and does no transgression—they give him a reward like that which goes to one who [goes and] does a religious duty."

J. R. Simeon b. Rabbi says, "Lo, it says, *Only be sure that you do not eat the blood, for the blood is the life* [Deut. 12:23].

K. "Now if blood, which the soul of man despises—he who keeps away from it receives a reward,

L. "robbery and fornication, which the soul of a man desires and after

which he lusts—he who keeps away from them how much the more
will attain merit—

M. "for him, and for his descendants, and for the descendants of his descendants, to the end of all generations!"

M. Mak. 3:15

Once more we see that where the principal sanctions are described, the purpose and passion of these sanctions also are set forth. In the case of flogging, the scriptural passages underline the covenant that joins God and Israel, emphasize God's love for Israel, and stress God's forgiveness of sin, once atoned for. We find ourselves, therefore, in precisely that same frame of reference in which the death penalty is described and explained. The convicted felon confesses not so as to mitigate the punishment, but so as to secure the future. The flogged person too is restored for the long future to the circle of Israel the people. The sanctions, then, prove transient. The one put to death is properly buried and appropriately mourned. The one who is flogged remains "a brother," so: "once he has been flogged, lo, he is tantamount to your brother." What has triggered someone to insert here sayings that express Simeon's interest in extirpation is hardly clear. But that insertion, in this very context, alerts us to the deepest concern of the system, as we shall now see, since flogging on its own is no clear counterpart to extirpation.

We move toward the temporal context of sanctions to underline the highly teleological program expressed through these modes of punishment and their implementation. The system of sanctions encompasses actions that have not yet been taken, situations that have not yet come into being. This surprising fact points toward a politics of an apocalyptic order indeed. To state the matter simply: one can be legitimately punished—even executed—not only for what one has done, but for what one *might* do. This conception points toward a politics aimed very far beyond a range of the mere civil order. It is not that the stakes in political violence are higher; it is that they are different from those we are likely to recognize because the politics' passion flows from the now determinate future. At stake in the maintenance of public order are issues of such overriding importance that, we shall now see, preemptive execution, prior to the commission of acts warranting the death penalty, is deemed legitimate.

Accordingly, the politics encompasses judgments on what a person is likely to do: "Let him die while yet innocent, and let him not die when he is guilty." And that principle applies to a variety of persons deemed likely to commit sins or felonies that carry the death penalty. The conception that such persons are to be killed now, before they err, is made explicit and fully represents the system's norm. We must wait to account for this conception until we can survey the entire range of the sanctions as these find explanation, thus achieving a glimpse of the system's points of passionate concern.

A. A rebellious and incorrigible son is tried on account of [what he may] end up to be.

B. Let him die while yet innocent, and let him not die when he is guilty.

I   C. for when the evil folk die, it is a benefit to them and a benefit to the world.

D. but [when the] righteous folk [die], it is bad for them and bad for the world.

II   E. Wine and sleep for the wicked are a benefit for them and a benefit for the world.

F. But for the righteous, they are bad for them and bad for the world.

III G. Dispersion for the evil is a benefit for them and a benefit for the world.

H. But for the righteous, it is bad for them and bad for the world.

IV I. Gathering together for the evil is bad for them and bad for the world.

J. But for the righteous, it is a benefit for them and a benefit for the world.

V   K. Tranquility for the evil is bad for them and bad for the world.

L. But for the righteous, it is a benefit for them and a benefit for the world.

M. Sotah 8:5

A. He who breaks in [Ex. 22:1] is judged on account of what he may end up to be.

B. [If] he broke in and broke a jug, if bloodguilt applies to him, he is liable.

C. If bloodguilt does not apply, he is exempt.

M. Sotah 8:6

A. And these are those who are to be saved [from doing evil] even at the cost of their lives:

B. he who pursues after (1) his fellow in order to kill them—

C. after (2) a male, or after (3) a betrothed girl;

D. but he (1) who pursues a beast, he (2) who profanes the Sabbath, he (3) who does an act of service to an idol—they do not save them even at the cost of their lives.

M. Sotah 8:7

This collection requires little explanation. A–B declare the principle of conglomeration. The five-part construction which follows is clear as given. The point of M. Sotah 8:6 is that the one who breaks in at night may be killed without the householder's incurring bloodguilt. B–C add the corollary that if he breaks in by day and breaks a jug, the thug is liable to pay, because if the owner should kill him, bloodguilt applies. If he breaks in by night, he is not liable to make up the loss of the jug, because he is not subject to bloodguilt. In line with M. B.Q. 3:10, when a "fine" is assessed (the death penalty), there is no requirement of compensation for damages. If the thug may be put to death (as at C), he need not pay for the jug. M. Sotah 8:7 states the same basic point as M. 8:5A–B, and M. 8:6A refines the matter, as indicated.

But why does the politics take so keen an interest in the relationship between the convicted felon and God? And how does that profound concern form the source for systemic passion throughout? Time and again we have noticed that in describing sanctions, the paramount consideration is the future. But what future? It is not the present condition of a potential felon, nor the this-worldly condition of Israel the nation in its land. It is the future—whether the future of the potential felon or the future that is designated "the world to come," that is to say, a future not of this world at all, and that does not encompass considerations of everyday actions (for the felon) or politics (for the holy state). The sanctions serve as the point of contact between the here and now and a determinate age that is scarcely defined but always assumed, an age in which people live forever. In other words, the apocalyptic character of a politics that punishes people now so that they will not do what they are expected to do finds its teleology in what everyone will yet gain, which is life beyond death. And since there is life beyond death, people really do not die; their existence goes on essentially unaltered beyond the grave. Consequently, at stake for the felon is that ongoing life that is (merely) interrupted by the earthly court's penalty for this-worldly felony. The felon confesses so that, after death, he may yet stand in relationship to God. Of course, he is put to death for having precluded the future of his victim, whom he has murdered. The potential felon or sinner likewise is punished even before he has sinned. But look at the compensation! On the other side of the execution and the grave the felon regains relationship with God and resumes autonomous existence: life.

And why all this? To understand the answer, we recall that the penalty inflicted by Heaven is extirpation, the premature death of the felon or sinner. That accomplishes the expiation of the felony or the sin. Then the felon or sinner enters that right relationship with Heaven that allows life to go forward "in the world to come." Clearly, then, just as execution by the court corrects matters, so execution by Heaven does the same. The counterpart to the death penalty inflicted by the earthly or by the Heavenly court is one and the same: atonement yielding life eternal. Sin and crime are for the here and the now; but life eternal beyond the grave is for all Israel.

So the politics of this Judaism finds its teleology in eternity; its account of the theory of power over the nation, Israel, appeals in the end to the conception of an entire nation outliving the grave. This is stated very simply in the opening lines of the protracted account of who gets, and who does not get, a share in the world to come. The importance of the passage requires us to consider it in full detail. It is the single most important political statement in the

Mishnah; and it is quintessentially a political statement, about the state of the people, Israel, and about the state that they create, complete with the program of sanctions, spelled out in Mishnah-tractate Sanhedrin, of which the following comes as the climactic formulation:

A. All Israelites have a share in the world to come,
B. as it is said, *Your people also shall be all righteous, they shall inherit the land forever; the branch of my planting, the work of my hands, that I may be glorified* [Is. 60:21].

M. San. 10:1

The proof-text at B bears a definition of the world to come, with its reference to (1) the land, to (2) permanent possession of the land, to (3) Israel's possession of the land as God's doing. Here then is the world to come: locativity attained at the end, the fulfillment of a utopian politics in some one place. But that one place is not of this world at all. It finds its boundaries not in space but in time and space joined in union with God. It constitutes life eternal in the land of Israel under God's protection. And this offers a vision of eternity that is, as a matter of fact, deeply political in its essence. For the system's teleology speaks of a political entity, this people forming a nation, that is, "Israel," with its system of penalties and sanctions, that is, its politics, located in a particular place, the "land," and a permanent possession of enduring life in that community, that "people" that is "your people" and "righteous." But, we note, the principle is static, not dynamic. No matter what happens now or in the short term, and without regard to who does or does not do what is expected, all Israel has a share in that coming world. Clearly, we have here a politics of eternity, not a politics of time at all.

So here is the systemic teleology and source of passion, in politics in particular, fully exposed in a simple assertion that everybody will get that "world to come" that is none other than the "Israel" of the here and now. They will never die, and (by way of definition) they will always possess the sanctified territory in which God does God's planting. No wonder that death at the hands of the earthly court or extirpation by the Heavenly court proves emphemeral; everybody, that is, every Israelite, will live forever pretty much in the place and in the manner of the present, except that all will be righteous, none will die, and God will secure the society and state of that unending present coming in the indeterminate future.

Then, if that is the systemic teleology, is there any *political* penalty at all? Of course there is, and it is specifically defined for kings and for ordinary folk alike (but never for identified priests [the Mishnah refers only to a wicked high priest] or for sages, identified or otherwise). First, some actions permanently exclude a person from ongoing existence, from beyond the grave:

C. And these are the ones who have no portion in the world to come:

D. (1) He who says the resurrection of the dead is a teaching which does not derive from the Torah, (2) and the Torah does not come from Heaven; and (3) an Epicurean.

E. R. Aqiba says, "Also: he who reads in heretical books,

F. "and he who whispers over a wound and says, *I will put none of the diseases upon you which I have put on the Egyptians, for I am the Lord who heals you* [Ex. 15:26]."

G. Abba Saul says, "Also: he who pronounces the divine Name as it is spelled out."

M. San. 10:1

Clearly, the true mortal sins comprise doctrinal violations directed against God. These include, for example, denying the resurrection of the dead as a teaching of the Torah. Such a denial effectively denies the world to come— and what one denies one cannot have. As for denying that the Torah comes from God, practicing the sin of Epicureanism, reading heretical books, using God's name in healing, or expressing God's ineffable name, these form mere concretizations of the same species of sin. Unlike sins or crimes committed against other human beings—or even against the law of the Torah and the social order—these sins or crimes directly and immediately engage God. They misuse God's name, deny God's Torah, and, above all and first of all, reject the view that God has provided life as the permanent condition of creation. Why should utterances in these matters make so profound a difference, overriding all other crimes or sins? Because in misusing God's name and in denying the Torah, the Israelite places his or her will over the will of God in an explicit and articulated way.

And that brings us back to the observation that the systemic passion expresses a theological anthropology. Indeed, the various forms of blasphemy that provoke political penalties (whether from Heaven or on earth) deny that the human being is like God—if the Torah does not teach that the human being gets "the world to come," which is to say, lives beyond the grave, then the Torah does not represent the human being as like God, who lives forever. These two notions unite into a single sanction: denying eternal life for the human being means rejecting the image of God as it defines human beings, and (species of the same genus of crime and sin) misusing the name or the image of God provokes the same odious penalty. So the teleological reading of the sanctions at hand allows us clear entry into the passionate concern of the politics as a structure and system. What motivates the politics is the issue of death or life.

No wonder, then, that those who have no access to "the world to come"— in this context, in light of the definitive proof-text, to eternal life beyond the grave—require specification. Kings and commoners, prophets and ordinary people, all are listed, with their crimes or sins alongside. The kings are those who caused Israel to sin. Then come entire political entities, complete communities, "the generation of the flood," "the generation of Babel," "the men of Sodom." These are gentiles, but not individuals. They are political entities, and what these have in common is that, as entire communities, they form counterparts to Israel as a whole nation.[10] They rebelled against God, so they lost eternal life. Then come individual Israelites too.[11]

Which Israelites lose the world to come? The counterpart of rejecting God is rejecting the Land. In light of the definitive proof-text with which we began, that hardly presents a surprise. The spies who rejected the land have lost their portion in the world to come. So too has the generation of the wilderness, which did not believe and trust. Clearly, then, the counterparts to the kings who made Israel sin and the gentiles who warred against God, are the Israelites who rejected the Land, on the one side, or who rejected God, on the other.

A. Three kings and four ordinary folk have no portion in the world to come.

B. Three kings: Jeroboam, Ahab, and Manasseh.

C. R. Judah says, "Manasseh has a portion in the world to come,

D. "since it is said, *And he prayed to him, and he was entreated of him and heard his supplication and brought him again to Jerusalem into his kingdom* [2 Chron. 33:13]."

E. They said to him, "To his kingdom he brought him back, but to the life of the world to come he did not bring him back."

F. Four ordinary folk: Balaam, Doeg, Ahitophel, and Gahazi.

M. San. 10:2

I A. The generation of the flood has no share in the world to come,

B. and they shall not stand in the judgment,

C. since it is written, *My spirit shall not judge with man forever* [Gen. 6:3]—

D. neither judgment nor spirit.

II E. The generation of the dispersion has no share in the world to come,

F. since it is said, *So the Lord scattered them abroad from up there upon the face of the whole earth* [Gen. 11:8].

G. *So the Lord scattered them abroad*—in this world.

H. *and the Lord scattered them from there*—in the world to come.

III I. The men of Sodom have no portion in the world to come,

J. since it is said, *Now the men of Sodom were wicked and sinners against the Lord exceedingly* [Gen. 13:13]—

K. *Wicked*—in this world,

L. *And sinners*—in the world to come.

M. But they will stand in judgment.

N. R. Nehemiah says, "Both these and those will not stand in judgment,

O. "for it is said, *Therefore the wicked shall not stand in judgment, nor sinners in the congregation of the righteous* [Ps. 1:5]—

P. "*Therefore the wicked shall not stand in judgment*—this refers to the generation of the flood.

Q. "*Nor sinners in the congregation of the righteous*—this refers to the men of Sodom."

R. They said to him, "They will not stand in the congregation of the righteous, but they will stand in the congregation of the sinners."

IV S. The spies have no portion in the world to come,

T. as it is said, *Even those men who brought up an evil report of the land died by the plague before the Lord* [Num. 14:37]—

U. *Died*—in this world.

V. *By the plague*—in the world to come.

V W. (1) "The generation of the wilderness has no portion in the world to come and will not stand in judgment,

X. "for it is written, *In this wilderness they shall be consumed and there they shall die* [Num. 14:25]," the words of R. 'Aqiba.

Y. R. Eliezer says, "Concerning them it says, *Gather my saints together to me, those that have made a covenant with me by sacrifice* [Ps. 50:5]."

Z. (2) "The party of Korah is not destined to rise up,

AA. "for it is written, *And the earth closed upon them*—in this world.

BB. "*And they perished from among the assembly*—in the world to come," the words of R. 'Aqiba.

CC. And R. Eliezer says, "*Concerning them it says, The Lord kills and resurrects, brings down to Sheol and brings up again* [1 Sam. 2:6]."

DD. (3) "The ten tribes are not destined to return,

EE. "since it is said, *And he cast them into another land, as on this day* [Deut. 29:28]. Just as the day passes and does not return, so they have gone their way and will not return," the words of R. 'Aqiba.

FF. R. Eliezer says, "Just as this day is dark and then grows light, so the ten tribes for whom it now is dark—thus in the future it is destined to grow light for them."

M. San. 10:3

From historical, we turn to contemporary political entities, communities acting all together in such a way as to lose their eternal life. What follows identifies a city, that is, a political entity, that has no portion in the world to come. It explains how collective punishment is applied.

A. The townsfolk of an apostate town have no portion in the world to come,

B. as it is said, *Certain base fellows have gone out from the midst of thee and have drawn away the inhabitants of their city* [Deut. 13:14].

C. And they are not put to death unless (1) those who misled the [town] come from that same town and from that same tribe,

D. and unless (2) the majority is misled,

E. and unless (3) men did the misleading.

F. [If] (1) women or children misled them,

G. or if (2) a minority of the town was misled,

H. or if (3) those who misled the town came from outside of it,

I. lo, they are treated as individuals [and not as a whole town],

J. and they [thus] require [testimony against them] by two witnesses, and a statement of warning, for each and every one of them.

K. This rule is more strict for individuals than for the community:

L. for individuals are put to death by stoning,

M. therefore their property is saved.

N. But the community is put to death by the sword,

O. therefore their property is lost.

M. San. 10:4

The city as a whole is penalized, as was Sodom, when it conforms to the stated conditions. The importance for the larger argument is self-evident.[12]

As if to underline the proposition that what people do together dictates their fate, we end with the apostate town. That is as it should be, since we began with an account of those convictions and actions that constitute examples of apostasy. Here we conclude with the sanction inflicted upon an entire community by the nation at large. And that too is as it should be, since political sanctions preserve the public order that secures for the nation now and in time to come ("the world to come") ongoing life.

Not surprisingly, the penalty for the apostate group is to be gathered together and killed together, to be subjected to that one form of the death penalty that does not right the relationship with God. Only as individuals can we correct that relationship. This penalty, then, extinguishes for all time the political entity that has ultimately and finally denied God. There is a certain exact justice in such a sanction: one loses what one has denied. But it is a terrible justice indeed, imposing upon the system as a whole responsibility for matters private as much as public, matters that the human being rightly or wrongly settles for himself or herself. Freedom to affirm is also liberty to perish.

As we review the catalog of those who have lost life beyond the grave, we notice a curious disjuncture between the initial catalog and the illustrative materials. Our account of who has no share in the world to come begins with those who commit crimes or sins against God. Such crimes or sins are individual, since they concern matters of conviction, on the one side, and misappropriation of divine power by the individual, on the other. But the account goes on to deal with kings and ordinary folk, as public figures. Its kings are those who made Israel sin; its ordinary folk are false prophets, again, persons who have access to legitimate power and who have misused it. And then, as if to underline the utterly public and shared political sanction at hand, the catalog provides a series of gentile, then Israelite political entities that are denied eternal life. This means that a share in the world to come is something one gains, or loses, as part of an entire community and that the condition of the public interest dictates the fate of the private person. Entire generations of gentiles, groups and an entire generation of Israelites form such entities.

So the passion and motivation point to the proposition that the political entity, Israel, will endure forever. That political entity, Israel, moreover is made up of persons who will never really die, in that they will live forever in the world to come. And my characterization of matters is right at the surface, even though, admittedly, evidences of passion and encompassing concern prove difficult to locate in a document so laconic as the Mishnah and in a system so centered upon stability and order as the initial politics of Judaism. Wanting to find out what people so cared about as to identify with the purpose of shared society and collective action yields only one ineluctable result. People individually did not want to die and collectively wanted to stay right where they were and do pretty much what they then were doing. So, as we saw in those simple but definitive words, "life in the world to come" means life in the Land, secured by God, living and not dying.[13]

Now one may ask what such a teleology has to do with the politics of the here and now. In light of the account of sanctions now reviewed, the question bears its own self-evidently valid answer. The system as a whole is meant to secure that here and now of life in the Land, the life of the people sustained by the Land, the life beyond death for individuals and for nation alike. And that teleological and eschatological vision forms not only the goal of politics but also the explanation and justification for the most violent media available to the political entity, which is denial of life. None then can miss the appropriate quality of the passion and its complement, the pathos, of the politics of this Judaism: to live forever, to lose life forever. That is to say, to live forever, like God, or to lose life forever, unlike God. Faced with such a choice, who could remain indifferent?

To conclude: a tripartite plan, in which Heaven, earth, and mediating Temple collaborate to realize a complete political structure and system bespeaks a single passion. Constant caring about what people do, passionate concern to correct and sustain right thought and right action, flow from the paramount appeal to the systemic theory of God in relationship to the Israelite individual and also to the entire holy society, Israel. The task of the social order, and thus of its politics, requires people working together in a holy community to aim at the sanctification of the here and now. In line with the sanctification of creation on the eve of the seventh day, when all things were in place and subject to their correct name, sanctification is understood as the stable and proper ordering of all things in the plan and program of Heaven. But the here and the now form the vestibule, prologue to the eternal life of Israel, political entity and social fact, through all time.

Politics works by common agreement because all persons share in the task of securing that good order, consensus, common consent that makes possible life beyond death for the individual and the nation alike. The system works not because everybody agrees, but by appeal to law and obedience to law. And yet, in the end, everyone agrees to the essential rightness and justice of the system. As we shall now see, what the politics is meant to accomplish, its definition of the responsibilities of the political system, finds definition in that sense of the rightness of things that undergirds the entire structure.

7

Responsibility

Intention

A politics undertakes responsibility to exercise power purposefully so as to achieve systemic, that is to say coherent, social goals. To identify the range of systemic responsibility, we now predictably turn to sanctions and how these are represented. In the Mishnah's portrayal of the politics of its Judaism, naked power in the form of sanctions is imposed in such a way as explicitly to set forth the ends for which these regrettable but necessary means are constituted. Even the death penalty serves to secure for the sinner or criminal eternal life. Not only so, but the system characterizes those in command as objective, so that it is the responsibility for law and its goals that motivates their action.[1] So, as portrayed in accounts of sanctions, the judge does not enjoy killing or maiming people; the priest does not relish disposing of, or taking for himself, a large share in the valuable beasts and produce of the population; the king or the anointed priest does not look forward to leading men to their death in battle. All of these points at which the politics, through institutions and a bureaucracy, exercise naked power over persons and property alike mark the sharp edges of shared and public responsibility. These are the things that everyone does together, through power vested in persons who stand for institutions and an ongoing administration and bureaucracy. That is why, if we wish to analyze the theory of power in a material setting, we have also to pay close attention to the theory of that responsibility that legitimates power in the everyday world as much as myth validates the uses of power in the intangible world.

Let us take, for example, the representation of the anointed priest who leads the army into battle. He has the right to maim or kill retreating soldiers. Obviously, it is part of the task. Moreover, when the war is not optional but obligatory, then no one has any choice; all must do their duty. A shared, public, and common responsibility governs, and the system takes over to require every person, male and female, young and old, to die if need be. I can think of no more explicit statement of how one's responsibility to carry out the sanctifying religious duties incumbent upon the political entity as a whole validates the use of legitimate violence by agencies of government than the following:

A. *And the officers shall speak further unto the people [and they shall say, What man is there who is fearful and fainthearted?] Let him return to his home* [Deut. 20:8].
B. R. Aqiba says, "Fearful and fainthearted—just as it implies:
C. "He cannot stand in the battle ranks or see a drawn sword."
D. R. Yosé the Galilean says, "*Fearful and fainthearted*—this is one who trembles on account of the transgressions which are in his hand.
E. "Therefore the Torah has connected all of these, so that he returns home because of them [and will not be publicly shamed]."
F. R. Yosé says, "As to a widow married to a high priest, a divorce of woman who has undergone the rite of *halisah* to an ordinary priest, a *mamzer*-girl or a *Netinah*-girl married to an Israelite, an Israelite girl to a *mamzer* or a *Netin*—lo, these are the ones who are *fearful and fainthearted*."

M. Sotah 8:5

A. *And it shall be when the officers have made an end of speaking to the people that they shall appoint captains of hosts at the head of the people* [Deut. 20:9] and at the rear of the people.
B. They station warriors at their head and others behind them, and iron axes are in their hand.
C. And whoever wants to retreat—he has the power to break his legs.
D. For the start of defeat is falling back,
E. as it is written, *Israel fled before the Philistines, and there was also a great slaughter among the people* [1 Sam. 4:17].
F. And further it is written, *And the men of Israel fled from before the Philistines and fell down slain* [1 Sam. 31:1].

M. Sotah 8:6

A. Under what circumstances [do the foregoing rules apply]?
B. In the case of an optional war.
C. But in the case of a war subject to religious requirement, everyone goes forth to battle—
D. even a bridegroom from his chamber, and a bride from her marriage canopy.
E. Said R. Judah, "Under what circumstances? In the case of a war subject to religious requirement.
F. "But in the case of an obligatory war, everyone goes forth to battle—
G. "even a bridegroom from his chamber, and a bride from her marriage canopy."

M. Sotah 8:7

The exemptions do not apply in a holy war, so A–D. At E–G, Judah rejects the view by making yet a third distinction in types of war. He speaks of the wars of Joshua and of those against Amalek (F). The point throughout is simple. The political entity bears responsibilities so solemn that individual rights, even to life and property, let alone to happiness, are set aside and voided. These exercises of power are purposeful and responsible, and they typify the systemic account overall.

Power, including the sanctions involved in legitimate violence ("knee-capping" the coward, for instance), expresses responsibility. As between lack of objectivity and irresponsibility, which is to say, the capricious exercise of power for its own sake, and utter commitment to attaining, through power, the responsible purposes of God and holy Israel, the systemic statement makes its self-evident choice. But identifying those modes by which the system has expressed its definition of objective goals, its identification of its responsibilities, indeed its definition of matters for which politics was meant not to bear responsibility—these matters of definition require sustained attention on their own.

Now how are we to determine the definition of responsibility and with it evidences of the character of the systemic claim of objectivity? If we want to know for what the politics bears responsibility, we turn to the detailed picture of the law to ask, to whom and for what is the politics answerable? Clearly, on the surface the political system is answerable to God for the condition, as to sanctification, of holy Israel. But knowing that the politics answers to God or models itself upon the Heavenly court tells us only that the theory of politics repeats itself in all its details. That explains why what I propose to explain is both more general and also more particular. In general terms I believe I can explain in the language of public policy that *for* which the politics bears responsibility. I also claim to account in a very particular way for the politics' answer to the question, *to* whom is the exercise of power answerable in the conduct of one's range of responsibility? When we know the range of responsibility and the focus of responsibility, we can then outline the basis for the appeal to objectivity that anyone who exercises power in this system will set forth: not my will but my duty. And the transformation of will into public policy, and hence also answerability, accomplishes the goal of identifying the range of responsibility of Judaism's politics. For when we know for what and to what (or whom) politics is responsible and accountable (respectively), we also understand why, in the system's conception, the political figure, exercising power in the service of responsibility, claims to act in full objectivity and never in mere self-interest.

Political responsibility for what? The obvious mode of definition draws attention to all the topics covered by the initial systemic statement. But a survey of the topical program of the Mishnah[2] suggests that a mere paraphrastic summary of the subjects that the Mishnah's authorship chose hardly delineates the range of responsibility assigned by the system in particular to its political institutions and staff. This is for two reasons. First, since, as a matter of fact, the politics encompasses the purposes of the system, there is no distinguishing between political and other responsibilities—the system's framers recognize no frontier dividing secular from religious concerns, for instance.[3] Second, merely rehearsing the topical program by itself scarcely helps us to state in encompassing terms how the politics defines those responsibilities that, in general and throughout, transform naked power into purposeful politics. Institutions and personnel of politics, after all, coerce and compel, while the system takes for granted that many more actions are coerced by conscience, character, or simply the prevailing practice—hence by culture—than are compelled. It follows that the starting point for an analysis of the goals of Judaism's politics remains to be identified. Where shall we identify the distinctively political components of the systemic account of public responsibility?

Once more we must revert to the simple fact that sanctions embody power. In pursuit of the definition of systemic responsibility for politics, we begin with sanctions and how they are represented. How, in the very context of imposing sanctions, does the political statement of Judaism in its initial post-Temple phase signal the responsibilities that the political system takes upon itself? For example, how does the Mishnah represent women so as to portray a picture of the responsibilities of the system? But why consider women? Because women in this system have little power—more than children and slaves, less than men. As an interstitial case, then, women may typify those who are without power over others. With little power women are acted upon by men, but rarely act upon them. Hence they form a suitable arena for the consideration of systemic responsibility in the purest form: *lèse majesté*. In the system's account of responsibility for women we see how the system in theory transforms whim into political will and private and personal prejudice or suspicion into a quite objective procedure involving the exercise of naked, physical power. What better indicator of a systemic theory of political responsibility?

We begin with a sanction specifically imposed only on women. At stake in the representation of this sanction is that matter of responsibility that justifies singling out women for punishment not inflicted on men. The sanction in question derives from Scripture but receives systemic prominence in Mishnah-tractate Sotah.[4] We will first trace the scriptural version. Scripture specifies that a wife accused of infidelity undergoes a rite that *ex opere operato* determines her guilt or innocence. That is to say, the normal rules of procedure and justice do not pertain; the husband need not bring evidence or witnesses to sustain his accusation, which bears the demeaning status, therefore, of a mere complaint or suspicion. On those grounds, nonetheless, the wife is required to submit to rites that otherwise she would not willingly accept.

This case constitutes the most blatant and utterly naked exercise of power, of male dominance over the female, that the system portrays. Therefore, not surprisingly, it carries with it a portrait of the systemic goals, explicitly expressed. What is at stake here? The punishment fits the crime: the exercise even of naked dominance, as we see with the accused wife, is represented as balanced and equitable punishment for her alleged crime.

A.   By that same measure by which a person metes out [to others], they mete out [his or her fate] as well:

B.   She primped herself for the sin, the Omnipresent made her repulsive.

C.   She exposed herself for sin, the Omnipresent exposed her.

D.   With the thigh she began to sin, and afterward with the belly, therefore the thigh suffers the curse first, and afterward the belly,

E.   (But the rest of the body does not escape [punishment]).

M. Sotah 1 : 7

A.   Samson followed his eyes [where they led him], therefore the Philistines put out his eyes, since it is said, *And the Philistines laid hold on him and put out his eyes* [Judges 16:21].

B.   Absalom was proud of his hair, therefore he was hung by his hair [2 Sam. 14:25–26].

C.   And since he had sexual relations with ten concubines of his father, therefore they thrust ten spearheads into his body, since it is said, *And ten young men that carried Joab's armor surrounded and smote Absalom and killed him* [2 Sam. 18:15].

D.   And since he stole three hearts—his father's, the court's, and the Israelite's—since it is said, *And Absalom stole the heart of the men of Israel* [2 Sam. 15:6]—therefore three darts were thrust into him, since it is said, *And he took three darts in his hand and thrust them through the heart of Absalom* [2 Sam. 18:14].

M. Sotah 1 : 8

A.   And so it is on the good side:

B.   Miriam waited a while for Moses, since it is said, *And his sister stood afar off* [Ex. 2:4], therefore, Israel waited on her seven days in the wilderness, since it is said, *And the people did not travel on until Miriam was brought in again* [Num. 12:15].

C.   Joseph had the merit of burying his father, and none of his brothers was greater than he, since it is said, *And Joseph went up to bury his father . . . and there went up with him both chariots and horsemen* [Gen. 50:7, 9].

D.   We have none so great as Joseph, for only Moses took care of his [bones].

E.   Moses had the merit of burying the bones of Joseph, and none in Israel was greater than he, since it is said, *And Moses took the bones of Joseph with him* [Ex. 13:19].

F. We have none so great as Moses, for only the Holy One, blessed be He, took care of his [bones], since it is said, *And he buried him in the valley* [Deut. 34:6].

G. And not of Moses alone have they stated [this rule], but of all righteous people, since it is said, *And your righteousness shall go before you. The glory of the Lord shall gather you [in death]* [Is. 58:8].

M. Sotah 1:9[5]

Clearly, as I suggested, the punishment fits the crime;[6] the exercise of power rights the balance upset by a person's wrong action or in danger of being upset by a person's potential action. The purpose of the politics, then, is to bear the responsibility of sustaining the social order and defending it from disruption and disorder. The appropriate punishment serves not only to inflict the appropriate penalty; the sanction itself demonstrates the much more important fact that, through power, the social entity here on earth, holy Israel, sustains the stable and perfect order that it is meant to comprise. At stake stand not the sanction and its validity, but the system and its essential rightness. This explains why, at M. Sot. 1:9, we forthwith address the counterpart to the conception that the punishment fits the crime—the reward, too, fits the act of merit. That is, the system works not only through sanctions but also through acts of sanctification.[7]

The biblical law concerning finding a neglected corpse serves as the medium for making a further statement of corporate responsibility in our context. If a corpse is found unattended, it is assumed that the person has been murdered. This in turn means that the community has failed in its responsibility to secure the property and life of the deceased. This failure requires atonement, for bloodguilt consequently is imputed to the community. That circumstance offers us another explicit statement of what is at stake in the collective action of the community. Responsibility for the social order lies with the community, seen as a corporate entity. This is why, in the matter of passion and motivation, the language of appeal is to "all Israel." Accordingly, even though no identified individual bears, or could be imagined to bear, guilt, the community as a whole shares shame that what should not happen has happened.

A. The rite of the heifer whose neck is to be broken is said in the Holy Language,

B. since it is said, *If one be found slain in the land lying in the field . . .*

C. *then your elders and your judges shall come forth* [Deut. 21:1–2].

D. Three from the high court in Jerusalem went forth.

E. R. Judah says, "Five, since it is said, *Your elders*—thus two, and *your judges*—thus two, and there is no such thing as a court made up

of an even number of judges, so they add to their number yet one
more."

M. Sotah 9:1

A. The elders of Jerusalem took their leave and went away.
B. The elders of that town bring *a heifer from the herd with which labor
   had not been done and which had not drawn the yoke* [Deut. 21:3].
C. But a blemish does not invalidate it.
D. They brought it down into a rugged valley (and *rugged* is meant liter-
   ally, "hard," but even if it is not rugged, it is valid).
E. And they break its neck with a hatchet from behind.
F. And its place is prohibited for sowing and for tilling, but permitted
   for the combing out of flax and for quarrying stones.

M. Sotah 9:5

A. The elders of that town wash their hands in the place in which the
   neck of the heifer is broken, and they say,
B. *Our hands have not shed this blood, nor did our eyes see it* [Deut.
   21:7].
C. Now could it enter our minds that the elders of a court might be shed-
   ders of blood?
D. And we did not see him and let him go along without an escort.
E. And [it is] the priests [who] say, *Forgive, O Lord, your people Israel,
   whom you have redeemed, and do not allow innocent blood in the
   midst of your people, Israel* [Deut. 21:8].
F. They did not have to say, *And the blood shall be forgiven them*
   [Deut. 21:8].
G. But the Holy Spirit informs them, "Whenever you do this, the blood
   shall be forgiven to you."

M. Sotah 9:6[8]

Although the local authorities carry out the rite of expiation, Jerusalem, the
nation-state, is represented even in the local action (M. Sot. 9:1, 2).[9] So the
politics of the state ("holy people") as a whole, not only of an individual
town or region, is engaged by the failure to preserve the life of one individual.
The court and the priests carry out the rite, the court bearing responsibility
for the protection of life even of a stranger—"we did not see him and let him
go along without an escort"—and the priests seeking forgiveness and reconciliation with God. Thus the two operative agencies of politics, the court-
administration here on earth and the temple in its mediating role, accomplish
the rite. God in heaven then responds (M. Sot. 9:6G–H). We have here a
striking picture of the system as a whole, all components responding to a
single systemic failure. And that detail provides the key to the politics' understanding of the responsibility that legitimates power.

The responsibilities of government down here, as exemplified in the rite of the heifer to recognize responsibility and atone for collective shame and sin, find their definition in the responsibilities assumed in the dominion of God in Heaven. And these share a single definition because what God proposes to accomplish, the responsibilities for which God exercises power, corresponds to what the politics of this Judaism is meant to achieve below. What the agencies of state and government do on earth is what God wants them to do and what God's agencies do in Heaven. What holds the whole together is the correspondence of divine expectation and human intention. That conviction is hardly particular to the politics of the system; it is general to the system as a whole. It corresponds to that excessively general formulation to which I referred to at the outset.

But if we wish to understand, in particular, what renders objective and impersonal the decisions of king, high priest, and judge-administrator, we have to appeal to the conception that what "we"—that is, "we," the political classes—want is what God wants. We bear responsibility down here just as God does up yonder. The link is in the attitude, will, intentionality of earth and Heaven, for these correspond. The human being is like God in every particular, in the matter of attitude, will, and intentionality; there the point of consubstantiality is uncovered. And, it must follow, that is where issues of responsibility and purpose for the politics of the political entity of holy Israel are going to be sorted out. That observation draws us to the systemic center, the source of movement and activity.

One fundamental principle of the system of Judaism attested in the Mishnah is that God and the human being share traits of attitude and emotion.[10] They want the same thing; they want it at the same time, for the same reasons, and in the same way. The responsibility of the system finds its definition in this psychological correspondence: like God, the system's man is a responsible entity. And, we need hardly be reminded, man's responsibility is to keep things in proper balance and proportion, each thing in its proper category. But who is this man? What we shall now see is that the systemic responsibility subordinates the political classes—king, priest, scribe—to another component of the social order. This component occupies a classification entirely different from the political one. And when we identify that systemically critical figure, we shall have come to the disjunctive traits of the system. Consequently we will understand why political responsibility is not the main or even the most important component of the system's conception of social responsibility. For the point of correspondence—Heaven to earth—which we could not find where we expected it, in the King/king, we find in the will of God and the will of the householder.

The politics facilitates from the sidelines; it protects the borders of the system. But as I shall now show, it is the householder who stands at the center of the circle of sanctification. The reason I so claim is simple: in the systemic account, when the system builders wish to show how God responds to the attitude of a human being, it is in the context of the householder's attitude toward, and evaluation of, the crop. True, everyone conforms with God's will, or the political system takes appropriate action—naked power guards the frontiers. But that negative alternative is not the main locus of existence. Life goes on not in reaction against power as threat, but in response to the inner resources of goodwill and sound persuasion. Responding to God's will takes the form not only of coerced obedience but of active partnership in a shared activity. And who above all shares in this partnership? It is not the king, nor the high priest, nor even in particular the scribe.[11] When the systemic statement identifies the point at which God's will and man's will meet, it is in other than political circumstances, and it is the householder, not a political actor at all, who is God's partner. The householder, who stands wholly outside the repertoire of political persons and classifications, bears the burden of systemic responsibility, willing to do God's will. When we grasp the shift from the politics of power to the polity of joint participation in the scarce resources of the land, we shall see in microcosm the stunning disjuncture of the politics of this Judaism, its separation from the economics of Judaism.[12]

A single striking example of the fact suffices to show the rule that prevails throughout. Once we grasp the case, we shall readily understand the rule, and from the rule we shall grasp the general principle that anwers the questions, responsible for what, to whom? To this end, let us turn in tractate Maaserot (rules of tithing) to the matter of the partnership between God and the householder in the ownership of the Holy Land. Maaserot makes clear that man and God respond in the same way to the same events since they share not only ownership of the Land but also the same viewpoint on the value of its produce. When the farmer wants the crop, so too does God. When the householder takes the view that the crop is worthwhile, God responds by forming the same opinion. The theological anthropology that thus brings God and the householder into the same continuum prepares the way for understanding what makes the entire Mishnaic system work. For the centrality of human intentionality in the detailed laws of tithing draws our attention not so much to what motivates the entire system of the Mishnah as to how the authorship of the Mishnah chooses to set forth its position on any critical topic.

Martin Jaffee details the situation in his discussion of Mishnah-tractate Maaserot. I cite his exposition in the context of the partnership, in the ownership of the Holy Land, of God and the householder:[13]

> Mishnah-tractate Maaserot (Tithes) defines the class of produce which is subject to Scripture's diverse agricultural taxes, and determines when payment of these taxes is due. . . . The tractate's questions are: When, in the course of a crop's growth, may it be used to satisfy the obligation to tithe? When, further, in the course of the harvest of the crop, must the tithes actually be paid? It is in the answers to these questions that we uncover the relationship between the human being and God that the Mishnah's authorship sets forth. For the Mishnah's answer to this two-fold question is generated by Scripture's assumption that the agricultural offerings of the Land of Israel are a sacred tax which Israelites owe to God for the prop-

erty they take from his Land (Lv. 27:30). Accordingly, the tractate points out that produce *may* be tithed as soon as it ripens, for at this point the crop becomes valuable as property. Payment of the tithes is not due, however, until the farmer or householder actually claims his harvested produce as personal property. This occurs, in Mishnah-tractate Maaserot's view, whenever a person brings untithed produce from his field into his home, or when he prepares untithed produce for sale in the market. Produce appropriated in this fashion is forbidden for consumption until it is tithed. Having claimed the produce for his own personal use, the farmer must remove those portions which belong to God before he may use it himself. The tractate thus addresses a theological problem. That is to determine, and then to adjudicate, the respective claims of man and God to the produce of the Land of Israel.

The point, well stated by Jaffee, is that the will of God and the purposes of the human being—the Israelite, of course—correspond. When the farmer by his deed demonstrates his attitude, that elicits from God a corresponding response. If the farmer takes possession of the crop for his own purposes, then God wants God's share of the same crop.

Then in the very modes of reflection upon the attitudes and purposes of the human being we discern the deepest layers of conviction that animate the system as a whole.

> At stake, in other words, is the relationship of Israel to the Lord of its ancestral land. . . . Produce first becomes subject to the law of tithes when it ripens in the field. God's claim to the tithes of the produce, that is, is made only when the produce itself becomes of value to the farmer. Only after produce has ripened may we expect the farmer to use it in his own meals, or sell it to others for use in theirs. Thus God's claim to it is first provoked, and must therefore be protected, from that point onward. As we have seen, the produce is permitted as food only if the farmer acknowledges God's prior claim, e.g., by refraining from eating it as he would his own produce. Should the farmer overreach his privilege, however, either by preparing to make a meal of the produce in his field or by claiming to be its sole owner, he loses his privilege to eat altogether, until he tithes. Once God's claim against the produce is satisfied by the removal of the tithes, the produce is released for use in all daily meals. It is now common food. . . . The God of Israel acts and wills in Mishnah-tractate Maaserot only in reaction to the action and intention of his Israelite partner on the Land. Nowhere do the framers of Mishnah-tractate Maaserot expect—or allow for—unilateral or uncontrollable actions proceeding from the initiative of God.[14]

Why is it here, and here principally, that we find that for which the politics, too, bears its share of responsibility? It is because at stake in the issue of responsibility is not only what people do, but how they feel, what they think, above all, the things they plan and intend.

People stand responsible not only for their actions but also for their intentions and, as we saw in the list of potential criminals punishable before the fact, for their improper attitudes. Intentionality initiates the system's power to differentiate among the foci of power: Heaven, earth, Temple. Responsibility transcends politics not because naked power is irrelevant to matters of attitude and intention—the contrary, we know full well, is the fact. The reason, within the system, is that responsibility comes to principal expression in other than political terms. The penalties activated by the householder's misappropriation of God's share of the crop, while present, play no critical role in the tractate that sets forth the correspondences between God's and the householder's plans for the crop. The issue of sanctions (whether imposed by God or by the Temple or by the earthly court) is not bypassed; it is simply not critical to what the framers of the tractate wish to expound (which is why the differentiation of institutional responsibility and authority plays no role in the tractate).

So what we learn in our account of responsibility is the place of politics in the system as a whole. Politics, we now recognize, is subordinate; while it bears a systemic message, its message does not predominate. In so stating, of course, we revert to our initial proposition, which is that at its foundations the political myth of Judaism appeals to the story of Eden and finds it dynamism in the conflict between God's purpose and Adam's will.[15] These conflict because they can conflict; they form a consubstantial realm of shared being, a transaction between equal powers, hence a conflict of power. That explains why more than the social order stands at stake in the politics of this Judaism. What matters is the cosmic relationship that joins God to holy Israel and governs all things. And this accounts for the fact that in the politics of this Judaism, life eternal for the political entity, Israel, also stands at stake. Then conflict between God's purpose and Adam's will is allowed. Still, there are rules and sanctions, and our task is to identify the limits. We shall see that the individual may struggle against God and sin against God, but at no point does the system concede that Israel all together may do so. The political examples of conflict are fantasies, but when we identify actual limits to the human will, they turn out to be corporate and public and collective, that is, political in a perfectly secular sense.

Thus far, then, we have established that politics bears responsibility *for* the social order and *to* Heaven. The link between the social order of holy Israel and the cosmic order in Heaven is forged in the shared if ineffable bonds linking God and humanity, the fragile yet firm web woven of plans, intentions, and attitudes. That accounts, as I just said, for the, to us, egregious responsibility that the politics undertakes for not only what people have done but also for what they might do, that is, for what their present intentions and plans signal that they are going to do. Why do we kill the potential sinner or criminal before he or she does anything at all? Because the determinant is attitude, which governs all else. And the attitude (it is assumed) now has come to ample demonstration, even though commensurate actions have yet to take place. That that intangible future also forms the object of political sanction— kill him first, before he does anything—we now realize forms the critical indicator of that for which the politics bears responsibility. And, I am inclined to think, the individual's attitude, not that of society, is at stake: society cannot form an improper affective intention, only an individual can.

But how to proceed from there? The upshot of our meeting with Mishnah-tractate Maaserot is that God and the human being share traits of attitude and emotion. They want the same thing, respond in the same way to the same events, share not only ownership of the Land but also their viewpoint on the value of its produce. When the farmer wants the crop, so too does God. The important concept is that man's intention triggers God's requirements. Without grasping the issue of intentionality, we shall not understand how and why attitude and plan form political, not merely metaphysical or theological facts.

But I refer to intentionality in a very specific aspect, the relationship between attitude and action. That is where one becomes fully responsible for attitude. Once we know how the framers of the Mishnah sort out that critical matter, we shall have a full definition of their conception of responsibility—which, as a matter of fact, we now know governs political responsibility as well. We now turn to the interplay of action with the intention and will of the human being. The discussion on intention works out several theories concerning not God and God's relationship to humanity, but the nature of the human will in respect to deed. This is, we now realize, an account also of the working of the divine will in response to the human attitude. The human being, like God, is defined not only as sentient but also as a volitional being who can will with effect, unlike beasts and angels. (Though surely presupposed, angels do not figure in the Mishnah at all.)

At the outset we eliminate from the politics categories of things and persons that for one reason or another do not possess an active will for which they bear responsibility. These form systemic categories but not political subsets. Consider animals. Here will or attitude cannot operate. So animals are functionally null. The same is so of slaves. Hence the politics exercises no sanctions when it comes to the behavior of beasts or slaves, except so far as these are implicated in the actions or responsibilities of human beings.[16] Similarly, consider angels. Their will and attitude, where these are represented in later documents, stand totally subservient to God's wishes.[17] Evidently, only the human being,[18] exemplified, for instance, by the person of the farmer, possesses and also exercises the power of intentionality. When a human being forms an intention—whether or not given material expression in gesture or even in speech—consequences follow. And it is at the point of assessing the relationship between intention and action that politics finds its way into the scheme. So the power that human intentionality possesses forms the central consideration in any account of political responsibility. When we have framed our theory of the interplay between what I want to do or want to make happen, and what I actually do or make happen, the intervention of the sanctions of power, whether inflicted on high or imposed down here, finds its place.

Now to the generative problematic: why the focus of political power upon personal attitude? It is because the attitude or intentionality of the Israelite, forming the counterpart of God's, defines the one area of effective power over which the social order bears no control, but for which the social order both bears responsibility and pays the consequences. The attitude of the individual householder toward the crop, like the attitude of the priest toward the offering that he carries out, affects the status of the crop or the offering. Attitude or intentionality classifies an otherwise unclassified substance; it changes the standing of an already classified beast; it shifts the status of a pile of grain, without any physical action whatsoever, from one category to another; it can even override the effects of the natural world. For example, the farmer's attitude can retain in the status of what is dry and so insusceptible to cultic uncleanness a pile of grain that in fact has been rained upon and wet down. An immaterial reality, shaped and reformed by the householder's attitude and plan, can override the material effect of a rainstorm. Clearly, the power of attitude or intention is very real.

The subject matter that serves as a principal medium for sages' theories of human will and intention, and hence for those of God as well, hardly appears very promising for political analysis. And that is to be expected because, we now realize, while attitude and action bear profound political meaning and play a critical role in politics ("our hands did not shed that blood"), the true realm governed by intentionality far transcends the very narrow limits of politics. And that is as it should be because, as I just said, coercion, even legitimate violence, has slight bearing upon matters of will and intention. Where politics can play its role, as in executing the person who holds demonstrably bad intentions before he or she does anything truly culpable, in theory the politics does its deed. The main exposition of the matter will come where politics scarcely ventures but where, as a matter of fact, the system clearly conceives people live out their lives—in the frame of the sheltering household.[19]

As before, the tractate that comes to the fore, tractate Makhshirin, deals with the farmer's disposition of his crop. But the topic of this tractate on its own will hardly lead us to anticipate what, in fact, interests sages in the exposition of that topic. The subject matter is the effect of liquid upon produce. This topic derives from the statement of Lev. 11:37: "And if any part of their carcass [a dead creeping thing] falls upon any seed for sowing that is to be sown, it is clean; but if water is put on the seed and any part of their carcass falls on it, it is unclean for you." Sages understand this statement to mean that dry seed is not susceptible to uncleanness, while seed that has been wet down is susceptible. They further take the view—and this is the point at which intention or human will enters in—that if seed, or any sort of grain, is wet down without the assent of the farmer who owns the grain, then the grain remains insusceptible, while if seed or grain is wet down with the farmer's assent, then the grain is susceptible to uncleanness. The upshot is that grain which a farmer wets down and which is touched by a source of uncleanness (e.g., a dead creeping thing) is then deemed unclean and may not be eaten by those who eat their food in a state of cultic cleanness that accords with the laws of the book of Leviticus pertaining to priests' food in the Temple.

The recurrent formula "If water be put" alludes to Lev. 11:34, 37 and refers to the deliberate wetting down of seed or produce. But at stake is the classification of the water. Water in the category of "If water be put" is water which, having served the farmer's purpose, has the power to impart susceptibility to uncleanness should it fall on grain. Water that is not in the category of "If water be put," water which falls on grain by some sort of accident, does not impart susceptibility to uncleanness to grain that is otherwise kept dry. It remains to observe that the reason the farmer wets down grain is that the grain is going to be milled, and milling grain requires some dampening of the seed. Accordingly, we have the counterpart to the issue of tithing. When the farmer plans to make use of the (now tithed) grain and indicates the plan by wetting down the grain, then the issue of cultic cleanness, that is, preserving the grain from the sources of cultic uncleanness listed in Leviticus 11 through 15, is raised. Before the farmer wants to use the produce, the produce is null. The will and intentionality of the farmer, owner of the grain, are what draws the produce within the orbit of the immaterial world of uncleanness and cleanness.

It would carry us far afield to review all of the tractate's treatment of the question of intentionality as just now summarized, so a single sequence suffices to place on display the way in which these principles come to concrete expression.

A. He who kneels down to drink—
B. the water that comes up on his mouth and on his moustache is under the law, If water be put. [That water imparts susceptibility to uncleanness should it drip on a pile of grain, since the farmer has accomplished his purpose—getting a drink—by stirring up that water and getting it into his mouth or on his moustache.]
C. [The water that comes up] on his nose and on [the hair of] his head and on his beard is not under the law, "If water be put." [That water does not have the power to impart susceptibility to uncleanness should it fall on a pile of dry produce.]
D. He who draws [water] with a jug—
E. the water that comes up on its outer parts and on the rope wound round its neck and on the rope that is needed [in dipping it]—lo, this is under the law, If water be put.
F. And how much [rope] is needed [in handling it]?
G. R. Simeon b. Eleazar says, "A handbreadth."
H. [If] one put it under the waterspout, [the water on its outer parts and on the rope, now not needed in drawing water] is not under the law, If water be put.

M. Makhshirin 4:1

A. He on whom rains fell,
B. even [if he is] a Father [principal source] of uncleanness—
C. it [the water] is not under the law, If water be put [since even in the case of B, the rainfall was not wanted].
D. But if he shook off [the rain], it [the water that is shaken off] is under the law, If water be put.
E. [If] he stood under the waterspout to cool off,

F. or to rinse off,

G. in the case of an unclean person [the water] is unclean.

H. And in the case of a clean person, [the water] is under the law, If water be put.

M. Makhshirin 4:2

A. He who draws water with a swape-pipe [or bucket] [and pieces of fruit later fell into the moisture or water remaining in the pipe or bucket],

B. up to three days [the water] imparts susceptibility to uncleanness. [Afterward it is deemed to be unwanted (Maimonides).]

C. R. Aqiba says, "If it has dried off, it is forthwith incapable of imparting susceptibility to uncleanness, and if it has not dried off, up to thirty days it [continues to] impart susceptibility to uncleanness."

M. Makhshirin 4:9

What must get wet in order to accomplish one's purpose sages deem wet down by approval. But water not needed in one's primary goal is not subject to approval. The pericope consists of M. 4:1A–C and D–H, the latter in two parts, D–E + F–G and H. The point of A–C is clear. Since, in dipping the jug into the water (D–E), one cannot draw water without wetting the outer parts and the rope, water on the rope and the outer parts is deemed affected by one's wishes. Simeon b. Eleazar glosses. At H one does not make use of the rope and does not care whether the water is on the outer parts, since he can draw the water without recourse to either. Accordingly, water on the rope and on the outer parts does not impart susceptibility to uncleanness.

The pericope at M. 4:2 is in two parts, A–D and E–H, each in two units. The point of A + C is that the rain does not come under the person's approval. Therefore the rain is not capable of imparting susceptibility to uncleanness. If by some action, however, the person responds to the rain, for example if he shakes off his garments, then it falls under his approval. B is certainly a gloss, and not an important one. The principal source of uncleanness, that is, the *Zab* of Leviticus 15, derives no benefit from the rain and therefore need not be explicitly excluded. At E, however, the person obviously does want to make use of the water. Therefore it is rendered both susceptible to uncleanness and capable of imparting susceptibility to other things. G makes the former point, H the latter. Perhaps it is G that has generated B, since the distinction between unclean and clean is important at G–H and then invites the contrast between A + B and E + G, that is, falling rain versus rainwater pouring through the waterspout and deliberately utilized.

The dispute sets M. Makhshirin 4:9A–B against C. We deal now with a wooden pipe or bucket. Do we deem the bucket to be dried off as soon as it is empty? No, B says, the water in the bucket, detached with approval (by definition), remains able to impart susceptibility for three days. Aqiba qualifies the matter. If the water drawn with approval was dried out of the bucket, whatever moisture then is found in the bucket is not wanted; the man has shown, by drying out the bucket or pipe, that he does not want moisture there. If it is not dried out, then whatever liquid is there is deemed to be detached from the pool with the approval and therefore able to impart uncleanness for a very long time. Only after thirty days do we assume that the wood is completely dry of the original water detached with approval.

Now if we reflect on the detailed rules we have observed, one thing will have struck the reader very forcefully. What Scripture treats as unconditional the authorship of the Mishnah has made contingent upon the human will. Specifically, when Scripture refers at Lev. 11:34, 37 to grain's being made wet, it makes no provision for the attitude of the owner of the grain, his intention in having wet the grain, or his will as to its disposition. What is wet is susceptible; what is dry is insusceptible. The effect of the water is *ex opere operato*. Yet, as we see, that very matter of the attitude of the householder toward the grain's being made wet forms the centerpiece of interest in the Mishnah. The issue of intentionality thus forms the precipitating consideration behind every dispute we have reviewed. Significantly, the priestly authors of Leviticus could not have conceived such a consideration.

The introduction of that same concern can be shown to characterize the Mishnah's treatment of a variety of biblical rules and to form a profound and far-reaching systemic principle. That principle bears responsibility for a variety of details of considerable consequence, including, as a matter of fact, the whole of the systemic politics' understanding of issues of responsibility. Here we move on to the matter of the conduct of the cult and the role of intentionality in the cult, consistent with what has gone before. Scripture maintains the power of the sacred acts willy-nilly, not taking account of the attitude of the actor. The Mishnah's conception of intentionality intervenes. The importance of the matter for our consideration of politics cannot be missed. Judaism's is a politics in which power corresponds with intentionality and in which one's intention or will represents the one matter over which a person exercises full control. Hence the politics weighs the will or intentionality of one party against that of another, and the definition of responsibility will encompass one's responsibility for one's own attitude. To see how this is worked out in the Mishnah, we do well to contrast its position with that of Scripture on the same matter.

1. *"Whatever touches the altar shall become holy"* [Ex. 29:37]. It would be difficult to find a less ambiguous statement. But here is the rule of the Mishnah's sages: Intentionality plays no role, exercises no power; sanctity works *ex opere operato*.

2. *"The altar sanctifies that which is appropriate to it"* [M. Zebahim 9:1]. "And what are those things which, even if they have gone up, should go down [since they are not offered at all and therefore are not appropriate to the altar]? The flesh for the priests of Most Holy Things and the flesh of Lesser Holy Things [which is designated for priestly consumption]" [M. Zeb. 9:5].

To understand the conflict between statement 1 and statement 2 we have to

understand how an animal enters the category of Most Holy Things or Lesser
Holy Things. It is the action of the farmer, who owns the beast and designates
it for a purpose within the cult, that imparts to the beast that status of Most
Holy Things or Lesser Holy Things. In both cases, the rule is that such a beast
yields parts that are burned up on the altar and other parts that are given to the
priests to eat or to the farmer. The point is this: it is the farmer himself who
has designated his beast for sacrifice in the status of Most Holy Things or
Lesser Holy Things. It is then the farmer's disposition of the offering that
places it into the classification that yields meat for the officiating priest out of
the carcass of the sacrificial beast. Here, in principle, we have something
surely appropriate to the altar. But because of the designation—the realization
of the act of intentionality of the householder, the owner of the beast—the
beast has fallen into a classification that must yield meat to be eaten, and that
meat of the carcass that is to be eaten must be taken off the altar, though it is
fit for being burnt up as an offering to God, and given to the owner or to the
priest as the rule may require.

It would be difficult to find a more profound difference, brought about by a
keen appreciation for the power of the human will, between the Scripture's
unnuanced and uncontingent rule and the Mishnah's clear revision of it. It
would, further, carry us far afield to catalog all of the innumerable rules of the
Mishnah in which intentionality forms the central concern. The rather arcane
rules of Mishnah-tractate Makhshirin show us how sages thought deeply and
framed comprehensive principles concerning will and intentionality and then
applied these principles to exceedingly picayune cases, as we should by now
expect. A simple conclusion seems well justified by the chapter we have examined in its broader conceptual context. The will of the human being forms
the one source of power and autonomous dominion that competes with the
will and intentionality of God.

It is there, therefore, that the politics must locate its focus. But politics cannot bear responsibility for the conflict between God's will and man's will—
only for the outcome. So politics' role in the Judaism at hand is subordinated
not because power does not matter, but because there is a form of power that
sanctions, whether from above or from down here, simply do not affect. And
human freedom resides in that power that lies beyond politics altogether. Let
me emphasize the result: *where legitimate violence cannot extend, there politics comes to an end.* So politics, structure and system alike, deals only with
one kind of power. The political classes—king, priest, scribe—bear only limited responsibility, and politics consequently stands somewhat off-center in
the structure and order of the system of Judaism. The householder stands at
the heart of matters because he is the one whose will with effect and profound
consequence either conforms to or conflicts with God's—at least in the things
that count, the condition of place and of the Holy Land in particular.

From the cases at hand, concerning tithing on the one side, cultic cleanness
on the other, we may generalize as follows:[20] will and deed constitute those

actors of creation which work upon neutral realms, subject to either sanctification or uncleanness—the Temple and table, the field and family, the altar and hearth, woman, time, space, transactions in the material world and in the world above as well. An object, a substance, a transaction, even a phrase or a sentence is inert but may be made holy when the interplay of the will and deed of the human being arouses or generates its potential to be sanctified. Each may be treated as ordinary or (where relevant) made unclean by the neglect of the will and inattentive act of the human being. Just as the entire system of uncleanness and holiness awaits the intervention of the human being, who imparts the capacity to become unclean upon what was formerly inert or removes the capacity to impart cleanness from what was formerly in its natural and puissant condition, so in the other ranges of reality the human being stands at the center on earth, like God in Heaven.

The human being, in God's image, after God's likeness, male and female, is counterpart and partner in creation in that like God he has power over the status and condition of creation, putting everything in its proper place, calling everything by its rightful name. That explains not in general but in exquisite detail the union of theology and politics in Judaism. The human being and God are the two beings that possess the active will. The human being further mirrors God in that he exercises the will, forming attitudes and intentions. That theory of the human being, a philosophical issue concerning the nature of will and attitude meets the theory of God's relationship with humanity, a theological concern concerning the correspondence of God's and humanity's inner being. And this fact accounts for what validates the system of sanctions, defining that for which the politics bears ultimate responsibility: what people want to do. The validation of politics appeals to a responsibility that far transcends the realm of politics.

The one thing that we conceive to be personal and private turns out, within the politics of this Judaism, to elicit the most sustained and ongoing concern from the political structures and system. What people do, and even what they *want* to do, fall subject to politics. Through its severe restriction on the range and realm of the power of politics, that fact expresses the theology that turns loving God into a commandment, an attitude into a duty. "You will love the Lord your God with all your heart, with all your soul, and with all your might" turns out to form not merely the systemic ethos, its worldview writ small, but, we now realize, the definition of its ethics, its way of life. In this context, it forms its politics—a politics writ somewhat awry.

And when we turn back to the circumstance in which the system comes to expression, we see a deeper layer of meaning altogether. All of this deep thought is precipitated by the critical issue facing Israel, the Jewish people. For them, defeated on the battlefield and deprived of their millennial means of serving God in the Temple in Jerusalem, the crucial question becomes "what, now, can a human being do?" In response, the politics imputes to the individual Israelite householder precisely what circumstances have denied. Addressing an age of defeat and (in consequence of the permanent closure of the Temple in Jerusalem) despair, the Mishnah's framers' principal message is that the human being stands at the center of creation, the head of all creatures upon earth; he corresponds to God in Heaven, in whose image he is made. The way in which the Mishnah makes this simple and fundamental statement is illustrated on nearly every page of the document. It imputes to the human being the power to inaugurate and initiate sanctification and uncleanness, processes that play a critical role in the Mishnah's account of reality. And it predicates that power on the human being's will, his intentionality. That is, the will of the human being, expressed through his deed, is the active power in the world. And, we now see, that power is not really political at all, for to it the petty sanctions at hand, even extirpation or execution, remain beside the point. Why? Even though I die young or am put to death, I will live beyond the grave. And that "I" stands for me, my will, my intentionality, my attitude. Then, to what really matters in the social order, politics proves subordinated and merely contingent.

Why is that the fact? Because the true arena for politics and the exercise of power, even legitimate violence and other forms of coercion, finds its boundaries within the will and plan of the private person. That means nothing can be so public and so deeply a matter of political coercion as the one thing to which the community cannot gain access—what in the privacy of my heart I feel, think, want, propose, intend. Except as it so shapes attitudes that people will want what the community requires them to want, the politics proves null at the very point at which the stakes rise highest. As matters would be phrased in later writings, "Nothing whatsoever impedes the human will." But of course, looking back on the age at hand, we know that everything did.

The "Israel" of the Mishnah never concretely achieved its stated political goals.[21] For example, it never set up a government of priests and kings; it never regained the order and state of rest that people imagined had once prevailed in creation, in Eden at the beginning. And that observation brings us to the final point in our analysis of Judaism's political system. How did the politics imagine the system actually functioned? At this point we make the movement downward to the here and now from the heights of mythico-theological discourse on the nature of Adam and Eve in the Eden of Israel. In the humble details of everyday life we shall see the applied rationality of a system that identifies the political entity as a holy people destined never to die, made up of persons who will, if they will it, live through all eternity. True, in this Judaism politics stands subordinate, its range of responsibility limited. But even in politics the stakes prove very high, the responsibilities solemn indeed.

8

Transcending Power

Proportion and Governance

When the system's politics considers how the law functions, as opposed to how the law is enforced, it appeals not to institutions and their bureaucracies nor to penalties for violating the rules. Rather, it appeals to the self-restraint and inner discipline of the society. How so? By an act of free will, by recognizing the rules and understanding their inexorable working, people conduct themselves so as to keep the law among those who do not obey or who, more commonly, are suspected of not obeying it. If people keep the law in some detail, others avoid violating it.

Then we must ask ourselves, what, precisely, is the *polis* (the political entity[1]) that is supposed to define the arena for the politics of this Judaism? Its invisible walls hardly surround all Israel (every Jew): the political theory recognizes that not everybody keeps all the laws. Through the law of the Mishnah, it sorts out the wholly obedient from the less perfectly obedient, separates both from the disobedient and all from the sinner or criminal or felon. It does not merely distinguish the sinners and felons from the rest. Here the disobedient remain within the community; their violation of the law remains unpunished; it is merely coped with.

That hardly attests to a politics resting on elaborated power, worked out through institutions of an autocephalic character and fully able to impose sanctions. In many ways, what we have is a twofold conception of politics. The one is set forth as a structure of myth, institutions, bureaucracy, and administration. The other makes its way as a system of actualities of passion, responsibility, and everyday functioning. The two political theories intersect but prove asymmetrical. For if there are courts in session in Heaven and on earth, with king and high priest, army and Temple, sages everywhere doing the business of state, then why the sage advice not to assist transgressors? Why not just beat them up, if one can? The answers outline the system's sense of proportion.

A political system appeals to more than passion and sanctions to mark out the borders of acceptable conduct, that is, to impose and enforce norms. If passion accounts for the movement of a system, and responsibility accounts for its direction, neither serves to explain how, on a day-to-day basis, the theory imagines that the politics actually works. The system functions within those carefully marked out borders, that is to say, in a way that is normal and routine. And that fact explains why, when this Judaism sets forth its politics, it pays ample attention to the everyday, which is to say, to the balance and proportion between violence and willing obedience. In the everyday world people in the politics of this Judaism are assumed to go along and also to get along.

This Judaism seldom appeals to the politics of legitimate violence. Rather, as its laconic and dull language suggests, it assumes willing collaboration, routine. Clearly, it intends to treat norms as merely descriptive and only ordinary. Of course, then, my characterization of the systemic statement's language points toward its most profound apologetic: these laws say now how they ought to be, but how they really are; in conforming, people simply do what is natural and right. I cannot imagine a more powerful polemic than the one contained in the descriptive language of a working system of law made up for what was, in fact, utopia.[2]

In such a linguistic setting the word "law" is readily defined as "the external reference of formalized norms."[3] That then serves to describe how the politics functions. The modes by which the politics' operations are described convey the politics' profoundly polemical purpose. That purpose is to claim that, down here as up there in Heaven, we have and obey rules that (merely) describe how things are meant to be and therefore actually are, and only incidentally prescribe and provoke the imposition of sanctions. Doing things in accord with the law means to conduct oneself and form a society in conformity with how things in any case are meant to be. Life in a society thus in conformity with the descriptive norms is the natural social condition. It seems natural because created by God, and it comprises the political reality of public policy that is meant by God to characterize the life of Israel, the holy people. If, therefore, we wish to know how the politics of this Judaism imagines the functioning of the system, we must turn, as is our way, to claims that the norms function naturally and inexorably, just as we expect the laws of gravity to work.

Consider this example of such a claim:

A. Whoever has only fifty zuz and yet conducts business with them, lo, this man may not collect for produce designated for the poor.

B. And anyone who does not need to collect such produce [designated for the poor] but takes it will not depart from this world before he in fact depends on other people.

C. And any man who is not lame, dumb, or handicapped but pretends to be will not die of old age before he actually has such a defect.

D. And anyone who needs to collect such produce but does not collect it

will not die of old age before he is able to support others from that
which belongs to him.

M. Peah 8:9

The sanction for violating the rule, A, with its implicit generalization that
one may not lie about one's own condition to gain what one has no right to
take, is imposed neither by an earthly court nor even by Heaven. Here is another version of the same conception:

L.   But any judge who accepts a bribe and on that account changes his
     judgment will not die from old age before his eyes grow weak,

M.   as it is stated, *And you shall take no bribe, for a bribe blinds officials
     and subverts the case of those who are in the right* [Ex. 23:8]

M. Peah 8:9

A fixed rule, a "natural law,' operates here.[4] If one does *X*, the inevitable
and necessary result—in political language, the sanction—is *Y*. Clearly, then,
the system's claim merely to describe how things are is itself constitutes an allegation of sanctioned effect, working *ex opere operato*. The correct balance,
proportion, and composition derive not from the *ought* but from the *is*. And
this forms the richest and most abundant source of power of them all. We
recall in this connection the language of Weber. He writes "The decisive
means for politics is violence. . . . Whoever contracts with violent means for
whatever ends—and every politician does—is exposed to its specific consequences." But that view is contradicted by the political theory of the Mishnah's Judaism. For in the politics of this Judaism, political sanctions that
convey power work well because they are represented in such a way that
power does *not* have to work at all. People accommodate themselves to the
rules and also to a realm in which there are those who do not keep the rules—
a very odd conception, but a stabilizing and irenic one.[5] The fact calls into
question the certainty of contemporary political theory that politics finds its
adequate definition in the legitimate uses of violence, because the contemporary theory reduces the system to elemental brutality and ignores its component of the systemic message that politics reenforces not through violence at
all. Politics serves as a medium for forming and expressing consensus.

That kind of power lies in the conduct of the community, which is conceived to make its own observations and draw consequences from them. What
defines the correct proportions and places for actions and things? It is that
people know the rules that describe and, therefore, also prescribe position and
proportion. They obey those rules. If others do not, the sanction lies in conduct such as is represented in the following potpourri:

A. He who undertakes to be trustworthy [that is, one who is assumed to tithe all of his produce] tithes what he eats, sells, and purchases, and does not accept the hospitality of an *am ha'ares* [in context: one who does not do these things].

B. R. Judah says, "Also one who accepts the hospitality of an *am ha'ares* is trustworthy."

C. They said to him, "If he is not trustworthy concerning himself, how should he be trustworthy concerning others, [e.g., concerning food he feeds or sells to others]?"

M. Dem. 2:2

A. He who undertakes to be a *haber* [associate of a group that scrupulously observes the laws of levitical cleanness] does not sell to an *am ha'ares* [in context: one who does not keep those laws] wet or dry produce . . . does not purchase from him wet produce,

B. does not accept the hospitality of an *am ha'ares,*

C. does not receive him as a guest while the latter is wearing his own clothes.

M. Dem. 2:3

A. He who gives his tithed produce to the mistress of an inn so that she may prepare it for him to eat—tithes that he gives to her and what he receives back from her,

B. since she is suspected of exchanging her own doubtfully tithed produce for his tithed produce.

C. Said R. Yosé, "We are not responsible for deceivers, but he tithes only that which he receives from her."

M. Dem. 3:5

A. A woman may lend to her neighbor suspect of not observing the law of the Sabbatical year a sifter, sieve, millstone, or oven, but she may not sift or grind flour with her [since the grain was gathered in violation of the law].

B. The wife of a *haber* may lend to the wife of an ordinary Israelite a sifter or sieve, and she may sift or grind or shake dry flour with her.

C. But from the time that the ordinary Israelite woman pours water over the flour, rendering it susceptible to uncleanness, the wife of a *haber* may not touch the flour, because one does not assist those who commit a transgression.

D. And all of these allowances were made only in the interest of peace.

M. Sheb. 5:9

A. He who is suspected of transgressing the Seventh Year—they do not purchase from him flax, even if it is combed, but they purchase from him spun flax and woven flax.

M. Bekh. 4:8

The point throughout is the same. People are assumed to draw the correct conclusions and act upon them. The system works—so it is portrayed—because people know what will happen if they keep the law and also if they do not.[6] Thus violence and willing compliance are held in proportion to one another.

How, we may ask, does the systemic document explain and thus legitimate the functioning of the system? It seems to me self-evident that obedience to those who exercise power down here responds to the authority represented by the earthly court, which is God.[7] But I think a further principle held to be self-evidently true is that in his politics the law constitutes a statement of what is fair and just. Consequently, to accept the system's sanctions is to conform to the way things obviously are supposed to be. That view comes to expression not only in the character of the political discourse, noted just now, but also in numerous specific allegations of how the system imposes the sanction of "measure for measure." Consider the following: "He who takes payment for judging—his judgments are null. He who takes payment for testifying—this testimony is null" (M. Bekh. 4:6). So too, if you violate a given law, you are not trusted as to *that* law:

> A. He who is suspected of breaking the law of firstlings—they do not purchase from him meat of gazelles or untanned hides.
> B. R. Eliezer says, "They purchase from him the hide of a female."
> C. And they do not purchase from him bleached wool or dirty wool. But they purchase from him spun wool and wool made into garments.
>
> M. Bekh. 4:7
>
> A. He who is suspected of transgressing the Seventh Year—they do not purchase from him flax, even if it is combed, but they purchase from him spun flax and woven flax.
>
> M. Bekh. 4:8

So the appeal to Heaven comes about not because of the charisma imputed to earthly surrogates but because of the routine and order—the inner rationality—attributed to the workings of the law overall, and that is, as a matter of established fact for the system, both in Heaven and on earth. This stands for a different type of myth, one that legitimates power because is is regular and routine, legal and orderly. Yet that hardly tells the whole story of why coercion is valid and legitimate, of how the politics of this Judaism functions according to a fine sense of proportion.

The picture of how things work comprises a more fundamental and persuasive claim: the system operates to secure the good order of the world. Good order involves avoiding confusion, making extralegal decrees to secure the goals of the law—the law permits one thing, but good order prohibits it, so wisdom takes precedence, and power imposes sound public policy over the logical or theoretical requirements of the law. That is, in practice, beyond the law a power exists that transcends what we might have anticipated.

A system so rich in confessions of weakness, with patient negotiation substituted for legislation, hardly prepares us for the explicit claim that sages' rule so functions as to set aside the law when public policy requires, as in the following sustained representation of how the system works:

     A. At first [the husband] would set up a court in some other place and annul it.

     B. Rabban Gamaliel ordained that people should not do so,

I   C. for the good order of the world.

     D. At first he used to change his name and her name, the name of his town and the name of her town [i.e., to give an adopted name].

     E. And Rabban Gamaliel ordained that one should write, "Mr. So-and-so, and whatever alias he has," "Mrs. So-and-so, and whatever alias she has,"

II   F. for the good order of the world.

M. Git. 4:2[8]

In this passage, which deals with proper writs of divorce, the support of widows and the poor (M. 4:3, the *prosbol*), the sensible treatment of slaves, and sound negotiation with gentiles—that is to say, with the system's marginal or interstitial components—the law gives way. I find here the counterpart for the allegation that the laws describe how things really are. Now we see the system in fact requires that when the law represents how things ought not to be, it gives way to the rationality required by the politics. The system possesses power to solve its problems.

In addition, the politics encompasses the economy. Sages' courts are represented as controlling prices, on the one hand, and ensuring that "true value" is exchanged in commercial transactions of sale or barter, on the other. The following story alleges that sages control matters as critical to "the good order of the world" as support for the poor and for women and proper arrangements for slaves:

     A. The woman who is subject to a doubt concerning [the appearance of] five fluxes,

     B. or the one who is subject to a doubt concerning five miscarriages,

     C. brings a single offering.

     D. And she [then is deemed clean so that she] eats animal sacrifices.

     E. And the remainder [of the offerings, A, B] are not an obligation for her.

     F. [If she is subject to] five confirmed miscarriages,

G. or five confirmed fluxes,

H. she brings a single offering.

I. And she eats animal sacrifices.

J. But the rest [of the offerings, the other four] remain as an obligation for her [to bring at some later time].

K. There was the following case: A pair of birds in Jerusalem went up in price to a golden denar.

L. Said Rabban Simeon b. Gamaliel, "By this sanctuary! I shall not rest tonight until they shall be at [silver] denars."

M. He entered the court and taught [the following law]:

N. "The woman who is subject to five confirmed miscarriages [or] five confirmed fluxes brings a single offering.

O. "And she eats animal sacrifices.

P. "And the rest [of the offerings] do *not* remain as an obligation for her."

Q. And pairs of birds stood on that very day at a quarter-denar each [one one-hundredth of the former price].

Here the sage's ruling is supposed to control prices by governing the demand for sacrificial birds.[9] Evidently, good order further means the power to solve problems, to deal with the effects of important events.

The politics of Judaism certainly claimed in its own behalf that its institutions and authorities could cope with crises and solve problems. Since the single most critical issue, to us, is how (in fantasy at least) to accommodate the effects of the Temple's destruction, we find of special interest the allegation that sages' courts could well address the changes required in the life of the community and the synagogue liturgy in consequence of its loss.

The following sets forth a picture of the sound functioning of a politics entirely in control of its circumstance. Once more, the capacity to deal with the absence of power has to be understood as a claim of considerable power indeed.

A. The festival day of the New Year which coincided with the Sabbath—

B. in the Temple they would sound the shofar.

C. But not in the provinces.

D. When the Temple was destroyed, Rabban Yohanen ben Zakkai made the rule that they should sound the shofar in every locale in which there was a court.

E. Said R. Eleazar, "Rabban Yohanan b. Zakkai made that rule only in the case of Yabneh alone."

F. They said to him, "All the same are Yabneh and every locale in which there is a court."

M. R. H. 4:1

Let me stress the main point: the problems caused by the destruction of the Temple did not find Israel without power to deal with its situation; the sages' court could do what had to be done. The passage's details then bear that implicit and important message. Still more stunning evidence that the Mishnah's statement of the politics of this Judaism represented itself[10] in control of the everyday conduct of Israel derives from the systemic picture of how to cope with political error. No one, after all, could maintain that the political institutions, the entire community, and the king and high priest, never erred. When power was misused, a truly strong politics could identify the error and correct it. The mode by which political error (such as collective sin or erroneous decisions by instruments of government) was corrected appealed to Scripture, for Scripture makes provision for collective expiation of guilt incurred on account of collective action affected through public institutions of government and instruction. It is this topic which is now worked out fully in relationship to, and essentially as an exegesis of, Scripture itself. But the reason for treating the matter here derives from Mishnah's and not Scripture's principles of organization. Mishnah-tractate Horayot takes up the application and elucidation of Leviticus 4. The Scriptures which refer to a sin committed in error are at issue. Specifically, when the court instructs the community to do something which, in fact, should not be done, we have a case of erroneous instruction to which, the Mishnah's authorship takes for granted, Lev. 4:1–5, 13–21, 22–26 and Num. 15:22–26 refer.

The Mishnah's authorship's problem is to define situations in which there has been a bona fide error on the part of the court. Here we invoke the stated Scriptures. Specifically those which treat an individual's inadvertent or deliberate sin will come into operation. So in all, the problem of the tractate is presented by Scripture, and Mishnah's particular contribution is clear. Let us now turn to the specifics of Scripture. Mishnah-tractate Horayot deals with cultic penalties for sin. Lev. 4:1–5 state:

> And the Lord said to Moses, "Say to the people of Israel, if any one sins unwittingly in any of the things which the Lord has commanded not to be done, and does any one of them, if it is the anointed priest who sins, thus bringing guilt on the people, then let him offer for the sin which he has committed a young bull without blemish to the Lord for a sin offering. He shall bring the bull to the door of the tent of meeting before the Lord, and lay his hand on the head of the bull, and kill the bull before the Lord. And the anointed priest shall take some of the blood of the bull and bring it to the tent of the meeting; and the priest shall dip his finger in the blood and sprinkle part of the blood seven times before the Lord in front of the veil of the sanctuary."[11]

Now, clearly, the premise is that the sin under discussion is inadvertent or unwitting. Whether the sinner be the ruler, the high priest, or the entire people, all stand subject to the conception that an erroneous ruling by the court has caused this unwitting sin. The theory of the system as set forth in the

Mishnah will examine possible decisions in this regard; it will explore, for example, whether the court and the public have acted together, or whether the court only issued a ruling while the public carried it out.[12] But Mishnah-tractate Horayot's message for us is simple: the court, that is, the political system, bears full responsibility for what it does. Consequently, the individual who accepts the court's decision is not liable if, on the account, he has sinned or committed a crime. This claim in behalf of the political system constitutes, for the politics of this Judaism, the allegation of total and complete responsibility, and therefore sovereignty under God and the Torah to be sure, possessed by the political system as a whole.

The upshot is that the system deals with political sin or crime in precisely the way in which it copes with individual sin or crime. When the government errs, as when a private person does, the task is to restore the balance and order broken by error, sin, or crime. That is accomplished through the appropriate means, the punishment fitting the character of the crime.

The operative criterion here is whether or not the sin or crime was committed deliberately against God, or inadvertently or unintentionally against God. And that leads us to ask: precisely what kind of operating and practical authority does the politics of this Judaism contemplate? And how does the system account on an everyday basis for the sanctions, including legitimate violence, that it posits? Does it turn to tradition, charisma, or law? The answer is clear from what has already been said: we deal with a politics of sustaining rationally, meaning a politics of routine and law.[13]

The religious politics before us does not appeal to charisma to account for the functioning of the system, let alone to justify obedience. We recall that Weber defines authority or domination in terms of "the probability that a command with a given specific content will be obeyed by a given group of persons."[14] That probability, so the Mishnah portrays matters, derives not only from the source of the law, but also from its rationality, with its appeal to order. Here then is a political myth, structure and system alike, that appeals not to charisma but soley to the routinization of political behavior. Then obedience is not coerced but evoked, and the politics of the Mishnah presents a theory of shared consent yielding consensus. The domination is not vested in persons but in God through the Torah—so the theory presents matters.

In the present context, the formerly neglected power represented by the sages' consensus finds a natural place. The law sages teach secures order and stands for common sense rationalities. Sages' consensus represents the law, and the law comes from tradition, and tradition validates the law by appeal to its source, which is Sinai. The court on its own can do nothing—so the theory holds—except repeat and clarify what the prior court has done. That appeal to the fundamental political myth, which refers all things to Heaven, secures stability and, by the way, also explains why majority and minority opinions register:

A. And why do they record the opinion of an individual along with that of the majority, since the law follows the opinion of the majority?

B. So that, if a court should prefer the opinion of the individual, it may decide to rely upon it. For a court has not got the power to nullify the opinion of another court, unless it is greater than the other in wisdom and in numbers.

C. If it was greater than the other is wisdom but not in numbers, in numbers but not in wisdom, it has not got the power to nullify its opinion, unless it is greater than it in both wisdom and numbers.

D. Said R. Judah, "Why do they record the opinion of an individual against that of a majority to no purpose? So that if a person should say, 'Thus have I received the tradition,' one may say to him, 'You have heard the tradition in accord with the opinion of Mr. so-and-so [against that of the majority].'"

M. Ed. 1:5–6

Here once more, as with the account of the politics' responsibilities, we find appeal to tradition, and that assuredly forms one commonplace mode of mythic legitimation of the exercise of power.

Why obey? Because domination of this particular politics is legitimate. How so? Among legitimations of domination catalogued by Weber are those of tradition, charisma, and legality; all three join together in the politics of this Judaism. Weber writes:

> First, the authority of the "eternal yesterday," i.e., of the mores sanctified through unimaginably ancient recognition and habitual orientation to conform. This is the traditional domination exercised by the patriarch and the patrimonial prince of yore.
>
> There is the authority of the extraordinary and personal gift of grace (charisma), the absolutely personal devotion and personal confidence in revelation, heroism, or other qualities of individual leadership. This is "charismatic" domination, as exercised by the prophet. . . .
>
> Finally, there is the domination by virtue of "legality," by virtue of the belief in the validity of legal statute and functional "competence" based on rationally created rules. In this case obedience is expected in discharging statutory obligations. This is domination as exercised by the modern "servant of the state" and by all those bearers of power who in this respect resemble him.[15]

In the Mishnah, the court on earth enforces laws established of old, back to Sinai. That claim to tradition is set forth. Sinai, of course, stands for the revelation to Moses. There can be no more formidable allegation concerning charisma than that: God talking to the prophet. And finally, the rules that are set forth are represented as rational in creation and obligatory. Accordingly, were we to classify the myth that describes the functioning of the politics of this Judaism, we should have to find a way of situating our myth in three distinct taxa.

Yet, we realize full well, that again is misleading, and Weber provides a model of somewhat asymmetrical dimensions for the system at hand. For while we can adduce in detail notional evidence for the presence of a variety of legitimating myths, in point of fact only one plays a political role. Indeed, appeal to charisma or revelation plays no role whatsoever in how the system works, in its political balance and proportion. The court on earth is made up of men who know the law through discipleship, not through prophetic gifts. While all is regular and orderly, the systemically disruptive force comes not from God but from the will of the human being. That is precisely the opposite of political charisma; it is the force for chaos that the system is meant to overcome. But the fact that disorder derives from the human will, not from God's communication with prophets, also imparts its indicative trait to the systemic politics. How so? The very indicative presence of human freedom, integral to the theory of the working of power, excludes this mythic structure from being classified as a politics of (mere) legality. A politics that identifies the human will as the motive and force for the system's actual working does not impose mere legality, it seeks to nurture order. Let me state with some emphasis: *Judaism's politics is not a system in which the letter kills, but one in which the spirit is accommodated.* And that suggests we deal with a myth that defines a fourth genus altogether, one that, while charismatic, traditional, and legal, recasts all three traits in a way distinctly its own. To prepare the way for identifying that fourth genus of political myth, let me provide a brief prospectus of what is to come.

To reckon with the correct classification, we have to ask, as with our inquiry into the political myth, not what legitimates power but what precipitates the activity of power. That is to say, where and under what conditions does the politics take action and exercise coercion? And that question produces only a single, now predictable and familiar, answer. It is that the free will of humanity collides with the regularity and order set forth by divinity. The system works to set right humanity's relationship with God and humanity's activity in conformity with God's rules. The question of the system, then, is how to set matters right. And the uses of power by the system, therefore legitimations of power within the system, accomplish the goal of drawing all things into conformity with the correct paradigm.

So once more we reach a familiar conclusion: we deal with a politics of Eden, a politics of restoration, and, it follows, the myth of legitimation at hand is one that promises return and renewal. We have then to classify the myth of the politics of this Judaism as a myth of return, one in which, by obedience to the law and its institutions, humanity—Israel in particular—regains its right condition and proper circumstance. That is not an appeal to a good and valid tradition, but an effort to circumvent a bad tradition, one that has led to a sorry situation. Legitimacy now marks the reversion to Eden, and that kind of myth, profoundly conservative and restorative, forms a classification entirely distinct from the taxa of tradition, legality, and charisma.

Leaving matters here, however, would grossly misrepresent the actualities of the first of the political writings of this Judaism, for we should imagine that somewhere in the initial system is an account of power so exercised as to restore the balance broken by the fall from Eden. But the representations of actual administration, decisions made by the courts for instance, are wholly other. They are not only concrete and specific, they also are trivial and nit-picking. In this context we therefore are constrained to ask, does the systemic statement portray concrete acts of power carried out by courts?

Indeed it does, and a brief survey of diverse incidents alleged as fact by the Mishnah allows us to see precisely what courts can do and how they do it. Here is a sample of the allegations in the Mishnah that the courts made practical decisions and carried them out. Because of the importance of the proposition these passages are meant to illustrate and demonstrate, I give a sizable repertoire of brief entries.

A. The people of Tiberias brought a pipe of cold water through a spring of hot water.

B. Sages said to them, "If this was done on the Sabbath, the water is in the status of hot water that has been heated on the Sabbath itself. It is prohibited for use in washing and in drinking. If this was done on the festival day, the water is in the status of hot water which has been heated on the festival day. It is prohibited for use in washing but permitted for use in drinking."

M. Shab. 3:4

A. As to a bolt with a knob on its end—

B. said R. Eleazar, "In the synagogue in Tiberias they permitted using it on the Sabbath, until Rabban Gamaliel and elders came and prohibited it for them."

C. R. Yose says, "They treated it as prohibited. Rabban Gamaliel and elders came and permitted it for them."

M. Er. 10:10

A. They asked R. Tarfon about such a case [namely, moving a domesticated beast which has died from the place at which it has died on the festival day] and about a dough offering which had contracted uncleanness.

B. So he went to the study house and asked. They told him, "One should not move them from where they are located [until after the festival]."

M. Bes. 3:5

A. More than forty pairs of witnesses came forward to the advent of the new moon. But R. Aqiba kept them back at Lud. Rabban Gamaliel said to him, "If you keep the people back, you will turn out to make them err in the future."

M. R.H. 1:6

A. A certain man in Asya was let down by a rope into the sea, and they drew back up only his leg.
B. Sages said, "if the recovered part included from the knee and above, his wife may remarry, and if only from the knee and below, she may not."

M. Yeb. 16:4

A. They brought before Rabban Gamaliel in Kepar Otenai the writ of divorce, and the witnesses thereon were Samaritan witnesses,
B. and he declared it valid.

M. Git. 1:5

A. Someone pulled apart the hairdo of a woman in the marketplace.
B. She came before R. Aqiba, who required him to pay her four hundred zuz.

M. B.Q. 8:6

A. In Sepphoris someone hired a bathhouse from his fellow for twelve golden denars per year, at the rate of one golden denar per month, and the year was intercalated, getting an extra month.
B. The case came before Rabban Simeon b. Gamaliel and before R. Yose.
C. They ruled, "Let them divide the month added by the intercalation of the year."

M. B.M. 8:8

A. Boethus b. Zonen brought dried figs by ship, and a jar of libation wine broke open and dripped on them, and he asked sages,
B. who permitted using the figs once they had been rinsed.

M. A.Z. 5:2

A. The womb of a cow was removed, and R. Tarfon had the cow [which he held to be in the status of "torn" and not suitable for Israelite consumption) fed to the dogs.
B. The case came before sages, and they declared it permitted. . . .
C. Said R. Tarfon, "There goes your ass, Tarfon."
D. Said to him R. Aqiba, "Rabbi Tarfon, you are exempt, for you are an expert recognized by a court, and any expert recognized by a court is free from liability of paying."

M. Bekh. 4:4

A. In Mahoz people dampened wheat in sand.
B. Sages said to them, "If thus you have been doing, you have never

prepared food in accord with the rules of cleanness in your entire lives."

M. Makh. 3:4

A. In Salmon one planted his vineyards by intervals of sixteen, sixteen *amah,* and he would turn the foliage of two rows to one side and sow the cleared land,

B. and in the next year he would turn the foliage to another place.

C. And the case came before sages, and they permitted his actions.

M. Kil. 4:9

I could readily multiply this list; the candidates for cataloguing are many. But a single point emerged: no Eden here! When the systemic statement portrays how things actually are, we discern no appeal to a restoration to a primal perfection. Quite to the contrary, all we have by way of applied politics is a program of petty decisions by small claims courts, rabbinical bodies busy with what outsiders could not take seriously.

The program of practical decisions reveals a local court of limited jurisdiction indeed. We find rulings concerning matters that—by the Mishnah's own evidence—only limited circles of Jews are supposed to have taken to heart. These include festival and Sabbath observance (in some minor details); the holy days of the calendar; personal status (e.g., a woman is indeed a widow); correct preparation of documents; small claims about minor matters. I see here no extravagant claim at all. Rather, we have a potpourri of cases of a distinctly trivial character, affecting at best only a handful of local residents. That is, the politics in its institutional form speaks of Israel, the holy people, in its cosmic relationships, but the politics as a working system reaches only the lowest layers of the social order, and then only in matters of an essentially trivial sort.

Here, therefore, is a politics of bravado and bombast but also of sagacity and restraint. The vision appeals to power, to enduring institutions that can carry out public policy, a working system that accomplishes its goals for the social order. But the actualities accord with weakness, so that much depends upon inner constraint.[16] The outer indicator of such constraint has also to be set forth. It is a change in the ordinary routine of everyday conduct that signifies the actor's conformity with a law that others may or may not keep. When a political system represents itself as functioning essentially on inner compliance and goodwill, it has also to define the limns of conduct with those who do not obey. Here is a case in which the weakness of the law enforcement program requires a strengthening of the law for those who keep it, and doing so on the basis of an inner sanction:

A. At first they held, during the Sabbatical year a man may gather wood, stones, and grass from his own field in the same manner as he gathers them from the field of his neighbor in other years.

B. When transgressors of the laws of the Sabbatical year increased in number, they ordained that one man should gather stones from the field of another, and the other should gather from his field, so long as they do not do so as a mutual favor.

M. Sheb. 4:1

The concern here is that men conduct themselves in such a way that everyone can see the law is properly kept. Therefore the descriptive law invokes rules and their consequences in a manner quite different from the rules that emerge when we enter the system through the path of sanctions. Now we notice that those who choose to accord with the law simply draw the right conclusions concerning those who do not. They then make their own judgments and impose upon themselves the necessary restraints. The behavior of the other is not subject to sanctions. All rests upon the one who lives within (not merely by) the rule that describes that person.

Why so? It is hardly a sanction to the outsider not to accept from him, or extend to him, the hospitality of one's home and hearth. Nor can the outsider care about the details of the sorts of food he can purchase from the insider. Then how does the system actually function? It operates by internalizing norms in such a way as to inculcate an attitude of care and thoughtfulness in relationships within, as well as on the borders of, the community. Descriptive rules telling how things are yield, then, twin modes of enforcement: self-restraint on the inside, suspicion and perpetual care in dealing with the outside. These then form the frontiers of the politics, and everyone not only keeps the law but on his or her own enforces it. That explains the functioning of the law when the courts are not in session and the agents of Heaven and earth alike are occupied elsewhere, that is to say, the way the law works when it is meant to be descriptive and not prescriptive. The negative sanction that sustains the descriptive character of the law is distrust. The positive one is reliance upon the other. Distrust leads to shunning. Confidence leads to acceptance in community.

These are not only powerful social forces; by reason of that socially sanctioned power, they also are profoundly political. They can be invoked where no legitimate violence is assumed possible or required. Then who exercises ultimate power? It is not the institutions and the bureaucracy which, in setting forth the system, we examined in detail. Nor is there an appeal to a myth of a political character. Ultimate power lies in the hands of those who conform to the natural law that defines the *polis*.[17] But the locative sense in which *polis* must always be understood, it is not a policy. It is, nonetheless, the political entity of this system. That entity is not locative but utopian: wherever in the Holy Land the Holy People is located, there we find the counterpart to the *polis* of the politics of Aristotle. The politics of Israel takes place in the holy Israel. That is the point made countless times, as in the following:

A. Nothing is prohibited on account on the laws of diverse kinds except wool and flax that are spun or woven together, as it is written, *You shall not wear* shaatnez [Dt. 22:112], something which is hackled, spun, or woven.

B. R. Simeon b. Eleazar says, "It is turned away, and it turns his father in Heaven against him."

M. Kil. 9:8

When we recall the persistent appeal in the context of the political myth to God's engagement in the political life of holy Israel, we find ourselves prepared for such a claim as is represented here.

To understand what is to come we must recall the observations (in chapter 7) about the consubstantiality of divine and human will, attitude, and intention: what God wants is what humanity should want, and God responds to the attitudes of human beings. The upshot for the present inquiry is simple: the counterpart to the positive sanction of enjoying God's favor and the negative one of being denied it ("his father in Heaven is turned away from him") is appeal to sages' approbation or disapproval. True, the politics of this Judaism is a politics that claims the power of life and death, the authority to deprive a person of property, to transfer goods from one party to another, to inflict physical injury. At the same time, the politics repeatedly appeals to the good or ill will of sages, and that sanction, falling outside of the system of explicit penalties and rewards, proves a critical factor in the representation of the system's functioning. Specifically, where the law is one thing but good public policy another, sages intervene and approve conduct beyond the minimal requirements of the law, as in the following instances:

A. One who repays a debt cancelled by the Sabbatical year—the sages are pleased with him.

B. One who borrows money from a convert whose children converted with him need not repay the debt to his children. But if the debtor repaid the children the debt owing to their father after the father's death, the sages are pleased with him.

C. All chattels are acquired through drawing them into one's possession. But anyone who stands by his word and does not withdraw from the transaction before the chattels have changed hands—the sages are pleased with him.

M. Sheb. 10:9

A. The cow of R. Eleazar b. Azariah would go out with a strap between its horns—

B. not with the approval of the sages.

M. Shab. 5:4

A. Six rules did the men of Jericho make. For three sages reproved them, and for three they did not reprove them.
B. These are the three for which they did not reprove them:
C. they grafted palms on the fourteenth of Nisan throughout the day; they did not make the prescribed divisions in reciting the Shema; they reaped and stacked wheat before the offering of the *omer,* and they did not reprove them.
D. And these are the three for which they reproved them: they permitted use of Egyptian figs, from stems which had been dedicated to the Temple; they ate on the Sabbath fruit which had fallen under a tree; they left over the corner of the field in the case of vegetables, and sages did reprove them.

M. Pes. 4:8

A. All those who enter the Temple mount enter at the right, go around, and leave at the left, except for him to whom something happened, who goes around to the left.
B. "What ails you, that you go around to the left?" . . .
C. "For I am excommunicated."
D. " 'May he who dwells in this house put it into their heart that they draw you near again.' "

M. Mid. 2:2

We recall in this context evidence that the politics exhibited a clear sense of the limitations of institutional power. We confront a system that works by consensus, even while claiming access to violence at its disposal. In this connection we call to mind specific allegations, however the law may describe reality, there are facts of power to contend with:

> Rabban Yohanan b. Zakkai decreed against calling courts into session for such a matter. For the priests pay attention to you when it comes to putting someone out but not when it comes to drawing someone near.
>
> M. Ed. 8:3

> . . . Elijah is not going to come to declare unclean or to declare clean, to put out or to draw near, but only to put out those who have been brought near by force and to draw near those who have been put out by force.
>
> M. Ed. 8:7

Here is an instance in which sages' approval or disapproval registers and years of law observance are declared null.

A. In Mahoz people dampened wheat in sand. Sages said to them, "If thus you have been doing, you have never prepared food in accord with the rules of cleanness in your entire lives."

M. Makh. 3:4

All that registers is disapproval. The account does not invoke any concrete penalty; it merely represents the announcement of a rule. This item then forms the counterpart to the systemic evidence that within Israel lie forces beyond sages' control. When, therefore, we ask how the system functioned, as opposed to how it is portrayed as a structure, the politics of this Judaism portrays a dual reality, as I said. And before us, I think, is how people conceded things really were.

Nor is incapacity to enforce the law upon all Israelites the sole constraint upon the power of the politics of this Judaism. Surrounding recalcitrant Israel are gentiles, and these represent power—if not a differentiated and well-labeled power concentrated in institutions and susceptible of clear identification. In the following, tax collectors are clearly Jews, but gentiles (supervising?) likewise are expected to join in what is self-evidently a transaction outside the framework of Judaism's politics and Israel's power:

A. If tax collectors entered a house, the house is unclean.
B. If a gentile is with them, they are believed to state, "We did not enter," but they are not believed to state, "We entered but did not touch anything."
C. Thieves who entered the house—unclean is only the place trodden by the feet of thieves.
D. And what do they render unclean?
E. Food, liquid, and open clay utensils.
F. But couches and seats and clay utensils bearing a tight seal are clean.
G. If there is a gentile with them or a woman, everything is held to be unclean.

M. Toh. 7:6

The gentile and the nonobservant Israelite, engaged in activities beyond the sanctions of the system and also outside of its control, attest to political realities that the politics of this Judaism acknowledges but cannot then account for. The system copes in the theory with Israelite disobedience and with felonies or sins committed by Jews. But the conduct of tax collectors and presumably other gentile agencies lies outside the range of even speculative politics. The system can account only for the consequences of powerful external forces as far as the private conduct of faithful Israelites is concerned. That is to say, the system addresses only the things that its component persons control. In effect, it defines the cultic status of chairs, beds, pots and pans.

However, any account of the politics' functioning that treats power and the systemic account of public policy as more or less the same thing misses the power of the system's political theory. In their portrayal of how Judaism's politics functioned, the system builders acknowledged weakness just as they set forth a claim to effective government. No well-crafted theory of politics can omit all reference to the world beyond, to the world outside the political control of (in this case) Israel's power, yet inevitably in conflict with that same power. The nuanced account of the effects of power covers the fully obedient in relationship to the only partially conforming, the sinner or felon within the power of the system (as represented), the person or agency utterly beyond the power of the system. That capacity for nuance attests to the strength and persuasive force of the political system at hand, which acknowledges strength and also weakness, thereby claiming that it can at the very least explain what it clearly cannot control.

Accordingly, the treatment of tax collectors, the partially observant, the disobedient sage, as well as the concession that within Israel freedom brings conflict with order, the will of the Israelite standing over against the will of God—all of these diverse modes of conceding and also *explaining* the facts of the social order form a persuasive case indeed, one for a simple proposition. The politics of Judaism not only describes how people acknowledge things really are; it also can account for, can set forth the governing rules of, those same realities. And to be able to explain—to know the rule even when the rule does not (yet) govern—that forms a considerable claim to the power of rational discourse. How so? True control takes far more forms than that of mere coercion. Control also comprises knowledge of how things work, of how they are but also are supposed to be.

Thus the legitimate rationality of the politics of this Judaism far transcends the range of power, the legitimate resort to violence to secure conformity to the social order. In this system, the ultimate sanction is right knowledge, revelation. To that sanction, politics in its concrete resort to legitimate violence, whether through earthly or Heavenly agencies, stands subordinated. The system invokes a politics, but it is not a political system.[18] The contrast with the politics posited by Weber therefore is easily drawn. Weber's politics is disembedded, the Mishnah's politics is systemically embedded. This Judaism is a religious system that accomplishes its goals through the social order and therefore, along the way, sets forth an economics and a politics and a philosophy. But any claim that a free-standing economics, politics, or philosophy emerges proves insufficient and merely partial. A religious system integrates rather than differentiates, and, by definition, every social component of a religious system must be embedded and wholly defined within the context of that religion. Religion then forms the independent variable; in its setting, all other variables prove subordinate, and so too politics. That simple fact, richly illustrated here, explains why Weber's comments on religion and politics prove monumentally irrelevant to religion.

A clear claim to precisely that kind of control in the end characterizes the power of Judaism's politics. Accordingly, sorting out the political theory of power encompasses the theoretical explanation of lack of power. And that acute and accurate sense for the true proportions of things accounts for the politics of this Judaism seen whole and complete: the structure, comprising myth, institutions, personnel, the system, with its passion, responsibility, and, most impressively, quite realistic sense for the right balance and order of the functioning politics as a whole. True, we uncover a politics of Eden, with two all-powerful wills, God's and humanity's, in conflict. True, at stake in such politics is life eternal for the political entity, holy Israel. And yet, to be serviceable, as the Mishnah's politics in its fundamental principles proved to be, the politics had to accord with perceived reality (if not in most of its details). How to solve the problem? Merely to concede that Israel is weak, therefore its politics have to accommodate weakness, hardly suffices.

What had to be done, and what was done, was to show that the condition of Israel politically corresponds to the basic structure of humanity in its very being. Politics becomes a statement not of worldly power but of ontological truth, and that accounts, in the case at hand, for the laconic and descriptive character of political discourse. This is how things are, because this is how we are: the world corresponds to the self, politics to psychology. And, when we remember humanity is "in our image, after our likeness," the pathos, not the power, of God intervenes as the central political principle of Judaism. That is how the politics of this Judaism not only explained power but also accommodated the reality of this-worldy weakness. Israel's powerlessness matched the individual's frailty. And, "in our image, after our likeness," humanity's vulnerability formed the counterpart to God's point of weakness: God cared what humanity wanted, attended to but did not control the attitude, emotion, sentiment, intentionality, of humanity. Weakness, incapacity, frailty—these are relative. To be weak in one way is to be strong in another. Power is pathos.

At stake in politics was not only the brave vision of power over death and beyond the grave. At issue also was an account of power that the prospective political community could find plausible. And weakness was made plausible as a function of restraint, accommodation as an expression of self-control. To be plausible the community did not have to imagine itself omnipotent. If the all-powerful God could give way, in infinite love, before the will of frail humanity, then no politics needed to posit that systemic claim to unflawed omnipotence that, in any case, Israel did not have. That is why an account of power in the case of the politics of Israel concludes with the recognition that, out there, there really are both tax collectors who can walk uninvited into one's very home, and, therefore, a power that could send them. To face that fact and not surrender to the admission of utter futility—that, I think, forms the single most powerful affirmation in the politics of this Judaism. And the success of this politics finds its measure in its power for a very long time and under remarkably diverse circumstances to make weakness plausible and reasonable.

When we speak of the description, analysis, and interpretation of systems, we have to compare not what one system deems rational with what another one identifies as logical and orderly and sane; rather, we have to see how, in comparison and contrast, two or more systems cope with what is chaotic and beyond all order—for that is the human situation common to all systems (so, at the end of this century, it seems to me). But of all systems we cannot speak, so we shall address just one other.

Before proceeding, let me call attention to where we now stand. This Judaism's theory of the social order encompasses a politics, puts to the fore a theory of the exercise of power, not merely propositions of a philosophical or theological character, perhaps accompanied by the exercise of persuasion or demonstration. We now know that this Judaism fabricates the view of an "Israel" that constitutes a political entity, that is empowered to commit acts of legitimate violence. Its "Israel" is not a merely voluntary community of the likeminded faithful. I now have demonstrated beyond any doubt that the politics of this "Israel" encompasses a state governed by an established, enlandised, and fully empowered civil service, in place and running things.

How then are we to gain perspective upon this farrago of fantasy about kings and high priests, with its power formally in the hands of a genealogical caste but really exercised by "sages," a profession (not a class defined by relationship to means of production) of clerks or hired intellectuals? And what are we to make of the political definition of "Israel"? In setting forth my general theory of the work of comparison and contrast, I mean to explain precisely how I shall come up with answers to those questions.

PART THREE
THE POLITICS OF JUDAISM
IN SYSTEMIC CONTEXT

9

Judaism's Initial Politics

A Theory of Comparison and Contrast

In Judaism, as its first post-Temple statement suggests, you can legitimately impoverish, maim, or kill people who sin or commit crime, that is to say, people who do not conform in deed and in deliberation—you can penalize both attitude and action. Since attitude, emotion, and intentionality need not come to expression in the social order or bear consequences for society as a whole, they may be deemed narrowly religious in focus. So in the terms carefully defined now, this Judaism appears a political religion, a religion that not only addresses the social order and proposes political agencies for its governance, but that also encompasses within the political framework matters of narrowly religious definition. It comprises a religious politics, a political religion.

And that paramount systemic trait is odd, as I pointed out in the introduction, since other Judaisms (and, for several centuries to come, a wide variety of Christianities too) do not represent themselves as political religions. Among the writings of other Judaisms in antiquity (for instance, the fragments assembled as the apocryphal and pseudoepigraphic collections the Dead Sea scrolls, and the like), we find—at best—episodic references to political facts but no counterpart to the sustained political theory.

None portrays an account of the structure and system of politics as this-worldly disposition of coercion and legitimate violence affecting all "Israel"; none mirrors the Mishnah.[1] Other authors and authorships respond to political facts but do not invent them; they reject or affirm the conduct of the Temple as arbiter of power and mediator of the supernatural, but they do not theorize on what they will do when in charge. And they cannot conceive of what it means to be in charge.[2] Few other system builders who focused upon the social order[3] within the Judaisms and Christianities of the first three centuries of the common era sustainedly and systematically asked political questions at all. In that context, the answers take second place to the fact that the questions enjoyed primacy, as chapters 3 through 8 have shown us.

Accordingly, a rough and rapid negative comparison—who does not set forth a political Judaism at all?—draws us back to our initial inquiry: why a politics for this Judaism in particular? And what systemic purpose was supposed to be accomplished by the political structure and system we have now described? Addressing these questions allows us to transform a mass of inchoate information into interesting and useful data, for by undertaking to phrase a thesis, to ask a question and propose an answer, I may endow the facts with meaning. Since the specific question I find critical is, "Why politics at all, and why, in particular, *this kind* of politics rather than some other?" the reader must immediately wonder, "And precisely what kind of politics is that?" And since that question governs all else, we must not only describe the politics of this Judaism (which we have accomplished), we must also analyze that same politics. The work of analysis imposes a labor of characterization that transcends the report of systemic facts intelligibly arrayed in accessible categories such as Weber has supplied for us. We require a new guide to the theory of things; Weber did his service in helping us to start the work. But as soon as we recognized the difference between a freestanding politics and a systemically embedded politics, we found Weber's categories somewhat limited—and restrictive.

But what kind of guide now, and who in particular, will lead us? The guide must be a system builder, a philosopher. For reasons I shall set forth at length, here in theory, in the next chapter in fact, Aristotle will serve as our pathfinder and companion. But the path from description to the beginning of analysis and interpretation has first to be theorized and charted. Why? I propose to compare the Mishnah's politics with Aristotle's, the indicative character of the Mishnah's system with the fundamental and generative traits of Aristotle's system. That is a new venture and demands explanation even in its inception: why is it appropriate, even necessary, to compare writings hitherto deemed incomparable and apparently remote from one another?[4]

As I suggested in my introduction, to characterize one thing I have to adduce in evidence some other thing of the same sort; to know what kind of thing one thing is, I have to know two or more things of the same type. That knowledge, making possible comparison and contrast, allows me to describe the kind of thing I propose to account for. If of a given class of things I know only one thing, then I really understand nothing. I can describe facts or paraphrase statements, but I cannot explain anything beyond itself. Hence I cannot explain anything, for explanation requires appeal to more than the case; the case must serve as exemplary, or explanation turns in upon itself and becomes a mere recapitulation of unexplained traits. So to see the whole and identify its indicative traits, we require a sustained exercise of comparison. This means comparing one system's politics to another's. Since we must now attempt to understand the mode of thought of the system as a whole, we require a context in and against which we may grasp all of the data whole and in correct proportion and composition.[5]

If we now know what people have decided that they want to know, we have yet to gain perspective, through a process of comparison and contrast, upon the questions. That will provide us with insight into how the authorship before us has defined what it wishes to know. Knowing what two or more authorships have wanted to know in addressing issues of politics affords perspective on what each authorship has found of urgent interest, for in its address to questions of the legitimate and social use of violence, what one authorship stresses may scarcely intersect with the program found critical by some other authorship. If that is so, then merely because two authorships adventitiously have asked the same question or even reached the same conclusion, we cannot claim to know more than an accidental fact of no systemic weight of meaning. That explains why we go off in search of the key to the system of thought, by which I mean the logic by which questions (in this context: political questions) are generated and by which the right modes of thought for forming and answering those questions are made to appear to be self-evident. And, as is self-evident, in the nature of all knowledge, that search leads us beyond the limits of the evidence before us. Who knows only one thing understands nothing.

Before identifying an appropriate source of a system for comparison and contrast, I have first to specify the rules governing my choice. Now what exactly are the theoretical rules that govern inquiry through comparison and contrast? When we propose to compare one thing with something else, it is because we perceive among like things basic points of difference that bear significance. Accordingly, the first task is to establish likeness. But if things are exactly alike, then they are the same thing. So the second task is to identify points of difference.[6] Comparison in a methodical way is a methodical manipulation of difference. Once we show a system to be like some other, we then may ask how the one differs from the other. But the process, once inaugurated, reverses itself. Because there will be points of difference, we can discern commonalities and important traits of sameness. The order of argument then is clear.

The alternative to this view is the more commonly held program. First, people compare details. Second, they look for difference. They are wrong on both counts. Comparing details out of context yields no useful insight, because without defining the detail's context in a complete system, we cannot know that one detail in its setting bears the same weight and meaning as the other in its circumstance. Only by comparing one whole system to another (a Judaism to another system) and then turning to the systemic component of special interest to us (comparing the politics of that Judaism to the politics of that other system) shall we produce insight deriving from our grasp of the context of detail.[7] E. P. Sanders states the case with some force. He writes:

> What is clearly desirable then is to compare an entire religion, parts and all, with an entire religion, parts and all; to use the analogy of a building, to compare two buildings, not leaving out of account their individual bricks. The problem is now to discover two wholes, both of which are considered and defined on their own merits and in their own terms, to be compared with each other.[8]

What about starting with difference? Ignoring the issue of systemic like-ness—hence comparability!—causes problems for a different reason. Dis-cerning (mere) difference is an act of fabrication and imputation; it operates subjectively, deep within the murky recesses of impressions and instincts and inchoate hunches. Accordingly, I look first to the surfaces of things—points in common, systems that prove congruent—to establish a context for com-parison and contrast; I identify points of difference among two systems that I have already shown to be in some consequential way like one another. The alternative is to wander aimlessly in search of connections, likenesses, among things that have not been shown to begin with to stand in relationship at all.

Establishing systemic likeness and outlining the likeness and difference of the systemic component under study here form the first two layers of theoreti-cal inquiry. The third and final one is then to ask what is at stake. (The more familiar, American framing of the question is simply, "So what?") Having defined the arena for comparative study, what do I claim we learn that we did not know before we juxtaposed two congruent yet differentiable systems (in this context: intellectual compositions forming propositions for the social order made up of facts, viewpoints, bits of data)? What questions do I answer that I could not answer before the act of juxtaposition, comparison, and con-trast? Let me state the problem with heavy emphasis: *what* else *do we know, what* more *do we know, than we knew before we tried to apply what the one thing shows us to the case of two things?*

The answer to the questions "what else? what more?" furthermore requires taking account of the things people might have done, alternatives that others did choose. Confronting the (theoretical) range of choices as to politics, I pro-pose to make sense of the chosen.[9] In the comparison and contrast of systems set within a single, legitimated and defined continuum, I am able to make sense of one system by playing it off against the other. The useful end of the game of comparison, then, is to discover, through the might-have-beens of culture, the meaning of what was, for the work of interpretation begins when the task of description has made available two or more sets of interesting and well-composed facts. It begins when the work of description has shown that the one thing applies to the case of two things. Out of description, now done, emerges the labor of analysis, leading to interpretation, and both of these de-pend upon the exercise of comparison and therefore of contrast.[10]

To define the systemic context, let us now return to some simple facts. The most striking is also the most puzzling: this Judaism encompasses within its systemic statement a complete politics. It follows that this Judaism is politi-cal. I claim that that trait is surprising because, as briefly noted just now, not all Judaisms and Christianities made up a politics for themselves. Second, the social realities defining Israel's existence assigned politics to other-than-Israelite authorities. There was scarcely a working regime among the Jews that required a political theory or made credible this particular version of a theory of politics.[11] The Jews of the Land of Israel, who constitute the Mishnah's "Israel," in the second century hardly formed a political entity at all. Representing "Israel" as political, setting forth what I have called a political religion, seems implausible: *that* subject is surely not for that here and that now. True, later in the century, at the time of the Mishnah's publication ca. A.D. 200, some Jews exercised a measure of power, backed by Rome, over other Jews. But that purely local authority over matters of merely internal concern hardly made of them a state, complete with kings, high priests, temples, courts, and administration. In the time in which the Mishnah's authorship did its work, there were no Israelite kings, no high priests, no Temple and no orderly and well-situated government. So to appeal to the requirements of society is a poor initiative. As an account of how things are, in its laconic and merely descriptive language, the Mishnah can provoke only incredulity.

But let us place the fantastic nature of the politics into context. Since, in the Judaism as a whole we deal with not fact but fantasy, the question "why a politics?" is no more surprising in light of the facts of the age than "why a theory of the cult?" or "why an account of the mysteries of cultic uncleanness?" [12] The answer to the question of why this, not that, can appeal to facts of the age no more plausibly in one matter than in any other. In fact, the topical program of the system encompasses subjects chosen for reasons important to the system builders. When we understand the whole, we shall grasp the traits of the parts, beginning with their fundamental topical or thematic interests. But in a well-crafted system for the social order, since all things are meant to cohere and form a congruent statement, the answer provided for any one of the parts should in theory account for the choice of the other parts as well. And as a matter of fact, the historical or social facts of the day play no substantial role in the formation of the politics, the theory of the cult, the account of cultic uncleanness, and a wide variety of other subjects. Not only so, but those same historical or social facts ought to have produced tractates (sustained considerations) on a variety of subjects that the system does not treat at all. [13]

Since what I wish to know is why then the system builders found it necessary to encompass politics within their larger systemic statement, I have to identify in the enormous detail before us—the politics—that message definitive of the system as a whole that was meant to come to expression through the politics in particular. And for that purpose, too, I need to find out how, in some other politics, a message characteristic of the system as a whole could come to the surface through the politics in particular. Why in the case of this Judaism did the authorship make its statement through political as much as through theological, philosophical, or economic statements? That question takes on weight when we know what in the case of some other systemic composition an authorship did in the same way. Clearly, then, to grasp the statement of a system, we have to place it into context and also into comparison as well. The alternative is merely to paraphrase.

What is like may be contrasted with what is unlike. But what establishes likeness? And where to begin? First, in my view, we have to identify likeness, then observe difference. So to begin with I seek to compare what is alike in basic structure and system and, as a happenstance, exhibits points of commonality and difference in detail. At stake are not facts but how facts are assembled into a coherent statement and structure. Facts out of context serve not at all; facts in context draw attention beyond themselves, outward to their systemic settings. If we know how, in Papua New Guinea, the clear counterpart to a high priest and a king divide power and rule a state (head man, magician, tribe, to use rough and ready counterparts), and if we compare and contrast this case with how the high priest and the king in the Mishnah's Judaism distribute the powers of government, we learn nothing we can use for comparison and contrast, for these are mere facts. Further, we scarcely have access to a statement of the politics of Papua New Guinea's nonliterary social entity, and thus lack a usable counterpart to the Mishnah for purposes of comparison and contrast. That is to say, the Mishnah constitutes an encompassing statement on a variety of subjects, all of them pertinent in the composition of a portrait of the life of holy Israel. But Papua New Guinea's seven hundred and fifty language communities share no such encompassing statement in writing, to my knowledge, to which I could compare the Mishnah's system (except the ones written by anthropologists, and they hardly count in the present context).

Seeing things whole, sorting things out in accord with the system's rules of differentiation, classification, category formation, in all explaining why this, not that: these intellectual tasks phrase the questions that come first. Only in the context of systemic analysis are we able to focus upon the particular topic at hand; we move from systemic proposition to the particularities of politics (or of economics, or of philosophy), and not the other way around. Does it follow that, for purposes of comparison and contrast, any system of coherent thought about principal issues of social being serves equally well as any other? In theory, yes.

But in practice some serve better than others. True, we may well compare the politics of the Judaism set forth by the Mishnah with the politics of a social system set forth by an Indian or Chinese metaphysician or philosopher, as much as with the politics of Plato, Aristotle, Augustine, Aquinas, Hobbes, Hegel, or Marx. In all cases the conditions for theoretical analysis are met: a system of encompassing thought about humanity in society, in which among the topical program are issues of power and its legitimate utilization. Accordingly, no obstacle stands in the way of drawing into alignment for purposes of theoretical analysis, comparison, and contrast, the politics of this Judaism and the politics of Plato, Hobbes, or Marx.

But a special circumstance, which I shall now explain in some detail, requires us to pay closest attention to a single system builder, one among the many great intellectual figures who encompassed within their well-crafted systems of thought concerning the social order fundamental questions about the exercise of power under in a cloak of legitimacy. That figure is Aristotle.

But his role is so critical to the venture that justifying my choice requires an entire chapter (chapter 10) and considerable attention to detail. When we know why he best serves the purposes of comparison and contrast for the politics of this Judaism, we shall find our way to the critical and central questions, the answers to which will allow us to see in context and with full clarity as to proportion and structure the politics of this Judaism. The hermeneutical fulcrum of inquiry, then, will be located at the point at which the politics of this Judaism and the politics of Aristotle come together. There we find validation for the act of comparison. And that act of comparison will not take place merely as a matter of caprice—topical comparison—or even of well-balanced and proportioned weighing out of comparable alternatives—systemic comparison. The comparison of like things to show the difference, rather than of unlike things to show the similarity, will prove necessary, inexorable, profoundly logical. And that is how we shall proceed.

Let me state in advance the outline of the argument to come, so that the reader will see *in nuce* how I have attempted to meet the conditions for comparison and contrast that I have identified in this discussion. The economics of Judaism and of Aristotle take identical positions on the householder—the person who commands the means of production. For both, he constitutes the building block of the political economy. In the systematic thought of each party, the householder, commanding the fundamental unit of production, forms the point of departure. For both parties, too, the householders together form the village, and, as we shall see, it is at that point, in the agglomeration of villages made up of householders, that Aristotle defines politics, the life of the city or *polis*. The sages of the Mishnah concur as to the village; critical to their system is its principal social entity, the village, comprising households. Indeed, the model, from household to village to "all Israel," comprehensively describes whatever of "Israel" the authorship at hand has chosen to describe. In this aspect, however, the sages part company from Aristotle, whose basic social metaphor, the city, differs at its foundations from that of sages who leap from village to "Israel." My task is first, in chapter 10, to establish these facts, and then, in chapter 11, to explain them. Finally, in chapter 12, I shall draw those conclusions as to the comparison of systems, and of politics within systems, that in my judgment define the stakes for my entire analysis of the politics of this Judaism.

10

Why Aristotle in Particular?

It is natural to begin with Aristotle, who was in a class by himself among
the political theorists and sociologists of antiquity: he studied the politics
and sociology of the Greek city more closely than anyone else; he thought
more profoundly about these subjects and he wrote more about them than
anyone.

G. E. M. de Ste. Croix

Three considerations make Aristotle's system uniquely valid for comparison
with the Mishnah's.[1]

First, the Mishnah's generative mode of inquiry is the same as that pursued
by Aristotle in his natural philosophy. It depends on the formation of genera
made up of species.

Second, if we wish to compare a politics with another politics, we have also
to compare an economics with an economics, for since a politics tells who
may do what to whom, it consequently dictates who gets to keep what. That
constitutes a judgment extending to the disposition of scarce resources.[2] In
antiquity, the only economics of importance is that of Aristotle.[3]

Third, in addition to these two rather general considerations, there is a particular one that makes the comparison ineluctable. For both accounts of the
social order in its structure and system, the building block of the social entity
is identified as the irreducible unit of production, and the formative component in the social entity is the person who controls the means of production. In
both cases this is the householder. So the two systems are methodologically
congruent; they both treat politics as part of an account of the larger social
order; and they concur that the householder is the building block of politics.
With these fundamental points in common, we shall (in chapter 11) undertake
a comparison yielding an important contrast: the building block of Aristotle's
politics and economics is one and the same, the householder,[4] but that is not
the case for the politics of this Judaism. This fact produces the analytical

question that allows us (in chapter 12) to enter deep into the heart of the politics of this Judaism. And that, of course, is our goal.

As a matter of fact, in their method the Mishnah's framers analyzed problems in the manner of Aristotle. In the philosophy of Judaism, the fundamental purpose of all intellectual inquiry is to discover the way things are and therefore are supposed to be.[5] It aims, then, to secure for each thing its correct place in the natural order. If we know the category to which an apparent singleton belongs, then we define the rule that governs that item too. We secure for what appears abnormal a normal status, and for what seems odd a routine position with other things of its class. In so doing, we accomplish rational explanation; we find a genus for what appears to be sui generis, beyond rationality. Classification therefore is the medium by which we explain. By definition, therefore, that mode of thought applies in a single way to all domains of being—the natural and the social in the natural world and the supernatural realm as well. A single rationality pertains to the givens of all being, here and above too. The power of intellect, obeying the laws of correct classification or organization of things, holds the whole together in perfect balance, sense, and consequence. At stake in identifying the principles of classification therefore is the correct understanding of the dynamic of the philosophy of Judaism.

In philosophical method I see three basic principles repeatedly invoked by the Judaic system represented by the Mishnah. The first is to identify the correct definition or character of something and to preserve that essence. So we begin with the thing itself. Our premise is that we can identify the intrinsic or true or inherent traits of a thing, the thing seen by itself.[6] But we then ask in what way something is like something else, and in what way it differs. Our premise is that in some ways things are like other things; traits may be shared. So we proceed to the comparison of things. That requires us to identify the important traits that impart the definitive character or classification to a variety of distinct things. So we proceed to a labor of comparison and contrast. The third principle is that like things fall into a single classification, with its rule, and unlike things into a different classification, with the opposite rule. That conception, simple on the surface, defines the prevailing logic throughout the entire philosophy. At no point do we find any other logic in play. The problems develop, as we shall see in the next chapter, when we turn to concrete problems of classification.

The system of ordering all things in their proper place and under the proper rule maintains that like belongs with like and conforms to the rule governing like—the unlike goes over to the opposite and conforms to the opposite rule. When we make lists of the like, we also know the rule governing all the items on those lists. We also know one other thing, namely, the opposite rule, governing all items sufficiently like to belong on those lists, but sufficiently unlike to be placed on other lists. That rigorously philosophical logic of analysis, comparison and contrast, serves because it is the only logic that can serve a system that proposes to make a statement concerning order and right array.

The mode of thought, of course, comes from natural philosophy, out of which natural science has evolved. But while the speciation of genera is not Aristotle's alone, it is Aristotle who set matters forth with the greatest clarity and power. The method is simply stated. Faced with a mass of facts, we are able to bring order—that is to say, to determine the nature of things—(1) by finding out which items resemble others and (2) determining the taxic indicator that forms of the lot a single classification, and then (3) determining the single rule to which all cases in that classification conform. That method of bringing structure and order out of the chaos of indeterminate facts pertains, on the very surface, to persons, places, things; to actions and attitudes; to the natural world of animals, minerals, vegetables; to the social world of castes and peoples, actions and functions; and to the supernatural world of the holy and the unclean, the possession of Heaven and the possession of earth, the sanctified and the common.

As to method, can we situate the taxonomic method of the sages—premises and rules—in the same category as the method of Aristotle?[7] We begin with the simple observation that the distinction between genus and species lies at the foundation of all philosophical knowledge as Aristotle discovers that knowledge. Adkins states the matter in the most accessible way. He writes: "Aristotle, a systematic biologist, uses his method of classification by genera and species, itself developed from the classificatory interests of the later Plato, to place man among other animals. . . . The classification must be based on the final development of the creature."[8] But to classify, we have to take as our premise that things are subject to classification, and that means they have traits that are essential and indicative, on the one side, but also shared with other things, on the other. The point of direct intersection between our Judaism's philosophy of hierarchical classification and the natural philosphy of Aristotle lies in their shared and critical conviction concerning the true nature or character of things. Both parties concur that there *is* such a true definition of what things really are—a commonplace for philosophers, and generative of interesting problems about Ideas, Form and Substance, Actual and Potential, and the like. But only Aristotle and the Mishnah systematically and thoroughly carry into the material details of economics that conviction about the true character or essence of definition of things. The economics of the Mishnah and the economics of Aristotle begin in the conception of "true value," and the distributive economics proposed by each philosophy then develops that fundamental notion. The principle is so fundamental to each system that comparison of one system to the other in those terms alone is not only justified but necessary.

But how are we to know the essential traits that allow us to define the true character of things, to classify them? This is the point at which our comparison becomes particular, since what we need to find out is whether there exist between Aristotle's and Judaism's philosophies only shared convictions about the genus and the species, or particular conceptions as to how these are to be identified and organized. The basic conviction on both sides is this: objects are not random but fall into classes and so may be described, analyzed, and explained by appeal to general traits or rules. The component of Aristotelianism that pertains here is "the use of deductive reasoning proceeding from self-evident principles or discovered general truths to conclusions of a more limited import; and syllogistic forms of demonstrative or persuasive arguments."[9]

The goal is the classification of things, which is to say, the discovery of general rules that apply to discrete data or instances. Minio-Paluello states,

> In epistemology . . . Aristotelianism includes a concentration on knowledge accessible by natural means or accountable for by reason; an inductive, analytical empiricism, or stress on experience in the study of nature . . . leading from the perception of contingent individual occurrences to the discovery of permanent, universal patterns; and the primacy of the universal, that which is expressed by common or general terms. In metaphysics, or the theory of Being, Aristotelianism involves belief in the primacy of the individual in the realm of existence; in correlated conceptions allowing an articulate account of reality (e.g., 10 categories; genus-species-individual, matter-form, potentiality-actuality, essential-accidental; the four material elements and their basic qualities; and the four causes—formal, material, efficient and final); in the soul as the inseparable form of each living body in the vegetable and animal kingdoms; in activity as the essence of things; and in the primacy of speculative over practical activity.[10]

The manner in which we accomplish this work is to establish categories of traits. These will yield the rules or generalizations that make possible both classification and, in the nature of things, hierarchization (to which we turn in chapter 12).

Enough has been said to justify using a shared method when comparing Aristotle's and Judaism's philosophies, but I have yet to specify what I conceive to be the generative point of comparison. It lies in two matters. The paramount consideration is the shared principles of formal logic. This I find blatant in the Mishnah, and all presentations of Aristotle's philosophy identify it as emblematic. The second consideration is obviously the taxonomic method, viewed from afar. Let us turn to the former first.

When we follow a simple account of the way in which we attain new truth, we find ourselves quite at home. Allan's account follows:[11]

> Induction . . . is the advance from the particular to the general. By the inspection of examples . . . in which one characteristic appears conjoined with another, we are led to propound a general rule which we suppose to be valid for cases not yet examined. Since the rule is of higher generality than the instances, this is an advance from a truth "prior for us" toward a truth "prior in nature."

My representation of the Mishnaic mode of presentation of cases that, with our participation, yield a general rule, accords with this inductive logic. But that impression requires qualification:

> On the other hand, sometimes two general truths, which are self-evident or not open to reasonable doubt, necessarily imply a third truth, of more limited scope. Such a procedure is deduction or demonstration. It advances from what is prior in nature towards which is prior for us, and, because it does this, has a completeness and a constraining force which is always missing in induction. It shows not merely that a fact is true but why it is true.

The theory of deduction forms the centerpiece of Aristotle's logic, so Allan maintains. We have already examined instances of the same deductive reasoning in the Mishnah.

And this observation carries us to the more important of the two principles of sound intellectual method, the taxonomic interest in defining through classification. As a matter of fact, this definitive trait of natural philosophy is what we find in common between Aristotle's and the Mishnah's philosophical method. These points in common prove far more than those yielded by the general observation that both systems appeal to the identification of genera out of species. In fact, what philosophers call the dialectical approach in Aristotle proves to be the same approach to the discovery or demonstration of truth as we find in the Mishnah. Owens sets the matter forth in the following language: "Since a theoretical science proceeds from first principles that are found within the thing under investigation, the initial task of the philosophy of nature will be to discover its primary principles in the sensible thing themselves." [12] I cannot imagine a formulation more suited to the method of the Mishnah than that simple statement.

Not only in scientific method, but also in substantive propositions concerning economics, the philosophers of the Mishnah stand in the circle of Aristotle—the only important thinker in economics in antiquity. [13] Still, my choice of Aristotle over Xenophon and Plato requires explanation, and we do well to begin with an account of the fundamental intellectual context in which economics as Aristotle was to define the field developed. For that purpose we review Polanyi's introduction to Aristotle's economics in its larger context. I refer to Polanyi because he, it seems to me, has taken the broadest perspective on Aristotle's economic thought:

> Whenever Aristotle touched on a question of the economy he aimed at developing its relationship to society as a whole. The frame of reference was the community as such which exists at different levels within all functioning human groups. In terms, then, of our modern speech Aristotle's approach to human affairs was sociological. In mapping out a field of study he would relate all questions of institutional origin and function to the totality of society. Community, self-sufficiency, and justice were the focal concepts. The group as a going concern forms a community (*koinonia*) the members of which are linked by the bond of good will (*philia*). Whether *oikos* or *polis* [household or village], or else, there is a kind of *philia* specific to that *koinonia*, apart from which the group could not remain. *Philia* ex-

presses itself in a behavior of reciprocity . . . , that is, readiness to take on burdens in turn and share mutually. Anything that is needed to continue and maintain the community, including its self-sufficiency . . . is "natural" and intrinsically right. Autarchy may be said to be the capacity to subsist without dependence on resources from outside. Justice . . . implies that the members of the community possess unequal standing. That which ensures justice, whether in regard to the distribution of the prizes of life or the adjudication of conflicts or the regulation of mutual services, is good since it is required for the continuance of the group. Normativity, then, is inseparable from actuality.[14]

So, Polanyi goes on, for Aristotle trade is "natural" when it contributes to the community's self-sufficiency. The just price derives from goodwill, *philia*, as a matter of reciprocity which is of the essence, Polanyi says, for all human community. "Prices are justly set if they conform to the standing of the participants in the community, thereby strengthening the goodwill on which community rests. . . . In such exchange no gain is involved; goods have their known prices, fixed beforehand." [15]

The theory of trade and price therefore elaborates the general theorem of the human community: "Community, self-sufficiency, and justice: these pivots of his sociology were the frame of reference of his thought on all economic matters, whether the nature of the economy or policy issues were at stake." [16] The economy concerns the household in particular, that is, "the relationship of the persons who make up the natural institution of the household." Why the interest, then, in economics at all? Polanyi's answer is that people had to link the requirements of communal existence and communal self-sufficiency to two matters of policy, trade and price. The fundamental notion was the self-sufficiency of the community, which yielded the principles that trade that served to restore self-sufficiency was in accord with nature; trade that did not was contrary. That is, prices should strengthen the bond of community. This is why Aristotle called commercial trade "hucksterism"—it had no bearing upon the sociology that mattered to him. He had no perception of the price-mechanism of supply and demand. Commerce was administered and institutional.

Aristotle was not the first to deal with economic questions. From the time of Thucydides Greeks knew the difference between real wealth such as fixed assets, real estate, and the like, which they valued, and money wealth, liquid capital and movables, which they did not value so highly. For Thucydides, the war against Troy involved the wealth of the community—measured in land and its products, quantities of arms, of treasures, of utensils, of metal, large houses, and slaves. In the time of the Peloponnesian War wealth took the form of coin, which could command all forms of real wealth.[17] But the economic theory of the important philosophers was primitive and unimportant in their larger work, which concerned politics, not economics. General principles with bearing on economic theory or policy, of course, can be identified—for example, Democritus' recognition of the subjective and relative character of utility.[18] But Plato's ideas on economic subjects are random.[19] Joseph A.

Schumpeter introduces Graeco-Roman economics with these words: "rudi-
mentary economic analysis is a minor element—a very minor one—in the
inheritance that has been left to us by our cultural ancestors, the ancient
Greeks." [20] The reason for that fact, many maintain, is that prior to the development of the market, economic activities were insufficiently differentiated to
attract particular attention. [21] When writers such as Xenophon, all the more so
the Romans later on, spoke about economics, they provided rules for household management, observation rather than analysis. [22]

Plato proposed to describe economics within the context of the ideal state,
which was to be large enough "to allow appropriate scope for the play of each
man's natural talent." [23] That is why a small state was adequate. In that context, Schumpeter describes Plato's perfect state:

> Plato's Perfect State was a City-State conceived for a small and, so far as pos-
> sible, constant number of citizens. As stationary as its population was to be its
> wealth. All economic and non-economic activity was strictly regulated—warriors,
> farmers, artisans . . . being organized in permanent castes, men and women be-
> ing treated exactly alike. Government was entrusted to one of these castes, the caste
> of guardians or rulers who were to live together without individual property or fam-
> ily ties. [24]

Schumpeter explains the "rigid stationarity" by appealing to Plato's dislike of
"the chaotic changes of his time. . . . Change, economic change, was at the
bottom of the development from oligarchy to democracy, from democracy to
tyranny." Plato's caste system rests upon the perception of the necessity of
some division of labor. [25] The emphasis lies upon the "increase of efficiency
that results from allowing everyone to specialize in what he is by nature best
fitted for." Plato's theory of money is that the value of money is on principle
independent of the stuff it is made of. [26] These points are of interest, of course,
but compared with Aristotle's economics, Plato's proves episodic and random,
not part of a well-composed system of the social order.

Aristotle too proposed to think through the requirements of the state, and it
is in that context, as with Plato, that his economic thought, that political economy that characterizes the Mishnah's system as well, went forward. Aristotle
dealt with property and the art of managing the household (in Greek, called
"economics"). The fundamental of Aristotle's economics is the distinction
between *oikonomikē* and *chrēmatistikē,* the former involving wealth consumed in the satisfaction of wants and the use of commodities or goods for
that purpose, the latter, wealth-getting, money-making, and exchange. [27]
"Chrematistics" includes both unnatural and natural means, barter, the former, retail trade and money making the latter. Exchange is natural, therefore.
Things have a primary and a secondary use; the primary use of a shoe is for
wearing, the secondary, for trading or exchanging. As to value, Plato had
maintained that one "should not attempt to raise the price, but simply ask the
value," while Aristotle introduces the notion of subjective value and the

usefulness of the commodity: "In the truest and most real sense, this standard lies in wants, which is the basis of all association among men."

So Haney: "An exchange is just when each gets exactly as much as he gives the other; yet this equality does not mean equal costs, but equal wants."[28] In book 5 of the *Nicomachean Ethics* and book 1 of the *Politics,* economic analysis, a subsection of other matters, comes to the fore. In the case of the *Ethics,* Aristotle treats economics in the context of justice. Aristotle concerns himself with distributive justice, such as that involving honors, goods, and other possessions. Justice means equality. Corrective justice involves private relations between individuals, in which "it may be necessary to 'straighten out' a situation, to rectify an injustice by removing the (unjust) gain and restoring the loss."[29] Aristotle had in mind fraud or breach of contract, not an "unjust" price.[30] In *Politics,* Aristotle addresses as the context in which (fair) exchange is discussed the forms of human association, which are the household and, made of households, the *polis.* Here he deals with issues of authority—dominance and subjection—which form the center of political theory. And in that context, he treats, also, property and modes of acquiring it, asking whether "the art of acquiring" property is the same as "the art of household management," that *oikonomikē* which we met earlier.[31] What Aristotle contributed to economic theory covers the economic organization of society, the matter of communal versus private property, and value and exchange.[32] On this latter topic, Spiegel states:

> Aristotle makes the important distinction between use and exchange, which later was to be expanded into the distinction between value in use and value in exchange. The true and proper use of goods . . . is the satisfaction of natural wants. A secondary or improper use occurs when goods are exchanged for the sake of monetary gain. Thus, all exchanges for monetary gain are labeled as unnatural. This includes specifically commerce and transportation, the employment of skilled and unskilled labor, and lending at interest. The exchange of money for a promise to pay back the principal with interest is considered the most unnatural one. . . . Lending at interest yields gain from currency itself instead of from another exchange transaction which money as a medium of exchange is designed to facilitate. Money begets no offspring; if nevertheless there is one—interest—this is contrary to all nature.[33]

The essential point, Spiegel notes, is the emphasis on the mutuality of give and take. Each gives to the other something equivalent to what he receives from the other.

As Finley notes, we cannot translate the abstraction "the economy" into Greek. Finley's judgment of Xenophon as an economist is this: "In Xenophon there is not one sentence that expresses an economic principle or offers any economic analysis, nothing on the efficiency of production, 'rational' choice, the marketing of crops."[34] From that kind of writing, for the reason given by Finley, economics could not come: "Without the concept of relevant 'laws' (or 'statistical uniformities' if one prefers) it is not possible to have a concept of 'economy.'"[35] Schumpeter for his part sees Aristotle as a figure of "more than slightly pompous common sense."[36] But the analytic intention makes him an interesting figure. As to economic problems, the interest was subordinate; social and political analysis predominated in his program. Schumpeter described Aristotle's general contribution to social science in these words:

> [1] that not only was Aristotle, like a good analyst, very careful about his concepts but that he also coordinated his concepts into a conceptual apparatus, that is, into a system of tools of analysis that were related to one another and were meant to be used together . . . ; [2] that . . . he investigated processes of change as well as states; [3] that he tried to distinguish between features of social organisms or of behavior that exist by virtue of universal or inherent necessity and others that are instituted by legislative decision or custom; [4] that he discussed social institutions in terms of purposes and of the advantages and disadvantages they seemed to him to present.[37]

Aristotle's economics, in *Politics* 1:8–11 and *Ethics* 5:5, comprise an economic analysis based upon wants and their satisfactions, so Schumpeter: "Starting from the economy of self-sufficient households, he then introduced division of labor, barter, and, as a means of overcoming the difficulties of direct barter, money—the error of confusing wealth with money duly coming in for stricture. There is no theory of 'distribution.'"[38]

When, in all, I turn to Aristotle for my source of comparisons, it is on the basis of the view of Schumpeter that among all those who refer to economic data we have a systematic mind only in Aristotle. No one else in antiquity, with the possible exception of Plato,[39] produced economic theory or appealed to theory at all, even though they made practical observations that economic analysis could have precipitated (e.g., profitable use of land depends on distance from the market or center of consumption).[40] Even if Plato were as substantial a figure in economic theory as Aristotle (and I find no historian of economic theory who takes that view), all other things being equal, we should still have to choose Aristotle over Plato, all the more so over Xenophon, for our particular comparative exercise.

We come now to the last of the three considerations that lead to the comparison of the Mishnah's politics with Aristotle's, the simple fact that the two systems share convictions about the centrality of the householder in the economic system. Having something fundamental in common, they may well be contrasted, also, in other aspects of their larger visions of society. And both conceive, as a matter of method, that the social order rests upon the means of production, and social relationships spin out issues of disposition of scarce resources. That fundamental fact validates the claim that the two systems are fundamentally alike and permits comparing them. That fact also explains why, it must follow, the differences between the two systems matter and so provide perspective on the character of the Mishnah's politics.[41]

Not only as a matter of method do both Aristotle's and the Mishnah's modes of formulating the social order begin with economic considerations. As a matter of fact, both systems identify the same component of the social entity in particular, in the same language, as the principal figure in the economics of their respective accounts of political economy. That is the one who is held by both system builders to control the means of production.[42] In the mythic and symbolic language shared by Aristotle and the Mishnah's authorship, that party, in command of the irreducible minimum of productive capacity, is called the householder. And since for the philosophy of the sages of the Mishnah and for the system of Aristotle, it is the householder that defines the starting point for social thought, we are on firm ground indeed in comparing the system of the one to that of the other. That fact imparts systemic significance to the points of difference in the politics of each system that we shall presently (in chapter 11) identify.

Before proceeding, let me define the householder as the Mishnah understands that classification of person. Only then will the comparison between Aristotle's and the Mishnah's householders prove concrete. The Mishnah's definition of the householder in wholly economic terms, as the one who commands the means of production—or, more accurately, who commands those means of production which the framers of the system propose to notice— proves critical. When we see the household as an economic unit, the social side to matters loses all importance; indeed, it hardly matters whether or not we introduce considerations of kinship. As noted, co-residence is not always essential in designating a person a part of a household. Propinquity means only that one is within a reasonable distance, which is to say, one is part of the village, but the village takes form out of households and is (merely) a construction of households, having no other independent social forms. Accordingly, the entire system knows as its basic social unit and building block what is also its basic economic unit, defined as the component of the whole that controls the means of production, the "farm" in all that "farm" entails.

Control of the means of production bears consequence for the shape and structure of all other relationships in society. Only by studying these shall we fully understand what is at stake in our analysis of the householder and his systemic position. The householder's will proves paramount in all matters, not only economic decision making; this is shown most dramatically by the systemic opposite of the householder, the slave, whose will is never effective.[43] In this regard we should not confuse the rights of the male as householder with the male's rights and power as husband. To be sure, the householder, always a male, as husband has cultic rights over his wife. For example, he can confirm or nullify her vows. But, more to the point, as master of the household, he controls all property so that, for the duration of the marriage, the wife's and minor children's property is his to do with as he wishes. And his disposition of real property through gift or inheritance is equally autocephalic. True, biblical rules of primogeniture may apply as to the disposition of estates, but the householder may give away the property and in so doing may ignore the received rules of testamentary succession. That total control of real wealth sets aside the inherited laws that dictate in some measure who gets what. In these and other ways, we see that while the householder to begin with commands the economic unit, that control bears secondary implications for his control of other matters. We may therefore affirm that the one who controls the means of production and who defines and constitutes the unit of production effectively is in charge of all else. But not quite, as we shall presently observe.

In the Mishnah's economics (as in Aristotle's) we have an economic theory that ignores most of the participants in the economy, which is supposedly subject to legislation and direction.[44] In order to understand the highly restricted and selective dimensions of the Mishnah's economics, we conclude by reverting to the question, who in the system of the Mishnah could become a householder? The answer is, any Israelite. But that answer carries in its wake a certain disingenuousness, for "Israel" stands for males, specifically males possessed of sufficient wealth to acquire land, however miniscule. It is further taken for granted that the Mishnah's entire system addresses Jews; gentiles are not represented as householders, though their presence in the neighborhood is persistently acknowledged. So the Mishnah's economics excluded women, half of the "Israel" to which the Mishnah referred, not to mention gentiles, who formed a sizable part of the population in areas of the Land that Jews occupied, as well as areas that Jews did not occupy in appreciable numbers. The same economics, more to the point, also made slight provision for regulating of the affairs of those Jews and gentiles who lived by pursuing crafts not connected to the work required for the household (the farm). It neglected those who lived by trade and investment or by the sweat of their brow (as day laborers)—and however many other sorts and classifications of people and work one can imagine.

What of the economically active members of the community of Israel, the Mishnah's counterpart to Aristotle's *polis?* What of the people who had capital and knew how to use it? If they wished to enter that elevated "Israel" which formed the social center and substance of the Mishnah's Israel, they had to purchase land. Then matters again turn out as they did in the Greek cities described by Finley: in both cases money-holding citizens turned to the land "from considerations of status, not of maximization of profits," whereas "the non-citizens [kept off the land] of necessity lived by manufacture, trade and moneylending."[45] The consequence—to abbreviate Finley's interesting argument—is that "what we call the economy was properly the exclusive business of outsiders." In the case of the economics of Judaism, by contrast, economic theory encompassed the market as much as the household. The same message pertained, the same statement resonated. We shall now see precisely what it was. For when we know what we now do about the household, we can describe a steady-state society, but we have not yet gained access to what the system, through its disposition of the household as the systemically active unit of economic activity, proposed to lay down as its statement concerning, and through the creation of, that steady-state world.

In its identification of the householder as the building block of society, to the neglect of the vast panoply of "others," nonhouseholders, the Mishnah's authorship reduced the dimensions of society to only a single component. But this is the sole option open to a system that, for reasons of its own, wished to identify productivity with agriculture, individuality in God's image with ownership of land, and social standing and status, consequently, with ownership and control of the land—the land in this context constituting the sole systemically consequential means of production. Now if we were to list all the persons and professions who enjoy no role in the system, or who are treated as ancillary to the system, we have to encompass not only workers—the entire landless working class!—but also craftsmen and artisans, teachers and physicians, clerks and officials, traders and merchants, the whole of the commercial establishment, not to mention women. Such an economics, disengaged from so large a sector of the economy of which it claimed, even if only in theory, to speak, can hardly be called an economics at all.

When describing the way in which the social order rationally manages scarce resources, that is, its economics, the authorship of the Mishnah nonetheless speaks in particular for the Israelite landholding, proprietary person. The Mishnah's problems are the problems of the householder; its perspectives are his; its sense of what is just and fair expresses his sense of the givenness and cosmic rightness of the present condition of society. And these householders are men of substance and of means, however modest, aching for a stable and predictable world in which to tend their crops and herds, feed their families and dependents, keep to the natural rhythms of the seasons and lunar cycles, and, in all, live out their lives within strong and secure boundaries on earth and in heaven. This is why the sense of landed place and its limits, the sharp lines drawn between village and world, on one side, Israelite and gentile, on the second, Temple and world, on the third, evoke metaphysical correspondences. Householder (which is Israel) in the village, and Temple beyond, form a correspondence. Only when we understand the systemic principle concerning God in relationship to Israel in its land shall we come to the fundamental and generative conception that reaches concrete expression in the here and now of the householder as the centerpiece of society.

Let us now consider how the two parties concur as to their definition of the household—as we recall, only when we have fully analyzed their points of agreement will the differences between the politics of each take on systemic consequence such that we may interpret the politics of this Judaism.

To begin with, Aristotle and the framers of the Mishnah share an interest in economics, while other system builders in their respective settings do not. Both of them, distinctive in their contexts, found necessary to the construction of their systems sustained inquiry into the economic foundations of society. That fact characterizes, among Judaic system builders, only the sages of the Mishnah and their continuators. And of course, as I have suggested, Aristotle stood alone as an economic thinker in antiquity. Polanyi's characterization of Aristotle's mode of thought, cited above, applies without variation to that of the authorship of the Mishnah: "Whenever Aristotle touched on a question of the economy he aimed at developing its relationship to society as a whole." And, as a matter of fact, in the encompassing system of thought on economics of both Aristotle and the Mishnah's authorship, the beginning of all inquiry lies in the character and capacities of the one who controlled the means of production. That one was conceived to be, and was called, the householder.

For Aristotle, the theories of trade and price therefore elaborate the general theorem of the human community: "Community, self-sufficiency and justice: these pivots of his sociology were the frame of reference of his thought on all economic matters, whether the nature of the economy or policy issues were at stake." [46] The economy concerns the household in particular, that is, "the relationship of the persons who make up the natural institution of the household." Why the interest, then, in economics at all? Polanyi's answer is that people had to link the requirements of communal existence and communal self-sufficiency to the following two matters of policy: trade and price. The fundamental notion was the self-sufficiency of the community, which yielded the principle that trade that served only to restore self-sufficiency was in accord with nature, trade that did not was contrary; prices should strengthen the institutions of the community, namely, the household. When we turn to the Mishnah's politics, we shall see the parallel conception, that the householder formed the basic building block of the political structure and system.

The postulate of self-sufficiency governed all else; such trade as was required to restore self-sufficiency was natural and right, but that alone. [47] The fundamental principle, which will find ample instantiation, also, in the Mishnah's economics, is therefore natural self-sufficiency attained by the *oikos* and the *polis* made up thereof; it is political economy. Polanyi writes: "The institution of equivalency exchange was designed to ensure that all householders had a claim to share in the necessary staples at given rates, in exchange for such staples as they themselves happened to possess. . . . Barter derived from the institution of sharing of the necessities of life; the purpose of barter was to supply all householders with those necessities up to the level of sufficiency." [48] Accordingly, Aristotle's economic theory—as did his politics—rested on the sociology of the self-sufficient community made up of self-sufficient, if mutually dependent, households—a contradiction in terms, since self-sufficiency and mutual dependency surely are not compatible as theories of economic exchange.

Aristotle's approach, however, does not comprise an economics and a politics kept separate but joined in a larger intellectual structure. Rather Aristotle presents us with a political economy, in which economics is embedded in a larger theory of the social order. That cogency of political economy is seen in his joining of economic to political issues when he refers to the household. We cannot overstress the fact that for *both* politics and economics, the irreducible, minimal unit of production, deemed to be the household, formed the building block and foundation for all higher structures. For one probative example, wealth is measured by the household and the town or *polis,* that is, the political unit of the social order, so that Aristotle defines wealth as "a means, necessary for the maintenance of the household and the *polis* (with self-sufficiency a principle in the background), and, like all means, it is limited by its end." [49]

The basic thrust of the economics bears a political message, a lesson for the maintenance of the self-sustaining political unit or *polis.* Indeed, the aim of economics is to sustain the politics. And the goal of politics is to maintain the balance and order of the household and *polis.* Consider the following. In a system that appeals for validation to the teleology of nature, exchange by itself is natural: "Shortages and surpluses . . . were corrected by mutual exchange. . . . When used in this way, the art of exchange is not contrary to nature, nor in any way a species of the art of money-making. It simply served to satisfy the natural requirements of self-sufficiency." [50] Clearly, money makes possible the correct exchange of value. Quite logically, then, he regards the usurer (e.g., the one who offers consumer loans) as practicing the art of money-making in an unnatural way: "interest makes [money] increase," and that violates the purpose of money, which is merely for the sake of exchange. But Aristotle also states that profit is made not according to nature, but at the expense of others. Indeed, Aristotle in general insists on the "unnaturalness of commercial gain." Therefore he does not consider the rules or mechanics of commercial exchange. Finley notes: "Of economic analysis there is not a trace." [51]

The Mishnah's system focuses upon the society organized in relationship to the control of the means of production, that is, it focuses on the farm, for the household is always—as a matter of fact—the agricultural unit. The Mishnah's authorship set forth the same fantasic conception as Aristotle, one of a simple economy. Each system invented a neat world of little blocks formed into big ones, households into villages, villages, for Aristotle, into the *polis.* There were then no empty spaces, but also no vast cities (for a reason characteristic of the system as a whole, as I shall specify presently). As the Mishnah's authorship saw matters, community or village (which is not the same as the *polis*) is made up of households, and the household (*bayit/oikos*) constitutes the building block of both society or community, and also of economy. It follows that the household forms the fundamental, irreducible, and, of course, representative unit of the economy, the means of production, the locus and the unit of production. The household constituted "the center of the productive economic activities we now handle through the market." [52] Within the household all local, as distinct from cultic, economic, therefore social activities and functions, were held together. For the unit of production comprised also the unit of social organization and, of greater import still, the building block of all larger social, now also political, units with special reference to the village. [53]

In the conception at hand, which sees Israel as made up, on earth, of households and villages, the economic unit also framed the social one, and the two together composed, in conglomerates, the political one, hence a *political economy* (*polis, oikos*), one that is initiated within an economic definition formed out of the elements of production. The Mishnah makes a single cogent statement that the initial unit of society and politics finds its definition in the irreducible unit of economic production. It conceives no other economic unit of production than the household, though it recognizes that such existed; its authorship perceived no other social unit of organization than the household and the conglomeration of households, though that limited vision omitted all reference to substantial parts of the population perceived to be present (the craftsmen, the unemployed, the landless, and the like). Had Aristotle been shown a copy of the Mishnah and taught how to make sense of it, he would have found its economics entirely familiar.[54]

Let me define in general terms the householders as the framers of the Mishnah perceive them. Householders were farmers of their own land, proprietors of the smallest viable agricultural unit of production—however modest that might be. They stood at the center of a circle of a sizable corps of dependents: wives, sons- and daughters-in-law, children and grandchildren, slaves, servants. And others came within their circle who were not part of the hierarchy of the household (such as craftsmen and day laborers, for instance). Accordingly, at the outer fringes of the Mishnah's household were such ancillary groups as craftsmen and purveyors of other specialties, wagon drivers, providers of animals and equipment for rent, moneylenders, shopkeepers, wholesalers of grain and other produce, peddlers and tradesmen, barbers, doctors, and butchers, scribes and teachers, and, of course, the ultimate dependents, the scheduled castes: priests, Levites, and the poor. This list tells us, as we shall observe presently, that, in the system of the Mishnah the economic classes of traders and other purveyors of liquid capital ("capitalists," those who systematically and purposefully [re]invest wealth in ongoing moneymaking ventures, not merely the bazaar merchants) stood essentially outside the conceptual framework of the Mishnah's political economy.

As principal and head of so sizable a network of material relationships, the householder saw himself as pivot of the village, the irreducible building block of society, the solid and responsible center of it all. In the corporate community of the village, other components, each with a particular perspective and program of pressing questions, surely existed, and the householder could have been only one of these. But in the perception of the Mishnah, he is the one that mattered. And the Mishnah's framers could not have erred, for the householder controlled the means of production and held the governance of the basic economic unit of the village as such. Traders and peddlers and others outside the economy of the household also functioned outside the framework of the village as such; by definition, they were not settled, landed, stable. Their economic tasks required them to travel from place to place, for instance, to collect produce and resell it at the market. But so far as the Mishnah's picture of society in its economic relationships and productive aspects is concerned, the whole held together through the householder. It expresses this phenomenon in mythic terms: he who owns something is the only one who may sanctify it; in Heaven, God sanctifies, and, on earth, the householder, the farmer, does the job.

Clearly, then, the social foundation of the Mishnah's economy rested on the household, which in turn formed the foundation of the village—the village was imagined to comprise the community of households in the charge of small farmers who were free and who owned their land.[55] In fact, the entire economics of this Judaism addresses only the social world formed by this "household." No economics in the system of the Mishnah pertained to commercial, professional, manufacturing, trading, let alone laboring, persons and classes. Rulings referred to these classifications of economic persons and activities, to be sure. But the household forms the focus.

"The household," furthermore, in the Mishnah is a technical term.[56] Landless workers, teachers, physicians, merchants, shopkeepers, traders, craftsmen, and the like by definition cannot constitute or even affiliate with a household; we have here an amazingly narrow economics. The definition of the market and its working, and the conception of wealth, viewed within both market and distributive economics, sort out affairs only as these pertain to the household. That is to say the economics of Judaism omitted reference to most of the Jews, on the one side, and to the economic activities and concerns of labor and capital alike, on the other. These formidable components of the social entity "Israel" the system at hand simply treats, from an economic perspective, as null. No one else but the householder and his establishment plays a generative role in economic thinking. All are, within economics, systemically inert—except in relationship to that householder. By contrast, in passages in which proprietary responsibilities and obligations play no role, for example, in matters having to do with the cult, religious observance, or the sacred calendar, the Mishnah's authorship speaks not of the householder but of "he who . . . ," or "a man," or other neutral building blocks of society not defined in terms of proprietary status of landholding.[57]

Whether, in fact, all "Israel," that is, the Jews in the Land of Israel, lived in such villages or towns, each made up of a neat array of householders and their dependents, we do not know. But, self-evidently, it is difficult to imagine a reality composed of such a neat arrangement of building blocks. The Mishnah's authorship itself recognizes that the village—all the more so larger settlements altogether—consisted of more than households and householders; the authorship even recognized that "household" is an abstract entity, not a concrete and material social fact, as we shall see in a moment. But even without such passages, we should find it exceedingly difficult to imagine a society made up wholly of smallholders and people assembled in neat array around them. None can envisage a society or community lacking such other social categories as large holders, landless workers in appreciable numbers, crafts-men laboring for a market independent of the proprietary one of house-holders, and numerous other categories of production and classifications of persons in relationship to means of production.

That skewed perception of the economy makes all the more indicative of the character of the Mishnaic system and its thought the fact that we deal with a single block, a single mold and model. In imagining a society which surely encompassed diverse kinds of persons, formed in various molds and in accord with a range of models, the authorship of the Mishnah has made its statement of its vision, and that vision dictates the focus and requirements of analysis. Household as the building block of village—the two fundamental units of Israelite society together form an abstraction, not a concrete physical or social entity. In effect, it is not simply a house separate from other houses, or a family distinct from other families, either of which is easy to demonstrate. Nor is the household a concrete description of how people really lived; it does not depend on the spatial arrangements of houses; it does not comprise social units made up of distinct household-houses (or, as we shall see in a moment, families as equivalent to households). The supposition of Mishnah-tractate Erubin, for example is that households are in a village, that people live cheek by jowl in courtyards, and that they go out into the fields from the village. So the notion of the isolated farmstead is absent here. That is important in relat-ing the household to the village, *oikos* to *polis,* and it also shows how abstract is the conception of the household, since it is conceived as a unit even though, in fact, the households were not abstract and distinct units at all.

And what, exactly, is necessary—if not sufficient—to define the house-hold? Solely its economic, not its social or mythic (genealogical), configura-tion. Let me emphasize: the singularity of the household lay not in its physical, let alone its genealogical, traits, but—as I assumed at the very out-set—solely in its definition as a distinct unit of economic production. *What made a household into a household was its economic definition as a whole and complete unit of production, and the householder was the one who con-trolled that unit of production.* That economic fact made all the difference. The Mishnah's framers did not consider that all of the household's members were related (indeed, that was not the fact at all), nor that all of them lived in a single building distinct from other single buildings. For the Mishnah's author-ship, what made the household into a social unit was the economic fact that, among its constituents, all of them worked within the same economic unit and also worked in a setting distinct from other equivalently autonomous eco-nomic units. In the idiom of the Mishnah, they *ate* at the same table—"eat-ing" should be understood as an abstraction, not merely as a reference to the fact that people sat down and broke bread together. That seems to me an inter-esting point.

Nor is the "household" of which courtyards are composed only Jewish. "He who dwells in the same courtyard with a gentile, or with an Israelite who does not concede the validity of the *erub* . . . ," so Mishnah-tractate Erubin 6:1. This concession of householder status to the gentile neighbor in a courtyard once more underlines the economic and functional definition of the household, as distinct from its genealogical and cultic meaning.[58] The premise of the household as an autonomous unit and building block of society contradicts the realities described by the Mishnah's framers. The social unit of the courtyard has numerous cultic effects, but it is not an economic unit and is not recognized as such. "The householder" has no counterpart in "the shareholder of a courtyard." The one forms an economic unit, the other does not (e.g., in M. Er. 6:3–4, the courtyard is a cultic unit bearing no economic weight whatsoever). This again shows us the precision in the framers' use of the terms "household" and "householder"—the precision, but also the utter abstraction of the conception. The householder thus forms a very specific classification of person, bearing particular definition and playing a role in discourse mainly when issues of property and substance have to be sorted out.

Within the villages any Israelite male was assumed to possess the potential to become a householder, that is, in context, to become the master of a domain, a landholder.[59] The single most important difference between the conception of the householder in the Mishnah and the conception of landholding for the Greek thinkers who in theoretical economics formed the counterpart to the Mishnah's authorship lies in that one fact. As Finley states, "It was the Greeks who most fully preserved for citizens a monopoly of the right to own land, and who in the more oligarchic communities restricted full political rights to the landowners among their members."[60] While, as we shall see, the householder by definition always is assumed to own land and to command a domain, the Mishnah knows as full participants in its politics—that is, as "citizens" or more appropriately subjects of the kingdom (of Heaven) for which it legislates—landless persons, women, slaves, children, and the other persons and classes entirely outside the categorization and hierarchization accomplished in its economics by the unit of the household. When the Mishnah's system speaks of cultic or ritual responsibilities, or all the inhabitants of a town, including those who belong to categories for which landholding is irrelevant, the Mishnah speaks of "a man," or "he who . . . ," or "all the residents of the town," and not of "the householder."

The householder as the principal building block of economics precluded other classifications of economic actors. There is, after all, production of other than agricultural products (e.g., goods and services). Production encompasses making pots and chairs, but the craftsman does not define an economic unit, that is, a householder, if he does not also own and farm land (perhaps through day laborers). The shopkeeper, the tradesman, the merchant, and the capitalist also command wealth and engage in productive activities of all kinds. But they too do not control those means of production that make a difference to the system of the Mishnah. The framers of the system consider land, and only land, basic to the productive entity "society," so that only the householder, who is by definition a landholder who farms, constitutes the focus of consideration and concern. Given what they wished to say, when they spoke of the rational utilization of scarce resources, the framers of the Mishnah addressed issues of production in the household, as well as the paramount position of the householder in matters of market and of wealth. But when they addressed the legitimate use of violence, they defined the political entity in a completely different manner.

The householder, then, is a classification serving solely economic components of the system of Judaism as a whole. A technical term, which occurs when we speak of either market or distributive economics, "the householder" operates in the discussion of the rational disposition of scarce resources, that is, in the fourth and first divisions of the document, respectively. In the rest of the Mishnah, the differentiation between householder and any other Jew makes no difference. Therefore the language of the document ignores that differentiation, for it is a fixed trait of the Mishnaic language, and therefore of the Mishnaic system, that differentiation in language and hence hierarchization served as an instrument of thought only where for systemic reasons a distinction made a difference. That point is critical to our understanding of the householder, who is not the same as any Israelite for the Mishnah's authorship, but who forms the center of interest, the principal unit of productive activity, the class of person who forms the building block of the village. The political economy of the Mishnah is defined by the householder forming with other householders a village: *oikos* become *polis*. The problem in the analysis of the politics of this Judaism is contained within that formulation. For the *polis*—the village—does not then generate the politics of this Judaism, but, by definition, it does form the politics of Aristotle.

Having defined the household in context, let us turn to its systemic activity; here again we shall see that the household is a fundamentally apolitical category. The household served as a hierarchizing category for the economy by setting all things into relationship with all other things within that realm of the social order. Just as the priest served as the hierarchizing category for the Temple, the king for the realm, so the householder did for the control and disposition of scarce resources. And his distinctive task is clearly set forth. Where he was in control and in charge, at the head of the line, he was to hold things together in good composition. The Mishnah's theoretical conception of its ("Israel's") political economy, that is, the village or *polis* comprising the household or *oikos*, therefore, is neat and orderly, with all things in relationship and in proper order and proportion. The economy encompassed other economic entities, in particular craftsmen and traders, both of them necessary for the conduct of the household. But each was placed into relationship with the household, that is, once more hierarchized, the one as a necessary accessory to its ongoing functioning, the other as a shadowy figure who received the crops in volume and parceled them out to the market. The relationships between householder and craftsman, or between householder and hired hand, are sorted out in such a way as to accord to all parties a fair share in every transaction. Class interest viewed in a narrow, selfish framework of course did not exist. Class responsibility did, and the responsible party stood to the fore. Responsibilities of the one as against the other are spelled out. The craftsman or artisan, to be sure, is culpable should he damage property of the householder, but that judgment simply states the systemic interest in preserving the present division of wealth so that no party to a transaction emerges richer, none poorer.

The household, therefore, should be understood in three aspects. First, it marked a unit of production, and the householder was the master of the means of production. This was a farming unit in particular. That defines the household's indicative character and quality. Second, the household also marked a unit of ownership, and the householder was the master of a piece of property. Commanding means of production meant, in particular, running a farm. Third, the household also encompassed an extended family unit. But a household without land simply was no household, for the term bore economic, not only social, valence: a family unit by itself did not constitute a household. That is one side of the matter. The other is equally critical. Merely owning a piece of property, without using the property for farming, also did not make a man (and certainly not a woman!) into a householder. To state matters negatively, the authorship of the Mishnah cannot conceive of ownership in the absence of productive use of property and therefore calls into question the permanence of absentee ownership, that is, the organization of properties not managed by their owners.[61]

The upshot is stated simply: Judaism's economics forms a system in which a principal and generative consideration derives from control of the means of production. And, as a matter of fact, the political economy of the Mishnaic system proves partial and highly selective, for the economic unit does not dictate the definition, or even the perception, of the political. The householders form a social group which also is an economic one but, as a matter of fact, is not a political one. And that fact should prove surprising. For, on the one hand, I doubt that a more thoroughgoing definition of society in terms of its economic categories and building blocks, that is, by appeal to the means and unit of production, can be located in any other Judaism. The householder functioned as the principal economic actor, making the decisions for himself and his dependents.[62] But the household, while forming one of the two social constructs of the Mishnah's world, plays no role in the other. It makes up the village, but, appealing now to Aristotle's language, the village is no *polis*. The village, which is made up of households, thus the *oikos* and the *polis,* for Aristotle yields a political economy.[63] Since the household for the Mishnah does not comprise, with other households, a political entity of any kind, we must wonder why not.

In the economics of Judaism the householder is systemically the active force, and all other components of the actual economy (as distinct from the economics) prove systemically inert.[64] But that is hardly the case for Aristotle.

His economic actor and his political actor are one and the same and are defined in the same terms. The economic and political entities are well defined by Finley when he observes, "All Greek states . . . restricted the right of land ownership to their citizens. . . . They thereby . . . erected a wall between the land, from which the great majority of the population received their livelihood, and that very substantial proportion of the money available for investment which was in the hands of non-citizens." [65] But the politics of this Judaism does not define economic entities, as I have stressed. It defines other entities, for other purposes altogether. According to the theory of Judaism, anyone might own land, even though few did.[66] That meant that in economic terms citizenship extended very broadly, to all Israelites. The hierarchization effected by economics differentiated in economic terms. It separated householders from all others, who were in turn arrayed in relationship to the household. But—and this is the principal consideration for my argument—in political terms matters appeal to a different hierarchy altogether, different taxa signifying different categories and a distinctive ordering of those categories. The contrast in the principal of category formation between Aristotle's unitary conception that the citizen also was a landholder, while the outsider was neither citizen nor landholder, and the Mishnah's dual conception, points to the difference that requires sustained attention: why this, not that?

11

Aristotle's *Politics* and the Politics of Judaism

> It follows that the *polis* belongs to a class of objects which exist in
> nature and that man is by nature a political animal. . . . Nature . . . does
> nothing without some purpose, and for the purpose of making man a politi-
> cal animal, she has endowed him alone among the animals with the power
> of reasoned speech. Speech is something different from voice. . . . Speech
> serves to indicate what is useful and what is harmful, and so also what is
> just and what is unjust.
>
> Aristotle

Aristotle's politics forms an important chapter in his larger inquiry into the properties of things and into how, by nature, things are meant to be. His system's teleological focus, its concentration on the realization of what things may in their nature become illuminates politics too.[1] That is why, when Aristotle reaches his stunning generalization about the nature of the human being, he forthwith adduces in evidence the traits of humanity. How otherwise explain the odd juxtaposition of politics and anthropology or account, in the setting of the *polis* as the political entity, for appeal to politics as the natural outcome of humanity's power of speech! Psychology, politics, economics, anthropology—all deliver the same message about the priority of how things are by nature.

But politics bears a particular burden of the larger systemic message. For Aristotle, according to Martha Nussbaum, politics and economics bear the same task, namely, the proper distribution of scarce resources to the correct recipients (for economics), and the appropriate distribution of capacities or opportunities for the realization of capabilities (for politics).[2] Nussbaum expresses the union between economics and politics in affording the correct and natural distribution of scarce resources and the effects of power as follows:

> The aim of political planning is the distribution to the city's individual people of
> the conditions in which a good human life can be chosen and lived. The distributive
> task aims at producing capabilities. That is, it aims not simply at the allotment of

commodities, but at making people able to function in certain human ways. A necessary basis for being a recipient of this distribution is that one should already possess some less developed capability to perform the function in question. The task of the city is . . . to effect the transition from one level of capability to another. This means that the task of the city cannot be understood apart from a rather substantial account of the human good and what it is to function humanly.[3]

It follows that we understand Aristotle's politics in the correct context only when we identify the ubiquitous systemic message carried in particular by the politics—and can explain why the subject of politics forms the particularly suitable medium for that message. The same, we shall see, is true for the politics of this Judaism. By identifying and accounting for the generative difference between the Aristotle's political system and that of the Mishnah, we better understand not only the politics but also—and especially—the respective systems for which each politics forms an indicative component.

To begin with, let us review Aristotle's idea (surveyed in the preceding chapter) that the householder is the generative component not only of economics but also of politics, that he operates in structure and system alike. Taking R. G. Mulgan's description of Aristotle's politics as our model, we look first not at the household, but at the *polis,* which is to say, at the political community. Mulgan quotes Aristotle:

> "Every *polis* is a community of persons formed with a view to some good purpose. I say 'good' because in their actions all men do in fact aim at what they think good. Clearly then, as all communities aim at some good, that one which is supreme and embraces all others will have also as its aim the supreme good. That is the community which we call the *polis,* and that type of community we call political."[4]

But what constitutes that "community of persons"? This seems to me the critical question here. Mulgan notes that of the two lesser communities that comprise the *polis* and precede it in time, the household and the village, the household is much more important in Aristotle's ethical and political theory. Though the village provides a necessary link between the household and the *polis* in the chain of historical development, Aristotle ignores it as an integral part of the fully developed *polis.* The household, on the other hand, continues to have important functions for him. It operates as an educational institution. Indeed, it is the center of life for over half the population of the city, that is, for women, children, and slaves. Consequently, for Aristotle the head of the household is the pivotal figure. He acts as a link between the political community and the smaller community of the household.[5]

Mulgan identifies the political community as supreme, most powerful; the *polis* comprises the institutions that control the rest of society. Mulgan notes, "This conception of the political community is similar to the modern notion of the state, which is usually defined in terms of the monopoly of legitimate coercion."[6] The *polis* controls other communities, which are included in it and form parts of it: "All forms of community are like parts of the political community." [7] Accordingly, the political community is coextensive with the society of the city-state. [8]

Aristotle's principal political polemic forms part of a larger systemic program, the investigation of what accords with nature or exists by nature. This investigation pursues that which derives from basic human motives and promotes the human "good." True, Aristotle argues that the polis is an institution and came into being at some point in history. But he holds that the political community or *polis* is natural in the sense that it derives from basic human motives and promotes the human good. [9] Mulgan explains the matter, giving its crux as follows:

> Aristotle begins his argument that the *polis* is natural with a sketch of the development of the *polis* from the household and the village. He considers the *polis* as if it were a biological organism and tries to discover its nature by examining the pattern of its growth and development. The first stage is the household which is based on two fundamental distinctions in human nature. One is the difference between male and female which enables the human race to reproduce itself. The other is the difference between ruler and ruled, in particular between the man who has the intellectual capacity for ruling as a master and the man who can do no more than carry out his master's orders. These two instinctive relationships, male and female and master and slave, together with that of parent and child, . . . form the household.
>
> The household provides only the simplest necessities and so a number of households unite into a village which can supply more than men's daily needs. But the village is still too small, and so several villages unite in a further community, the *polis*, which alone is large enough to be self-sufficient. The original impetus for this larger community comes from the need for the necessities of life, but it continues to exist for the sake of the good life. That is, men first form the *polis* for relatively modest reasons, but, once created, it makes possible the realization of more elevated aims which men then come to see as the main reason for its existence. Being self-sufficient, the *polis* marks the final stage in a process of natural growth and development; indeed, as it is the final stage, it is itself the "nature" of human development, the "essence" which is realized at the end of natural growth. [10]

The important point from our perspective is the role of the household in this judgment concerning the *polis*. Mulgan cites Aristotle as follows: "Therefore the *polis* is a perfectly natural form of community, as the earlier communities from which it sprang were natural. This community is the end of those others and its nature is itself an end; for whatever each thing is when fully grown, that we call its nature, that which man, household, or anything else aims at being." [11] In other words, the *polis* is natural because it is the natural outcome of the full maturing of the household and because the household itself is natural, being founded (in Mulgan's words) on "innate biological differences." Evidently, it is therefore quite *natural*, in Aristotle's clearly defined sense, for the household to serve as the fundamental building block in the political structure that comes to full realization in the *polis*. This is not to assign priority in importance to the household over the *polis*. Indeed, as we shall see in a moment, Aristotle assigns the *polis* priority over the household and over any individual in it, "for the whole must be prior to the parts." But it does mean that there cannot be a *polis* without a household, and vice versa. Accordingly, the household must be seen to constitute an essential component in the political community. For my comparison (worked out further in chapter 12), the critical point is very simple and, I think, self-evident: for Aristotle, the household constitutes a principal category in the political structure.

That fact cannot be taken for granted, for other social classifications were available for inclusion within the political structure. To take a blatant example, Aristotle knew about the ethnos, or nation-state, a political entity that would exceed the *polis* in size.[12] But he regarded such states as too large for good government, since not every citizen of the *polis* can participate. Mulgan details the politics' systemic quality with great clarity:

> Aristotle's preference for the *polis* is not due to ignorance of the existence of other types of state; he is aware of possible alternatives, especially the ethnos or nation-state which was often larger than the *polis*. But such states, though large enough to provide the right level of material prosperity, will not be able to offer the good life. Once a community has grown beyond a certain size it cannot be well governed and cannot provide the political participation which every citizen of the ideal *polis* will expect. . . . The whole life of ethical virtue, as described in the Ethics, assumes the community of the *polis*. Aristotle's argument that the *polis* is natural because it is self-sufficient and therefore the culmination of a natural process of social evolution thus rests ultimately not on biological or historical fact but on his conception of the good life.[13]

The upshot is very simple. For Aristotle, politics like economics begins with the household, and political structures and the systems that make them work form conglomerates of households. Innate or natural traits of households and householders form the justification for the claim that "man is a political animal," which is to say, "an animal that lives in a *polis,* or *polis*-animal."[14] And that is not only a fact that derives from innate properties. It also forms a judgment of how things should be: it comprises a teleological justification for the *polis,* made up of households, as how things are meant to be: "Man is therefore a *polis*-animal also in the sense that, if he is to realize his moral potential, he needs the order and control which are provided by the government of the *polis;* the moral perfection of the members of the *polis* can be achieved only by means of publicly administered law."[15] And this brings us to Aristotle's conception of the household as a political entity, the smallest irreducible whole political unit.

The representation of the household in this way should not be misunderstood. Aristotle does not maintain that the *polis,* forming later, is therefore subordinate to the household in the political structure:

> The *polis* has priority over the household and over any individual among us. For the whole must be prior to the parts. Separate hand or foot from the whole body and they will no longer be hand or foot. . . . It is clear then that the *polis* is both natural and prior to the individual.[16]

"Prior" in this sense constitutes a teleological, not a temporal, judgment. But the *polis* is prior in another sense." A third [thing] is said to be prior to other things when, if it does not exist, the others will not exist, whereas it can exist without the others," so the *polis,* which develops from the household and the village, "is posterior in the order of becoming, but prior in the order of nature, because it is the end towards which man's social development is directed." [17] The *polis* can exist without a particular household, but it cannot come into existence without the corpus of households of which it is composed. In Mulgan's judgment, what we have is a restatement of the conviction that the *polis* is natural.

The household, joined to the *polis* through the formation of the villages and the agglomeration of the villages into the *polis,* retains fundamental importance in Aristotle's politics. It existed by nature, allowing for the expression of the natural instincts of reproduction and self-preservation and providing the basic necessities of life. These natural tasks accommodating innate traits, then, defined the household, which "provides for the procreation and rearing of children and which produces much of the economic wealth of the *polis.*" [18] The household also undertakes fundamental political tasks within the larger life of the community. These are educational, on the one side, and socially controlling (over women, children, and slaves), on the other. So Aristotle relates the household to the political entity:

> Every household is part of a *polis,* and the virtue of the part ought to be examined in relation to the virtue of the whole. This means that children and women too must be educated with an eye to the whole constitution of the *polis*—at least if it is true to say that it makes a difference to the goodness of a state that its children should be good and its women good. And it must make a difference; for women make up half the adult free population and from children come those who will participate in the constutition. [19]

The householder, then, forms the critical link between the political community and the household, that is to say, the smaller political community that, in conglomeration with other such units, makes up the political community or the *polis.* Hence we see the embeddedness of the economics in a political economy.

Not only so, but the economic tasks of the household form a principal part in the political role of that same social entity. As we have already noted, the second of the two innate traits of the household is the possession and acquisition of wealth. [20] Aristotle's politics in no way can be distinguished from his economics, as we have already observed. But why should that be so? The reason is that integral to his system as a whole is this claim that the innate traits of humanity are what account for the development of the household, then of the village, then of the town or *polis.* That uniformity in social classification, using the same building block throughout, derives from the method of classifying things by their traits and then appealing from the traits of things to their purpose. Accordingly, it is teleology that accounts for the natural condition of things. That innate quality that makes the household the simplest whole unit of society also applies to the *polis* or political community as the complex composition of such simple whole units of society.

It now suffices to repeat that for both systems—the Mishnah's and Aristotle's—the one who controls the means of production, the householder, also defines the basic unit of economic activity. And, we now better understand, the householder, also defines for Aristotle the basic unit of political activity.[21]

For the Mishnah's politics, the household plays no role whatsoever. It is not an indicative category. Nor does the householder serve as the subject of a single statement of a political character. Rather, the subjects of all these sentences are figures within the monarchy, cult, or bureaucracy (king, priest, scribe). That separation of the economic actor from the political one is especially astonishing since all economic thought prior to the eighteenth century treats economics as part of the science of political economy, that is, as an aspect of public policy (i.e., a mode of distribution of wealth by appeal to considerations extrinsic to wealth). Mulgan states matters for Aristotle, by extension revealing for us the truly exceptional character of Judaism's separation of politics from economics:

> Wealth and production are aspects of the general life of the *polis*, like education, warfare, or drama, and so are equally subject to ethical evaluation and political control. The question of "economics" in Aristotle illustrates a more general difficulty which we face when we try to understand Greek political thought. We tend to divide our thoughts and activities into different, autonomous categories, such as the economic, the religious, the moral, the legal, the political, and the educational. For the Greeks some of these distinctions did not exist and those that did were much more blurred than they are for us. Greek society . . . was more "integrated," less "differentiated," than our own. Though we cannot avoid using words like "economics" when we discuss Aristotle's political theory, we must not let them distort his meaning. At the same time, the absence of such sharp distinctions in his view of society may help us to a better understanding of our own society. Though more differentiated than Greek society, it is not so sharply divided as our categories sometimes suggest. Aristotle's approach to politics reminds us that the spheres of economics, law, morality, and education are not isolated but closely interdependent.[22]

What Mulgan says of Aristotle's economics and politics—that they embedded within a social system and its purpose—applies with no important variation to the economics and politics of all modes of political and economic theory prior to the Enlightenment. Then, and only then, economics was disembedded and developed into an autonomous intellectual construction.

Before proceeding, let me briefly explain the analytical conception of "embeddedness" which forms the exegetical fulcrum of this study of politics in systemic context. Until the eighteenth century, thought about the social order considered economics part of a larger intellectual composition, a design for the social order as a whole. That is to say, economics from Aristotle to

Quesnay and Riqueti, in the eighteenth century, dealt with not the science of wealth but rather "the management of the social household, first the city, then the state." [23] As we have now seen, the same is so of politics, which in Aristotle's case comprised a medium expressing a larger thesis, a thesis that came to full exposure in respect to the economics and, as a matter of fact, to the philosophy of the social order. Until the French physiocrats, for system builders all three—economics, politics, philosophy—were meant to say the same thing in regard to different aspects of the society. They corresponded to the social order as it attained concreteness in a particular way of life, social entity, worldview, respectively. Accordingly, in the matter of economics as embedded in a larger theory of society, economics formed a component of the larger sociopolitical order and dealt with the organization and management of the household (*oikos*). The city (*polis*) was conceived as comprising a set of households. An "embedded" economics served, as did a politics or a philosophy, to convey a systemic statement; economics was not deemed a science unto itself but a chapter in a theory of society. The same, we may say very simply, applied to politics, hence, political economy. [24]

Since, in the case of the initial system of post-Temple Judaism, the basic building block of the economy is not the fundamental and irreducible social unit of which the politics is composed, we find in this Judaism no system of thought that we may call a political economy and that we might link to the politics of this Judaism. The economics is not embedded in the social system and structure but defines a categorical entity—an imperative—on its own. How it is that Judaism could produce a politics distinct from economics in its fundamental structure and system? How could it comprise a disembodied economics? [25]

From this point, two tasks lie before us. The first is to show as fact the negative proposition that the household in the politics of this Judaism does not play the role that it does in the economics of Judaism; the second is to explain why, and characterize through comparison and contrast the Mishnah's system in particular.

What evidence sustains the claim that the householder in the politics of this Judaism does not constitute a political category, a topic of political discourse? The answer is not merely the silence of the Mishnah's politics on the householder as a political entity. It is that the social unit of the village, made up of households, does not form a political entity in the way in which it does for Aristotle's politics. Households, however many, do not aggregate into a village, nor villages, however large, into a *polis*, a city or a town that defines a political entity. No political role in the politics of this Judaism is assigned to the social entity constituted by either the village or the town. No political role is assigned to the householder because he forms the critical component of a social unit that itself is politically inert. The *élan vital* of this Judaism's Israel's politics is social, but society is other than Aristotle considers it to be.

The systemic message comes forth at points of differentiation: what the system builders wish to sort out defines the focus of their interest and the medium of their systemic message.[26] In point of fact, the framers of the Mishnah scarcely differentiate among urban settings, village or town or city, and hence the difference between the one and the other bears no systemic consequences. To see that point clearly, we have to gain perspective on the village and the town in the system of the Judaism of the Mishnah. What do we find in the Mishnah's repertoire? I discern remarkably few allusions to an urban setting in which distinctions as to the setting—*polis* or town as against village, town composed of villages made up of households, for instance—make much difference. For example, when people refer to a city on which it has not rained (M. Ta. 2:1), or a city that has been taken in a siege (M. Ket. 2:9), there is no consequence I can see for a larger theory of the difference between a village or town and a city. On the other hand, when, at M. Qid. 2:3, we find a clear reference to the difference between life in the one place and that in the other, we do reach a point of some interest. The passage has a man falsely swear to a prospective bride that he is a villager when in fact he lives in the city, or vice versa. The unmet stipulation nullifies the woman's agreement to become betrothed to him. A husband may not take his wife from a town to a city and vice versa (M. Ket. 13:10D). So there was a clear distinction. But the difference that the distinction makes is unspecified; nor have I found in the later commentaries a very plausible explanation of the difference. Clearly it involves conditions of everyday life and has no bearing on any larger systemic interests. Nor does the equivalent distinction make a difference at M. Meg. 2:3.

Overall, moreover, I find no tendency to evaluate life in the one place as better or worse than life in the other; the location is simply a fact of life. The notion of dwelling together with gentiles in the same city is a commonplace (e.g., M. Makhshirin 2:5). Likewise, there are references to large and small cities (e.g., M. Erubin 5:8), and these references produce no grounds to think sages held a higher opinion of one than of the other or thought there were consequential differences. A large city is defined as one in which there are ten men of leisure (M. Megillah 1:3), a small town as one in which there are fewer than that number. The usage of KPR, small town, is unusual; generally the framers of the Mishnah used the word for town, 'YR, sometimes clearly meaning a large one, sometimes meaning a small one, and often having no clear intent.

That, sum and substance, is the whole story for the Mishnah. There is clear and present distinction between city and town, but it makes very little difference. Where a distinction is made, we cannot say what difference it makes. The simple fact is that the Mishnah's authorship does not imagine a difference between village and town or city, that is, for Aristotle, *polis*.[27] More to the point, that same authorship never conceives the village or town to form a political unit. That is to say, when the authorship refers to political issues, it does not invoke the category town, or village, and it further does not speak of the householder as a political, as well as an economic, building block.

The distinction that does make a considerable difference for the politics of this Judaism was Jerusalem as against everywhere else. Jerusalem was where the politics took place. And, I stress, that forms a fundamental fact of the politics of this Judaism, in contrast to the view of Aristotle, for whom the location of a given *polis* is irrelevant. Aristotle describes an ideal political community; while it must have certain physical characteristics, it does not have to be in this place or that, but can exist anywhere that meets certain conditions. By contrast, the politics of this Judaism is locative.

The difference, of course, is readily explained. Jerusalem was the metropolis of Judaism. Mother of cities, from its perspective there were no differences among its offspring. Jews inherited in Scripture a sizable corpus of images and myths associated with the Heavenly city, poised as it was in Heaven over the earthly Jerusalem. Certainly, all Israel hoped for the rebuilding of Jerusalem and the reestablishment of the Temple. The law itself made ample provision for life in Jerusalem. Whole tractates, such as Maaser Sheni, took up the definition of the city and of food that entered the sacred limits of the city. Others, such as Sheqalim, dealt with the officials of the city and the Temple and their work. So in the Judaism of the Mishnah, there is only one social entity that can correspond to the *polis* in the thought of Aristotle, and that is Jerusalem: the unique *polis,* the metropolis.

Jerusalem is the location of the temple, the king, the high court; it constitutes the political place par excellence. But it also was the only such place, and no other place situated itself in relationship to that place. So Jerusalem's critical status within the political structure of Judaism bore hierarchical, and also locative, consequence. In relation to Jerusalem, everywhere was nowhere in particular, and Jerusalem was above everywhere else. Then the politics of this Judaism served a larger hierarchical purpose of assigning a place in the social order to one place above all other places, and the focus of the politics upon Jerusalem made its statement as well. But that statement is made in a voice of silence for, after all, Jerusalem was now inaccessible. So the political structure and system of Judaism addressed an imaginary world; an Israel without a king, high priest, or even access to Jerusalem called for a king to govern, a high priest to preside, a Jerusalem to form the center.

And here we gain perspective on the politics of this Judaism, for, we now realize, this politics forms a mere chapter in a story with its own beginning and purpose. The system of Judaism before us formed an exercise in the study of sanctification and its effects, and therefore, for systemic reasons, Jerusalem was *the* "city," and its "cityness" derived from its holiness.[28] And so far as "city" or "town" forms for Judaism the counterpart to *polis,* and the locus of power makes that a necessary comparison, then "city" formed a utopian and hierarchizing category, not a locative and political entity. To state the matter very simply, for the Judaic system Jerusalem served the hierarchizing purpose of distinguishing one place from everywhere else. And that distinction made no political differences whatsoever, because—let me stress—*only Jerusalem was empowered, and from Jerusalem all power flowed.*[29]

That sanctification formed a scheme of hierarchization is captured eloquently in the Mishnah in its balancing of sanctification and uncleanness in the following language:

> Ten levels of uncleanness pertain to man . . .
> (1) He whose atonement is incomplete is prohibited in regard to Holy Things but permitted to eat heave offering and tithe;
> (2) he who is unclean as one who awaits sunset to complete his purification is . . .
> (3) he who is unclean as having suffered a pollution . . .
> (4) He who is unclean by reason of intercourse with a menstruating woman . . .
> (5) He who is unclean as a *Zab* [Lev. 15]
> (6) He who produced three appearances of flux . . .
> (7) He who is unclean as a leper . . .
> (8) He who is certified as a leper;
> (9) If a limb . . .
> (10) And if there is on the limb . . .
>
> M. Kelim 1:5

> There are ten degrees of sanctification:
> (1) The land of Israel is holier than all other lands. And what signifies its sanctification? For they bring from it the *omer* and the first fruits and the Two Loaves, which they do not present from any other land.
> (2) The cities surrounded by a wall are more holy than the land.
> (3) Within the wall of Jerusalem the space is more holy than theirs.
> (4) The rampart is more holy than that space.
> (5) The court of women is more holy than that space.
> (6) The court of Israel is more holy than that space.
> (7) The court of the priests is more holy than that space.
> (8) The area between the porch and the altar is more holy than that space.
> (9) The sanctuary is more holy than that space.
> (10) The Holy of Holies is more holy than that space.
>
> M. Kelim 1:6–9 (pass.)

Space here is differentiated by appeal to cities like Jerusalem ("surrounded by a wall") and to condition within Jerusalem (3–10). The counterpart to the differentiated space of Jerusalem is the differentiated condition of cultic uncleanness. The counterpart to the differentiated space of Jerusalem is not locative—it does not operate through distance from Jerusalem—but hierarchial, in a different categorical framework altogether.

Jerusalem formed an abstraction. But in the system the issue was not the concrete reality of the city or its abstraction and material inaccessibility. Systemically Jerusalem stood for something else, something other, a social entity with no analogy down here in the village or town or city. It stood for someplace, a center as against an undifferentiated periphery of no-places. And that standing made of Jerusalem an instrument of locative hierarchization.[30] The power of Jerusalem to hierarchize also defines the place of Jerusalem in this Judaism. Where the system builders locate opposites, we find the critical message, and Jerusalem is holy in the way that uncleanness is unholy, point by point, stage by stage. Uncleanness is a matter of status, of hierarchy of what I may do or may not do if I am unclean, balanced against where I may go or may not go when I am clean.

Incidental to all this are the political classifications king, priest, scribe, which form epiphenomena of the hierarchization of all else but do not themselves impose order or hierarchy on anything else, except as their systemic tasks permit. To hierarchization the matter of place is simply irrelevant, except for Jerusalem. But place, in Jerusalem, is not locative but an expression of the order of things. The political structures and system the Mishnah's philosophers have in mind find categories in the correspondence between Heaven and earth which takes place at or over Jerusalem. And that is not a locative conception; it is, by definition, utopian.[31] The politics of the Mishnah's philosophers concerned power everywhere in general but—as a matter of social fact then and there—nowhere in particular. The specificity of Jerusalem then hardly masks its utopian quality. To put matters very simply, in the politics of this Judaism, Jerusalem is not *about* place, not at all. For if, beyond Jerusalem, no particular place is distinguished from any other, so that (in our case) the politics works (or does not work) without regard to location, then Jerusalem too hardly lays claim to take place somewhere in particular. As the cited passage of the Mishnah expresses the point, *Jerusalem defines not location but relation.*[32]

So if Aristotle were to interrogate a sage about the *polis,* inquiring where precisely the locative community figures in the politics of this Judaism, what sort of answer would he get? The *polis,* a particular community in a specified place, makes its appearance only once, so far as I have noticed, in the political sector of the system of the Mishnah. This occurs at M. San. 10:4: "The townsfolk of an apostate town have no portion in the world to come." These people form part of a catalog of those who lose life beyond the grave because of crimes or sins against God. A share in the world to come is something one gains as part of an entire community—the community of all Israel—but one may lose that share also as part of an entire community that is discerned as a community in relationship to God in particular. Among the components of the political community that has acted collectively and is to be subjected to collective sanctions, we find a variety of castes or classes singled out for consideration—women, children, temporary residents, bypassers—but among them the householder does not appear.

And that fact brings us back to the striking absence of the householder, who really does have power, in the politics of this Judaism. At no point does the householder define a categorical imperative that is either the subject or the object of power. In the context of sanctions that pertain to a village/town/*polis* as such, he is not a presence, does not define a political category. Indeed, the householder appears in the Mishnah only when the management of farms or estates plays a role. Why can the conception of the householder play no role whatsoever in the politics of this Judaism? Because the politics of this Judaism, to begin with, is not a dimension of location. It is not based on the land. Possession and management of the means of production, comprising a particular place or space, has no bearing upon politics. Why? The issues settled by legitimate use of violence are simply different from those worked out by the allocation of scarce resources—and economics is subordinated.[33]

Landholding, then, does not bear consequences for the politics of this Judaism. Controlling the irreducible unit of means of production bears no political weight; it does not help to define one political classification as against some other. Holding or not holding the land never defines the legitimacy of violence in a political circumstance. The case just now noted, concerning the apostate city, proves the opposite. Mere residence, not qualified by landownership, defines guilt. I cannot point to a single component of the theory of politics that appeals to possession of the land for definition of a categorical component of the system.[34] The politics of Judaism never appeals to enlandisement as a political category, that is, as the requirement for participation in the political process, in the way in which the economics defines the household as the farming unit but also ignores those farming units that do not comprise households. So clearly, control of means of production does not constitute the kind of power that the politics of this Judaism contemplates. That fact is underlined by the discontinuity between the political institutions of the system as a whole—king, priest, sage—and the actual politics of the village or town. These rest in the hands not of king or priest, but only of sage. Sages are not represented as landholders or as employees of landholders. And in the village, the sages work as ad hoc administrators, not as part of a coherent politics of administered power.

These observations about the difference between a politics that omits reference to control of means of production and one that encompasses that form of power within a larger theory of the distribution of power draw us back to our basic work of comparison. The primary locus of power dictates, for both systems, the answer to the question of where politics takes place at all. Aristotle's premise is that power inheres in the community (*koinonia*), and the community finds its definition by the nature or natural condition revealed in the citizens, who encompass all landholders and therefore most householders.[35] So Mulgan:

> Aristotle begins his analysis of the *polis* by describing the *polis* as a community (*koinonia*), a concept which is fundamental for his political theory. . . . Commu-

nities should properly have morally valuable purposes, . . . and the true *koinonia* will pursue the true good. . . . Another essential characteristic of any *koinonia* is that it involves . . . both friendship and justice. . . . In politics the most important . . . principle is distributive justice which governs the distribution of goods and benefits to different members of the same group, and it is this aspect of justice which is an essential feature of every *koinonia*.[36]

Power, then, flows from the community to the individual, and the foundation of the politics is the community that comprises the *polis*. That is, the male, free citizens—all landholders, defined as householders—form the institutions of politics that all together comprise the *polis*.

For the politics of this Judaism, holy people, divided into castes of a hierarchical order, constitute the political entity; holy land, ordered in relationship to the holiest place, Jerusalem, constitutes the definitive locus. The power parcelled out is the power of the sacred, and politics' task is to order all persons and classes of persons who are eligible according to appropriate taxic indicators with regard to their sanctification (that is, by caste, not by wealth). In such a system no place exists for the householder because the kind of power that concerns this politics is not the power he enjoys to allocate scarce material resources in a rational manner. This politics concentrates on the power to allocate holiness in a rational manner. So to politics the householder is simply irrelevant. What he governs has no bearing upon matters of consequence. The distributive economics of Judaism makes the important decisions upon material goods and services; the issues of politics then concern entirely other matters. The hierarchization of all persons and places and things in proper place and order aims at the highest point, which is defined as the most holy. The householder in such a system is not subject to hierarchization at all, forming as he does no category that appeals for identification, standing, and status to taxic indicators of the sacred.

These distinctions flow from still more fundamental propositions about how things are by nature. What, specifically, do we mean by "nature"? For Aristotle, the answer derives from the teleology signalled by the natural traits of things, and for the Mishnah's sages from their supernatural traits, signalled by the inherited qualities imputed by scriptural science.[37] Aristotle speaks of the this-worldly and given characteristics of the human being in general, yielding, as a matter of fact, the *polis*. The sages in their politics speak of "Israel," that is, the holy people. What explains the formation of the political unit? For Aristotle, householders forming villages (villages making up towns or cities) frame the *polis*. That is, nature defines the social entity, defines how things are.

For sages, by contrast, "Israel" forms a supernatural category made up of people born to Israel the supernatural social entity. It comprises children of very particular persons, Abraham, Isaac, and Jacob. So birth—hence caste, or marriage into a caste for a woman—carries with it a supernatural definition signified by genealogy. And, as a matter of fact, that genealogy has its heaviest bearing upon caste arrangements (priest, Levite, Israelite). Once more a politics of hierarchization results. In it nothing is merely natural or ordinary; in the formation of the social entity governed by the politics of this Judaism, there are no givens, only gifts of grace—and the chief gift is one's place in the social order, one's caste-standing as to sanctification. Aristotle appeals to the natural as what promotes the human good. That is not what is at stake in the Mishnah's Judaism, and it predictably plays no role in Mishnaic Judaism's politics.

If I had to describe the most striking differences between the two political systems at hand, I should address more than the systems' disagreement on how to evaluate the political consequences of control of the means of production.[38] I would refer particularly to Aristotle's striking power to take up questions of competition, control, political change, on the one hand, and the Mishnah's steady-state conception of politics on the other. Whereas constitutional change has a principal interest for Aristotle, issues of instability and disorder in the political context receive no attention in the Mishnah.[39] In Aristotle's mind, constitutional change can be contemplated. People can force change through violence (illegal means); they can gain power within an existing constitutional framework; as members of a governing body they can implement change peacefully by taking a deliberate decision to alter the rules. By contrast, the Mishnah includes no provision for constitutional change. Its silence with regard to the transfer of power and the revision of institutional structures differs strikingly from Aristotle's thoughtful treatment of these topics. But then, for Aristotle, change forms part of his politics' topical program; it is something to be considered. For the Mishnah's framers, I maintain, disorder is unthinkable, antisystemic. A system that proposes to bring about order (to be defined in the coming chapter) will find only danger in change and reform of public institutions alike. And this accounts for the avoidance we see.

But the main point of difference is that for Aristotle the household forms the point of departure for politics, and for Judaism it does not. And from that one point of difference, we can account for all of the other differences just now catalogued. Let me state the upshot of this comparison with emphasis:

Aristotle works out a system that joins economics to politics by appeal to a single and uniform teleology. The Mishnah's philosophers set forth a system that distinguishes economics from politics by appeal to a single and uniform principle of classification.

Politics in each setting bears its share of the burden of the system, and from what the two systems have in common, we see only points of contrast and differentiation. Now, to accomplish the final task, we turn to the question, for this Judaism what requirement of the systemic message has provoked the invention of a politics? To answer that question, we must find a mode of analysis that serves for the Judaic and Aristotelian systems both. When a single manner of inquiry yields different answers for different systems, and we can therefore explain why this, not that, we have reached the end of our study.

12

The Mishnah's Politics of Hierarchization

Inquiry into the ancient state and government needs to be lowered from
the stratosphere of rarefied conceptions, by a consideration not only of
ideology, of "national" pride and patriotism, of *der staat,* of the glories
and miseries of war, but also of the material relations among the citizens or
classes of citizens as much as those more commonly noticed between the
state and the citizens.

M. I. Finley

The contrast between Aristotle's and Judaisms's politics alert us to two important points of difference. First, the Mishnah's economics and its politics seem
disjoined. The householder functions as the building block for the house of
Israel, for its *economy* in the classic sense of the word—but the politics of the
house of Israel does not know him.[1] Second, Aristotle's keen interest in recognizing, explaining, and even controlling change contrasts vividly with the
Mishnah's framers' apparent incapacity to recognize change at all. The one
thing the Mishnah does not want to tell us is about change. It does not encompass history as the story of how things come to be what they are.

What do we learn from the difference between Aristotle's and the Mishnah's
politics about the Mishnah's system of the social order? At stake is an account
of what we may call the Mishnah's rationality,[2] its sense of how things are and
are meant to be. Accordingly, when we compare the politics of this Judaism
with that of Aristotle, we find ourselves moving beyond the boundaries set by
the topic before us. Our question concerns no longer principal components of
systems, but generative conceptions thereof. It addresses the basic sense for
the fittingness, the logic, the right ordering of things. When we can identify
the rationality of a system, then at the deepest layers of perception we can
compare that system with some other. And that is the right way to conclude,
for at stake in politics, for both Aristotle and Judaism, is not politics at all.

As a matter of fact, both Aristotle and the philosophers represented in the
Mishnah utilized politics to make a point that in each system far transcended
the subject at hand.[3] That point, in the case of the politics of this Judaism,

addresses the relations among classifications of persons and the relationships among those classifications.[4] These relations, while transcending the matter of legitimate violence, encompassed politics within a larger frame. That fact tells us why the Mishnah's particular Judaism also invoked politics in making its larger statement. The system required a politics because an important part of its message in the system builders' judgment could come to expression only in a politics.[5] The question therefore becomes, "What was that message, and why was politics, in particular, the correct medium for stating it?"

True, the Pentateuch itself set forth a politics, and so the choice of politics as a mode of spelling out the systemic message can hardly present any surprises. The character of the pentateuchal system assuredly found definition in the establishment of an "Israel" that was fully empowered, and fully enlandised as well. But framers of other Judaisms and Christianities did not appeal to a politics to set forth their systemic compositions, not at all. As a matter of fact, other Judaisms and Christianities set forth their systemic program in entire indifference to the issues of politics. And this point requires serious consideration so that the issue before us—why a politics at all?—will gain its rightful weight.

The topical program of the Mishnah, when compared with the themes deemed urgent by other system builders of some of the Judaisms and Christianities of the time, is marked by its sustained and systematic interest in civil law and government.[6] For example, the writings of apocalyptic Judaisms scarcely include any counterpart to the design for an everyday and functioning political struture and system (all the more so for an economics, it goes without saying). The Judaism of the Essene community of Qumran designed a political structure and system mainly for itself; it rejected the prevailing politics and assigned to its community the sole legitimate politics and also, of course, the sole standing as authentic Israel. Whether this be deemed a counterpart to the Mishnah's politics requires attention in its own terms; I am inclined to doubt it. Finally, the Judaism that would emerge in the writings that would continue the Mishnah, the two Talmuds in particular, recognized the existence of institutions of power for the Jews without encompassing those institutions within its politics as legitimate and important components of the legitimate use of power. The exilarch in Babylonia and the patriarch in the Land of Israel in no way form counterparts in the politics of the two Talmuds to the king and high priest of the politics of this Judaism.[7] So in the context of other Judaisms, the interest in political structures and systems of the one before us should not be regarded as merely characteristic of any Judaism because of the pentateuchal precedent.

The profoundly political character of this Judaism becomes still more astonishing when we look at the writings of early Christian figures, at the Gospels and the letters of Paul, for instance. There we search in vain for any political discourse that might bear implications for political institutions and their operation. Jesus is represented as having been perceived by the Romans as a political figure, but the Gospels formulate no political structure or system in his name, and the entire range of politics—appeal to legitimate use of violence, whether natural or supernatural—finds its boundaries at the limits of the church communities. The conception of a Christian state is beyond imagining. True, to Jesus are attributed sayings that respond to political facts, but none that will frame such facts; and Paul is utterly apolitical. Indeed, sayings cited in Jesus' name argue against any Christian politics whatsoever.

And that conforms to a familiar fact, that the earliest writings of Christianity hardly contain the raw materials for political theory of any kind; the exercise of power lies beyond the imagination of the Christian system builders and thinkers even after the advent of Constantine. From the formation of the Mishnah, ca. 200, two centuries would pass before a Christian writer would set forth a political theory of ambition and weight. But the parallel with the politics of post-Temple Judaism even then is inexact, for Augustine, the first Christian political thinker, did his work well after Christianity had gained the standing of a political power, when Christian emperors and bishops had wielded power and enjoyed the right of exercising legitimate violence in Christianity's name for more than a century.

If a system of Christianity such as Augustine set forth encompassed a politics, it was because Christianity by nature of its institutional position formed a political power within the Roman empire. That did not make it necessary for Augustine to think up a politics for his Christianity, but it made it plausible and natural for him to do so.[8] By contrast the authorship of the Mishnah, even though remembering a Jewish state perhaps, ever knew what it meant to put a person to death for a felony, to take away people's property in the name of collecting taxes, to beat, to maim, to expel and send into exile, in the name of the legitimate rule of the law enforced by the legally constituted and just state. Augustine was a bishop; he knew what power was about; the sages of the Mishnah, if they held any power at all, were at best local busybodies. From the perspective of competing figures, they seemed mere meddlers and no-accounts and bunglers, pretending to make up their minds and bear weighty opinions about matters concerning which, in point of fact, they utterly lacked experience. So why a political Judaism?

To answer that question we must address it to philosophy: why is it that a philosophy attends also to politics? The task of identifying the role of politics in the systemic composition and defining the unique message that was assigned to politics by the system seems to me quite clear. Having identified Aristotle as our guide and model, we turn back to the position and systemic tasks of politics in his philosophy, and with that perspective as our guide, we shall return to the Judaism at hand. We do well to begin with the judgment of the great M. I. Finley: "In the *Politics* Aristotle defined man as a *zoon politikon,* and what that meant is comprehensible only in the light of his metaphysics; hence correct translation requires a cumbersome paraphrase—man is a being whose highest goal, whose telos (end) is by nature to live in a *polis.*"[9]

It follows that sustained and cogent thought on politics, in particular, formed a critical component of Aristotle's larger thought on the nature of humanity. Political science encompasses all other areas of learning: "Now since political science uses the rest of the sciences, and since, again, it legislates as to what we are to do and what we are to abstain from, the end of this science must include those of the other sciences, so that its end must be the good for man." [10] If Aristotle wishes to discuss "the whole of human good," he must address a politics, and, as Mulgan states at the outset of his exposition, "An account of Aristotle's political theory must therefore begin with his conception of human good." [11]

Let us dwell for a moment on how politics delivers the systemic message concerning human good. Aristotle equates "human good" with "the good life." What are the traits of happiness? "The happy man will be someone who values the philosophical contemplation of eternal truths above all else and will devote a considerable amount of his time to it." [12] And again, Mulgan states, "The subject matter of political science is human action." [13] Aristotle's main purpose in the *Politics* is "to provide a handbook or guide for the intending statesman"; "political science" is also "statesmanship." [14] Aristotle writes primarily for the ruler, the statesman or legislator who will be making important political decisions, rather than for the ordinary citizen; his political science is statesmanship, not civics. [15] And what does Aristotle wish to accomplish through his political philosophy? "The overtly practical purpose of Aristotle's political science explains the close dependence of the *Politics* on his conception of human good. Political decisions must be based not only on knowledge about the workings of politics but also on some view of the ends or goals which the community ought to be pursuing." [16] So the goals which the statesman ought to achieve constitute Aristotle's starting point; next come generalizations or rules about how these goals can be achieved in different types of political situation; finally, Aristotle applies the rules to actual situations. [17] The role of political thought in the definition of human good therefore is critical:

> The happy man will be someone who values the philosophical contemplation of eternal truths above all else and will devote a considerable amount of his time to it. . . . This conception of the good life provides the background and inspiration for most of Aristotle's political theory. The connection between his ethical ideals and his political science is most clearly expressed in the last chapter of the *Ethics,* where, having completed his account of the good life, he raises the question of how it is to be implemented. People are unlikely to become good unless the government and the laws are directed toward the achievement of human good. The complete "philosophy of human nature" must therefore include the study of laws and constitutions and how best to frame them. . . . The influence of Aristotle's ethics on his politics will be most apparent in his discussion of the nature of the *polis* and in his account of the ideal state which is intended to implement the ethical ideal. [18]

Evidently, Aristotle attends to political science because he is interested in the nature of the human being and especially in human action.

This fact explains why politics forms a medium for the expression of Aristotle's larger system of thought on the nature of the human being and human society: "The overtly practical purpose of Aristotle's political science explains the close dependence of the *Politics* on his conception of human good. Political decisions must be based not only on knowledge about the workings of politics but also on some view of the ends or goals which the community ought to be pursuing." [19] The principal point is that the politics of Aristotle forms part of a larger inquiry into how things are by nature. In this connection we rapidly review what formed the centerpiece of our inquiry into the role of the household in Aristotle's *polis*. Aristotle's philosophical program, we remember, is to investigate what accords with nature or exists by nature. In this context the correct mode of thought derives from the discovery and classification of the traits and characteristics of things by nature.

So Mulgan states: "Because this world is constructed according to a coherent and rational pattern, it is proper . . . that each species should develop and exercise its own natural characteristics. By doing so, it realises its 'essence' and performs its work of function." [20] The appeal to nature, beginning with biology and ending with the political community, then accounts for the place of the politics in the larger system, to which politics likewise proves natural and necessary. The subject matter accounted for, the message delivered through this topic as through many others spelled out, we may now turn to the counterpart for the initial Judaism.

When we come to Judaism and ask, "What is the message of politics, and why does politics serve as a particularly appropriate medium for the message?" we do best to begin not with similarity but with difference, for having established grounds for comparison, we can now explore the incongruities of the two systems. [21] Seen in this light, each system will then serve through the outline of its shadow to highlight the indicatively different systemic traits of the other. To understand the message for which politics served as a medium, and to explain why that particular medium uniquely served the purposes of the system builders, we return to our discussion of the systemic myth, spun out of the facts of power in its most brutal political form, from which, after all, all else flows.

Why a political Judaism? And what message did this Judaism find possible to express uniquely, or most powerfully, in the medium of a fabricated political structure and system? The principal message of politics in the system of Judaism derives, we recall, from our capacity to differentiate among the applications of power by reference to the attitude of the person who comes into relationship with that power. We remember that if the deed is deliberate, then one institution among the set of politically empowered institutions exercises jurisdiction and utilizes supernatural power. If the deed is inadvertent, another political agency exercises jurisdiction and utilizes the power made available by that same supernatural being. Why does this seem to me of such fundamental importance? *Because where a system differentiates, there it delivers its critical message.* So the point at which the system tells us "why this, not that" marks its exegetical fulcrum. And that, we recall, lies in the systemic identification of the two powers that do conflict, God's and the human person's. The entire politics works out the issues of power that to begin with are generated out of that conflict. And, by the way, the politics then identifies political agencies to deal with the several distinct types of conflict between those two wills.

The system's entire message stands within that resolution of the power of will that is implicitly and tacitly contained within the labor of hierarchization, beginning at the very foundations of all being. As I shall now explain, the question answered by the politics for the system, and by the system as a whole, is this: what happens when God's will, which is supreme, confronts conflict ("rebellion," "sin," "disobedience") with the human will, which is subordinate? The answer is, God's will be done. And this—this politics—is how. Why a politics? Because the system recognizes that the human will does constitute power. It is, moreover, a power to be reckoned with, taken into account, deemed legitimate even in its violent confrontation with God. And therefore—because of its very legitimacy—the power formed of the human will is to be met with the equal, and equally legitimate, violence that the political system, acting in God's behalf, effects. The hierarchization of power sets forth the systemic problem, and the theory of the politics of this Judaism defines the self-evidently valid solution.

The conflict worked out by politics then is between God's will, expressed in the law of the Torah, and the human being's will, carried out in obedience to the law of the Torah or in defiance of that law. Here, as we noted in the beginning, we find a reprise of Eden's politics and of all the other mythic formulations of the conflict between God's power and humanity's, between God's commandment and humanity's freedom to obey or to disobey. The politics of Judaism emerges as a reprise, in stunning detail, of the story of God's commandment, humanity's disobedience, God's sanction for the sin or crime, and humanity's atonement and reconciliation. When Adam and Eve or Moses and Aaron exercise their own will and defy God, they set their power, their free choice to obey or disobey, against God's power, his capacity to command—without coercion. And because of God's limitation, we have here a conflict of human and divine wills that stand in equal contest with one another.

This again precipitates the systemic question, how are equal powers ordered? The power of the will of the one against the strength of the will of the other (a will limited by self-restraint, to be sure) forms not so much the theme of the system before us as its problematic. That, in my view, accounts for the system's profound engagement with issues of hierarchization. The dynamic of the system derives from the capacity of human attitude and intention to define culpable action, and, as I said, that central theme draws us back to the myth of Adam and Eve in Eden. Once more we note the principal message: God commands, but humanity does what it then chooses. In the interplay of those two protean forces, each a power in its own right, the sanctions and penalties of the system apply.

Let me then say why I think this Judaism found a politics necessary, a political statement integral. And let me define the statement that this Judaism made through its politics. Politics served the critical systemic task of differentiation: why this, not that. It proved necessary because it sorted out the effects of the human will among three media of divine intervention: Heavenly court above, earthly court below, Temple altar in between. Power, as we noted earlier, works its way in the interplay between what God has set forth in the law of the Torah and what human beings do intentionally or inadvertently, obediently or defiantly. Accordingly, a politics was necessary, a political statement integral to Judaism. And given the subject matter of politics, the legitimate uses of coercion, we may hardly find astonishing the inclusion of a politics in the initial Judaism.

But what was the shape of the particular statement that emerged? To answer that question, we turn from the myth to the method: how, precisely, did the sages of the Mishnah work out their politics? When we know the answer to that question, we shall understand the character of the system's details, just as, when we know the main purpose of Aristotle's system, we can also account for the character of his fictive politics. This is why the answer to our question draws us to an account of Judaism's counterpart to Aristotle's thesis about the priority of the natural over the conventional, his insistence upon the principle—prior to all propositions—that both political and nonpolitical institutions derive from the very nature of things. This quality enables them to realize the potential that is inherent in that nature, that is justified by the traits of human nature. Accordingly, here we shall juxtapose and compare things that, when we began this inquiry, could not have appeared to us to be congruent or—as we shall see in a moment—even related. Since, in my view, one of the marks of an analysis' success is the possibility it raises for us plausibly to juxtapose and compare what to begin with appeared utterly incomparable, we seem to have made some progress.

Knowing Aristotle's mode of thought, and therefore fundamental purpose in making his system, we can account for his topical program in general and the particular relevance of politics within that program. That is, if only after the fact, we can account for his uses of politics. But can we identify within the method of the Mishnah's sages an equivalently fundamental method or mode of thought? To answer that question, we turn from generalities about myth to the concrete cases at hand. When the framers of the Mishnah speak, it is only in and through detail. But if, as I maintain, their statement is systematic and forms a system, then how they treat any detail of any substance should indicate how they think about all details. From that indication, consequently, we should be able to generalize about the methods and modes of thought at hand.

And once we can describe how the system builders think, we can identify what is the generative tension and critical concern of the system as a whole, a tension worked out, a concern expressed, also in the realm of politics.

For that purpose we move, as we did before, from the myth of power to the institutions thereof. When the Mishnah's sages address the description of institutions, what do they want to know about them? That is to say, given a topic, they will have a particular program of inquiry they propose to follow. From a scarcely limited corpus of facts, they will want to find out or invent answers to one set of questions rather than to some other. A particular aspect of the facts will attract their interest. This aspect I term a generative problematic, for it generates the problems the system builders identify and propose to solve. In the case at hand, we turn to the two most consequential matters, to the political structures and sanctions which together constitute the formation of coercive power that defines a politics—any politics.

And this inquiry draws us to two issues, the relationship between king and high priest, and the catalog of judicially inflicted penalties. These issues seem utterly unrelated, yet they yield a single mode and method of thought and produce results that fall within a single classification. Specifically, they compare and contrast and therefore hierarchize. In the matter of institutions, exemplified by the treatment of the king and the high priest, we find silence about questions that engage us. For example, the authority and role of king and high priest in the administration of the everyday affairs of particular localities, and the way in which people leave and enter office, do not appear. But we do learn in exquisite detail the relative position of the high priest and the king (the king stands higher in the hierarchy of power and authority than the high priest). The Mishnah's framers want to accomplish the hierarchization of these two important loci of power, so they compare the king to the high priest and in detail make explicit the standing imputed to each.

The generative problematic concerns hierarchization, which is to say, comparison and contrast of species of the same genus. The two heads of state are alike but different, and the king is the superior figure. The high priest and the king form a single genus but two distinct species, and the variations between the species form a single set of taxonomic indicators. The one is like the other in these ways, unlike the other in those ways. We recall the passage (first encountered in chapter 4) beginning as follows:

A. A high priest (1) judges, and [others] judge him;
B. (2) gives testimony, and [others] give testimony about him;
C. (3) performs the rite of removing the shoe with his wife. . . .

M. San. 2:1

A. (1) The king does not judge, and [others] do not judge him;
B. (2) does not give testimony, and [others] do not give testimony about him;

C. (3) does not perform the rite of removing the shoe, and others do not perform the rite of removing the shoe with his wife. . . .

M. San. 2:2

The formal traits of the matched sets make immediately clear the mode of thought at hand which, in context, is hierarchization through the comparison and contrast of the traits of officeholders. We know the proper place of each because we can identify the rules that govern them both, and, further, we know the meaning of the application of a rule to one species but not to another of the same genus. The comparison is the point, and what we learn is that the king enjoys a higher standing than the high priest. Then what the system builders want to know about the king and the high priest is the answer to a hierarchical question. That explains why they adduce in evidence the facts they have chosen, rather than other facts that could have been discovered or made up in answer to a generative problematic of another character entirely.[22]

That indicative trait of the system as a whole explains why, as a matter of fact, their entire politics is a politics of hierarchization. At stake are the right arrangements, the proper and correct positions, for all persons and all things. The questions that delineate the hierarchy cover who is on top, who underneath, and who comes first, who next. Just as Aristotle everywhere seeks the answer to one question, systematically worked out in diverse areas, so do the sages of Judaism. Aristotle consistently wishes to know what is good for humanity, a question he answers by appealing to the natural traits of persons and things; similarly, the philosophers of the Mishnah want to answer their question. And they too answer their question by appealing to the natural traits of persons and things, traits that they work through inductively in quest of the pertinent rule or generalization.

Aristotle, we recall, appeals to the capacity of humanity to speak, and this forthwith forms a fact of nature that dictates a trait of politics as well:

> Nature . . . does nothing without some purpose, and for the purpose of making man a political animal, she has endowed him alone among the animals with the power of reasoned speech. Speech is something different from voice. . . . Speech serves to indicate what is useful and what is harmful, and so also what is just and what is unjust."

The same mode of thought—appeal to the traits of things in search of generalization—accounts for the hierarchical positions assigned to king and high priest. So we juxtapose the sentences of Aristotle beginning "Nature . . . does nothing" with those of the Mishnah that declare, "A high priest judges and others judge him, the king does not judge, and others do not judge him," etc. Aristotle's thinking about the political implications of the natural ability of humanity to be able to speak forms the counterpart to the Mishnah's authorship's thinking about the comparison of the king and the high priest. Incongruous? Only if we do not grasp the systems and what is at stake in them. The

Mishnah's sages dealt with politics because they wished to address fundamental issues of power, and they imposed upon politics the generative problematic of hierarchization because that defined their mode and method of thought. What they wanted to find out, in the description of the social order, was the right ordering of things, and what they managed, then, to say, through politics in particular, was that God disposes of the effects of human freedom.

That is not to suggest that all Israelites were conceived to be equal and to stand in the same relationship to Heaven within the grid of sanctification. The contrary is the case. Although a system of hierarchization by definition concerns itself with the opposite of the equalization of relationships, proposing to show how persons (things, places, conditions as to cultic cleanness—just about anything!) are not equal, in the politics at hand, the upshot of hierarchization is that diverse castes are unequal, but all male Israelites may overcome the hierarchical structure imposed by caste by entering the category of sage. The sage, after all, truly possesses and manipulates power, for power comes from God, and the sage is the master of the message of Heaven.

Now that we have the Mishnah's modes of thought in hand, let me conclude with a reprise of the main conceptions on which this politics of Judaism rests. The framers of religious systems that concern themselves with the structure and order of society answer urgent questions set for them in the life of society, questions of economics, philosophy, and politics. To these issues of the social order, governing the material and intellectual foundations of the social entity and the proper administration, through sanctions, of its collective life, they respond with what are to them self-evident answers. The religious system, then, comprises identification of the urgent question and the composition, out of accounts of the ethics, ethos, and politics dictated (commonly) by Heaven, of final solutions to that critical problem. The Mishnah provides one striking example of how people in writing set forth the ethics, ethos, and ethnos that all togther comprise a Judaism, how they give a cogent answer to an urgent question. Since in this Judaism we deal with a social entity that in the minds of its inventors also constitutes a political entity in particular, we here consider how in their imagination intellectuals proposed to sort out issues of legitimate violence. For the political entity, "Israel," in this Judaism exercises the form of coercion that consists of the power to tell people what to do and then to make them do it.

In describing, analyzing, and interpreting the politics of this Judaism we have dealt with high abstractions. But we cannot permit matters to conclude with so theological a judgment of what is at stake. Remembering the words of M. I. Finley that stand at the head of this chapter, we have to ask how the politics of this Judaism sorted out "the material relations among the citizens or classes of citizens as much as those more commonly noticed between the state and the citizens." The answer is that this politics did not sort out the material relations among citizens or classes of citizens. This is a politics that appealed to indicators of an other-than-material order when it classified persons, social entities—all living things—within an order and a hierarchy. Independent variables, in the imagination of the system builders, derived from other considerations than the control of the basic means of production. Perhaps it would be more to the point to say the system builders thought that the systemically interesting means of production were not those that produced material things. What mattered was holiness, and how holiness ("the holy" or "the sacred") was defined would then indicate who produced it, that is, who sanctified whom, and how.

So the systemic issues of hierarchization dealt with the ordering of different things on the basis of different traits from those things that are signified by the indicators of material productivity, and that explains why, if Marxist can identify with their views the politics of Aristotle, they cannot similarly appropriate the politics of this Judaism. Only in that light can we take into account an economics that utterly ignores most of the actual economy[23] and a politics that treats as null such obviously puissant classes at that composed of householders. Now we see the full meaning of the simple fact that sages ignored when treating politics what proved the critical and central component of their thought when treating economics. When sages in the Mishnah set forth a politics, they concerned themselves not with material relations at all, but with power relationships, and these, they conceived, flowed not from any relationship among classes of citizens but from that between all Israelites and God. So the distinctions are between like entities—yet signal vast differences.

From their intellects, the Mishnah's system builders have composed a world at rest, perfect and complete, made holy because it is complete and perfect. In mythic terms, the Mishnah confronts the fall from Eden with Eden, with the world on the eve of the Sabbath of Creation: "Thus the heavens and the earth were finished and all the host of them. And on the seventh day God finished his work which he had done, and he rested on the seventh day from all his work which he had done. So God blessed the seventh day and hallowed it, because on it God rested from all his work which he had done in creation" (Gen. 2:1–3). The Mishnah's framers have posited an economy embedded in a social system awaiting the seventh day and that day's divine act of sanctification which, as at the creation of the world, would set the seal of holy rest upon an again-complete creation. There is no place for action and actors when what is sought is no action whatsoever, but only unchanging perfection. There is room only for a description of how things are, for the present tense, for a sequence of completed statements and static problems. All the action lies within, in how these statements are made. When nothing remains to be said, nothing remains to be done. There is no need for actors, whether political entities such as king, scribes, priests, or economic entities, householders.

The Mishnah's principal message, expressed through the categorical media of economics and politics alike, the message that makes the Judaism of this document and of its social components distinctive and cogent, is that man stands at the center of creation, at the head of all creatures upon earth; he corresponds to God in Heaven in whose image he is made.[24] Who this man is—whether householder in economics, whether priest, monarch, or sage in politics—shifts from topic to topic, but the priority of the human (male's) will and attitude in the disposition of important questions everywhere forms the premise of discourse. The way in which the Mishnah makes this simple and fundamental statement by imputing to man the power to inaugurate and initiate those corresponding processes which play so critical a role in the Mishnah's account of reality, sanctification and uncleanness. The will of man, expressed through the deed of man, is the active power in the world. Will and deed constitute the operators in creation working upon neutral realms subject to either sanctification or uncleanness. They affect the Temple and table, the field and family, the altar and hearth, woman, time, space, transactions in the material world and in the world above. An object, a substance, a transaction—even a phrase or a sentence—although inert, may be made holy when the interplay of the will and deed of man arouses or generates its potential to be sanctified. Conversely, each may be treated as ordinary or (where relevant) made unclean by neglect of the will or by an inattentive act of man.

Take the case of how uncleanness and cleanness work. These two categories are not systematically inert or neutral, but systematically indicative. The entire system of uncleanness and holiness awaits the intervention of man, which imparts the capacity to become unclean upon what was formerly inert, or which removes the capacity to impart cleanness from what was formerly in its natural and puissant condition. So too in the other ranges of reality; man stands at the center on earth just as God stands at the center in Heaven. Man is counterpart and partner and creation in that, like God, he has power over the status and condition of creation. He can put everything in its proper place, call everything by its rightful name. So, stated briefly, the question taken up by the Mishnah and answered by Judaism is, what can a man do? And the answer laid down by the Mishnah is, man, through will and deed, is master of this world, the measure of all things. Since when the Mishnah thinks of man it means the Israelite, who is the subject and actor of its system, the statement is clear. The man is Israel, who can do what he wills. In the aftermath of the two wars, the message of the Mishnah cannot have proved more pertinent.

We conclude with the obvious point about utopia, that it exists no-where in particular. The politics of Judaism began in the imagination of a generation of intellectuals who, in the aftermath of the Jerusalem government's and Temple's destruction (70) and the military defeat Jews suffered three generations later (132–135), had witnessed the end of the political system and structure that the Jews had known for the preceding millennium. Initially set forth in the Mishnah, the political theory of Judaism laid out political institutions and described how they should work. In that way these intellectuals, who enjoyed no documented access to power of any kind and who certainly seem unable to coerce many people to do very much, sorted out issues of power. They took account, in mind at least, of the issues of legitimate coercion within

Israel, the holy people, which they considered more than a voluntary association, more than a community formed around a cult.[25]

Their Judaism encompassed a politics because through politics they found it possible to express their systemic message, one that put everything in its proper place and order, correctly differentiating, compellingly hierarchizing. And that systemic message explains why their system's social entity, that is, their Israel, formed a political entity as well. Their "Israel" was supposedly able to govern in its holy land through the exercise of coercive power, not merely through a voluntary community that persuaded compliance. The setting was an age of endings and, consequently, beginnings. Everyone knew what was now behind. Within the half century before the time of the authorship of the document, the Temple of Jerusalem had been destroyed, together with the political structures based upon it, and a major war meant to recover the city and reinstitute an autonomous, even independent, Jewish state had been lost. But no one could anticipate what would now happen.

Whatever politics had before now had no call upon the future, unless the coming generations restored the now lost structure and system. And the founders did not. Instead, they made up a system for which, in concrete, historical time, no counterpart had actually existed in the world and age of which sages had firsthand knowledge. Indeed, whatever the political facts deriving from the Israel of times past—or from Roman practice in their own day, for that matter—the authorship had in hand, they were drastically reworked. All received information and fabricated conceptions served equally to form the essentially fresh and freestanding structure and system that sages made up. From the middle to the end of the second century, the work of rethinking the politics of this Judaism went forward. And, therefore, embedded within the religious system represented by the Mishnah and correlative and successor writings was set forth a politics that would define the reference point of Judaism from that time to the present. But that does not mean the politics of this Judaism in its initial statement ever attained realization in the structure of actual institutions and in the system of a working government.

The system of the initial Judaism, while influential for nearly two millennia, never actually dictated how people would do things at all. By the time the systemic document made its appearance a new politics had gotten under way, one that accorded to holy Israel in the Holy Land, that is, to Jews in Palestine, limited rights of self-government that were mainly focused upon matters of no interest to the provincial authorities (e.g., issues of personal status, transactions of petty value, ritual and cultic questions that meant nothing to anybody who mattered).[26] But that new politics, with its jurisdiction over things of no account and its access to power of no material weight, in no way corresponded to the formidable conceptions of legitimate violence, exercised through enduring institutions and a well-organized bureaucracy and appealing to a sustaining political myth, that are set forth here. Nor in the realities of Jews' limited self-administration in the third and fourth centuries, down to ca. 400, do we find actual examples of the workings of the passion, responsibility, and proportion and balance of a concrete system of political life, such as the document's authorship has made up for itself. But the one trait that would characterize all subsequent systems is the one dictated by the initial system. Politics would require the working out of issues of hierarchization, and sages would dictate the composition and construction of Israel's social order.

Notes

PREFACE

1. An account of a politics usually encompasses what people actually do, as well as the theory of what may be done and how that will get done. But in the case of this Judaism we have no information whatsoever on what was going on, only on how sages described what should happen. We know as fact only that the system at hand posits authority in king and high priest, and that ca. A.D. 200 there was no king or high priest governing the Jews of Palestine. Herod had been the last autonomous king, and the last governing high priest had perished more than a century and a quarter earlier. The wholly fictive character of the politics then is transparent. In our inquiry into the next stage in the political theory of Judaism, that marked by the Talmud of the Land of Israel and related writings, we shall find more attention to political facts, as distinct from fantasies.

2. Let me briefly define the Mishnah (to which we return at length in chapter 2). Written in the aftermath of the destruction of the Temple in A.D. 70 and of the Jews' political system and institutions at that time, composed in the ruin of the war led by Bar Kokhba to regain Jerusalem, rebuild the Temple, and restore the Jews' government and political autonomy (132–135), the Mishnah's code, completed in 200, sets forth how things ought to be. Beyond the Pentateuch ("the [written] Torah"), ca. 450 B.C., the Mishnah comprises the initial document of the Judaism that has proved authoritative and definitive from antiquity to our own day, the Judaism of the dual Torah, oral and written. In the mythic framework of that Judaism, the Mishnah (long after the fact to be sure) enjoys paramount standing as the first writing down of the oral part of the Torah revealed by God to Moses at Mount Sinai.

3. Further definition will be provided in chapter 2.

4. New York: Praeger, 1988. Sicker includes a bibliography for political theory in reference to Judaism. For the titles that deal with, or refer to, late antiquity, I regret I cannot say I found any use whatsoever. See my *Economics of the Mishnah* (Chicago: University of Chicago Press, 1990), for a judgment of the available writings on the counterpart subject. For politics there is, to my knowledge, no equivalent to the inestimable Eliezer Kleiman, Hebrew University of Jerusalem, whose articles on the economics of the Talmud show how the technical analytical work is to be done.

INTRODUCTION

1. I have explained this matter at some length in my *Judaism and its Social Metaphors* (Cambridge: Cambridge University Press, 1988).

2. That is why contemporary political theory in the tradition of Max Weber will not serve to guide category formation for the present work.

3. I have shown in my *The Philosophical Mishnah* (Atlanta: Scholars Press for Brown Judaic Studies, 1989), 1–4, that the Mishnah constituted a philosophical writing, and in my *Judaism as Philosophy: The Method and Message of the Mishnah* (Columbia: University of South Carolina Press, 1991) I have defined precisely the character of that philosophy. That accounts for my referring to the authorship of the Mishnah as philosophers. Their writing was received and transformed by different kinds of thinkers altogether.

4. In H. H. Gerth and C. Wright Mills, *From Max Weber: Essays in Sociology* (New York: Oxford University Press, 1958), 77–128. All page references refer to this article.

5. But that is not to suggest that the contemporary politics of the state of Israel or of the organized Jewish communities elsewhere in the world (to the degree that these form political entities at all) are understood, best or at all, by appeal to the politics defined by the Judaism studied here. I do not deal with that question. For one thing, no one has yet demonstrated that there is anything remotely resembling a political tradition of an ongoing, linear kind that characterizes Judaic religious systems or that accounts for Jews' political behavior. True, some assume just that. But rigorous analysis lies in the future.

6. As, in the case of this same Judaism, through economics!

7. My framing of the entire inquiry derives, of course, from the theory of the study of religion worked out by Jonathan Z. Smith in various papers, most recently in his *Imagining Religion: From Babylon to Jonestown* (Chicago: University of Chicago Press, 1982).

8. This is not meant as just another book about the Mishnah, and readers familiar with my *Judaism: The Evidence of the Mishnah* (Atlanta: Scholars Press for Brown Judaic Studies, 1987), second edition, augmented, will surely want to skip chapter 2.

9. My view is that the description, analysis, and interpretation of one politics in its systemic context require the comparison and contrast of that system with another politics in its setting. Just as we cannot study a religion without the comparison of religions, so we cannot study a politics without comparing the political systems, or the theories thereof. Solely through comparison and contrast do we gain perspective on the thing we know. It follows that if we wish to place the politics of Judaism into theoretical context, we must find the likeness of this politics and some other politics, and the difference of this politics and another one. That explains why a third of the book is devoted to the work of comparing politics.

10. For a general introduction to the context of Greco-Roman political thought I consulted Kurt Raaflaub, "Die Anfänge des politischen Denkens bei gen Griechen, " *Pipers Handbuch der politischen Ideen,* ed. Iring Fetscher and Herfried Münkler (Munich and Zurich: Piper, 1988), 189–271.

11. As the politics is expounded in the clear and authoritative work of R. G. Mulgan, *Aristotle's Political Theory: An Introduction for Students of Political Theory* (Oxford: Clarendon Press, 1977).

12. In my book of of essays, *The Study of Judaism* (Atlanta: Scholars Press for Brown Judaic Studies, 1989), there are many passages relevant to the subject treated here, but not necessary for my argument and analysis. See chapter 8 of that book for the full abstracts from the Mishnah to which I briefly refer here. In that same freestanding essay I also include some discussions of problems that seemed to me important but that impeded the exposition of our current pursuit. In this way I have tried to set forth an intellectually economical account of my subject. The same collection of essays places this book into the twin contexts—the social description of religion, the political economy (hence, social ecology) of religion—defined by the field of learning to which I hope to contribute (and indeed, to help renovate) and into the context of my intellectual autobiography.

13. I have also had to refer to other works of mine for fairly substantial discussions of problems important here, since a reprise is not possible, but the upshot is important. I refer, for instance, to *The Formation of the Jewish Intellect: Making Connections and Drawing Conclusions in the Traditional System of Judaism* (Atlanta: Scholars Press for Brown Judaic Studies, 1988), where I set forth the list-making logic of the Mishnah and show how it works, and to *Uniting the Dual Torah: Sifra and the Problem of the Mishnah* (Cambridge: Cambridge University Press,

1989), which identifies the logical foundations of the Mishnah's modes of thought and argument. These works stand on their own, as this book is meant to, but the results, as to the fundamental systemic intellect represented by the Mishnah, coincide with the ones presented here and vastly enrich them.

CHAPTER ONE

1. M. I. Finley, *Politics in the Ancient World* (Cambridge: Cambridge University Press, 1983), 8.

2. As will become clear later on, I use the term "his" advisedly.

3. We return to this matter in chapter 12.

4. I owe the point on Hobbes to the reader of this book for the University of Chicago Press. On disembedded economics and the disintegration of political economy, see my *Economics of the Mishnah* (Chicago: University of Chicago Press, 1990).

5. These terms are described in length in chapter 2.

6. I use the more familiar A.D., rather than the theologically more appropriate C.E. (Common Era), and B.C., not B.C.E. (Before the Common Era) simply to stick to what people know. This book includes enough that is unfamiliar as it is.

7. I fear this usage of "ethics" is idiosyncratic and so beg the reader's indulgence.

8. None familiar with the character of Judaism in the state of Israel can quarrel with that obvious judgment. But the diaspora Judaisms, where Jews are numerous, commonly take up positions on political questions as well, and the faith forms a community that finds it appropriate to appeal to sanctions of various kinds in effecting public policy. It must follow that all Judaisms that emerge from the Mishnah and its continuator documents are political.

9. I have worked out the economics in *The Economics of the Mishnah* (Chicago: University of Chicago Press, 1989).

10. I have spelled out the philosophy in *Judaism as Philosophy: The Method and Message of the Mishnah* (Columbia: University of South Carolina Press, 1991).

11. The considerable literature on the political situation of the Jews of Palestine in the first and second centuries is catalogued, through 1964, in my *History of the Jews of Babylonia* (1965; 2d rev. ed., Leiden: E. J. Brill, 1970), vol. 1, *The Parthian Period*. Salo W. Baron, *Social and Religious History of the Jews* (New York: Columbia University Press, 1952) vol. 2, also serves. There is no need to demonstrate here the established facts that the old political order ended in 70 and was obliterated by the defeat of Bar Kokhba in 135. The new order, in which the Jews as an ethnic group were governed in some matters of mainly internal concern by an ethnarch, the patriarch or *nasi,* clearly was in place ca. A.D. 200. It was then that the Mishnah's politics came to publication as part of the entirety of the Mishnah's account of the social order. These simple and well-accepted facts explain my characterization of the politics of Judaism in its initial statement as a politics of the interim, describing not past or future or, none can deny, the present, that is, the actual time—mid-second century—in which the politics was made up and written down.

12. But my comparison is to the philosophical politics of Aristotle, rather than, for example, the theological politics of Augustine, because the Mishnah is fundamentally and profoundly a philosophical document, not a theological one. I show that fact in my *The Philosophical Mishnah* (Atlanta: Scholars Press for Brown Judaic Studies, 1989), chapters 1–4, and I spell out the philosophy in the context of Aristotle's method and Plotinus's Middle Platonic doctrine in my *Judaism as Philosophy: The Method and Message of the Mishnah* (Columbia: University of South Carolina Press, 1991). In my *Transformation of Judaism: From Philosophy to Religion* (Champaign-Urbana: University of Illinois Press, 1991), I have discussed Augustine's *City of God* in comparison with the political economy of the Judaism of the Talmud of the Land of Israel and related Midrash compilations. In that context, so I insist, we no longer can speak of a philosophical system at all.

13. And it explains why in describing, analyzing, and interpreting the politics of Judaism we have in hand an opportunity to examine a religious formation of politics perceived quite outside the reference-points delineated for us by Max Weber, and by later scholars in his tradition. Weber's categories do not work well for the study of an embedded politics. In the end, then, we have to recognize the systemic autonomy of the Mishnah's political categories.

14. While admittedly not expert in the literature, I have seen no sustained interest, in accounts of politics in antiquity, in the politics of Judaism (at least, beyond the Hebrew Scriptures), and none of the books I consulted knows that the Mishnah constitutes a political document.

15. True, sanctions are abnormal, obedience normal. The indication of political success is when the politics works, day in, day out, year in, year out. The measure of success derives in the case before us from this Judaism's achieving its goals not through coercion but through collective effort and assent.

16. I explain the Weberian origins of these categories later in this chapter.

17. I provide a full account of the available theories for the formative age of Judaism in my *Judaism and Its Social Metaphors: Israel in the History of Jewish Thought* (Cambridge: Cambridge University Press, 1988).

18. See Bernard Lewis, *The Political Language of Islam* (Chicago: University of Chicago Press, 1988), 25ff.

19. There are, in fact, two politics to be discussed in the analytical and interpretive part of this book (part 3), the Mishnah's and Aristotle's. And, in fact, both political structures and systems neglect the same set of issues, while focusing upon another set of issues. The questions I bring and the traits of the two systems that are compared define the issues.

20. We return to this matter in chapter 2.

21. I owe this approach to matters to Professor Frances K. Goldscheider, my colleague and dear friend, who told me that sociologists have a full program of questions that require answers for the building of settlements on distant planets. My sense is that this is much as the Jesuits (among others) had answers in the sixteenth and seventeenth centuries for the questions of society building in the Spanish and Portuguese New World, and as the Puritans had for New England. Nothing started *de nova,* because people had thought through precisely what they would need to know. The Mayflower Compact, after all, was signed aboard ship, before a single structure had been built on shore.

22. All pages are from "Politics as a Vocation," cited in note 4 to this book's introduction.

23. Gerth and Mills, 333ff.

24. That then sets the stage for chapter 4, and, consequently, chapter 5 as well. We shall see in part 2 that the same procedure, beginning with the concrete application of power through sanctions, guides us in identifying appropriate data to determine how the politics was supposed to function.

25. I need hardly add that I claim no expert knowledge of Greek political theogy and take my observations for purposes of comparison and contrast only by naked eye, and then only of the most obvious and accessible sightings: moon, sun, but not distant or faded stars.

26. Cited by R. G. Mulgan, *Aristotle's Political Theory* (Oxford: Clarendon Press, 1977), 3.

27. That may be said of most political theories—and most of those evolve less subject to intervention by practitioners of statecraft.

28. In our century we prefer "class" or "caste" or other more abstract and impersonal categories.

29. Whom we shall meet again in chapter 2 and chapter 10.

30. The embeddedness of economics within a larger theory of social and political economy, characteristic of Aristotle's system, does not characterize the relationships between economics and politics in Judaism. My guess is that the possibility of a disembedded economics came about only with the collapse of Christian belief (via Aquinas to Aristotle) for the eighteenth-century philosophers. That opened the way to modes of inquiry formerly closed by the profoundly embedded, therefore distributive, economics of the Christianity of the tradition of Aristotle. But, of

course, economics followed and explained the economy, and the formation of market economics as the regnant medium of material relationships in Western Europe came about long after the rise of capitalism.

CHAPTER TWO

1. These fall into two categories, compilations of exegeses and amplifications of the Mishnah and equivalent documents serving Scripture, that is to say, the oral and the written forms of the Torah, respectively. The former comprise, among other writings, the Tosefta, the Talmud of the Land of Israel, and the Talmud of Babylonia, and the latter, Sifra to Leviticus, Sifré to Numbers, Sifré to Deuteronomy, Mekhilta attributed to R. Ishmael, Genesis Rabbah, Leviticus Rabbah, Pesiqta deRab Kahana, and other compilations, all completed between the third and the seventh centuries A.D.

2. The diachronic measure is taken by showing not only how a later formation has found its own definitions of matters, but how a later formation has realized in itself conceptions or principles implicit or hidden within an earlier one. Or how a later formation set aside the received categories! I have shown that the successor system to the Mishnah's undertook its own category formation, integrating matters differentiated by the earlier system, for instance, as I argue in my *Transformation of Judaism.* But no one can maintain that the Mishnah's inner tensions and generative logic have reached full exposure only within the formulations of the Mishnah itself. What we find later on can be shown to bring to the surface results of premises, resolutions of tensions, contained even at the outset. But this must be demonstrated, not merely postulated.

3. No criterion of age or of longevity pertains, for how long does a system have to survive to be classified as a system? A system that meets the definition at hand—worldview, complemented by a way of life, addressed to a clearly denoted Israel—however long it lasts constitutes a system. The reason is that a religious system presents a fact not of history but of immediacy, of the social present. The issue of survival by itself proves irrelevant to the analysis of a system. A system is like a language. A language forms an example of language if it produces communication through rules of syntax and grammar. That paradigm serves full well however many people speak the language, or however long the language serves. Two people who understand each other form a language community even, or especially, if no one understands them. For however long, at whatever moment in historic time, a religious system grows up in the perpetual present, an artifact of its day, whether today or a long-ago time. The only appropriate tense for a religious system is the present. A religious system always *is,* whatever it was, whatever it will be. Why so? Because its traits address a condition of humanity in society, a circumstance of an hour—however brief or protracted the hour and the circumstance.

4. So the phrase "the *history* of a *system,*" presents us with an oxymoron.

5. I put "Israel" into quotation marks to underline that the word can stand for a variety of types of social entities and that an "Israel" will form a component of a Judaism and bear the systemic message of that Judaism. I have laid out these matters on their own in my *Judaism and its Social Metaphors* (Cambridge: Cambridge University Press, 1988). The question of the social entity of a religious system is not primary in the present work, though I should imagine that the politics of a Judaism will play an important role in bearing the systemic judgment upon its Israel. I hope, therefore, in future reflection to make sense of the relationship between the politics of this particular Judaism and its "Israel." But we are still at the stage of laying out the principal components of the system viewed as a social system and therefore read as an account of social science: systematic learning about society. That accounts for my tripartite program: economics, politics, philosophy—a full picture of the social theory of a religious system.

6. That position of extreme nominalism is factually incorrect, as I shall now argue. But the argument affords no comfort to the position of idealism that finds only one Judaism throughout or that identifies in diverse Judaisms a single essential or underlying Judaism. For reasons now spelled out, a position between nominalism and idealism proves descriptively entirely in order.

7. Such a paradigm should impart to all Judaisms a political character, but it does not. Why the Mishnah's heirs and continuators persisted in encompassing within their systems a well-framed politics, while others among the Pentateuch's many heirs and continuators did not, I cannot say. But from the Mishnah to the nineteenth century, we have considerable difficulty in locating an essentially apolitical or nonpolitical Judaism, a construction of a social entity, world-view, and way of life with no interest whatever in the day-to-day uses of legitimate violence. Clearly, the nineteenth century's Judaisms, Reform, Historical or Conservative, and Orthodox, radically reframed the inherited pattern of a political religion.

8. I treat the question of enlandisement in chapters 10 and 11, with the upshot in chapter 12. In my view the premises of Aristotle's politics are profoundly locative, while those of the Mishnah's politics are wholly utopian. This is spelled out in due course. So far as the Mishnah's politics are properly characterized as applicable to no place in particular (though obviously, only to the Holy Land in general), they must be regarded as a step away from the deeply locative politics of Deuteronomy but, of course, well within the entirely utopian politics of Leviticus.

9. It would carry us far afield to recapitulate the methods and results, spread over a variety of books of mine, summarized in that sentence. Readers may generously assume that the work has been one and that the statement is a minimal claim indeed.

10. I use the word "utopian" in its ordinary sense: never-never land. But in the concluding chapters, the other sense of "utopia," which is "nowhere in particular," as against the contrary word (invented by Jonathan Z. Smith), "locative," will form a principal component of my analysis. See Smith's *Imagining Religion: From Babylon to Jonestown* (Chicago: University of Chicago Press, 1982).

11. What I can answer is "why this" for economics and politics. The answer for politics is contained in chapter 12. The part of the question covering "why not that" seems to me more difficult to address, and I am not entirely sure of the correct methods for conducting the description and analysis, yielding an interpretation in response to the question. Perhaps on the other side of the present three-dimensional inquiry I shall have a clearer idea of not only "why this" but also "and why not that."

12. The modes of thought of the document derive from *Listenwissenschaft,* that is, list making, and therefore are deeply hierarchical in basic character; that is the argument of chapter 12. This exposition rests on two books of mine that cannot be recapitulated here, *The Making of the Mind of Judaism* (Atlanta: Scholars Press for Brown Judaic Studies, 1987) and *The Formation of the Jewish Intellect: Making Connections and Drawing Conclusions in the Traditional System of Judaism* (Atlanta: Scholars Press for Brown Judaic Studies, 1988).

13. Further discussion of the Mishnah's Judaic system in the context defined by politics is in chapter 12.

CHAPTER THREE

1. A fundamental premise of my mode of systemic analysis is that where a system differentiates, there it lays its heaviest emphasis and stress. That is how we may identify what particular questions elicit urgent concern, and what other questions are treated as null.

2. Given the authority of Scripture and the character of the Pentateuch as a design of a holy state, on holy land, made up of holy people, living a holy life, we should not be surprised by silence, on the surface at least, about the reason why. People everywhere acknowledge and confess God's rule and the politics of the Torah, in its written form as the Pentateuch, claiming legitimacy attained through conformity to the law and politics. But we cannot take for granted that Scripture has supplied a myth. That is something to be shown in context, as we shall see in just a moment.

3. I do not distinguish crime from sin, since I do not think the system does. At the same time our own world does make such a distinction, and it would be confusing not to preserve it. That accounts for the usage throughout.

4. I explained this matter in chapter 1.

5. It goes without saying that appeal to Scripture at this point is irrelevant, for reasons specified in chapter 2. People used Scripture in building their system; they did not begin their system building by perusing Scripture. But when our analysis of the application of power invites attention to Scripture, we surely are justified in seeing what we find there.

6. *The Social Study of Judaism,* chapter 8, contains the relevant sources, which may be consulted to sustain this point in the exposition.

7. In line with the Mishnah's usage, I refer to God and God's heavenly court with the euphemism of "Heaven," and the capital *H* expresses the simple fact that "Heaven" always refers to God and God's court on high. The Mishnah is not clear on whether its authorship thinks God personally intervenes throughout, but there is a well-established belief in divine agents, e.g., angels or messengers, so in speaking of Heaven or Heaven's intervention, we take account of the possibility that God's agents are meant.

8. I am puzzled by the fact that in the Mishnah "kingdom of Heaven" never occurs in what we should call a political context; rather, it occurs in the context of personal piety. My sense is that this usage should help illuminate the Gospels' presentation of sayings assigned to Jesus concerning "the kingdom," "my kingdom," "the kingdom of God," and the like. Since the Mishnah presents a highly specific politics, the selection of vocabulary bears systemic weight and meaning (something I have shown in virtually every analytical study I have carried on); these are in context technical usages. But their meaning in their own context awaits the kind of systemic analysis conducted here on the political vocabulary of Judaism, treated systemically and contextually and not just lexicographically.

9. The ordeal inflicted on the wife accused of infidelity is not germane here. I deal with it in due course.

10. In chapter 4 we shall see another mode of establishing the law, which is sages' debate. But there too the form or convention requires the confirmation that sages have in the end reached a decision that, in accord with other sources, in fact has come from Sinai.

11. A fine distinction, perhaps, but a critical one, and the distinction between charisma and routine is not a fine one at all.

12. I cannot refer to "God" as "he" or as "she," hence the recurrent circumlocution, which is admittedly not ideal. The Judaic system before us of course took for granted the maleness of God, with little to say about the explicit statement to the contrary at Gen. 2:27.

13. The distinction between secular felony and religious sin obviously bears no meaning in the system, useful as it is to us. I generally will speak of "felon or sinner," so as not to take a position on a matter unimportant in my inquiry.

14. I remind the reader once more that the full repertoire of sources is in *The Social Study of Judaism,* chapter 8, in the section devoted to this chapter.

15. It would not serve to present here translations of all the pertinent texts, which would prove tedious and provide more information than is directly pertinent to the argument. All of these many details given in *The Social Study of Judaism,* chapter 8, for the section on this chapter, sustain the judgment I shall propose at the end, when I show how the power exercised by the several foci of politics, Heavenly, earthly, and intermediary, intersects and how in important ways each focus of power exercises responsibility for its own jurisdiction as well: Heaven, earth, the space between. Then we shall easily reconstruct the political myth, not as a set of generalities, but as a statement, through inarticulate detail, of a few overriding propositions. The survey to follow does lead to a single important point about the myth, even though in the interim the reader may wonder where it is all heading.

16. The sources on these are set forth in *The Social Study of Judaism,* chapter 8.

17. For that purpose, the reader may now wish to review in *The Social Study of Judaism,* chapter 8, the catalogue of those who are put to death by the earthly court through the four modes of execution introduced just now. There I have given the entire corpus of sources on the death penalty, here only briefly referred to.

18. Weber defines a state as a political association with access to the use of physical force: "a human community that (successfully) claims the monopoly of the legitimate use of physical force within a given territory" (PV 77, 78). A political question, then, means "that interests in the distribution, maintenance, or transfer of power are decisive for answering the questions and determining the decision." But we see in this and subsequent chapters political questions that far transcend the narrow limitations of power, yet that by any definition of politics involve politics. Politics then and now as well derives from the larger social order and cannot be interpreted outside of the larger system that expresses itself, also, through politics. To use violence to achieve one's will forms too narrow a definition of politics, because, for one thing, it ignores a variety of other ongoing, institutionally founded media by which the system appeals to coercion that is effective yet in no way based upon violence.

19. This is not to suggest that the distinction behind the system's differentiation is important only in the myth of Eden. Quite to the contrary, the authorship of the laws of Leviticus and Deuteronomy repeatedly appeals to that same distinction. But our interest is in myth, and I find in the myth of Eden the explanation for the point of differentiation that the political myth of Judaism invokes at every point. So, as I have said, the sanctions lead to the systemic question that requires mythic response, and once we know the question, we can turn to Scripture for the myth (as much as we can find in Scripture ample expansion, in law, of that same myth).

C H A P T E R   F O U R

1. This conforms to my finding concerning the philosophy of Judaism, which turns out to express ontological monotheism; the fundamental unity of being sets forth the hierarchical classification of all things.

2. As we shall see in chapter 5.

3. In chapter 12 I shall spell out what I conceive to be that purpose and message. At this point it suffices to say that we deal with a system of hierarchization. When the institutions are portrayed, they are related to one another, king above high priest, for instance. But when we examine the portrait and find that the hierarchization bears no important distinctions, we find yet another, and a very powerful, statement of hierarchization. King may be above high priest, but that does not matter, because sage is above all. So the silences convey a striking message about the triviality of one form of hierarchization, as much as explicit statements convey another important message about what being on top really requires and means. To elaborate on this point here would divert attention from the analysis of the data that sustain these descriptions and lead to the analysis and interpretation given later on.

4. We shall presently see such an elaborated and differentiated account of another agency, the Temple, and that shows us what might have been done for both monarchy and the sages.

5. The system builders cannot imagine a hegemony based on institutions, though that again explains nothing.

6. Portraying sages' court as the one that declares war and calls out the army presents a piquant irony in the aftermath of two wars that led to disaster.

7. I cannot point to a line in the Mishnah that acknowledges, in political terms, Rome's governance of the Land of Israel.

8. And this is not to be expected in a prescriptive, rather than a descriptive or explanatory, account. The upshot is to underline the carefully framed program of systemic consequence that is worked out in the politics too.

9. Further discussion of institutions of local governance is in *The Social Study of Judaism*, chapter 8 (supplements for this chapter).

10. We shall return to this matter in chapter 8 of this book.

11. And here I can think of no systemic reason for the silence on the everyday. Indeed, in the next stage in the politics of Judaism we shall see ample discussion of precisely how things are run hands-on, and on a daily basis.

12. But not as an identifiable economic class or genealogical caste.

13. Readers will allow, I hope, that I could adduce in evidence a great many more.

14. That acknowledgment forms the counterpart to the one that tacitly admits there were gentile authorities over Jews, and recusant Jews.

15. The remainder is in *The Social Study of Judaism,* chapter 8 (section devoted to this chapter).

16. Omitting reference to the competition runs parallel to ignoring forces that affect the Jews but fall outside of sages' control, and Jews who do not keep the law or acknowledge sages' authority.

17. Further discussion of the local courts appears in *The Social Study of Judaism,* chapter 8 (section devoted to this chapter).

18. Of course, there is no conception of a budget. But that concept in political economy would be long in coming, and if there is a counterpart to a budget in Plato's *Republic,* or even in the great Aristotle's *Politics,* I do not know what it was.

19. Further relevant abstracts are in *The Social Study of Judaism,* chapter 8 (section devoted to this chapter).

20. Further treatment of the various courts is provided in *The Social Study of Judaism,* chapter 8 (section devoted to this chapter), where Mishnah-tractate Sanhedrin 1:2–3 and 4:1–2 are given.

21. This comparison will become important to us in chapter 12 as well.

22. The formal traits of the matched sets of six items are clear as indicated. The interpolated materials, M. San. 2:1G–J, K–O, M. San. 2:2E–J, M. San. 2:3B–E, present three disputes between Judah and Meir or sages, the point of which is clear as given. Judah obviously has generated the conceptions of the disputes. K–O differ. They simply introduce extraneous material, outside both the frame of the disciplined construction and the equally disciplined dispute-materials.

23. A–D present miscellaneous rules; A refers to the rule at M. San. 1:5. M. San. 2:4E–N and M. San. 2:5 provide a systematic exegesis of Deut. 17:15–19.

24. I find puzzling the claim that the Gospels' representation of the trial of Jesus in any way finds explanation in details of the Mishnah and its continuator writings. It is hard to imagine the high priest, as the Mishnah portrays him, in charge of such a proceeding, and I cannot point to a single passage in the Mishnah that suggests the high priest would conduct a political trial of this kind (or any other kind of trial). And yet not a few explanations of the trial of Jesus appeal to the Mishnah and still later writings to account for one detail or another. It is hard for me to see how, in general, these writings pertain in any way whatsoever, hence, on what basis any detail in them can serve to explain any detail of the trial as it is portrayed. We have already noticed that "the kingdom of Heaven" has no political connotation whatsoever in the passages in which it occurs. Yet accounts of "the Kingdom of Heaven" in the sayings of Jesus also appeal to the politics of Judaism as set forth in the Mishnah, contrasting "Judaism's" political with "Christianity's" otherworldly and more spiritual conception of the kingdom of Heaven. That may well be so in general, but the passages of the Mishnah that know "the kingdom of Heaven" are not the ones that speak of politics at all.

25. For antiquity, of course, "party," as it is used today, is grossly anachronistic. Critics of Morton Smith's *Palestinian Parties and Politics That Shaped the Old Testament* (rpt. New York: Columbia University Press, 1987) have been quick to point this out in dismissing the book's main thesis. His work is woefully anachronistic.

26. The remainder is in *The Social Study of Judaism,* chapter 8 (section devoted to this chapter).

27. The remainder is in *The Social Study of Judaism,* chapter 8 (section devoted to this chapter). There I supply the texts that are pertinent to this topic.

28. But then, the system must also represent as requiring attention the things that sages said they could settle, and the things that sages ignore must also be treated as systematically inconsequential. Consequently, to assess the full institutional-political program of Judaism, we should

review the account of the topical plan of the Mishnah given in chapter 2. There we see what mattered, and, it follows, we also can outline the political platform—the range of policy and responsibility—of the politics of Judaism, for in one way or another, every item in the topical plan of the document formed a matter of public policy and was accessible to the power of coercion of one kind or another.

CHAPTER FIVE

1. As to the disposition of the funds, in *The Social Study of Judaism,* chapter 8 (section devoted to this chapter), I include the accounts of their use.

2. And we remember in this context how the high priest is treated with contempt, assumed not to know how to carry out the Atonement rite but to require instruction by sages (so M. Yoma 1:5, cited earlier). The picture is the same.

3. *The Social Study of Judaism,* chapter 8 (section devoted to this chapter), contains tractate Avot chapters 3 and 4.

4. The tractate's next chapters reveal how the professional ideal serves also as the personal model for the entire male population of the political system under description. See *The Social Study of Judaism,* chapter 8.

5. Why the system framers did not make up a set of offices and name bureaucrats in charge of them is not explained in the information at hand, let alone in the facts of the political realities of some age remote from our authorship—a century, two centuries, a millennium earlier, for instance.

CHAPTER SIX

1. That is, how they work and who imposes them.

2. Indeed, one of the marks of a well-crafted systemic statement is the ample explanation in one detail of a variety of important considerations. Ideally, each systemically active detail contains the main outlines of the entire systemic composition.

3. The entire issue of theological anthropology of Judaism seems to me to require a study in its own terms. I have repeatedly drawn back from that study. But in philosophical-theological terms, the remarkable study by Michael Wyschogrod, *The Body of Faith: Judaism as Corporeal Election* (New York: Seabury Press, 1983), seems to me right on target, and a reworking of the problem within the discipline of history of religion is certainly plausible and feasible. But in working out the problem, he totally botched the job, and the work has to be redone.

4. That is more than adequate proof of the utterly theoretical character of the politics of Judaism.

5. I cannot imagine more elegant proof of the purely theoretical and utterly utopian character of the politics of Judaism than these eloquent silences. But they derive, as we shall see, from systemic logic, not from the mere naiveté of intellectuals. Sages in the Mishnah were well informed about jealousy, envy, and other negative sources of positive action. But they did not appeal to those sources of passion when they chose to describe their politics at its cutting edge.

6. I of course reached these conclusions the other way around.

7. This matter will take on concrete meaning later on.

8. I have spelled out that fact in my *Messiah in Context: Israel's History and Destiny in Formative Judaism* (1983; rpt. Lanham: University Press of America, 1988).

9. The modest accretions do not obscure the fact that we have a sizable and effective narrative which is smooth and flowing. The narrative of the stoning in part is spun out of relevant verses, e.g., M. 6:1B, M. 6:4G. This, curiously, requires two different forms of "stoning," the one, pushing the man down (evidently onto stones, which are not mentioned), the other, piling stones up on his heart. There also is some problem in the meaning of M. 6:4B–C. There are differing

views of how the passage should be interpreted; I have chosen the simplest. Third, there are inter-polated disputes, specifically M. 6:2E–F, which indicate that M. 6:2D avoids taking a position on a controverted matter, M. 6:3B–C, which again prove that M. 6:3A avoids a dispute by keeping vague what is at issue, and, at M. 6:4H–M, two disputes along the same lines. Three disputes involve Eliezer-Judah and sages on the penalty imposed on a woman. Yosé, further, glosses, and therefore differs from, M. 6:4/0. Finally, we observe interpolated homiletical mate-rials at M 6:2B–C and M. 6:4R–S.

10. Gentiles considered as individuals, not part of political entities, do not come under con-sideration. The sins or crimes that deny a person the world to come all pertain to beliefs or actions of Israelites (as M. 10:1D–2 and E make clear). The ethnic venue of "Epicurean" is not so self-evident as the others; I take it the sense is that it is an Israelite who maintains Epicurean beliefs or attitudes. The context surely requires that view.

11. Once more it seems to me that Israelites are treated as persons whose individual actions bear consequence, while gentiles are not.

12. The remainder of the passage is given in *The Social Study of Judaism,* chapter 8 (section devoted to this chapter).

13. In his *Jewish Symbols in the Greco-Roman Period,* Erwin R. Goodenough underlined the passion for eternal life contained within the symbols used by Jewish artists for synagogues and cemeteries. Here in the depths of the Mishnah, in its politics for Israel, I find the same source of passion, in a context never considered by Goodenough, since these literary evidences fell (quite properly) outside of his range of analysis. That the results converge is suggestive.

CHAPTER SEVEN

1. Thus, for example, no public mourning when a criminal or sinner is put to death, but a rite of reconciliation with the judges.

2. Available in chapter 2.

3. Much is made in studies of politics in non-Western and premodern societies of a simple fact. True, we cannot distinguish secular from religious. But why that distinction serves an essen-tial analytical or heuristic purpose is not clear, any more than we know why our incapacity to distinguish sinner from criminal makes much of a difference. Systemically, there is none. And the system is the thing.

4. It would carry us far afield to catalog those scriptural sanctions particular to women that are not given systemic prominence within the Mishnah's order and structure. Facts of Scripture do not, we recall, invariably take an active and definitive role in the Mishnah's system; more than a few such scriptural facts prove systemically inert and unimportant. One simple objective indicator is that an inert fact does not come to development, expansion, prominent place in the repertoire of topics in the Mishnah, while a systemically active fact does. To expand on this point is hardly required in light of my discussion in chapter 2 of the place of Scripture in the Mishnah.

5. The traits of the passage need not detain us for long. M.'s homily takes for granted that the accused wife is guilty. M. 1:7 completes the foregoing, then is matched at M. 1:9, but only in a most general way. In fact there is not the slightest effort at M. 1:7 to cite Scripture or otherwise to balance M. 1:9's interests, and M. 1:8's two elements—A and B–D—also are not matched.

6. But the explanation of what happens to the accused wife in the rite misses the point at hand, which is why the wife should be subjected to an essentially extrajudicial ordeal. But the author-ship clearly assumes that the penalty the guilty wife suffers is amply validated, and it makes the main point. Why the punishment fits the crime is really a distinct issue.

7. In chapter 12 we shall see how the concern for stability spills over into a sustained interest in hierarchization. For if the social order is meant to be held together and in one piece, it means that each entity within the order (person, thing, for instance) must be kept in place, and to be kept in place means to be kept in one's place, the particular locus that is appropriate. And that is the simplest language I can imagine for hierarchization: to be in place is to be in one's rightful locus.

The system is utopian in that it speaks of no place in particular; it is locative in that it speaks of all things in their particular places. Hierarchization then substitutes for locativity, and the utopian system serves to hierarchize. Whether an enlandised, materially locative system does so as well is not a problem to be worked out against the facts supplied by this particular Judaism!

8. The pericope at M. 9:1 is in two units, A–B and C–E. A–B revert to the theme of M. 7:1–2, but it is only at M. 9:6 that what must be said in Hebrew plays a role. The cited verse, then, should be Deut. 21:7. There is no point at which the proof-text begun at B serves the purposes of A. It follows that A is a superscription attached as part of the redactional work. The use of B indeed is in connection with C–E. The anonymous view is that three go forth, but Judah shows that the cited verse requires five. Narrative style characterizes M. 9:5A–D. The Jerusalemites measure the distance between the corpse and the surrounding towns, M. 9:1. They then go home, and the elders of the town which has to carry out the rite do their duty. The place in which the rite takes place, F, cannot be used for agricultural purposes. The narrative concludes with M. 9:6, and that is where our important point occurs, with two more legal-analytical pericopae to come. A–B, as we noticed, are the point at which M. 9:1–8 are relevant to M. 7:1–2. C–E are a secondary interpolation making an interesting point. Then the exposition of the Scripture is concluded.

9. This is another way—a rather striking one at that!—of expressing the nonlocative character of the system. As to particular place, only Jerusalem matters. Every other place is no place in particular.

10. This turning in the argument underlines once more the necessity of a systematic account of the theological anthropology of this and other Judaisms. Failing to outline the definition of what it means to be "humanity in our image, after our likeness," we still find ourselves sketching only the outlines of the system.

11. Though tractate Avot is explicit that one should make his will conform to God's, so that God's will conform to his; that God approves those whom people approve; and similar observations. I take these pieces of good advice to apply to all Israelites, even though the context is that of the sages' instruction to their own disciples.

12. I shall expand on this observation at length in part 3. It forms one of the principal results of this study.

13. In *The Social Study of Judaism,* chapter 8 (supplement to this chapter), I provide a more extensive repertoire of Jaffee's exposition, in his own words and edited by me, to underline the points made here.

14. Martin Jaffee, *The Mishnah's Theology of Tithing* (Atlanta: Scholars Press for Brown Judaic Studies, 1985), 6.

15. But not Eve's. Women's will does not have equal status in the Mishnah.

16. For a more nuanced view, see Paul Virgil McCracken Flesher, *Oxen, Women, or Citizens? Slaves in the System of the Mishnah* (Atlanta: Scholars Press for Brown Judaic Studies, 1988).

17. Angels and demons play no role in the Mishnah's representation of its Judaism. That such conceptions were commonplace is beyond doubt. But then God's active role in the Mishnah is no more vivid. Why later and successor systems introduce the personalities of God, angels, and demons requires attention in due course. The basic facts on the personality of God are in my *The Incarnation of God: The Character of Divinity in Formative Judaism* (Philadelphia: Fortress Press, 1988). I expand on this matter in the final chapter of my *Judaism as Philosophy: The Method and Message of the Mishnah* (Columbia: University of South Carolina Press, 1991).

18. I think, the male human being only. But in this context, women do participate.

19. That is not to suggest for one minute that people really did live only on farms. The system ignores the others when exposing its fundamental conceptions. The economics, we notice, omits from its theory most of the economy. That is to say, just as the economics is not really about the economy, so the politics is not really about the political structure and system at all. These form occasions for the exposition of what the system proposes to say. And all we can really explain is why these occasions, and not other (in theory equally suitable) pretexts.

20. And I know no contradictory cases in the Mishnah, which is why I am prepared to generalize as I do here.

21. But I think that Israel amply accomplished its systemic goal, which was to establish a realm of force and meaning for Israel's attitude and will. And in time that force yielded even a solution to the political crisis precipitated by the defeats of 70 and 135. But first came the reconstruction of the will, then the rehabilitation of the Jews' capacity to form a politics. This too forms a subject for the investigation of the next stages in the successor systems.

CHAPTER EIGHT

1. I invoke the concept of the *polis* only as a metaphor. In part 3 we shall try to locate the counterpart in the politics of Judaism to Aristotle's *polis*. That is a separate issue; the metaphor seems to me illuminating in the present context.

2. For the Mishnah, language is a self-contained formal system for description of a reality. The political community represented by the Mishnah (in this context: persons reflecting on the legitimate uses of violence to achieve social norms) stands strongly not only against nuance but also against change. The language is meant to be unshakable, and its strict rules of rhetoric are meant not only to convey, but also to preserve, equally strict rules of logic or, more practically, equally permanent patterns of relationship. What was at stake in this formation of language in the service of permanence? Clearly, how things were said was intended to secure eternal preservation of what was said. Change affects the accidents and details. It cannot reshape enduring principles, and language will be used to effect their very endurance. Use of pat phrases and syntactical clichés divorced from different thoughts to be articulated and different ways of thinking testifies to the prevailing notion of unstated but secure and unchanging reality behind and beneath the accidents of context and circumstance.

3. Jeffrey C. Alexander, *Theoretic Logic in Sociology* 3, 83, 113.

4. But I do not mean to enter into the discussion of the concept of natural law in Aristotle. That lies far beyond my capacities.

5. If there is a single line of the Mishnah that tells me how to account for the failure of descriptive law, that is to say, what happens when the fixed results of a specified action do not come about, I do not know what it is. On the negative side, for example, what about a judge who takes bribes but does not go blind? Where and how the politics of Judaism addresses flaws in the natural law I cannot say, nor can I point to remissions of the laws. These silences invite speculation, but this is not the occasion for it. In any event we cannot assume we know the systemic answers to these questions, if, for example, we merely send the questions back to Job or Jeremiah. Quite to the contrary, we shall have to look in the second and third systems emerging from this, the first one, for within the logic of the initial structure and system is a profoundly generative question, one that will demand answers and receive them. Since the question is a political one, the answer too must be political. This seems to me a gaping hole in the system's presentation of its politics.

6. And that raises the stakes considerably, when we remember the mythic power within the system. One has to want what one should want, intend what one is expected to intend. The human will is to be remade so that by nature it conforms to the Torah. The corresponding reflections in Paul's theology and in Fourth Ezra's reflection on the tragic flaw, "the good that I would that I do not," hardly require sustained attention in this context.

7. The Temple offerings for instance, are explained in that way at M. Zebahim 4:6: "For the sake of six things is the animal offering sacrificed: for the sake of the animal offering, for the sake of the one who sacrifices it, for the sake of the Lord, for the sake of the altar fires, for the sake of the odor, for the sake of the pleasing smell. And as to the sin offering and the guilt offering, for the sake of the sin expiated thereby."

8. The remainder of the passage is in *The Social Study of Judaism,* chapter 8.

9. This is another fine construction, because the perfectly balanced legal ruling, A–E, F–K, is cited in the *ma'aseh,* O–Q=F=K, except for the italicized word. The *ma'aseh* itself is clear as

stated, and to the *ma'aseh* O–Q are absolutely essential, though, of course, not necessarily in the given formulation. The woman in A has produced blood for five consecutive months on three days running. But she does not know whether these five incidents occurred when she was in her cycle of menstrual days or when she was in her cycle of *zibah* days. If in the latter, then she is confirmed as a *Zabah*. B has a woman who has five times produced some sort of an abortion but is not sure of its character (M. 1:4). One burnt offering and one sin offering suffice. The woman then is deemed clean so as to eat Holy Things. The offerings for the other four appearances of flux or miscarriages are null. By contrast, in the other case—five confirmed fluxes, meaning three consecutive days of flux during the *zibah* days—the woman is definitely unclean and owes the five sacrifices, all of which are to be brought. But after bringing only one of them she is clean for the purposes of eating Holy Things (J).

10. This is not to deny that the systemic statement could have represented matters as in fact they were. But for systemic analysis, the facts matter no more than they do in the systemic theory, as the very next component of my repertoire and argument now shows: the sacrifice by a political authority, in consequence of making a mistake. A theory borrowed from Leviticus 4, the concept bore no relationship to the politics of the second century, let alone to the liturgical possibilities. So whether fact or fancy, the representation is the thing.

11. The remainder of the relevant versus of Scripture appear in *The Social Study of Judaism*, chapter 8 (section devoted to this chapter).

12. I present the outline of Mishnah-tractate Horayot in *The Social Study of Judaism*, chapter 8 (serving this chapter). The discussion of Horayot comes accompanied by a sizable abstract of the document as well.

13. And only when we can identify the character of that rationality shall we understand the politics of Judaism. That accounts for the program of part 3, which is the definition of one rationality by comparison and contrast with another rationality for a component of the social order that derives from another system's politics but falls into the same classification.

14. Cited by Jeffrey C. Alexander, *Theoretic Logic in Sociology* 3, 83.

15. "Politics as a Vocation," in Gerth and Mills, *From Max Weber: Essays in Sociology*, 78–79.

16. I have expanded on this point in *Vanquished Nation, Broken Spirit: The Virtues of the Heart in Formative Judaism* (New York: Cambridge University Press, 1987). The political implications of the discussion in that monograph bear upon the present topic, but it would carry us far afield to work them out in detail and explicitly. The main point is that the politics really does correspond to the requirements of the social order in which, in theory at least, the politics was supposed to function. Psychology then forms a principal plank in the political platform of Judaism, and politics defines a major component of Judaism's theology of emotions. A political religion will be political in more than its politics. Or to state matters more accessibly, a system says the same thing in everything.

17. In invoking Aristotle's categories, I mean only to underline the ironics of the present theme.

18. I am inclined to think that without politics Aristotle's system cannot have delivered the most important components of its message. But my argument here and in part 3 is that while this Judaism made important parts of its systemic statement through politics, politics does not bear the most critical components of the systemic statement at all.

CHAPTER NINE

1. Where, for example, in the Essene Judaism of the Dead Sea Scrolls do we find impoverishing or maiming people? Ostracism, exclusion, or periods of separation hardly form the counterpart to this Judaism's amazing claim that all Jews are subject to one law and form a single political entity, "Israel." The exclusionary character of the Essene Judaism, its insistence that there is a discredited "Israel" out there of which it forms the remnant, differentiates that sectarian

politics from this national politics, so it seems to me. In any event, I find the character of this politics lacking any counterpart in other Judaisms' politics.

2. We return to that fact in chapter 12.

3. As distinct from issues of metaphysics, theology, or philosophy, thus excluding Philo. But I do not mean to suggest that the kind of analysis conducted here can be fruitless when brought to Philo's writings. My view, as an outsider to Philonic studies, is that the Mishnah's program for the social order finds no counterpart in Philo's principal range of interests. I shall be glad to be corrected by studies of other Judaisms parallel to this one, beginning with Philo's.

4. That framing of matters is slightly disingenuous, since in my *Economics of the Mishnah* (Chicago: University of Chicago Press, 1990) I of course have already undertaken precisely this comparison. But while the results of that study form the foundation of this one, my best judgment is that each must sit upon its own theoretical foundations, hence the importance to me of spelling out here the theoretical basis for the comparisons now to be undertaken.

5. The sole valid context for seeing things whole derives from the broader context provided by comparison, as I just said, one whole seen in contrast to another. Why does that seem to me so urgent? The reason is that only in that way do we grasp the choices people have made, the issues they have chosen, the questions they deem urgent, the answers they find self-evident: the systemic statement complete and in its lapidary form.

6. To state matters somewhat abstractly, what the one thing shows me can be applied to two things only when both things show the same one thing. Why do I insist that finding what is unlike in the like is legitimate, in a way in which finding what is like in the unlike is not? The reason is that in the former case, the absolute datum is similarity, and that is not imposed, imputed, or invented, but obvious, demonstrable (which is to say, subject to falsification), and superficial.

7. This position of mine is of course a commonplace in the comparative study of religion as practiced today. Among many excellent statements of it I recommend E. P. Sanders' *Paul and Palestinian Judaism: A Comparison of Patterns of Religion* (London: SCM Press Ltd., 1977).

8. E. P. Sanders, *Paul and Palestinian Judaism: A comparison of Patterns of Religion* (London: SCM Press Ltd., 1977), 16.

9. No one can claim that the Mishnah's sages closely studied alternative systems of politics and selected the one they found congruent to their larger purposes. It is the fact that the Greek philosophers did just that. But the kind of writing in our hands carries on philosophical thought in a very different idiom and makes no place for the exposition of that conscious choice among alternatives, a choice based on rationality and a consideration of the properties of things for instance, that makes the Greek philosophers so persuasive. The idiom of this writing, by contrast, leaves its authorship not only not terribly persuasive, but not even very interesting—until we realize what it is that, as philosophers, they were setting forth, and how they were choosing to do so. The aesthetics of philosophical writing bears a profound message as to the character of the philosophical enterprise, and I cannot think of a more stunning demonstration of that fact than in the comparison of the politics, within the larger systems, of the Mishnah's sages and of Aristotle. But in my planned next monographs and book on the philosophy of Judaism, I shall show in much greater detail, and over a broader sample of the document, the full philosophical program of the Mishnah's authorship, and, with that in hand, the aesthetic comparison of philosophical systems (surely Aristotle's and the Mishnah's) will go forward. Then and only then will the wit, and not only the wisdom, of this Judaism become somewhat accessible to us, for in aesthetics lies the full exposure of intelligence. Said more simply, how people say what they wish conveys a more profound message than what they choose to say, because the range of truth is limited, but the possibilities for conveying truth are as infinite as the range and kinds of intelligence meted out to human minds.

10. This theoretical statement is a reprise of my essay, "Alike and Not Alike," in response to Jonathan Z. Smith's essay "No Need to Travel to the Indies: Judaism and the Study of Religion," in J. Neusner, ed., *Take Judaism, For Example: Studies toward the Comparison of Religions* (Chicago: University of Chicago Press, 1983).

11. It would vastly exaggerate the power of the patriarchate, that is, the *nasi,* as represented

in the Mishnah and other sources of the age, to represent that institution as a successor government, proportionate to the autonomous regime that was destroyed in the war of 66–73. It seems clear that in the third and fourth centuries, the patriarchate gained some considerable standing. But in the aftermath of Bar Kokhba's defeat in 135, at which point our document's politics was taking shape (nearly the whole of the Division of Damages, so often cited in chapters 3 through 8, while of course referring to earlier times and writings, took shape only after 135), the patriarchate as it would develop in the third and fourth centuries was only beginning to reconstitute itself. And, much more to the point, the politics of this Judaism knows no patriarchate. The tripartite structure of monarchy, priesthood, and court system makes no place for the patriarchate (though the court system later on would be represented as an agency of the patriarchate). Hence if there was a considerable Jewish politics in the time the Mishnah took shape, the authorship of the Mishnah did not propose to explain it, nor did they even deign to take account of its actualities.

12. Filling up a fourth of the entire document in volume, but then completely ignored, except for one tractate, in all of the two Talmuds, continuator writings that took up and amplified the Mishnah!

13. I see no requirement at this point in the argument to spell out a large thematic program either omitted altogether or treated in a trivial way. A mere comparison of the two Talmuds' topical and thematic programs and the proportions of those programs devoted to given topics or themes with the Mishnah's authorship's topical and thematic program and the proportions of that program suffices to tell the entire story. I have done that work for such subjects as theory of history and eschatology, exegesis of Scripture ("midrash"), theory of revelation, theory of psychology, theory of society (the social entity "Israel"), and so on and so forth. Nothing is gained by reviewing the results here, since at this point they are not relevant. It is the simple fact that, just as the topics that are treated present puzzles, so the topical omissions found urgent by continuators of the system are equally astonishing.

CHAPTER TEN

1. The epigraph is from G. E. M. de Ste. Croix, *The Class Struggle in the Ancient Greek World: From the Archaic Age to the Arab Conquests* (London: Gerald Duckworth, 1981), 69. My colleague Professor Martha Nussbaum kindly called my attention to that book. In connection with Aristotle's politics, see R. G. Mulgan, *Aristotle's Political Theory: An Introduction for Students of Political Theory* (Oxford: Clarendon Press, 1977). I consulted various other works, of course, but Mulgan provided the clearest and the fundamental account of the matter, and, not being a scholar of ancient philosophy (as I stressed in the preface), I chose to rely on his as what seemed to me the best textbook account in the English language. I consulted, among other works in the vast literature on the subject, the following as well: Ernest Barker, *The Political Thought of Plato and Aristotle* (1906; rpt. New York: Russell & Russell, 1959); Ernest Barker, *Greek Political Theory: Plato and His Predecessors* (1917; rpt. New York: Barnes & Noble, 1947); M. I. Finley, *Politics in the Ancient World* (Cambridge: Cambridge University Press, 1983); Mason Hammond, *City-State and World State in Greek and Roman Political Theory until Augustus* (Cambridge: Harvard University Press, 1951); Donald Kagan, *The Great Dialogue: History of Greek Political Thought from Homer to Polybius* (N.Y.: Free Press, 1965); Bernard Lewis, *The Political Language of Islam* (Chicago: University of Chicago Press, 1988); Whitney J. Oates, "The Ideal States of Plato and Aristotle," in *The Greek Political Experience: Studies in Honor of William Kelly Prentice* (1941; rpt. N.Y.: Russell & Russell, 1969), 197–213; R. F. Stalley, *An Introduction to Plato's Laws* (Indianapolis: Hackett, 1983); and Erwin I. J. Rosenthal, *Political Thought in Medieval Islam: An Introductory Outline* (Cambridge: Cambridge University Press, 1958). I have already cited the work of Bernard Lewis on Islamic political vocabulary. Nothing in my account of Aristotle's politics is original; I depend entirely on Mulgan, which I checked against other accounts of the facts. Kagan, at 205, has a good description of the teleological view of Aristotle' defense of the *polis;* he traces its development: village, association of households; and

polis, association of villages. See de Ste. Croix, 69–81, on Aristotle's sociology of Greek politics. I found Lewis's lexicographic definition of politics less helpful than more analytical readings of Aristotle's politics. And let me repeat—I do not claim to contribute to the study of Aristotle's politics, except in the context of the history in antiquity of political thought, on the one side, and of comparative politics, on the other. I do not claim to tell specialists on Aristotle anything they did not know about Aristotle.

2. In so stating matters, of course, I reveal my own political and economic place within American conservatism. Others, who judge the givens of the social order differently, will analyze and assess matters in quite another manner. That Marxist scholarship will concur is a happy accident; American economic and political conservatives understand the basic importance of economic considerations in the making of the good society. My critique of the Marxist reading of some matters will find its place in later footnotes.

3. I shall expand on this point presently. The only other candidates are Plato and Xenophon. Xenophon's advice to a good farmer can scarcely be called an economics, and, while Plato does set forth the materials of which an economics can be formed, his statements are not systematic and cogent in the way in which Aristotle's are.

4. That is not to suggest that only a householder could be a citizen in a Greek city. That is not the case. But to be a citizen, one had to have the wealth to enjoy the leisure to engage in politics, and the principal form of investment was in real estate and hence farming. So while one did not have to own land and supervise a farmer in order to qualify as a citizen, in point of fact citizens ordinarily were also householders. We return to this qualification later on. I owe it to one of the readers of this manuscript for the University of Chicago Press, who through his criticism made a fundamental and exceedingly valuable contribution to my study.

5. I have shown this in detail in my *The Mishnah as Philosophy.*

6. A subset of this principle, of course, is the conception of true value, value inherent in a thing, shared between the philosophers of the Mishnah and Aristotle.

7. The issue is not one of direct connection. No one conjures up the fantasy and anachronism of the Mishnah's authorship's tramping down a Galilean hill from their yeshiva to the academy in a nearby Greek-speaking town, Caesarea or Sepphoris, for example, there studying elementary Aristotle and listening to the earliest discourses of neo-Platonism, then climbing back up the hill and writing it all up in their crabbed back-country idiom as the cases and examples of the Mishnah. But as a matter of fact, in its indicative traits of message and method, the Mishnah's philosophical system is a version of one critical proposition of neo-Platonism, set forth and demonstrated through a standard Aristotelian method. While we cannot show, and therefore do not know, that the Mishnah's philosophers read Aristotle's work on natural history or his reflections on scientific method, e.g., the *Posterior Analytics,* we can compare our philosophers' method with that of Aristotle, who also, as a matter of fact, set forth a system that, in part, appealed to the right ordering of things through classification by correct rules.

8. A. W. H. Adkins, *From the Many to the One: A Study of Personality and Views of Human Nature in the Context of Ancient Greek Society, Values, and Beliefs* (Ithaca: Cornell University Press, 1970), 170–71.

9. Minio-Paluello, Lorenzo, "Aristotelianism," *Encyclopaedia Britannica* 1:1155.

10. Minio-Paluello.

11. Op. cit., 126ff.

12. Joseph Owens, *A History of Ancient Western Philosophy,* 309ff.

13. M. I. Finley, "Aristotle and Economic Analysis," in M. I. Finley, ed., *Studies in Ancient Society* (London and Boston: Routledge and Kegan Paul, 1974), 28.

14. Karl Polanyi, "Aristotle Discovers the Economy," in Karl Polanyi, Conrad M. Arensburg, and Harry W. Pearson, eds., *Trade and Market in the Early Empires: Economies in History and Theory* (Glencoe: The Free Press, 1957), 79.

15. Polanyi, 80.

16. Polanyi, 80.

17. William I. Davisson and James E. Harper, *European Economic History* I, *The Ancient World* (N.Y.: Appleton-Century-Crofts, 1972), 126.

18. Henry William Spiegel, *The Growth of Economic Thought* (Durham: Duke University Press, 1971), 13.

19. Spiegel, 15.

20. Joseph A. Schumpeter, *History of Economic Analysis* (New York: Oxford University Press, 1954), 53. But we should not ignore Polanyi's quite contrary view, "He will be seen as attacking the problem of man's livelihood with a radicalism of which no later writer on the subject was capable—none has ever penetrated deeper into the material organization of man's life. In effect, he posed, in all its breadth, the question of the place occupied by the economy in society" (66). He was, Polanyi says, "trying to master theoretically the elements of a new complex social phenomenon in *statu nascendi*" (67). The debate on the value of Aristotle's economics carries us far from the purpose at hand, which is only to outline the ideas of economic theory in circulation in antiquity so as to place within that outline economic ideas found in the Mishnah.

21. Davisson and Harper, 122. But that is the very point that Polanyi finds important.

22. See Finley, 27.

23. Robert Lekachman, *A History of Economic Ideas* (New York: Harper, 1959), 6.

24. Schumpeter, 55.

25. Schumpeter, 56.

26. Schumpeter, 56.

27. Lewis H. Haney, *History of Economic Thought: A Critical Account of the Origin and Development of the Economic Theories of the Leading Thinkers in the Leading Nations* (New York: Macmillan, 1920), 58.

28. Haney, 60.

29. Finley, 30.

30. Finley, 30.

31. Finley, 40.

32. Spiegel, p. 25.

33. Spiegel, p. 26.

34. Finley, 23. But others differ, for their own reasons, from Finley's judgment. The issue is not one on which I can venture an opinion.

35. Finley, 49.

36. Schumpeter, 57.

37. Schumpeter, 58.

38. Schumpeter, 60.

39. I say "possible" because, as I have explained, I do not see Plato as an economic thinker of the dimensions of Aristotle. But if others differ, they still will have to pay attention to the first consideration introduced here, which is the congruity of the Mishnah's and Aristotle's fundamental modes of thought through classification, comparison, and contrast. And, it goes without saying, even after two hundred years Christianity had produced nothing worthy of comparison. Schumpeter (71) observes that Christian thought of the first six centuries produced no economics: "The opinions on economic subjects that we might find—such as that believers should sell what they have and give to the poor, or that they should lend without expecting anything . . . from it— are ideal imperatives that form part of a general scheme of life and express this general scheme and nothing else, least of all scientific propositions." But even when we examine the great intellectuals of the tradition, we find no analysis of an economic character. The church fathers did preach against wanton luxury, in favor of charity and restraint. True, too, there can have been a theory behind such advice as that of Tertullian, "to content oneself with the simple products of domestic agriculture and industry instead of craving for imported luxuries or a theory of value behind his observation that abundance and rarity have something to do with price." But if there was a theory, it never came to expression or sustained exemplification. While the great intellectuals of the church addressed the political problems of the Christian state, they did not attend to economics, so Schumpeter: "The How and Why of economic mechanisms were then of no interest either to its [the church's] leaders or to its writers."

40. Schumpeter, 71.

41. Whether or not Aristotle's framing his political economy around the figure of the classification of person who controls the means of production, and whether or not the Mishnah's philosophers' identification of that same figure as the starting point (and ending point) of their economics makes either system Marxist is not a question taken up here. It is critical to the argument of de Ste. Croix. In this connection I call attention to Martha C. Nussbaum, "Nature, Function, and Capability: Aristotle on Political Distribution," *Oxford Studies in Ancient Philosophy*, 1988, and *Proceedings of the Eleventh Symposium Aristotelicum*, ed. G. Patzig.

42. Whether such a one actually did control the means of production is not at issue. In my *Economics of Judaism*, I point out that the economics of the Mishnah simply ignores most of the participants in the economy. Craftsmen, professionals, capitalists or entrepreneurs in capital, manufacturing, trading—these considerable participants in, and sectors of, the economy are treated only in relationship to the unit of production comprising the household. Entire classifications of persons in the economy, women and slaves and foreigners, for instance, play no role. The issues of economics are framed not only from the viewpoint of the householder but also within the frame of reference of the householder; the other issues, and they are many, are simply ignored.

43. See Paul Flesher, *Oxen, Women, or Citizens? Slaves in the System of the Mishnah* (Atlanta: Scholars Press for Brown Judaic Studies, 1988).

44. The reader will already have noticed that the politics likewise ignores most of the participants in the power system of the society that is described, such as women, children, and slaves, not to mention the components of the social order that are defined by other than cultic or political activity: the economic entities are not assumed to exercise legitimate violence or to participate in that exercise. But more of this later on.

45. Finley, 50.

46. Polanyi, p. 80.

47. Polanyi, p. 88.

48. Polanyi, 90. I also consulted Karl Polanyi, *The Livelihood of Man*, ed. Harry W. Pearson (New York: Academic Press, 1977), in particular 145–276.

49. Finley, 41.

50. Finley, citing *Politics* 1257a, 24–30.

51. Finley, 44.

52. Lekachman, 3.

53. But in classical Greece, while only citizens could own land, it is not the case that one had to own land in order to be a citizen. I owe to a reader for the University of Chicago Press the following clarification: "For Aristotle, citizenship is a matter of having the right to participate in judicial or legislative decision-making, and in many Greek states it was not necessary to be a landowner to have this right. Furthermore, Aristotle thinks of the ideal citizen as someone who has sufficient leisure not to engage in farming as a regular activity, since that would take time away from the more important business of politics. For this reason it might mislead the reader to suggest that Aristotle's ideal citizen is a farmer."

54. I qualify that statement in line with the comment given in the note above.

55. I paraphrase Claude Mossé, *The Ancient World at Work* (New York: W. W. Norton, 1969), translated from the French by Janet Lloyd, 49.

56. Proof is that "the householder" appears only in circumstances that require differentiation by taxa pertinent to the householder, e.g., factoring, land sales, and the like. Where differentiation by other taxa is demanded, not the householder but some other classification of the social entity, e.g., woman, or priest, or Israelite, or person, serves very nicely. The householder serves as the subject of sentences the predicate of which concerns economic questions. When political issues are addressed, the subject of the sentences is never the householder, as the survey in chapters 3 through 8 has already shown. Here again, a review of *Social Study of Judaism*, chapter 8, will produce not a single example of a political discourse attending to the householder. The fact that the language of the Mishnah differentiates among topical or thematic requirements seems to me not to have been fully appreciated.

57. But the conclusion that the Mishnah therefore speaks for the householder in particular and

represents his "class" interests ("class" being an excessive metaphor in this context) cannot follow, since the Mishnah in other topics speaks for others altogether, as the politics has already shown us!

58. By contrast, the household formed for purposes of sharing a lamb sacrificed for the Passover offering by definition cannot include a gentile, and a convert must be circumcised before he can partake of the meat of the shared beast. Here "household" stands for cultic family, not economic unit of production. It is a social category lacking economic dimensions; hence "householder" never occurs in the context of the Passover sacrifice and who shares in it. We find instead an odd usage, *haburah* or circle of participants. Once more the precision of word choice in the pages of the document points to the systematic conventions that governed the formulation of the document.

59. I cannot point to a passage in which it is assumed that a woman is head of a household. But women can own land and engage in the economic activities of a household, so I imagine that, in theory, the system could accommodate a woman householder. In practice, however, a woman is always taken to relate to a man, first her father, then her husband, and, when her husband has died, to her male sons or stepsons, who support her as a widow. It is further taken for granted that when a woman is divorced or widowed, she will remarry within a brief spell, so that the marriage settlement is meant to tide her over until she does so. Or she reverts to her "father's house," which means that she rejoins the household of her father, if he is alive, or of her brothers, if her father is dead. See Judith Romney Wegner, *Chattel or Person? The Status of Women in the Mishnah* (New York: Oxford University Press, 1988).

Nor can I point to a single passage that suggests gentiles cannot hold land and conduct establishments, but the Mishnah legislates for "Israel." The fact that gentiles hold land is not a systemic fact but an inert one, and when the authorship of the Mishnah speaks of "householder," so far as I can see, it always takes for granted it addresses an Israelite one. Nonetheless, the fact that gentiles, like women, can own land drives a further wedge between the Mishnah's economics and its politics. For whether or not gentiles can conduct households in the way that Israelites can and do, gentiles assuredly cannot participate in the politics of Judaism; there is no classification that accommodates them.

60. Finley, 95.

61. That negative conception forms the underside of the positive conception of the householder in charge of a unit of production and in command (of course) of the means of production. We uncover the negative definition, specifically, when we consider how the authorship of the Mishnah disposes of the absentee landowner who holds property but does not work it or oversee its productive utilization. It follows, as I just suggested, that ownership is not an abstract right divorced from all material function, but entails management and productive utilization of property, and the householder embodies that command and everyday mastery of the means of production in a way in which the absentee landowner cannot. Ownership in the present context, identified as it is with supervision and utilization and usufruct, derives from the premise of the householder as active manager and administrator of the means of production, and ownership finds its meaning in the command of the unit of production. Ownership is not abstract and not unconditional but concrete and related to ongoing and hands-on administration: usufruct, not merely deed, proves a right of ownership or functional access and use, as the case may be. And that definition of ownership draws us once more within the orbit of the household as a unit of production, distinct from both the family and the industrial-scale agricultural unit. What makes a household a household is possession *and usufruct* of land: both. And it is the household that defines the building block of the village, the *oikos* of the *polis,* and in the systemic statement of the Judaism of the authorship of the Mishnah, the formation of households into villages comprises "all Israel."

62. The system of the Mishnah can imagine an unattached woman constituting a household on her own, but she is so rare and exceptional as to fall quite outside the imagination of the system builders. That is why I take for granted that the Mishnaic system speaks only of males when it talks about the householder, just as, when it addresses certain functions assumed to be carried out

only by women, such as cooking, it always uses the feminine form. See Wegner, cited in n. 59 above.

63. In so stating, I do not mean to suggest that only a landowner could be a citizen of a Greek *polis*. But, it is clear, in the politics of Aristotle, the *polis* is comprised of householders, and households were also deemed ordinarily to form units of production and social organization alike. The contrast between the utterly apolitical classification of the Mishnah's household and the centrality of the household in economics then is a valid one and properly drawn.

64. As such, of course, the economics of Judaism can hardly qualify as an economics at all, since the theory ignores most of the actuality. But in the context of Aristotle's conception of economics, the Mishnah's theory of the economy qualifies full well. In this context, we do well to point to what is at stake in an economics that treats as economically beyond the realm of theory the generality of participants in the actual economy.

65. Finley.

66. Critical to my argument, then, is the fact that not only Israelite men but Israelite women (like gentiles, noted above) could own land. If only an Israelite male may own land and exercise usufruct over it (wives who own land cede to their husbands usufruct of the bulk of their estates for the duration of the marriage), then we find ourselves entirely within Finley's framework; all we need do is change "citizen" to "free, male, adult Israelite," and the Greek economic theory proves entirely a comfortable fit. But that is not the fact. Women could own land but, as chapters 3 through 8 have shown us, did not form a political class at all. So power leading to legitimate violence was denied them, while the right to possess scarce resources was allowed in particular circumstances. I need hardly underline the centrality of gender considerations in the analysis of systems.

CHAPTER ELEVEN

1. I rely on Nussbaum, cited in the next note.

2. Martha C. Nussbaum, "Nature, Function, and Capability: Aristotle on Political Distribution," *Oxford Studies in Ancient Philosophy,* 1988, and *Proceedings of the Eleventh Symposium Aristotelicum,* ed. G. Patzig. What makes this paper of special importance is Nussbaum's demonstration that there is a counterpart to distributive economics in Aristotle's politics.

3. Nussbaum, 1–2.

4. R. G. Mulgan, *Aristotle's Political Theory: An Introduction for Students of Political Theory* (Oxford: Clarendon Press, 1977), 13.

5. Mulgan, 38–39.

6. Mulgan, p. 16.

7. Mulgan, p. 17, from the *Ethics.*

8. The Mishnah's political community in no way corresponds to the society of the city-state. Its political community is its Israel. That leads us to anticipate no role for the city at all, and, as we shall presently see, there is none. And that same fact also explains the utopian, antilocative quality of the politics of Judaism, even of a Judaism that has at its center the one city that counts, which is Jerusalem. But we are getting ahead of our story.

9. That is not to say that the *polis* came into existence on its own, like a wildflower, without the intervention of human thought and ingenuity. Aristotle does not maintain that no institutions are manmade.

10. Mulgan, 20–21.

11. Cited by Mulgan, p. 21.

12. Mulgan, 22. See also Mulgan, 141 note 22, on "the ethnos," which means a political community larger than the *polis,* e.g., nation or people or race, such as Greeks or Persians.

13. Mulgan, 22.

14. Mulgan, 23.

15. Mulgan, 25.

16. Mulgan, 30–31.

17. Mulgan, 31.

18. Mulgan, 38.

19. Mulgan, 39.

20. Mulgan, 47.

21. But I find here no important support for the thesis of G. E. M. de Ste. Croix, *The Class Struggle in the Ancient Greek World: From the Archaic Age to the Arab Conquests* (London: Gerald Duckworth & Co. Ltd., 1981), who sees Aristotle (along with almost everybody else) as some sort of proto-Marxist. True, what I have said certainly will be read by de Ste. Croix as ample demonstration of his position. But my explanation of the same facts, in the tradition of Weber, seems to me profoundly anti-Marxist, because what I see at stake are generative traits of systems, which I find (as explained in the introduction and as chapter 12 will show) in the composition of self-evident answers to critical and urgent questions. These form realms of intellect that, in context, serve as independent variables, rather than as reflexes of prior and more fundamental interests, e.g., of the material kind so critical to the Marxist reading represented by de Ste. Croix. This same argument, again in the tradition of Weber, animates my *Self-Fulfilling Prophecy: Exile and Return in the History of Judaism* (Boston: Beacon Press, 1986).

22. Mulgan, 52.

23. Elizabeth Fox-Genovese, "The Origins of Physiocracy: Economic Revolution and Social Order in Eighteenth-Century France," ms. See also Karl Polanyi, *The Lifelihood of Man,* ed. Harry W. Pearson (New York: Academic Press, 1977), 7.

24. We in the West understood that such an embedded economics was the norm, the disembedded economics of capitalism abnormal, because Christianity taught just that. And the reason—so it seems to me—is that Christianity, through Aquinas, drew its paramount economics from Aristotle. Hence, from the very outset of the economics of Christianity in the Middle Ages, it was perfectly normal to conceive of economics and politics as related by nature, as embedded. The non-Christian *philosophes* held no such concept to be normal and could and did develop a different rationality, encompassing, as a matter of fact, a different logic of economics too.

25. These questions form the program that yields the general proposition and thesis demanded at the outset of chapter 9.

26. And, to the contrary, failure to differentiate within an entity signals the system's lack of interest in the entity: hence systemic inertia, and, in this context, political as well. But I do not wish to argue only from silence.

27. See *The Social Description of Judaism,* chapter 8 (supplementary materials on chapter 11) on this point. I find no interest in the ethnic composition of the one as against the other. In general, the village is commonly treated as made up wholly or mostly of Jews, while the town or city is made up of a mixed population in which Jews do not necessarily form a majority. But I see no systemic meaning in that issue at all, which is why I relegate my discussion of it to *The Social Description of Judaism,* chapter 8.

28. Compare M. I. Finley, *The Ancient Economy* (Berkeley and Los Angeles: University of California Press, 1985), 123. I mean to emphasize that in the pages of the Mishnah we cannot distinguish town from country.

29. The picture of appeal to the high court in the Temple seems to me adequate proof of this self-evident proposition.

30. Within a system aimed at systematic hierarchization as a means of overcoming chaos—everything in proper place and classification, which is to say, everything in correct order, hence, once more, hierarchization. This point is developed in chapter 12.

31. Jerusalem stands for something but, at the time and in the circumstance of the composition of the Mishnah existed solely within the theory of things, as much a matter of imagination as king, high priest, and Temple. But that is not critical to my argument, as already indicated.

32. Because there is Jerusalem and there is everywhere else, Jerusalem too is nowhere, in particular, for no other place locates itself in relationship to Jerusalem. A status, a focus, a me-

dium for mediation—none of these political traits imputed to Jerusalem define locative character-istics; in accord with not a single one of them can we locate any other political entity, and there in fact is within the system no other political entity anyhow. Consequently, as I said, Jerusalem is not a place but a state, even, in context, a state of mind, and it follows that the politics of Judaism is not locative but utopian in a very concrete and immediate sense indeed.

33. And would soon be redefined altogether, so that in the second phase in the unfolding of Judaism and the move from philosophy to theology, there would be no economics in the this-worldly sense at all, rather, a complete revaluation of what we man by "scarce resources." But that is for the next phase in this cubic chess game of mine.

34. Of course, agencies of the political system deal with possession of land, but that is not the same thing.

35. We have already noted that to own land one had to be a citizen, even though to be a citizen one did not have to own land. That accounts for the framing of matters here. All landholders were householders and were citizens, but not all those who possessed wealth and could have been householders in an economic sense were landholders.

36. Mulgan, p. 14.

37. I use the word "science" very deliberately to signal facts established beyond all doubt by appeal to irrefutable sources of truth, for the Mishnah's sages' Judaisms as for all other Juda-isms—Scripture above all.

38. Other such differences may be noted briefly. The politics of Aristotle is abstract, general, accessible, that of the Mishnah concrete, particular, and recondite and arcane. We find in the Mishnah no conception of "the state," a category that is critical and ubiquitous for Aristotle. Modes of thought that for Aristotle yield analytical categories for the Mishnah's framers produce personifications of institutions. That is exemplified in the fact that in the Mishnah's system there is no classification "community" (counterpart to *koinonia,* for instance). Unlike Aristotle's poli-tics, in the Mishnah's I find no interest in questions of residence, possession of legal rights, e.g., the right of suing and being sued and the right to share in the administration of justice and in political office. (Indeed, by that criterion, the only citizens of the Jewish state are the king, priests, and scribes!) There is no consideration of a "constitution" such as Aristotle puts forward. Aristotle's conception of the constitution as "the arrangement which states adopt for the distri-bution of offices of power and for the determination of the sovereign and of the end at which the community aims" (Mulgan, 45) can mean nothing in the politics of Judaism, and his three ele-ments of a constitution, deliberative, official or magisterial, and judicial, find no counterpart. (The distinctions I have made in this text among executive, judicial, and legislative actions are not native to the Mishnah.) Aristotle's whole discussion of "rule of the best men"—oligarchy, aris-tocracy—has no point of intersection with the politics of Judaism. These are issues never dis-cussed in the Mishnah, because it is taken for granted that the qualifications of government are genealogy or Torah-learning.

39. Although as I shall argue, these define the generative problematic of the entirety of Mish-naic Judaism.

CHAPTER TWELVE

1. But if there is a disjuncture between the generative metaphor of the Mishnah's economics and the one that is spun out in its politics, the systemic message is the same in both cases. The message of the document as a whole concerns order and stability, and that means hierarchization of things and persons in proper place and order.

2. Obviously, I appeal to the sense of "rationality" used in Max Weber's ouevre.

3. This is precisely the question I treat in my *Economics of Judaism:* why did this Judaism work out an economics at all? There, in the same way, I asked Aristotle for perspective by inquir-ing why, for his philosophy, economics proved so central. In chapter 10 I have already spelled out

the priority of place of Aristotle among economic theorists of antiquity, so my turning to Aristotle in connection with economics is amply justified. I there referred briefly, also, to the fact that the Mishnah's and Aristotle's methods prove to intersect in important and fundamental ways as to philosophical method. So the grounds for this systemic comparison, not merely the contrast of components of systems, are solid and fully exposed.

4. I avoid the word "classes" because it bears meanings hardly demonstrated to be present here. Finley's writings on class and class structure in antiquity seem to me the model to be followed.

5. Just as I asked, why does this system invoke also economics in making its larger systemic statement?

6. But it is not unique in this, since Philo showed keen interest in setting forth a whole politics in the context of his larger structure and system.

7. I return to these questions in projected studies of the second and third layers in the unfolding of the Judaism of the dual Torah.

8. I do not claim that that is why he did so. My intent is only to contrast Augustine's situation with that of the Mishnah's authorship.

9. M. I. Finley, *Politics in the Ancient World* (Cambridge: Cambridge University Press, 1983), 25.

10. Mulgan, 3.

11. Mulgan, 3.

12. Mulgan, 6.

13. Mulgan, 8.

14. Mulgan, 8.

15. Mulgan, 9.

16. Mulgan, 9.

17. Mulgan, 10–11.

18. Mulgan, 6.

19. Mulgan, 9.

20. Mulgan, 18.

21. I must underline that both systems are to be classified as philosophical, as I have shown in *The Philosophical Mishnah* (Atlanta: Scholars Press for Brown Judaic Studies, 1989) 1–4 and in *Judaism as Philosophy: The Method and Message of the Mishnah* (Columbia: University of South Carolina Press, 1991). Any conception that the Mishnah has a theological perspective, while Aristotle does not, is wrong as to the Mishnah. The Mishnah forms a philosophy of religion, working out an ontological monotheism; but it contains scarcely a word of theology.

22. The same point of interest animates discussion on the modes of inflicting the death penalty. The generative problematic comes to expression in the initial introduction of the vast treatment of that topic, as we remember:

A. Four modes of execution were given over to the court [in order of severity]:
B. (1) stoning, (2) burning, (3) decapitation, and (4) strangulation.
C. R. Simeon says, "(2) burning, (1) stoning, (4) strangulation, and (3) decapitation."

M. San. 7:1

At stake in the dispute is the severity of suffering imposed by each mode of execution. Simeon's order, C, differs from that of B in the degradation and suffering inflicted on the felon. Here, again, we find at stake the matter of hierarchization of a genus and its species. These two examples suffice to make the simple point that, time and again, the framers of the Mishnah address to political topics the generative problematic defined by hierarchization. A sustained inquiry into the generative logic of the Mishnah demonstrates precisely the same fact. The Mishnah's authorship's system not only orders things in its treatment of facts but conducts its entire process of thought through modes of establishing connections and drawing conclusions that by definition hierarchize. In point of fact, the entire mode of thought of the Mishnah is that of *Listen-wissenschaft*, the science of list-making. I have dwelt on that point elsewhere, and it would carry us far afield to review it. But the upshot is the same, since list-making by definition is hierarchizing, a list constituting an ordering, either of the items on that one list, or of the contents of several lists that are juxtaposed. See my *Formation of the Jewish Intellect: Making Connections and Drawing Conclusions in the Traditional System of Judaism* (Atlanta: Scholars Press for Brown Judaic Studies, 1988).

23. I point this out in my *Economics of Judaism*. The economics scarcely encompasses the half of the population comprised by women, the classes of craftsmen, artisans, those comparable to what we should call the free professions, traders, merchants, other entrepreneurs—pretty much everybody but the householder defined as landholder, hence farmer. And while it was a subsistence economy, not everybody was a subsistence farmer.

24. Woman is subordinate and dependent. Man is the norm and the normal. That is why I can say only "man" rather than, in this context, "the human being."

25. The power exercised by gentiles, e.g., the Roman government, never entered the picture since it was not a legitimate politics at all.

26. The second politics of Judaism, the one portrayed in the Talmud of the Land of Israel and associated writings, therefore requires systematic description in terms of itself and its categories, as does what I conceive to be the third politics of Judaism, the one set forth in the Talmud of Babylonia and its companions.

Index of Biblical and Talmudic References

Arthur W. Woodman

General Index

Arthur W. Woodman